Golang Crash Course

Use Golang to build high-performance concurrent cloud-native applications

Venkatesh R

Shubham Raizada

www.bpbonline.com

First Edition 2026

ISBN: 978-93-65895-797

Distributors:

BPB PUBLICATIONS
20, Ansari Road, Darya Ganj
New Delhi-110002
Ph: 23254990/23254991

DECCAN AGENCIES
4-3-329, Bank Street,
Hyderabad-500195
Ph: 24756967/24756400

MICRO MEDIA
Shop No. 5, Mahendra Chambers,
150 DN Rd. Next to Capital Cinema,
V.T. (C.S.T.) Station, MUMBAI-400 001
Ph: 22078296/22078297

Published by Manish Jain for BPB Publications, 20 Ansari Road, Darya Ganj, New Delhi-110002 and Printed by him at Repro India Ltd., Rewari.

www.bpbonline.com

Dedicated to

*My parents, **Ramesh** and **Jamuna Rani**, for their unwavering love and guidance.*

*My beloved wife, **Geetha**, without her, this journey would not have been possible, and for being my constant pillar of strength, standing by me through every challenge and triumph.*

*My son, **Parthiv**.*

- Venkatesh R

*I dedicate this work to my parents, **Pankaj** and **Anita**, for inspiring me to relentlessly pursue my goals. To my sister, **Shruti**, for always being my biggest cheerleader. And finally, to my wonderful wife, **Aishwarya**, for her unwavering support and guidance, and for gracefully enduring the long weekends and the time I took away from us to make this possible.*

- Shubham Raizada

About the Authors

- **Venkatesh R** is a technology leader with more than 18 years of experience in AI, enterprise software engineering, cloud platforms and big data systems. He currently works as a lead architect (engineering director) at Visa, where he leads initiatives in data quality platforms, anomaly detection and advanced analytics systems. Over the course of his career, he has worked with organizations such as Walmart focusing on modernizing legacy architectures and building scalable cloud solutions.

  He holds several professional certifications in AI, cloud and big-data technologies and is an MBA graduate from the Indian Institute of Management, Bangalore.

- **Shubham Raizada** is a principal engineer at Atlassian, where he works on high-scale web applications and distributed systems. He holds a B.Tech in computer science from NITK Surathkal. Before Atlassian, he was at Walmart and Cohesity building data platforms and backend services with Golang, Kafka and Spark. He also spent time at Conviva building a streaming engine from scratch in Rust, that led to his open-source contributions to Apache OpenDAL.

  In his free time, he likes to dive into technical papers and share what he learns on his blog.

About the Reviewers

- **Pawan Tilara** is a senior backend engineer at Angel One, where he works on building scalable and high-performance backend systems in a fast-paced fintech environment. He specializes in API design, distributed systems, and service-oriented architecture, focusing on creating reliable and efficient fintech solutions. Originally from Uttarakhand, Pawan brings a strong engineering mindset and a passion for solving complex problems. Over the years, he has worked across multiple technology stacks, including Golang, Python, AWS, and PySpark, enabling him to design efficient, high-performance systems.

  His work primarily focuses on modernising legacy architectures, improving system reliability, and optimising performance at scale. Pawan enjoys working on challenging problems that require both technical depth and practical decision-making. With hands-on experience across distributed systems and cloud platforms, he continuously strives to build robust solutions that align with business needs while maintaining engineering excellence.

- **Saubhik Singh** is a senior software engineer based in Bengaluru, India, specializing in distributed systems, cloud infrastructure, and scalable backend platforms. He currently works at DigitalOcean, where he contributes to core storage infrastructure, including block storage and **network file storage** (**NFS**). He has led the design and execution of control plane architectures and large-scale microservices that handle millions of requests while maintaining high reliability and performance.

  With strong expertise in Go, Kubernetes, and cloud-native technologies, Saubhik focuses on building resilient, fault-tolerant systems and improving scalability, performance, and operational reliability in distributed environments. He also actively shares engineering insights and has spoken at gRPC Conf India on building production-grade distributed systems

Acknowledgements

Writing a technical book is never an individual effort. It is the result of support, encouragement and collaboration from many people around us.

First, we would like to thank our families for their constant encouragement and understanding during the writing of this book. Balancing professional responsibilities, research and writing require many long evenings and weekends and their patience made it possible to complete this work.

We are also grateful to the team at BPB Publications for their guidance and support throughout the publication process. Their editorial feedback, technical reviews and structured publishing process helped refine the content and improve the clarity of the material presented in this book.

Finally, we would like to thank the global community of Golang developers and contributors whose tools, libraries and open discussions have made Golang one of the most exciting programming languages in modern software development.

Preface

Modern software development has evolved rapidly over the past decade. Applications today must be scalable, highly available and capable of handling massive volumes of data and traffic. Traditional monolithic architectures are gradually giving way to distributed systems and microservices. In this evolving landscape, developers need tools that are efficient, reliable and easy to maintain.

Golang was created at Google to address exactly these challenges. It combines simplicity with performance and provides built-in support for concurrency, making it ideal for building scalable backend services, distributed systems and cloud-native applications.

One of the biggest strengths of Go is its philosophy of simplicity. Generally programming languages evolve by adding increasingly complex features but Golang focuses on clarity, readability and efficiency. This makes it easier for developers to write maintainable code while achieving high performance.

The goal of this book is to help readers learn Go in a practical and structured way. Rather than focusing solely on theoretical explanations, the chapters emphasize hands on understanding and real-world application. By the time you finish this book you will not only understand Golang's syntax and features but will also be able to design and build scalable backend services using modern development practices.

This book is divided into three main sections. The first section introduces the core concepts of Go programming. The second section explores Golang's powerful concurrency model. The third section demonstrates how Golang can be used to build modern microservices and scalable APIs.

Section I- Core concepts of Go programming

Chapter 1: Introduction to Go — This chapter introduces the Go programming language, its origins and its design philosophy. It explains why Go has become a popular choice for backend development and cloud infrastructure. You will also learn how to install Golang and configure the development environment and writing your first Go program. In addition, the chapter gives a broader perspective on how Go fits into the modern software ecosystem. It highlights real-world problems that Go was designed to address, especially in distributed systems. By the end of this chapter, you will not only understand what Go is, but also why it matters.

Chapter 2: Go Syntax and Language Fundamentals — This chapter focuses on the core building blocks of Go programming. It covers variables, constants, data types, operators and control structures. By the end of this chapter, readers will have a strong understanding of the fundamental syntax required to write Go programs. The chapter also emphasizes writing clean and readable code using Go's minimalistic syntax. You will see how Go simplifies common programming constructs compared to other languages. This chapter ensures you are comfortable enough to start writing structured programs independently.

Chapter 3: Functions and Error Handling in Go— Functions form the backbone of Go programs. This chapter explains how to define functions, pass parameters, return values and handle errors effectively. You will also learn Golang's approach to error handling and best practices for writing reliable functions. Beyond syntax, the chapter focuses on writing functions that are reusable and maintainable. It introduces advanced concepts like variadic and anonymous functions with practical examples. Error handling is explained not just as a feature, but as a design philosophy in Go. This helps you write predictable and production-quality code.

Chapter 4: Structs and Methods — Structs allow developers to create custom data types by grouping related data together. This chapter introduces structs, methods and how Golang encourages composition instead of traditional inheritance. The chapter further explains how to design data models that reflect real-world entities. You will learn how methods bring behavior to data structures. It also explores how composition leads to more flexible and maintainable code. By the end, you will be able to design clean and idiomatic Go structures.

Chapter 5: Arrays, Slices, and Maps — Data structures are essential for building practical applications. This chapter explores arrays, slices and maps in Golang and demonstrate how they can be used to store, manipulate and process collections of data efficiently. It also highlights the performance implications of using each data structure. You will learn how slices provide flexibility over arrays and why they are widely used in Go. Maps are explained through real-world use cases like lookups and indexing. This chapter builds your confidence in handling data effectively.

Chapter 6: Pointers — Pointers enable programs to reference memory locations directly. This chapter explains how pointers work in Golang, how they interact with structs and functions and how pointers can be used to optimize memory usage. The chapter also demystifies common misconceptions around pointers. You will learn when to use pointers and when to avoid them. Practical examples show how pointers improve efficiency in large data structures. This understanding is crucial for writing performant Go applications.

Chapter 7: Interfaces in Go — Interfaces provide a powerful way to define Behavior in Go. This chapter explains how interfaces enable flexible and modular program design without relying on inheritance. It also introduces Go's concept of implicit interface implementation, which keeps code simple and elegant. You will see how interfaces are used in real-world scenarios like testing and abstraction. The chapter emphasizes designing loosely coupled systems. This is a key step toward building scalable applications.

Chapter 8: Packages and Modules — This chapter explains how Golang organizes code using packages and modules. Readers will learn how to structure large applications, manage dependencies and build reusable components. It also covers best practices for naming, organizing, and importing packages. You will understand how Go modules simplify dependency management in modern development. The chapter prepares you for working on larger, collaborative projects. It ensures your codebase remains clean and maintainable

Section II- Concurrency in Go

Chapter 9: Introduction to Go Concurrency — This chapter introduces concurrency concepts and explains why Golang's goroutines make concurrent programming simpler and more efficient than traditional multi-threading models. It also clarifies the difference between concurrency and parallelism using practical examples. You will understand how Go handles multiple tasks efficiently. The chapter connects these ideas to real-world applications like web servers and data processing. This builds a strong conceptual foundation for advanced concurrency topics.

Chapter 10: Channels and Synchronization — Channels provide a safe way for goroutines to communicate. This chapter explains how channels work and how they help synchronize concurrent operations. You will also learn about buffered and unbuffered channels and their use cases. The chapter explains blocking behavior and how synchronization is achieved naturally in Go. Common pitfalls such as deadlocks are discussed with examples. This chapter strengthens your ability to manage concurrent workflows.

Chapter 11: Select Statements and Timers — This chapter introduces the select statement and demonstrates how it allows programs to listen to multiple channel operations simultaneously. Readers will also learn how to implement timeouts using time. After, graceful shutdown mechanisms, handling OS signals and preventing deadlocks. The chapter also shows how to build responsive and non-blocking systems. You will understand how timers and tickers are used in real applications. Practical scenarios demonstrate how to coordinate multiple events.

Chapter 12: Advanced Concurrency Patterns — In this chapter readers will explore advanced concurrency techniques such as worker pools, pipelines and synchronization mechanisms that help build high-performance systems. It also introduces patterns commonly used in production systems. You will learn how to control resource usage and improve system efficiency. Concepts like rate limiting and task distribution are explained. This chapter enables you to design scalable and efficient concurrent architectures.

Chapter 13: Error Handling in Concurrency — This chapter discusses common challenges in concurrent programs, including deadlocks, race conditions and panic recovery. It also focuses on strategies for handling errors across multiple goroutines. You will learn how to build fault-tolerant systems that recover gracefully from failures. Techniques for debugging and monitoring concurrent systems are also covered. This is essential for writing reliable production code.

Section III- Building Microservices with Go

Chapter 14: Introduction to Microservices Architecture — This chapter introduces microservices architecture and explains why Golang is well suited for building distributed systems. It also compares microservices with traditional monolithic architectures. You will understand the trade-offs involved in adopting microservices. The chapter highlights scalability, flexibility and fault tolerance. This sets the foundation for building modern distributed applications.

Chapter 15: Building a Simple REST API in Go — In this chapter readers will learn how to create a basic REST API using Golang's built-in HTTP libraries. It also explains how to handle routing, requests and responses effectively. You will learn how to work with JSON data in APIs. The chapter introduces middleware and server configuration basics. By the end, you will have a working understanding of web service development in Go.

Chapter 16: Advanced RESTful API Design — This chapter explores advanced topics such as API versioning, logging, monitoring and deployment using Docker and Kubernetes. It also emphasizes designing APIs that are scalable and maintainable. You will learn best practices for structuring endpoints and handling errors. The chapter covers performance optimization techniques. This prepares you for building production grade APIs.

Chapter 17: Securing Microservices — Security is a critical aspect of microservice design. This chapter explains authentication, authorization and techniques for securing communication. It also introduces concepts like JWT, OAuth and TLS in a practical context. You will learn how to secure service-to-service communication. The chapter highlights best practices for protecting sensitive data. This ensures your applications are secure and reliable.

Chapter 18: Testing Microservices — Testing is essential for reliable software systems. This chapter covers unit testing, integration testing and end-to-end testing for Go applications. It also explains how to use mocking to isolate components during testing. You will learn how to build comprehensive test strategies. Performance and load testing concepts are also introduced. This chapter reinforces the importance of quality in software development.

Chapter 19: Managing Data in Microservices — This chapter discusses database design, distributed data management and architectural patterns such as event sourcing and CQRS. It also explores challenges like data consistency and schema evolution. You will understand how to design systems with decentralized data ownership. The chapter highlights best practices for scalable data management. This brings together architecture, data and system design.

Appendix A: Go Tools and Resources — This appendix introduces the essential tools and ecosystem that support modern Go development. It explains Go modules for dependency management and highlights profiling and debugging techniques. Readers will also explore CI/CD practices for building and deploying applications. Together these resources help in bridging the gap between writing code and running it in production.

Appendix B: Glossary — This appendix provides a concise reference to key terms and concepts used throughout the book. Each definition is written in a simple and clear manner for quick understanding. This section acts as a handy guide for reference and revisiting the concepts during learning and implementation.

Appendix C: Answers to Exercises — This appendix contains detailed solutions to the exercises included across chapters. Each answer is explained to reinforce both concepts and problem-solving approaches. It helps readers validate their understanding. This section serves as a practical companion for revision and self-assessment.

By the end of this book, readers will have a strong foundation in Go programming and will be equipped to build scalable, secure and production-ready applications.

Code Bundle and Coloured Images

Please follow the link to download the
Code Bundle and the ***Coloured Images*** of the book:

https://rebrand.ly/fy3owp0

The code bundle for the book is also hosted on GitHub at
https://github.com/bpbpublications/Golang-Crash-Course.
In case there's an update to the code, it will be updated on the existing GitHub repository.

We have code bundles from our rich catalogue of books and videos available at **https://github.com/bpbpublications.** Check them out!

Errata

We take immense pride in our work at BPB Publications and follow best practices to ensure the accuracy of our content to provide an indulging reading experience to our subscribers. Our readers are our mirrors, and we use their inputs to reflect and improve upon human errors, if any, that may have occurred during the publishing processes involved. To let us maintain the quality and help us reach out to any readers who might be having difficulties due to any unforeseen errors, please write to us at: **errata@bpbonline.com**

Your support, suggestions and feedback are highly appreciated by the BPB Publications' Family.

Piracy

If you come across any illegal copies of our works in any form on the internet, we would be grateful if you would provide us with the location address or website name. Please contact us at **business@bpbonline.com** with a link to the material.

If you are interested in becoming an author

If there is a topic that you have expertise in, and you are interested in either writing or contributing to a book, please visit **www.bpbonline.com**. We have worked with thousands of developers and tech professionals, just like you, to help them share their insights with the global tech community. You can make a general application, apply for a specific hot topic that we are recruiting an author for, or submit your own idea.

Reviews

Please leave a review. Once you have read and used this book, why not leave a review on the site that you purchased it from? Potential readers can then see and use your unbiased opinion to make purchase decisions. We at BPB can understand what you think about our products, and our authors can see your feedback on their book. Thank you!

For more information about BPB, please visit **www.bpbonline.com**.

Join our Discord space

Join our Discord workspace for latest updates, offers, tech happenings around the world, new releases, and sessions with the authors:

https://discord.bpbonline.com

Table of Contents

1. **Introduction to Go** ... 1
  - Introduction ... 1
  - Structure ... 1
  - Objectives ... 1
  - Overview of Go ... 1
    - *Features of Go* ... 1
    - *Use cases of Go* ... 2
  - History of Go ... 3
    - *Evolution timeline* ... 4
    - *Reasons for choosing Go* ... 4
  - Installing and setting up the Go environment ... 4
    - *Setting up a workspace* ... 5
  - Writing your first Go program ... 5
    - *Explanation* ... 6
    - *Building the executable* ... 6
  - Understanding the main function ... 6
  - Go modules and dependencies ... 6
    - *Creating a Go module* ... 7
    - *Managing dependencies* ... 7
    - *go mod commands* ... 7
  - Conclusion ... 7
  - Questions ... 7

2. **Go Syntax and Language Fundamentals** ... 9
  - Introduction ... 9
  - Structure ... 9
  - Objectives ... 9
  - Variables and constants ... 10
  - Basic data types ... 13
    - *Basic data types, complex numbers* ... 17
  - Operators and expressions ... 19
  - Control structures ... 21
  - Loops in Go ... 26
  - Conclusion ... 32
  - Questions ... 33

3. **Functions and Error Handling in Go** 35
Introduction 35
Structure 35
Objectives 35
Declaring and calling functions 36
Function parameters and return types 37
Variadic functions 40
Anonymous functions 44
Understanding and handling errors in Go 48
Creating and handling custom errors 52
Best practices for error handling 57
Conclusion 57
Questions 57

4. **Structs and Methods** 59
Introduction 59
Structure 59
Objectives 59
Defining structs 59
Methods in Go 63
Pointers to structs 67
Embedding and composition 71
Comparing and copying structs 76
Conclusion 80
Questions 80

5. **Arrays, Slices, and Maps** 81
Introduction 81
Structure 81
Objectives 81
Arrays in Go 82
Working with slices 84
Creating and modifying maps 87
Multidimensional arrays and slices 91
Iterating over maps and slices 94
JSON in Go 98
Conclusion 102
Questions 103

6. **Pointers** 105
Introduction 105
Structure 105
Objectives 105
Introduction to pointers 105
Working with pointers in Go 108
Pointer receiver methods in Go 112
Pointer receiver methods 113
Syntax of pointer receiver methods 113
Advantages of pointer receiver methods 115
Conclusion 118
Questions 118

7. **Interfaces in Go** 119
Introduction 119
Structure 119
Objectives 119
Interface 119
Understanding interfaces in Go 121
Key characteristics 123
Defining and implementing interfaces in Go 124
Embedding interfaces in Go 128
Interface embedding 128
Interface satisfaction 132
Implicit interface satisfaction in Go 132
Explicit interface satisfaction in other languages 132
Interface satisfaction across multiple Interfaces 134
Type assertions and type switches in Go 135
Empty interface and dynamic types in Go 138
Best practices for using interfaces in Go 141
Conclusion 143
Questions 143

8. **Packages and Modules** 145
Introduction 145
Structure 145
Objectives 145
Creating and using packages in Go 145
Structure of a package 145
Package declaration 146
Creating a package 146

Using a package...147
Special cases...147
Organizing code with modules in Go...150
Structure of a Go module...150
Importing external libraries in Go...153
Importing external libraries...153
Best practices for importing external libraries...156
Conclusion...160
Questions...160

9. Introduction to Go Concurrency...161
Introduction...161
Structure...161
Objectives...161
Concurrency...161
Importance of concurrency...162
Real-world scenarios where concurrency matters...162
Challenges without concurrency...163
Advantages of concurrency in Go...163
Common misconceptions about concurrency...163
Go makes concurrency easier...163
Comparing concurrency models...164
Use cases demonstrating the need for concurrency...164
Goroutines...165
Creating goroutines...166
Anonymous functions with goroutines...166
Managing goroutines...167
Error handling in goroutines...169
Goroutines vs. functions...170
Goroutines in practical applications...170
Performance comparison between goroutines and threads...171
Threads...172
Goroutines...172
Goroutines and threads...172
Performance metrics...172
Benchmarks and examples...173
Scheduler differences...174
Summary...175
Concurrency patterns in Go...175
Fan-out/fan-in pattern...176
Pipeline pattern...177

Worker pool pattern 178
Publish-subscribe pattern 179
Select pattern 180
Cancellation with context 181
Rate limiting pattern 183
Conclusion 183
Questions 183

10. Channels and Synchronization 185
Introduction 185
Structure 185
Objectives 185
Introduction to channels 185
Creating and initializing channels 186
Reasons to use channels 186
Anatomy of a channel 186
Best practices 187
Common mistakes 187
Unbuffered and buffered channels in Go 187
Unbuffered channels 187
Use cases 187
Buffered channels 188
Use cases 188
Comparing unbuffered and buffered channels 189
Deadlock with unbuffered channel 190
Deadlock with buffered channel 191
Best practices 191
Sending and receiving data from channels in Go 191
Sending data to a channel 191
Receiving data from a channel 192
Blocking nature of send and receive 193
Non-blocking channel operations 194
Error handling in send and receive 195
Deadlock scenarios 196
Best practices 197
Channel direction in Go 197
Types of channel directions 197
Converting bidirectional to directional 199
Combining directional channels with goroutines 200
Best practices 201
Go channel synchronization overview 201

Synchronization ... 201
Synchronization through unbuffered channels ... 201
Synchronization through buffered channels ... 202
Select for non-blocking synchronization ... 203
Synchronization with close ... 204
Common synchronization scenarios ... 204
Best practices ... 205
Conclusion ... 205
Questions ... 206

11. Select Statements and Timers ... 207
Introduction ... 207
Structure ... 207
Objectives ... 207
Select statement for channels ... 207
Overview of the select statement ... 207
Syntax of select ... 208
Characteristics of select ... 208
Using select for multiple receives ... 208
Using select for send and receive operations ... 209
Combining select for continuous monitoring ... 210
Using select for channel multiplexing ... 211
Handling timeouts with select ... 212
Advantages of select in channel operations ... 212
Best practices ... 212
Timeouts and non-blocking operations in Go ... 213
Overview ... 213
Implementing timeouts using time.After ... 213
Non-blocking operations with select ... 214
Using select with default ... 214
Combining timeouts with non-blocking operations ... 215
Advantages of timeouts and non-blocking operations ... 216
Real-world use cases ... 216
Common pitfalls ... 217
Best practices ... 218
Timer and ticker functions in Go ... 218
Overview of timer and ticker ... 218
Timer functions ... 218
Ticker functions ... 220
Differences between timer and ticker ... 222
Ticker and timer use cases ... 222

Best practices for timer and timer functions 224
Graceful shutdowns using channels in Go......224
Overview on graceful shutdown 224
Importance of graceful shutdowns 224
Using channels for graceful shutdowns 225
Shutdown signal channel......225
Coordinating multiple goroutines 226
Handling OS signals for shutdown 227
Handling long-running tasks......228
Graceful shutdown in web servers 229
Best practices for graceful shutdowns 230
Conclusion......231
Questions......231

12. Advanced Concurrency Patterns 233
Introduction 233
Structure 233
Objectives 233
Worker pools and goroutine management in Go 233
Overview 234
Usage of worker pools 234
Basic components of a worker pool 234
Example of basic worker pool implementation 234
Code example 234
Advanced features of worker pools 235
Collecting results 236
Dynamic worker pools 237
Handling errors in worker pools 238
Use cases for worker pools 240
Pipelines and stream processing in Go 240
Overview of pipelines and stream processing......240
Pipelines 240
Components of a pipeline......240
Basic pipeline example 241
Advantages of pipelines 242
Advanced pipeline example 242
Multi-stage pipeline with multiple goroutines......242
Error handling in pipelines 243
Real-world applications......245
Mutexes and race conditions in Go 245
Overview of mutexes and race conditions......245

Race conditions ... 245
Definition ... 245
Detecting race conditions ... 246
Usage of the race detector ... 246
Solving race conditions with mutexes ... 246
Mutex ... 246
Using sync.Mutex in Go ... 247
Common mutex patterns ... 247
Deadlocks and avoiding them ... 250
Deadlock ... 250
Mutex versus other synchronization techniques ... 250
Real-world applications of mutexes ... 250
Condition variables and locks in Go ... 251
Overview of condition variables and locks ... 251
Locks ... 251
Condition variables ... 252
Using sync.Cond for coordination ... 252
Producer-consumer problem ... 252
Combining condition variables with locks ... 253
Real-world applications ... 255
Building concurrency-safe applications in Go ... 256
Definition ... 256
Core principles of concurrency safety ... 256
Common concurrency issues ... 256
Techniques for building concurrency-safe applications ... 256
Synchronization with mutexes ... 257
Using channels for safe communication ... 257
Atomic operations ... 258
Context for goroutine management ... 259
Testing and debugging concurrency ... 260
Real-world applications of concurrency-safe design ... 260
Rate limiting and throttling in Go ... 260
Overview of rate limiting ... 260
Usage of rate limiting and throttling ... 260
Key concepts ... 260
Implementing rate limiting ... 261
Implementing throttling ... 264
Time-based throttling ... 264
Real-world applications ... 264
Conclusion ... 265
Questions ... 265

13. Error Handling in Concurrency 267
Introduction 267
Structure 267
Objectives 267
Best practices for handling errors in concurrency 267
Overview 268
Importance of error handling in concurrency 268
Common challenges in concurrency error handling 268
Best practices for handling errors 268
Testing and debugging concurrency errors 273
Best practices 273
Deadlocks and their solutions 273
Deadlock 273
Example of a deadlock 273
Common causes of deadlocks 274
Identifying deadlocks 274
Strategies to avoid deadlocks 274
Real-world applications 278
Recovering from panics in concurrent programs 278
Panic 278
Importance of recovering panics 278
Using recover to handle panics 278
Panics in concurrent programs 279
Strategies for recovering panics in goroutines 280
Best practices for panic recovery 282
Real-world applications 283
Synchronizing state between goroutines 283
Importance of synchronization 283
Techniques for synchronizing state 283
Comparing synchronization techniques 287
Applications of Go synchronization 287
Common pitfalls and solutions 287
Best practices for Go synchronization 287
Conclusion 288
Questions 288

14. Understanding Microservices Architecture 289
Introduction 289
Structure 289
Objectives 289

Microservices 289

Overview 289

Understanding microservices architecture...290

Monolithic vs. microservices architecture..290

Components of microservices architecture 291

Advantages of microservices..291

Challenges of microservices 292

Real world use cases of microservices..292

Microservices deployment strategies..292

Usage of microservices..293

Need for Go microservices...294

Key reasons for choosing Go for microservices..294

Simplicity and readability...294

Concurrency model 295

High performance 296

Native support for networking and HTTP...296

Small binary size..297

Cloud-native and container-friendly 297

gRPC support for high-performance communication..298

Easy deployment and CI/CD integration 298

Strong community and ecosystem...298

Usage of Go for microservices...299

Avoiding the use of Go for microservices 299

Principles of designing microservices..299

Key principles of microservices design 299

Single responsibility principle 299

Loose coupling...300

Autonomy 300

Decentralized data management...300

API first communication 301

Asynchronous communication 301

Fault tolerance and resilience 301

Observability and monitoring 302

Security first 303

Example of real-world microservices design 304

E-commerce microservices architecture...304

Conclusion...304

Questions...304

15. **Building a Simple REST API in Go** ... 305
Introduction ... 305
Structure ... 305
Objectives ... 305
Setting up a web server in Go ... 305
Handling HTTP requests and responses in Go ... 310
Routing in Go web applications ... 317
JSON encoding and decoding in Go ... 321
Error handling in Web APIs ... 327
Conclusion ... 331
Questions ... 332

16. **Advanced RESTful API Design** ... 333
Introduction ... 333
Structure ... 333
Objectives ... 333
RESTful API best practices ... 333
Logging and monitoring API requests in Go ... 338
Implementing API versioning in Go ... 342
API documentation in Go with Swagger ... 346
Handling rate limiting and throttling in APIs ... 350
Building a Docker image and deploying to GKE ... 352
Conclusion ... 357
Questions ... 357

17. **Securing Microservices** ... 359
Introduction ... 359
Structure ... 359
Objectives ... 359
Importance of microservices ... 359
Authentication overview ... 360
Authorization overview ... 360
Architecture patterns for auth in microservices ... 361
Token-based authentication ... 362
Understanding JSON Web Token ... 362
Generating and validating JWT in Go ... 363
TLS or SSL for secure communication ... 366
Configuring TLS in Go using an HTTP server ... 367
Implementing role-based access control ... 369
Securing communication between services ... 372

Best practices for securing microservices 374
Conclusion....376
Questions....377

18. Testing Microservices 379
Introduction 379
Structure 379
Objectives 379
Unit testing and integration testing in microservices....380
Unit testing for microservices 380
Integration testing for microservices....381
Writing tests for RESTful APIs....383
Unit testing REST handlers in Go....383
Testing handlers with path params and JSON....384
Mocking external services and dependencies....388
Mocking in Go using interfaces 388
Using GoMock for auto-generated mocks 389
Mocking HTTP calls 389
Mocking databases....391
Mocking message brokers 393
Load testing and performance optimization....393
Profiling and benchmarking in Go....395
Implementing end-to-end testing....396
Implementing E2E tests in Go 397
Running E2E tests in Docker Compose....399
Best practices for testing microservices 400
Conclusion....402
Questions....402

19. Managing Data in Microservices....403
Introduction 403
Structure 403
Objectives 403
Importance of database design in microservices....403
Schema design strategies....404
Handling cross-service data access....405
Choosing between SQL and NoSQL 405
Service-specific database design patterns....405
Key design considerations 406
Common mistakes to avoid in database design....406

Working with SQL and NoSQL databases.....406
Polyglot persistence.....406
Relational databases in microservices.....407
NoSQL databases in microservices.....407
Comparing SQL and NoSQL.....408
Using SQL and NoSQL together.....408
Access patterns and storage decisions.....409
Implementing data migrations and versioning.....409
Data migration.....409
Importance of schema versioning.....409
Event sourcing and CQRS patterns.....412
Event sourcing.....412
Command Query Responsibility Segregation.....413
CQRS and event sourcing together.....413
Implementing event sourcing in microservices.....414
Managing distributed transactions.....415
Best practices for data management in microservices.....417
Conclusion.....419
Questions.....420

Appendix A: Go Tools and Resources.....421
Introduction.....421
Structure.....421
Go modules.....421
Key Go modules files.....421
go.mod.....421
go.sum.....422
Core Go commands for modules.....422
Dependency proxy and security.....422
Profiling and performance tools.....424
Built-in profiling with pprof of GO.....424
Visualizing profiles.....425
Debugging tools for Go applications.....426
Print debugging and structured logs.....426
Continuous integration and deployment pipelines.....429
Importance of CI/CD for critical Go projects.....429
Common CI/CD workflow for Go projects.....429
Popular Go libraries and frameworks.....431
Web frameworks.....431

Appendix B: Glossary **435**

Appendix C: Answers to Exercises **439**

Chapter 1 439
Chapter 2 440
Chapter 3 441
Chapter 4 441
Chapter 5 442
Chapter 6 443
Chapter 7 444
Chapter 8 444
Chapter 9 445
Chapter 10 445
Chapter 11 446
Chapter 12 446
Chapter 13 447
Chapter 14 447
Chapter 15 448
Chapter 16 449
Chapter 17 449
Chapter 18 450
Chapter 19 450

Index **451-455**

CHAPTER 1
Introduction to Go

Introduction

In this chapter, we will understand the **Golang** (**Go**) programming language, discussing its foundational elements and the unique features that make it ideal for building efficient, cloud-native applications and scalable systems. We will discuss Go's origins, the problem it was designed to solve, and its core language constructs. Moreover, we will understand how to install Go, set up our workspace, and write our first Go program. As we progress, we will also discuss Go's concurrency model, its approach to memory management, and the modular system for handling dependencies, equipping you with a strong base to start building applications in Go.

Structure

The following topics will be covered in this chapter:

- Overview of Go
- History of Go
- Installing and setting up the Go environment
- Writing your first Go program
- Understanding the main function
- Go modules and dependencies

Objectives

By the end of this chapter, we will understand the history and motivation behind the Go programming language. We will discuss the main features and characteristics that make Go suitable for systems programming. We will also understand how to set up the Go environment on our machine and verify the installation. Additionally, we will write and execute a simple Go program, explain the purpose of the main function and Go's package structure, and utilize Go modules to manage dependencies within a project. These objectives aim to provide the foundational knowledge needed to understand Go.

Overview of Go

Go is a statically typed, compiled programming language primarily designed for application programming, particularly for networked and concurrent systems, with simplicity and performance as key considerations. Go was developed by *Google* and is maintained by a growing open-source community. By adopting modern paradigms, Go solves common development problems, such as dependency management, concurrency, and cross-platform portability.

Features of Go

The following are the main features of Go:

- **Static typing and efficiency**: Go is statically typed, meaning types are checked at compile time. This ensures that errors related to types are caught early in development.
- **Simplicity in syntax**: Go has a clean and minimalistic syntax. It avoids complexities like inheritance and annotations, which are found in other modern languages.
- **Built-in concurrency**: The standout feature of Go is its native support for concurrency through goroutines. Unlike traditional multi-threading, goroutines are lightweight and easy to work with, allowing you to handle thousands of concurrent tasks effortlessly.
- **Memory management with garbage collection**: Go automatically manages memory through garbage collection, freeing developers from the complexity of manual memory management.
- **Platform independence**: Go enables developers to write once and compile to any platform, making cross-compilation seamless.

Use cases of Go

The following are some of the use cases of Go:

- **Cloud services and microservices:**
  - **Scalability and efficiency**: Go is widely adopted for building cloud-native applications, especially because of its efficiency in handling concurrent tasks. Its goroutines enable applications to manage thousands of tasks simultaneously without excessive memory use, making it ideal for scalable cloud services.
  - **Adoption by leading platforms**: Go powers core components of leading platforms like Kubernetes, Docker, and Prometheus, which have transformed cloud-native infrastructure. These tools benefit from Go's simplicity, performance, and cross-platform capabilities.
  - **Modular microservice architecture**: The simplicity of Go's syntax and concurrency model allows engineers to quickly build, test, and deploy individual microservices that can communicate with other services, a common approach in modern cloud architectures.
- **Web servers and APIs:**
  - **High performance**: Go's compilation of native machine code and its efficient standard library make it one of the fastest languages for serving web requests, often outperforming other popular web languages.
  - **Memory management**: With built-in garbage collection, Go automatically handles memory management, helping developers avoid memory leaks, a common issue in web applications. This makes Go suitable for high-load applications where stability and performance are critical.
  - **Examples in the industry**: Many companies, such as *Uber*, *Medium*, and *Dropbox*, use Go to build fast, reliable APIs. Go's simplicity also reduces onboarding time for new developers, accelerating project timelines.
- **Systems programming:**
  - **Network services**: Go is highly suitable for networked applications, such as proxies, VPNs, and network monitoring tools, due to its low-level capabilities and efficient concurrency model. Goroutines allow network services to handle multiple connections without traditional threading issues.
  - **Cross-platform compatibility**: Go compiles to a single binary for all major operating systems, making deployment easier in heterogeneous environments. This portability is especially advantageous in systems programming, where different parts of a system may run on different platforms.
  - **Security and reliability**: Go's memory safety and built-in garbage collection reduce common security vulnerabilities like buffer overflows and memory leaks, which are typical in systems programming languages like C/C++.

- **Data processing and analysis**:
  - **Concurrency for data pipelines**: Data pipelines often require handling and transforming large datasets in parallel. Go's concurrency makes it well-suited for **extract, transform, and load** (**ETL**) operations where multiple data streams are processed simultaneously.
  - **Scalable applications in data-intensive fields**: Companies like Google, for example, use Go for tasks that require efficient processing of massive amounts of data. Go's strong support for concurrent execution makes it a good choice for applications like real-time data processing and stream processing.
  - **Ease of deployment**: Go's statically compiled binaries make it easy to deploy data processing pipelines across multiple environments without dependency issues, which is critical in big data applications that often require flexible, scalable infrastructure.
- **DevOps and automation tools**:
  - **Infrastructure as code (IaC)**: Go has become popular in DevOps for tools that automate infrastructure deployment and management. The language's performance and reliability make it suitable for applications that need high levels of automation.
  - **Rapid development of CLI tools**: Go's straightforward syntax and standard library make it easy to build command line tools. For DevOps teams, custom CLI tools are essential for managing infrastructure and monitoring systems, making Go a natural choice for these use cases.
  - **High concurrency for monitoring and logging**: Monitoring applications that need to gather logs, metrics, and other data in real-time benefit from Go's ability to handle concurrent processes efficiently. Tools like Prometheus, written in Go, are popular choices for monitoring large-scale infrastructure.
- **Internet of Things (IoT) and edge computing**:
  - **Low resource consumption**: In IoT, devices are often limited in resources, and Go's lightweight runtime and efficient use of memory make it a good choice for these constrained environments.
  - **Real-time data handling**: Go's concurrency and native networking libraries allow for real-time data processing on edge devices, where data is processed locally before being sent to the cloud.
  - **Cross-platform edge applications**: With Go's single-binary deployment, IoT applications can be easily deployed across different types of devices, regardless of the underlying operating system. This portability is valuable in edge computing, where multiple device types often work together.
- **Machine learning (ML) and artificial intelligence (AI)**:
  - **Data preprocessing**: Although Python is a common choice for machine learning, Go is increasingly used for data preprocessing tasks in ML workflows. Its speed and ability to handle large volumes of data make it a valuable tool for preparing datasets before analysis or model training.
  - **Integration with Python**: Many Go packages enable seamless integration with Python, allowing data scientists to preprocess and serve models in Go, leveraging its performance for production environments.
  - **Scalability in production ML systems**: With machine learning models increasingly deployed in real-time applications, Go's performance and concurrency support make it a strong choice for serving models and integrating with other ML infrastructures.

History of Go

Go was created as a response to the challenges those developers faced when working on large-scale systems. At Google, engineers often worked with languages like C++, Python, and Java, each of which had trade-offs in terms of speed, ease of use, and concurrency. The goal of Google was to develop a language that had the simplicity of Python, the performance of C/C++, and the ease of concurrency as a first-class citizen.

Evolution timeline

The following is the history of Go:

- **2007**: *Robert Griesemer*, *Rob Pike*, and *Ken Thompson* started working on Go to address the challenges of large-scale software development.
- **2009**: Go is officially announced and released as an open-source project.
- **2012**: Go 1.0 is released, marking a stable version for production use. This version ensured backward compatibility for future versions.
- **2015**: Go 1.5 introduces a new compiler written in Go itself, along with significant improvements in performance and garbage collection.
- **2017**: Go 1.8 introduces significant changes in the runtime, including improved garbage collection and runtime performance.
- **2022**: Go 1.18 added generics, a highly requested feature, allowing type-safe reusable code without sacrificing simplicity.
- **Present**: Go 1.24 enhanced generics with type aliases, improved module tooling, and added cryptographic features for modern security needs.

Reasons for choosing Go

When evaluating programming languages for modern development, Go offers compelling advantages, particularly in performance, concurrency, and community support. Let us take a deeper look into the reasons for choosing Go:

- **Performance**: Go compiles directly to machine code, enabling high-performance execution that surpasses interpreted languages like Python. This low-level compilation optimizes the runtime efficiency and reduces the overhead typically associated with the interpretation or virtual machine layers, making it ideal for performance-critical applications, such as backend services and microservices.
- **Concurrent programming**: Go's native support for concurrency through goroutines and channels provides a simple yet powerful model for handling multiple tasks simultaneously. With goroutines, you can spin up thousands of lightweight threads (or green threads) without the resource-heavy management that traditional threads require. Channels further enhance this by enabling safe and efficient data exchange between goroutines, making Go highly suited for scalable, concurrent applications.
- **Community and ecosystem**: The Go ecosystem is thriving, with a rapidly growing community and a comprehensive standard library. The ecosystem includes a wide range of open-source tools and libraries that simplify everything from web development to data processing. Additionally, community-driven efforts have produced numerous resources and frameworks, strengthening Go's position as a go-to language for both newcomers and seasoned developers.

Installing and setting up the Go environment

Before you start writing Go programs, you must install and set up the Go environment on your machine.

Here is a step-by-step guide for different operating systems:

- **For Windows**:
    1. **Download Go installer**: Visit the Go download page (**https://go.dev/dl/**) and download the `.msi` installer for Windows.
    2. **Install Go**: Run the installer and follow the instructions.
    3. **Verify installation**:

a. Open the command prompt and run:

```
go version
```

b. If the installation is successful, the installed Go version will be displayed.

- **For macOS**:

1. **Install Go via Homebrew**:

a. If you have Homebrew installed, you can use it to install Go:

```
brew install go
```

2. **Verify installation**:

a. After installation, verify by running:

```
go version
```

- **For Linux**:

1. **Download Go**:

a. Download the tarball from the official site:

```
wget https://golang.org/dl/go1.19.linux-amd6'.tar.gz
```

2. **Extract the tarball**:

```
sudo tar -C /usr/local -xzf go1.19.linux-amd64.tar.gz
```

3. **Set up environment variables**. Add Go to your system's **PATH** by modifying your **.bashrc** or **.zshrc**:

```
export PATH=$PATH:/usr/local/go/bin
```

4. **Verify installation**:

```
go version
```

Setting up a workspace

Setting up a workspace in Go involves organizing and configuring your development environment (also called a local workspace) to efficiently write, compile, and run Go programs. This setup helps your coding process, making it easier to manage and execute code.

The following are the steps involved in setting up a workspace:

1. Set the **GOPATH** environment variable, which defines the root directory of your Go workspace. Typically, you can set it as:

```
export GOPATH=$HOME/go
```

2. Add the workspace's bin subdirectory to your PATH:

```
export PATH=$PATH:$GOPATH/bin
```

Writing your first Go program

Writing your first Go program is an exciting step into Go programming. This process is simple, but it introduces key concepts that are foundational to Go and applicable to most programs we will write. Let us start with a simple Go program.

Follow these steps to create and execute a **Hello, World!** program in Go:

1. **Create a new file:**

a. Open your preferred text editor and create a file named **hello.go**.

2. **Write the following code:**

```
package main

import "fmt"

func main() {
    fmt.Println("Hello, World!")
}
```

Explanation

The following is the guided breakdown to help you understand the steps involved:

- **Package declaration**: `package main` specifies the package that contains the `main` function, which is required for standalone programs.
- **Import statement**: `import "fmt"` imports the `fmt` package for formatted I/O operations.
- **Main function**: `func main()` defines the entry point of the program.
- **Print statement**: `fmt.Println()` prints the message to the console.
- **Run the program**:

```
go run hello.go
```

Building the executable

Building an executable in Go means converting your Go source code into a standalone file that can run independently without needing the Go environment. This is helpful when you want to distribute or deploy your program, as the executable will contain all necessary instructions for it to run on its own.

Compile the program into an executable as follows:

```
go build hello.go
```

This will create an executable file that you can run as follows:

```
./hello
```

Understanding the main function

In Go, the `main()` function is the primary entry point. This is similar to the `main()` function in C or Java, where program execution starts from this function. It is important to note that the `main()` function must be declared within the main package for a Go program to run as a standalone executable.

If the `main()` function or main package is missing, the Go compiler will throw an error because it does not know where to start execution.

In Go, you cannot have multiple `main()` functions within the same package. This ensures clarity in terms of program flow and where the execution begins.

Go modules and dependencies

In modern Go development, modules provide a mechanism to manage dependencies. A module is a set of Go packages organized within a directory that contains a `go.mod` file at its root.

This `go.mod` file specifies the module's characteristics, including its path, version, and dependencies, as follows:

Creating a Go module

Creating a Go module is the first step in organizing and managing dependencies for a Go project. Modules allow Go to handle external libraries, making your code more modular and easier to maintain. A module essentially groups related packages and keeps track of their versions.

Undertake the following steps:

1. In your project directory, run:

   ```
   go mod init <module_name
   ```

2. This creates a **go.mod** file, which tracks the version of Go and external dependencies.

Managing dependencies

Managing dependencies in Go involves handling external libraries or packages that your project relies on. Go modules simplify this by automatically tracking dependencies in a **go.mod** file, which is created once you initialize a module as per the previous step. Undertake the following steps to maintain the external dependencies:

1. To incorporate an external Go library (dependency) into your Go project, you can simply import the package (dependency) to your project, using the **go get** command:

   ```
   go get github.com/user/package
   ```

2. Go automatically manages dependencies in the **go.mod** and **go.sum** files.

go mod commands

The **go mod** commands are a set of tools for managing modules and dependencies in Go projects, allowing you to control, update, and organize external packages. These commands help you maintain a stable development environment by keeping track of dependencies and their versions as follows:

- **go mod tidy**: Cleans up any unused dependencies and adds missing dependencies to the **go.mod** file. It identifies all direct and indirect dependencies required and ensures they are included in **go.mod** with the appropriate versions.
- **go mod vendor**: Copies all dependencies into a vendor directory, which ensures consistent builds.

Conclusion

In this chapter, we understood the essential elements of Go, from its origins to its distinct features that make it a powerful choice for web and cloud-native applications. We set up the Go environment, established a workspace, and wrote a basic program to help you familiarize with Go's syntax and structure. With insights into Go modules and dependency management, we now have the tools to organize and handle external packages, ensuring that our projects are structured, maintainable, and ready for collaborative development.

In the next chapter, we will discuss Go's syntax and core language fundamentals. We will understand the defining variables and constants, working with basic data types, and constructing expressions using operators. We will also cover key control structures like if, else, and switch, along with the various ways to implement loops in Go. This foundation will enable us to create more complex and functional programs as we progress through the book.

Questions

1. What is Go, and why was it created?
2. What are the main features that make Go suitable for cloud services and microservices?
3. Describe the steps to install Go on your machine.

4. What is the purpose of the main() function in a Go program?
5. What are Go modules, and how do they simplify dependency management?
6. Explain how you can manage dependencies in a Go project.
7. What command is used to compile a Go program into an executable file?
8. Explain the purpose of the GOPATH environment variable.
9. What does the go mod tidy command do in a Go project?

Join our Discord space

Join our Discord workspace for latest updates, offers, tech happenings around the world, new releases, and sessions with the authors:

https://discord.bpbonline.com

CHAPTER 2
Go Syntax and Language Fundamentals

Introduction

In Go, variables, constants, and data types are fundamental components of the language, essential for handling data in any program. They allow programmers to store, manipulate, and categorize data efficiently. Loops are fundamental in programming, enabling the automation of repetitive tasks with precision and efficiency. Go employs a distinctive approach by offering a single, flexible looping construct: the for loop, yet it is versatile enough to handle various looping scenarios, from simple iteration to complex data traversals. Go's for loop can function as a traditional loop, a while loop, or even an infinite loop, providing flexibility and simplicity. Additionally, Go includes the range keyword, which offers a convenient way to iterate over collections like arrays, slices, maps, and strings. Understanding how to use for and range effectively is crucial for developing efficient, readable, and maintainable Go code.

Structure

This chapter covers the following topics:

- Variables and constants
- Basic data types
- Operators and expressions
- Control structures
- Loops in Go

Objectives

By the end of this section, you should be able to understand the use of constants and variables effectively. You will gain a comprehensive understanding of basic data types in Go, including integers, floats, Booleans, strings, and complex numbers. Additionally, you will be equipped to understand and apply the syntax and structure of the for loop in various contexts. This includes using the for loop as a traditional loop, as a while loop, and even as an infinite loop when necessary.

You will also learn to leverage the range keyword to iterate efficiently over arrays, slices, maps, and strings. Furthermore, you will be able to employ the break and continue statements to control the flow within loops effectively. Best practices for managing loops in Go will be covered, including guidance on avoiding infinite loops and simplifying iterations over collections. Lastly, you will understand the performance benefits and readability advantages of using the range keyword in appropriate scenarios, ensuring that your code remains both efficient and easy to read.

Note: The text following a double slash (//) in code snippets is a comment used to explain the corresponding code snippet, and that line will not be executed. Read through the comments for a better understanding of the code. For example:

```
// This is a comment
package main
import ("fmt")

func main() {
  // This is a comment
  fmt.Println("Hello World!")
}
```

Variables and constants

In this section, we will be learning about variables in depth.

The details are as follows:

- **Introduction to variables:**
  - **Definition**: Variables are symbolic names assigned to data stored in memory. They allow programs to store, retrieve, and manipulate data dynamically.
  - **Purpose of variables**: Variables give programs flexibility and allow them to perform operations based on dynamic input and processing.
  - **Syntax overview**: In Go, variables can be declared using the `var` keyword or shorthand `:=`.
    - **Example**:

      ```
      var a int = 10    // Declaring an integer
      variable 'a' with the value 10
      b := 20       // Shorthand declaration where Go
      infers 'b' as an integer
      ```

- **Declaring variables in Go:**
  - **The basic syntax for variable declaration:**

    ```
    var variableName type = value
    ```

    Here, `var` is the keyword, `variableName` is the identifier, `type` defines the variable type, and `value` initializes it.
  - **Type inference**: Go infers variable types if you do not specify them explicitly, especially when using `:=` in a variable declaration.

    ```
    name := "Go Programming // Go infers 'name' as type 'string'
    ```

  - **Shorthand declaration with :=:**
    - `:=` is used to declare and initialize a variable in one line without the `var` keyword.
    - **Restrictions**: The shorthand `:=` can only be used within functions, not at the package level.
    - **Example**:

      ```
      package main

      // Using var at the package level
      ```

```
var name = "Venkatesh"

// This would cause an error:
// age := 30 // Error: shorthand assignment is not allowed at package eve

func main() {
    // Using shorthand := inside a function
    age := 30
    greeting := "Hello, " + name
    println(greeting, "You are", age, "years old.")
}
```

- **Variable types and declaration styles**:
  - **Single declaration**:

    ```
    var x int        // Declares an integer variable 'x' with default value 0
    ```

  - **Multiple declarations**:

    ```
    var a, b, c int = 1, 2, 3
    var x, y = 10, "Hello"  // Different types in the same line
    ```

  - **Block declaration style**: Useful for grouping related variables together, especially in functions or for global declarations.

    ```
    var (
        name string = "Shubham"
        age int = 30
        height float64 = 5.9
    )
    ```

- **Variable scope in Go**:
  - **Local variables**:
    - Declared within functions, loops, or blocks.
    - Accessible only within the specific block in which they are defined.
  - **Global variables**:
    - Declared outside functions at the package level.
    - Accessible throughout the package.
  - **Example**:

    ```
    var globalVar int = 50 // package-level variable

    func main() {
        localVar := 20       // Local variable
        fmt.Println(globalVar) // Accessible here
        fmt.Println(localVar)  // Accessible here
    }
    ```

- **Constants in Go**:
  - **Definition**: Constants represent fixed values that do not change throughout the program.

- **Declaring constants**: Constants are declared with the **`const`** keyword, followed by the name, type (optional), and value.
- **Syntax**:

```
const PI = 3.14159
const NAME string = "GoLang"
```

- **Rules for constants**:
  - Constants must be initialized at the time of declaration.
  - Only certain types are allowed for constants, including Boolean, numeric, and string.
  - Constants cannot be modified after their declaration, enhancing program stability.

- **Types of constants**:
  - **Typed constants**:
    - Explicitly specify the constant type during declaration.
    - **Example**:

```
const AGE int = 25
const PI float64 = 3.14159
```

  - **Untyped constants**:
    - Go has the capability to infer the type, and it would be more elegant to allow the Go compiler to infer the type instead of declaring it manually.
    - This can be more flexible when used in expressions.
  - **Example**:

```
const SCORE = 95  // Untyped constant, can be used as int or float64 in expressions
```

- **Benefits of using constants**:
  - **Immutability**: Since constants cannot be modified, they make the code more predictable and reduce unintended errors.
  - **Memory efficiency**: Go optimizes constants to occupy minimal memory, improving program efficiency.
  - **Improved code readability**: Constants can be used to define fixed values with meaningful names, making code easier to read and understand.
  - **Example**:

```
const (
    TAX_RATE = 0.07
    DEFAULT_TIMEOUT = 30
)
```

- **Best practices for variables and constants**:
  - Use camelCase for variable names (**`userCount`**, **`totalAmount`**), and UPPERCASE for constant names (**`MAX_COUNT`**, **`API_KEY`**).
  - Keep variable names descriptive to improve code readability.
  - Avoid using unnecessary variables; directly use values when appropriate.
- **Example programs to illustrate variables and constants**:
  - **Program 1**: Using variables and constants in basic arithmetic:

```
package main
import "fmt"

func main() {
    const PI = 3.14159
    var radius float64 = 5

    area := PI * radius * radius
    fmt.Println("The area of the circle is:", area)
}
```

- **Output**: `The area of the circle is: 78.53975`
- **Explanation**:
  - `PI` is a constant representing the value of pi.
  - `radius` is a variable holding the radius of a circle.
  - We use both in an expression to calculate and print the `area`.

- **Program 2**: Demonstrating variable scope:

```
package main
import "fmt"

var globalVar = "I am global!"

func main() {
    localVar := "I am local!"
    fmt.Println(globalVar) // Accessible here
    fmt.Println(localVar)  // Accessible here
}

func anotherFunc() {
    fmt.Println(globalVar) // Accessible here
    // fmt.Println(localVar)  // Not accessible here; would cause an error
}
```

- **Explanation**:
  - `globalVar` is declared at the package level, making it accessible in both `main()` and `anotherFunc()`.
  - `localVar` is declared within `main()`, so it is only accessible there.

Basic data types

This section talks about the basic data types. The details are as follows:

- **Introduction to data types**:
  - **Definition**: Data types define the kind of data a variable can store, determining the values it can hold and the operations that can be performed on it.
  - **Purpose of data types**: By specifying data types, Go optimizes memory allocation and allows for type checking, reducing errors at compile time.

- **Overview of primitive data types**: Go has several basic data types, categorized into the following groups:
  - **Numeric types**: Integers and floating-point numbers.
  - **Boolean type**: Represents true or false values.
  - **String type**: Used for sequences of characters.
- **Integer types**: Integers represent whole numbers without decimal points. The types of integers are:
  - **Signed integers (can be negative or positive)**:
    - **int8**: Range from -128 to 127
    - **int16**: Range from -32,768 to 32,767
    - **int32**: Range from -2,147,483,648 to 2,147,483,647
    - **int64**: Range from -9,223,372,036,854,775,808 to 9,223,372,036,854,775,807
    - **int**: Platform-dependent (typically 32 or 64 bits)
  - **Unsigned integers (only positive values)**:
    - **uint8**: Range from 0 to 255
    - **uint16**: Range from 0 to 65,535
    - **uint32**: Range from 0 to 4,294,967,295
    - **uint64**: Range from 0 to 18,446,744,073,709,551,615
    - **uint**: Platform-dependent (typically 32 or 64 bits)
  - **Examples**:

```
var age int = 25            // Signed integer
var distance uint32 = 500  // Unsigned integer
```

  - **Best practices**:
    - Use int for general-purpose integer variables unless you need specific byte sizes.
    - Use unsigned types (`uint`) only when negative values are irrelevant.
- **Floating-point types**:
  - **Definition**: Floating-point types represent numbers with fractional parts (decimals).
  - **Types**:
    - **float32**: 32-bit floating-point number, roughly 6-7 decimal digits of precision.
    - **float64**: 64-bit floating-point number, roughly 15-16 decimal digits of precision (more commonly used).
  - **Examples**:

```
var price float32 = 19.99
var pi float64 = 3.141592653589793
```

  - **Precision**: `float64` is more precise and is the recommended type for calculations requiring high accuracy.
  - **Operations with floating-point numbers**:
    - Operations like addition, subtraction, multiplication, and division are supported.
    - **Example**:

```
var radius float64 = 7.5
var area float64 = 3.1415 * radius * radius
```

- **Boolean type**:
  - **Definition**: The Boolean type represents a truth value, either true or false.
  - **Usage**: Booleans are commonly used in conditional statements to control the flow of the program.
  - **Declaration**:

```
var isActive bool = true
var hasDiscount bool = false
```

  - **Example with conditions**:

```
var isAdult bool = age >= 18
if isAdult {
    fmt.Println("You are an adult.") // This statement gets executed only if the age is above or equal to 18
}
```

- **String type**:
  - **Definition**: The string type represents a sequence of characters.
  - **Characteristics**:
    - Strings in Go are immutable, meaning that once created, their values cannot be changed.
    - Represented within double quotes ("").
  - **Declaration**:

```
var name string = "Shubham"
message := "Welcome to Go programming!"
```

  - **String length**:
    - The `len()` function returns the length of a string.
    - **Example**:

```
var greeting string = "Hello"
fmt.Println("Length:", len(greeting)) // Output: Length: 5
```

  - **String concatenation**:
    - You can concatenate strings using the + operator. Strings are immutable; Go allocates a new memory space to hold the resulting string, rather than modifying either of the original strings.
    - **Example**:

```
var firstName string = "Shubham"
var lastName string = "Raizada"
fullName := firstName + " " + lastName
fmt.Println(fullName) // Output: Shubham Raizada
```

- **Type conversion in Go**:
  - **Implicit vs. explicit conversion**:
    - Go is a statically typed language and does not perform implicit conversions between different types.
    - The conversion must be explicit using the desired type.
  - **Syntax**:

```
var i int = 42
```

```
var f float64 = float64(i)   // Converts int to float64
var u uint = uint(i)         // Converts int to uint
```

- **Example**:

```
var temperature int = 30
var tempInFloat float64 = float64(temperature)
```

- **Default values of basic types**:
  - **Definition**: When variables are declared without an initial value, Go assigns them default values.
  - **Defaults**:
    - **int, float32, float64**: 0
    - **bool**: false
    - **string**: "" (empty string)
  - **Example**:

```
var count int            // Default is 0
var active bool          // Default is false
var description string // Default is ""
fmt.Println(count, active, description)
```

- **Working with constants of basic types**:
  - **Definition**: Constants are fixed values defined with the const keyword. They must be of a basic type and cannot be changed after declaration.
  - **Syntax**:

```
const PI float64 = 3.14159
const GREETING = "Hello, Go!"
```

  - **Usage**: Constants are useful for values that remain unchanged, such as mathematical constants, fixed string messages, and configuration settings.
- **Example program to illustrate basic data types**:
  - **Program**: Calculating the area of a circle and displaying a message using various data types.

```
package main
import "fmt"

func main() {
    const PI float64 = 3.1415
    var radius float64 = 5.5
    var area float64 = PI * radius * radius

    var message string = "The area of the circle is:"
    fmt.Println(message, area)
}
```

  - **Output**: `The area of the circle is: 95.03037499999999`
  - **Explanation**:
    - `PI` is a constant representing the mathematical constant π.
    - `radius` and `area` are floating point numbers.

    - `message` is a string variable, and `fmt.Println()` outputs the final message with the calculated area.

- **Best practices for using basic data types**:
    - **Choose the appropriate integer type**: Use `int` unless specific bit sizes (e.g., int8) are needed to save memory.
    - **Use float64 for floating-point calculations**: This provides better precision and is the default for most calculations.
    - **Descriptive names for Boolean variables**: Use names that convey true/false meaning, like `isEnabled` or `hasPermission`.
    - **Avoid implicit type conversions**: Always perform explicit type conversions to prevent unexpected behavior.

Basic data types, complex numbers

The details are as follows:

- **Introduction to complex numbers**:
    - **Definition**: Complex numbers are numbers that include both a real part and an imaginary part. They are commonly represented in the form *a+bi*, where:
        - *a* is the real part (a real number)
        - *b* is the imaginary part (multiplied by *i*, where *i^2=1*)
    - **Usage in programming**: Complex numbers are useful in fields like physics, engineering, signal processing, and computer graphics, where calculations often involve imaginary components.
- **Complex types in Go**:
    - Go has two built-in types for complex numbers:
        - **complex64**: This type represents a complex number with float32 precision for the real and imaginary parts.
        - **complex128**: This type represents a complex number with float64 precision for the real and imaginary parts.
    - **Choosing between complex64 and complex128**:
        - Use complex64 for smaller, less precise values to save memory.
        - Use complex128 for greater precision when dealing with high-accuracy calculations.
- **Declaring complex numbers in Go**:
    - **Syntax**: The complex function is used to create complex numbers in Go. It takes two arguments: the real and imaginary parts.
    - **Example**:

```
var z1 complex64 = complex(5, 7)       // complex64 type with real part 5 and imaginary part 7
var z2 complex128 = complex(2.3, 4.5)  // complex128 type with real part 2.3 and imaginary part 4.5
```

    - **Direct assignment**: Complex numbers can also be directly assigned as *a + bi*, where *a* and *b* are floating-point literals.

```
z := 3 + 4i // Creates a complex number with real part 3 and imaginary part 4
```

- **Accessing real and imaginary parts**:
  - **Functions**: **real()** and **imag()** are built-in functions that extract the real and imaginary components of a complex number, respectively.
  - **Example**:

```
z := complex(6, -8)  // complex number 6 - 8i
r := real(z)         // r is 6
i := imag(z)         // i is -8
fmt.Println("Real part:", r)
fmt.Println("Imaginary part:", i)
```

- **Use case**: This is particularly useful when you need to operate separately on the real and imaginary parts of a complex number.

- **Basic operations with complex numbers**: Go supports arithmetic operations on complex numbers, similar to real numbers. Operations are performed separately on the real and imaginary parts.
  - **Addition**: The sum of two complex numbers *(a+bi)+(c+di)* results in *(a+c)+(b+d)i.*
  - **Example**:

```
z1 := 2 + 3i
z2 := 1 + 4i
sum := z1 + z2  // Result: 3 + 7i
```

  - **Subtraction**: The difference between two complex numbers *(a+bi)–(c+di)* results in *(a–c)+(b–d)i.*
  - **Example**:

```
z1 := 5 + 6i
z2 := 3 + 2i
difference := z1 - z2  // Result: 2 + 4i
```

  - **Multiplication**: The product of two complex numbers *(a+bi)×(c+di)* is calculated as *(ac–bd)+(ad+bc)i.*
  - **Example**:

```
z1 := 1 + 2i
z2 := 3 + 4i
product := z1 * z2  // Result: -5 + 10i
```

  - **Division**: Division of complex numbers *(a+bi)/(c+di)* is calculated as: *(ac+bd)+(bc–ad)i/c^2+d^2.*
  - **Example**:

```
z1 := 5 + 10i
z2 := 2 + 4i
quotient := z1 / z2  // Result: 2.5 + 0i
```

- **Calculating the magnitude of a complex number**:
  - **Definition**: The magnitude (or modulus) of a complex number *a+bi* is the distance from the origin to the point *(a,b)* in the complex plane. It is calculated as: *sqrt a^2+b^2.*
  - **Example**:

```
import "math"

z := complex(3, 4)
magnitude := math.Sqrt(math.Pow(real(z), 2) + math.Pow(imag(z), 2))
fmt.Println("Magnitude:", magnitude)  // Output: 5
```

- **Built-in functions for complex numbers**:
  - **Creating complex numbers**:
    - **complex(real, imag)**: Creates a complex number from real and imaginary parts.
  - **Extracting real and imaginary parts**:
    - **real(z)**: Returns the real part of the complex number z.
    - **imag(z)**: Returns the imaginary part of the complex number z.
  - **Example of using built-in functions**:

```
z := complex(2.5, 3.5)
fmt.Println("Real part:", real(z))
fmt.Println("Imaginary part:", imag(z))
```

- **Practical examples and use cases**:
  - **Example 1**: Electrical engineering calculations:
    - Complex numbers are important for calculating impedance in AC circuits, combining **`resistance`** (real part) and **`reactance`** (imaginary part). For instance, complex (5, 3) represents an **`impedance`** with 5 ohms of **`resistance`** and 3 ohms of **`reactance`**. You can add these numbers to get the total. This method simplifies handling AC circuit calculations by representing **`impedance`** as a single complex number, as shown:

```
var resistance complex128 = complex(4, 0)  // Purely real resistance
var reactance complex128 = complex(0, 3)   // Purely imaginary reactance
impedance := resistance + reactance        // Combined impedance
fmt.Println("Impedance:", impedance)
```

  - **Example 2**: Signal processing with complex numbers:
    - Complex numbers are often used in Fourier transforms and signal analysis.

```
// Example of combining two signals as complex numbers
var signal1 complex128 = complex(5, 3)
var signal2 complex128 = complex(2, 4)
combinedSignal := signal1 + signal2
fmt.Println("Combined Signal:", combinedSignal)
```

- **Best practices with complex numbers in Go**:
  - **Precision**: Use complex128 over complex64 if precision is essential, as complex128 offers greater accuracy.
  - **Separate calculations**: If working with high-precision real and imaginary parts separately, use **`real()`** and **`imag()`** functions to avoid rounding errors.
  - **Avoid unnecessary complex numbers**: Only use complex numbers when dealing with calculations that inherently require imaginary components, such as physics or signal processing.

Operators and expressions

In Go, operators are symbols that perform operations on variables and values, creating expressions. An expression is a combination of operators, variables, constants, and functions that evaluates to a single value.

The following are the types of operators in Go:

<table>
<tr><th>Category</th><th>Operators</th><th>Description</th></tr>
<tr><td>Arithmetic</td><td>+,-,*,/,%</td><td>Perform basic math operations</td></tr>
<tr><td>Relational</td><td>==,!=,>,<,>=,<=</td><td>Compare two values</td></tr>
<tr><td>Logical</td><td>&&,||,!</td><td>Combine or invert Boolean expressions</td></tr>
<tr><td>Bitwise</td><td>&,|,^,<<,>>,&^</td><td>Operate on bits: AND, OR, XOR, left shift, right shift, and AND NOT</td></tr>
<tr><td>Assignment</td><td>=,+=,-=,*=,/=,%=,&=,|=,^=,<<=,>>=</td><td>Assign values or combine operations with assignment</td></tr>
<tr><td>Increment/Decrement</td><td>++,--</td><td>Increase or decrease by 1.</td></tr>
</table>

Table 2.1: *Types of operators*

- **Arithmetic operators**: Arithmetic operators are used to perform basic mathematical calculations, as follows:

Operator	Description	Example
+	Addition	5 + 3 = 8
-	Subtraction	10 - 4 = 6
*	Multiplication	7 * 3 = 21
/	Division (integer/floating)	10 / 3 = 3 (integer result)
%	Modulus (remainder)	10 % 3 = 1

Table 2.2: *Arithmetic operators*

Note: Integer division discards the remainder, returning only the truncated result. To achieve precise outcomes, use floating point division by converting integers to float64 before performing the operation. This ensures accurate decimal results.

- **Relational operators**: Relational operators compare two values and return a Boolean result (true or false):

Operator	Description	Example
==	Equal to	5 == 5 = true
!=	Not equal to	5 != 3 = true
>	Greater than	7 > 5 = true
<	Less than	3 < 5 = true
>=	Greater than or equal to	5 >= 5 = true
<=	Less than or equal to	3 <= 4 = true

Table 2.3: *Relational operators*

- **Logical operators**: Logical operators combine multiple conditions:

<table>
<tr><th>Operator</th><th>Description</th><th>Example</th></tr>
<tr><td>&&</td><td>Logical AND</td><td>true && false = false</td></tr>
<tr><td>||</td><td>Logical OR</td><td>true || false = true</td></tr>
<tr><td>!</td><td>Logical NOT</td><td>!true = false</td></tr>
</table>

Table 2.4: *Logical operators*

- **Bitwise operators**: Bitwise operators manipulate individual bits:

Operator	Description	Example
&	AND	5 & 3 = 1
|	OR	OR
^	XOR	5 ^ 3 = 6
<<	Left Shift	5 << 1 = 10
>>	Right Shift	5 >> 1 = 2

Table 2.5: Bitwise operators

- **Assignment operators**: Assignment operators assign and update values:

Operator	Description	Example
=	Simple assignment	a = 10
+=	Addition assignment	a += 5 = a = a + 5
-=	Subtraction assignment	a -= 2 = a = a - 2

Table 2.6: Assignment operators

- **Expressions in Go**: An expression is a combination of variables, constants, and operators that produces a result.

```
a := 10
b := 20
c := (a + b) * 5        // Arithmetic expression
d := (a > b) || (b < 30) // Logical expression
```

Control structures

Control structures are fundamental in programming, allowing the code to make decisions and execute certain parts based on conditions. Go provides robust control structures, including **`if`**, **`else`**, and **`switch`**, which are straightforward and easy to use.

Let us look at these in more detail:

- **The if statement**:
  - **Definition**: The **`if`** statement allows a program to execute a block of code only if a specified condition is true.
  - **Syntax**:

```
if condition {
    // Code to execute if condition is true
}
```

  - **Example**:

```
var age int = 18
if age >= 18 {
    fmt.Println("You are eligible to vote.") // Code to execute if the
age condition is true
}
```

- **Explanation**: In this example, the message will only be printed if age is 18 or greater.

- **The else statement**:
  - **Definition**: The **`else`** statement is used alongside **`if`** to execute an alternative block of code if the condition in **`if`** is false.
  - **Syntax**:

```
if condition {
    // Code to execute if condition is true
} else {
    // Code to execute if condition is false
}
```

  - **Example**:

```
var age int = 16
if age >= 18 {
    fmt.Println("You are eligible to vote.")
} else {
    fmt.Println("You are not eligible to vote.")
}
```

  - **Explanation**: Here, if age is less than 18, the program will print the alternative message.

- **The else if statement**:
  - **Definition**: The **`else if`** statement allows multiple conditions to be tested in sequence. It is used when there are several possible conditions, each with its own block of code.
  - **Syntax**:

```
if condition1 {
    // Code if condition1 is true
} else if condition2 {
    // Code if condition2 is true
} else {
    // Code if none of the above conditions are true
}
```

  - **Example**:

```
var marks int = 85
if marks >= 90 {
    fmt.Println("Grade: A")
} else if marks >= 75 {
    fmt.Println("Grade: B")
} else if marks >= 50 {
    fmt.Println("Grade: C")
} else {
    fmt.Println("Grade: F")
}
```

  - **Explanation**: Here, different blocks of code will execute based on the range in which the mark falls.

- **Short variable declaration in if statements**:
  - **Description**: Go allows you to declare and initialize variables directly within an `if` statement, which limits the scope of the variable to the `if` block.
  - **Syntax**:
    ```
    if variable := expression; condition {
        // Code if condition is true
    }
    ```
  - **Example**:
    ```
    if temperature := 22; temperature > 30 {
        fmt.Println("It's a hot day.")
    } else {
        fmt.Println("It's a cool day.")
    }
    ```
  - **Output**: `It's a cool day.`
  - **Explanation**: Here, temperature is initialized and used only within the if-else structure.
- **Best practices with if, else if, and else**:
  - **Keep conditions simple and clear**: Complex conditions can make code hard to read. Break down complicated logic into smaller parts if necessary.
  - **Use short variable declaration wisely**: Use short variable declarations within if only if the variable is not needed outside the block.
  - **Avoid deep nesting**: Instead of multiple nested if-else statements, consider using a switch when there are many conditions or breaking the logic into separate functions.
- **The switch statement**:
  - **Definition**: The `switch` statement is a multi-way branch that allows different code blocks to execute based on the value of an expression. It is a more readable alternative to multiple if-else statements.
  - **Syntax**:
    ```
    switch expression {
    case value1:
        // Code for value1
    case value2:
        // Code for value2
    default:
        // Code if none of the cases match
    }
    ```
  - **Example**:
    ```
    day := "Monday"
    switch day {
    case "Monday":
        fmt.Println("Start of the week!")
    case "Friday":
        fmt.Println("Almost weekend!")
    case "Saturday", "Sunday":
    ```

```
        fmt.Println("It's the weekend!")
    default:
        fmt.Println("Just another weekday.")
    }
```

- **Explanation**: This **switch** statement checks the value of the day and prints the corresponding message.

- **Switch without expression**:
  - **Description**: In Go, you can omit the expression in a **switch**, making it act like a series of if-else statements. Each case can contain any condition.
  - **Syntax**:

```
switch {
case condition1:
    // Code if condition1 is true
case condition2:
    // Code if condition2 is true
default:
    // Code if none of the conditions are true
}
```

  - **Example**:

```
temperature := 25
switch {
case temperature > 30:
    fmt.Println("It's a hot day.")
case temperature >= 20 && temperature <= 30:
    fmt.Println("It's a warm day.")
case temperature < 20:
    fmt.Println("It's a cool day.")
}
```

  - **Output**: **It's a warm day.**
  - **Explanation**: Here, the **switch** statement acts as an alternative to multiple if-else statements, making the code cleaner.

- **The fallthrough keyword**:
  - **Description**: By default, Go's switch does not fall through from one case to the next. However, if you want to execute the code in the subsequent case, you can use the **fallthrough** keyword.
  - **Example**:

```
grade := "B"
switch grade {
case "A":
    fmt.Println("Excellent!")
case "B":
    fmt.Println("Good job!")
    fallthrough
case "C":
    fmt.Println("You passed.")
```

```
default:
    fmt.Println("Try harder next time.")
}
```

- **Output**:

```
Good job!
You passed.
```

- **Explanation**: In this example, when grade is `B`, the program will print both `Good job!` and `You passed` because of the `fallthrough` keyword.

- **Type switch**:
  - **Description**: A `type switch` is a form of `switch` that tests the type of an interface variable. It is useful when you need to handle different types dynamically.
  - **Syntax**:

```
switch v := x.(type) {
case int:
    // Code if x is of type int
case string:
    // Code if x is of type string
default:
    // Code for other types
}
```

  - **Example**:

```
var i interface{} = "Hello"
switch v := i.(type) {
case int:
    fmt.Println("Integer:", v)
case string:
    fmt.Println("String:", v)
default:
    fmt.Println("Unknown type")
}
```

  - **Explanation**: Here, the type of `i` is checked, and the corresponding block of code is executed based on whether `i` is an `int`, `string`, or another type. As per our example, the value `Hello` for the interface matches the type `string` and executes the corresponding print statement within the string scope.

- **Best practices with switch statements**:
  - **Limit the use of fallthrough**: Go's `switch` statements do not automatically fall through, which is a feature designed to avoid errors. Use `fallthrough` only when necessary.
  - **Default case**: Always include a `default` case, if possible, especially when dealing with unexpected values.
  - **Switch over types with care**: Use type switches when you genuinely need type checking, as they can make code harder to understand if overused.

- **Example program using if, else if, and switch**:
  - **Program**: Determine the `day` type and display an appropriate message.

```go
package main
import "fmt"

func main() {
    day := "Wednesday"

    // Using if-else statement
    if day == "Saturday" || day == "Sunday" {
        fmt.Println("It's the weekend!")
    } else if day == "Monday" {
        fmt.Println("Start of the week.")
    } else {
        fmt.Println("A regular weekday.")
    }

    // Using switch statement
    switch day {
    case "Saturday", "Sunday":
        fmt.Println("It's the weekend!")
    case "Monday":
        fmt.Println("Start of the week.")
    default:
        fmt.Println("A regular weekday.")
    }
}
```

- **Output**:

```
A regular weekday.
A regular weekday.
```

- **Explanation**: This program demonstrates both if-else and switch for checking the type of day.

Loops in Go

Loops are essential in programming as they allow you to execute a block of code repeatedly until a specified condition is met. In Go, the only looping construct is the `for` loop, which can handle all forms of repetition, including while and do-while constructs in other languages. Go also provides the range keyword for looping over collections, as described in the following list:

- **The for loop in Go**:
  - **Definition**: The `for` loop is the primary loop in Go, and it allows code to be executed repeatedly based on a condition.
  - **Syntax**:

```go
for initialization; condition; post {
    // Code to execute in each iteration
}
```

  - **Components**:
    - **Initialization**: Sets the starting condition for the loop (e.g., `i := 0`).

        - **Condition**: The loop continues as long as this condition is true.
        - **Post**: Executes after each iteration, typically used to increment or decrement a counter.
    - **Example**:
```
for i := 0; i < 5; i++ {
    fmt.Println("Iteration", i)
}
```
    - **Output**:
```
Iteration 0
Iteration 1
Iteration 2
Iteration 3
Iteration 4
```
    - **Explanation**: This loop will print `Iteration` followed by the current value of `i` from 0 to 4.
- **Using for as a while loop**:
    - **Description**: In Go, a `for` loop without the initialization and post components behaves like a `while` loop, as it only checks the condition at the start of each iteration.
    - **Syntax**:
```
for condition {
    // Code to execute while condition is true
}
```
    - **Example**:
```
count := 1
for count <= 5 {
    fmt.Println("Count:", count)
    count++
}
```
    - **Output**:
```
Count: 1
Count: 2
Count: 3
Count: 4
Count: 5
```
    - **Explanation**: This loop will keep running as long as the count is less than or equal to 5, simulating a `while` loop.
- **Infinite loops with for**:
    - **Description**: A `for` loop without any conditions or components runs indefinitely. This can be useful in cases where you want the loop to continue until explicitly broken.
    - **Syntax**:
```
for {
    // Code to execute indefinitely
}
```

- **Example**:

```
for {
    fmt.Println("This will print indefinitely.")
}
```

- **Stopping an infinite loop**: To stop an infinite loop, use a **break** statement based on a specific condition.
- **Example with break**:

```
i := 0
for {
    if i >= 3 {
        break
    }
    fmt.Println("Looping:", i)
    i++
}
```

- **Output**:

```
Looping: 0
Looping: 1
Looping: 2
```

- **Explanation**: This loop will stop once **i** reaches **3**, even though it is designed as an infinite loop.

- **The range keyword**:
  - **Definition**: **range** is a keyword in Go used to iterate over elements in data structures like arrays, slices, maps, and strings.
  - **Syntax**:

```
for index, value := range collection {
    // Code to execute for each element
}
```

  - **Parameters**:
    - **index**: The current index or key (for maps).
    - **value**: The current element's value.
  - **Example with array**:

```
numbers := []int{1, 2, 3, 4, 5}
for index, value := range numbers {
    fmt.Println("Index:", index, "Value:", value)
}
```

  - **Output**:

```
Index: 0 Value: 1
Index: 1 Value: 2
Index: 2 Value: 3
Index: 3 Value: 4
Index: 4 Value: 5
```

  - **Explanation**: This loop will print each index and the corresponding value in the numbers array.

- **Using range with different data types**:
  - **Array**: Iterates over each element.

```
arr := [3]int{10, 20, 30}
for i, v := range arr {
    fmt.Println("Index:", i, "Value:", v)
}
```

    - **Output**:

```
Index: 0 Value: 10
Index: 1 Value: 20
Index: 2 Value: 30
```

  - **Slice**: Behaves the same as an array.

```
slice := []string{"apple", "banana", "cherry"}
for i, v := range slice {
    fmt.Println("Index:", i, "Value:", v)
}
```

    - **Output**:

```
Index: 0 Value: apple
Index: 1 Value: banana
Index: 2 Value: cherry
```

  - **Map**: Iterates over key-value pairs.

```
fruits := map[string]string{"a": "apple", "b": "banana", "c": "cherry"}
for key, value := range fruits {
    fmt.Println("Key:", key, "Value:", value)
}
```

    - **Output**:

```
Key: a Value: apple
Key: b Value: banana
Key: c Value: cherry
```

  - **String**: Iterates over each character (as Unicode).

```
str := "GoLang"
for i, char := range str {
    fmt.Printf("Index: %d, Character: %c\n", i, char)
}
```

    - **Output**:

```
Index: 0, Character: G
Index: 1, Character: o
Index: 2, Character: L
Index: 3, Character: a
Index: 4, Character: n
Index: 5, Character: g
```

  - **Example explanation**: For each data type, the range provides a way to access each element and, if applicable, its index or key.

- **Control statements within loops**:
  - **break statement**:
    - Terminates the loop immediately.
    - **Example**:

```
for i := 0; i < 10; i++ {
    if i == 5 {
        break
    }
    fmt.Println(i)
}
```

    - **Output**:

```
0
1
2
3
4
```

    - **Explanation**: The loop will stop when `i` equals `5`, even though the condition allows it to run until `i` reaches `10`.
  - **continue statement**:
    - Skips the current iteration and moves to the next.
    - **Example**:

```
for i := 0; i < 5; i++ {
    if i == 2 {
        continue
    }
    fmt.Println(i)
}
```

    - **Output**

```
0
1
3
4
```

    - **Explanation**: When `i` equals `2`, the loop skips that iteration and continues with the next value of `i`.
  - **goto statement**:
    - Used to jump to a labeled statement, but generally avoided as it can make code harder to understand.
    - **Syntax**:

```
labelName:
    // Code here
goto labelName
```

- **Best practices with loops in Go**:
  - **Avoid infinite loops unless necessary**: Only use infinite loops if you have a specific plan for breaking out of them, such as a **`break`** condition.
  - **Use range for simplicity**: Range is highly readable and should be used when iterating over collections, such as arrays, slices, maps, and strings.
  - **Limit the use of goto**: The **`goto`** statement can lead to confusing, difficult-to-maintain code. Prefer break and continue for controlling loop flow.
- **Example program using different loop variants**:
  - **Program**: Let us explore different loops and controls in Go. The standard **`for`** loop is used for regular iterations with an initializer, condition, and increment. A while-like **`for`** loop that checks a condition before each iteration, acting like a **`while`** loop in other languages. An infinite loop with a break that runs endlessly until a **`break`** statement stops it, and a **`range`** with an array that allows easy iteration over elements and their indices.

    These are some variations that provide flexibility in managing loop execution effectively:

```
package main
import "fmt"

func main() {
    // Standard for loop
    fmt.Println("Standard for loop:")
    for i := 0; i < 3; i++ {
        fmt.Println(i)
    }

    // While-like for loop
    fmt.Println("\nWhile-like for loop:")
    count := 0
    for count < 3 {
        fmt.Println(count)
        count++
    }

    // Infinite loop with break
    fmt.Println("\nInfinite loop with break:")
    j := 0
    for {
        fmt.Println(j)
        j++
        if j == 3 {
            break
        }
    }

    // Using range with an array
```

```
        fmt.Println("\nUsing range with an array:")
        nums := []int{10, 20, 30}
        for index, value := range nums {
            fmt.Printf("Index: %d, Value: %d\n", index, value)
        }
    }
```

- **Output**:
  - The standard for loop:

```
0
1
2
```

  - While-like for loop:

```
0
1
2
```

  - Infinite loop with break:

```
0
1
2
```

  - Using range with an array:

```
Index: 0, Value: 10
Index: 1, Value: 20
Index: 2, Value: 30
```

- **Explanation**: Demonstrates various forms of loops and how they work in Go.

Conclusion

We have successfully understood variables and constants in Go. We have a deeper understanding of the basic data types like integer, float, Boolean, and string. We have a strong foundation in complex numbers as well. In Go, the for loop is a powerful tool that serves multiple purposes, from simple repetition to complex iteration over collections. The addition of the range keyword makes it particularly convenient to work with data structures like arrays, slices, maps, and strings, enabling a clean and concise syntax for traversing elements. Effective use of for and range can lead to more readable and efficient code. Additionally, the control statements break and continue to offer further flexibility in managing loop behavior. By understanding and mastering these looping mechanisms, developers can handle repetitive tasks and data processing with ease, making Go programs both robust and maintainable.

In the next chapter, we will see functions and error handling, which are foundational aspects of Go programming, allowing developers to structure code modularly and manage errors effectively. By understanding how to declare, call, and work with functions—including variadic, anonymous, and deferred functions—developers can write cleaner, reusable, and efficient code.

Questions

1. What are the three main components of a for loop in Go, and what purpose does each serve?
2. How does Go's for loop behave when it is used without any conditions?
3. Explain how the range keyword is used to iterate over arrays and maps in Go.
4. What is the effect of using the break statement within a for loop? Provide an example.
5. Describe a scenario where using continue in a loop would be useful.
6. How can the for loop in Go mimic a while loop?
7. Why is the range keyword advantageous when working with collections in Go?
8. Write a for loop that prints all numbers from 1 to 10 but skips the number 5.
9. When should you avoid using an infinite loop, and how can you terminate one safely if needed?
10. Explain the significance of the goto statement in loop control and why it is generally discouraged.

Chapter 3
Functions and Error Handling in Go

Introduction

In Go programming, understanding functions and error handling is essential for writing efficient and maintainable code. This chapter explores the different aspects of functions in Go, from their declaration and usage to the advanced handling of errors. Functions serve as the basic building blocks in Go, allowing developers to encapsulate reusable logic that can be executed with varying inputs. Additionally, Go's unique approach to error handling promotes clarity and simplicity, ensuring that errors are treated as first-class values and are explicitly managed within the code. Mastery of these topics not only enhances code readability but also helps in creating robust applications.

Structure

The chapter covers the following topics:

- Declaring and calling functions
- Function parameters and return types
- Variadic functions
- Anonymous functions
- Understanding and handling errors in Go
- Creating and handling custom errors

Objectives

This chapter focuses on enhancing your understanding of functions and error handling in Go. You will learn how to declare functions, including those with single or multiple parameters and return types, gaining a solid grasp of the structure and syntax required. Additionally, this chapter will cover function scope and Go's support for first-class functions, enabling you to understand variable scoping within functions and leverage functions as first-class citizens. You will also explore how to implement and use variadic functions, which allow you to pass an arbitrary number of arguments, providing flexibility in function calls. The chapter will introduce anonymous functions and closures, demonstrating how to use unnamed functions and how closures can capture variables from their surrounding context effectively.

Error handling in Go is a significant focus, where you will learn the language's philosophy behind managing errors, how to use built-in error functions, and how to create custom error types to add more context to error messages. Best practices for error management will be covered, including how to use fmt.Errorf with %w for wrapping errors, ensuring clarity and traceability in error handling. Furthermore, you will understand how to create and manage custom errors, designing specific error types for different scenarios, and using errors.As and errors.Is for inspecting and handling errors accurately. The chapter also covers techniques for aggregating and handling multiple errors using errors.Join, which is particularly useful for managing errors in batch processing or validation scenarios. By the end of this section, you will be well-equipped to write clean, maintainable, and effective error-handling code in Go.

Declaring and calling functions

The details of how to declare and call functions are as follows:

- **Introduction to functions:** Functions in Go are fundamental building blocks, allowing you to encapsulate code into reusable modules that perform specific tasks. A function in Go takes input, performs operations, and optionally returns output. Following the **Don't Repeat Yourself** (**DRY**) principle, functions help avoid redundancy and enhance readability and maintainability.
    - **Structure of a function in Go:** Each function in Go has a well-defined structure:

    ```
    func functionName(parameterList) (returnType) {
        // Function body
    }
    ```

        - **func:** The `func` keyword is required to declare a function.
        - **functionName:** This is the identifier for the function. It should be descriptive to reflect what the function does.
        - **parameterList:** List of parameters (if any) that the function accepts. Each parameter has a type.
        - **returnType:** The type of value that the function returns. This part is optional if the function does not return any value.
        - **Function body:** Contains the code block to be executed when the function is called.
- **Declaring a simple function:** A function can be as simple as one that prints a message:

```
func greet() {
    fmt.Println("Hello, welcome to Go!")
}
```

    - `greet` is the function name.
    - There are no parameters or return values.
    - The function body contains a single statement that prints a message.
    - **Calling the function:** To execute the `greet` function, simply call it by name:

    ```
    greet()
    ```

    - **Output:**

    ```
    Hello, welcome to Go!
    ```

- **Void functions:** Void functions (functions that do not return anything) are declared without specifying a return type.
    - **Example:**

    ```
    func displayMessage(message string) {
        fmt.Println("Message:", message)
    }
    ```

  This function only performs a task (printing) and does not return a value.
- **Understanding scope in functions:** Variables declared inside a function are local to that function and cannot be accessed outside. This is known as function scope.
    - **Example:**

    ```
    func calculateSquare(num int) int {
        square := num * num
    ```

```
        return square
    }
    // fmt.Println(square)  // Error: square is undefined outside the function
```

- **Functions as first-class citizens:** In Go, functions are first-class citizens. This means:
    - Functions can be passed as arguments to other functions.
    - Functions can be returned from other functions.
    - Functions can be assigned to variables.
        - **Example**:

```
func greet() {
    fmt.Println("Hello!")
}
var sayHello = greet
sayHello()  // Output: Hello!
```

Function parameters and return types

The function parameters and return types are discussed as follows:

- **Understanding parameters in Go functions:** Parameters allow you to pass data into functions, making them flexible and reusable for different inputs. Each parameter in Go is defined by a name and type.
    - **Syntax of parameters:**

```
func functionName(param1 type1, param2 type2) returnType {
    // function body
}
```

        - Each parameter requires a type.
        - Parameters are separated by commas.
    - **Example**:

```
func greetUser(name string, age int) {
    fmt.Printf("Hello, %s! You are %d years old.\n", name, age)
}
```

    - **In this function:**
        - `name` is a parameter of type `string`.
        - `age` is a parameter of type `int`.
    - **Calling the function with arguments:**

```
greetUser("Shubham", 25)  // Output: Hello, Shubham! You are 25 years old.
```

- **Multiple parameters with the same type:** If two or more consecutive parameters have the same type, you can omit the type for all but the last parameter. This simplifies function declarations.
    - **Example**:

```
func add(x, y, z int) int {
    return x + y + z
}
```

In this example: `x`, `y`, and `z` are all of type `int`.

- **Calling the function:**

```
sum := add(3, 5, 7)
fmt.Println("Sum:", sum)  // Output: Sum: 15
```

- **Function return types:** A function in Go can have one or more return values. Return types are specified after the parameter list in the function declaration.
  - **Syntax for return types:**

```
func functionName(parameters) returnType {
    // function body
    return value
}
```

- **Functions with a single return value:** A function can return a single value by specifying its type after the parameter list. The return keyword is used to send the value back to the caller.
  - **Example**:

```
func square(number int) int {
    return number * number
}
result := square(5)
fmt.Println("Square:", result)  // Output: Square: 25
```

In this example, the **square** function takes an integer and returns its square.

- **Functions with multiple return values:** Go allows functions to return multiple values, which is particularly useful for returning both a result and an error status.
  - **Example**:

```
func divide(dividend, divisor int) (int, error) {
    if divisor == 0 {
        return 0, fmt.Errorf("cannot divide by zero")
    }
    return dividend / divisor, nil
}
result, err := divide(10, 2)
if err != nil {
    fmt.Println("Error:", err)
} else {
    fmt.Println("Result:", result)  // Output: Result: 5
}
```

  - **In this example:**
    - The function divide returns two values: an integer and an error.
    - If the divisor is zero, an error is returned; otherwise, the division result is returned.

- **Named return values:** In Go, you can name the return values in the function signature, which can be beneficial for readability and organization.
  - **Example with named return values**:

```
func rectangleProperties(length, width int) (area, perimeter int) {
    area = length * width
```

```
    perimeter = 2 * (length + width)
    return  // Automatically returns area and perimeter
}
```

- **In this example**:
  - `area` and `perimeter` are named return values, declared directly in the function signature.
  - By naming the return values, you do not need to specify them in the `return` statement explicitly; the values of `area` and `perimeter` are returned automatically. You can also explicitly return just `area` and `perimeter` if needed.
- **Calling the function**:

```
area, perimeter := rectangleProperties(5, 10)
fmt.Println("Area:", area, "Perimeter:", perimeter)  //
Output: Area: 50 Perimeter: 30
```

- **Using blank identifiers with return values:** When a function returns multiple values, but you are only interested in some of them, you can ignore the unwanted values using the blank identifier _. (Note the underscore, which is the blank identifier.)
  - **Example:**

```
func performCalculation(x, y int) (int, int) {
    sum := x + y
    product := x * y
    return sum, product
}
sum, _ := performCalculation(3, 4)
fmt.Println("Sum:", sum)  // Output: Sum: 7
```

  In this example the `product` is ignored by using the blank identifier _.

- **Passing arguments by value vs. reference:** In Go, all function arguments are passed by value by default. This means that any changes made to a parameter inside the function do not affect the original variable outside the function.
  - **Example of passing by value:**

```
func modifyValue(x int) {
    x = x + 10
    fmt.Println("Inside function:", x)  // Output: Inside function: 20
}
x := 10
modifyValue(x)
fmt.Println("Outside function:", x)  // Output: Outside function: 10
```

    In this example, the value of `x` inside `modifyValue` is modified, but the original `x` remains unchanged outside the function.
  - **Passing a pointer to modify the original value:** To modify the original value, pass a pointer to the variable using the * operator.

```
func modifyValue(x *int) {
    *x = *x + 10
}
x := 10
```

```
modifyValue(&x)
fmt.Println("Modified value:", x)  // Output: Modified value: 20
```

In this example, `x` is passed by reference (using `&x`), allowing **`modifyValue`** to modify the original `x`.

- **Returning functions (higher-order functions):** Go supports higher-order functions, meaning functions can return other functions. This allows you to build more flexible code by using functions as return values.
  - **Example of a function returning a function:**

```
func multiplier(factor int) func(int) int {
    return func(x int) int {
        return x * factor
    }
}
double := multiplier(2)
fmt.Println(double(5))  // Output: 10
```

  - **In this example:**
    - **`multiplier`** returns a function that multiplies its argument by factor.
    - **`double`** is a function that doubles its input, demonstrating how functions can return functions.

Variadic functions

In this section, we will take an in-depth look at variadic functions. The details are as follows:

- **Definition:** A variadic function is a function that can take an arbitrary number of arguments. Instead of specifying a fixed number of parameters, variadic functions allow you to pass in zero, one, or multiple values for a given parameter. This feature is particularly useful when the number of inputs is not fixed or known in advance, such as when calculating the sum of a list of numbers or building a message from multiple parts.
- **Syntax of a variadic function:** In Go, you declare a variadic parameter by adding an ellipsis (`...`) before the parameter type. This tells Go that the function can accept any number of values for that parameter, treating them as a slice within the function.
  - **General syntax:**

```
func functionName(fixedParams, variadicParam ...type) returnType {
    // function body
}
```

    - **fixedParams:** Any required parameters. These come before the variadic parameter.
    - **variadicParam:** The variadic parameter, prefixed with `...`, representing zero or more arguments of a specified type.
- **Basic example of a variadic function:** Let us start with a simple example where we use a variadic function to calculate the sum of any number of integers.
  - **Example:**

```
func sum(numbers ...int) int {
    total := 0
    for _, number := range numbers {
        total += number
    }
    return total
}
```

- **In this example**:
  - **sum** is a variadic function that accepts any number of **int** values.
  - Inside the function, numbers is treated as a slice (**[]int**), and we can iterate over it to add up the elements.
- **Calling the function with different numbers of arguments:**

```
fmt.Println(sum(1, 2, 3))       // Output: 6
fmt.Println(sum(4, 5, 6, 7, 8)) // Output: 30
fmt.Println(sum())              // Output: 0 (no arguments provided)
```

- **How variadic parameters work:** Inside a variadic function, the variadic parameter is actually a slice of the specified type. This allows you to use slice operations, such as iteration or indexing, to work with the arguments.
  - **Example:**

```
func printNames(names ...string) {
    for i, name := range names {
        fmt.Printf("Name %d: %s\n", i+1, name)
    }
}
printNames("Shubham", "Venkatesh", "Raj")
// Output:
// Name 1: Shubham
// Name 2: Venkatesh
// Name 3: Raj
```

  - **names** is a variadic parameter of type **string**.
  - It is treated as a slice inside the function, so we can iterate over it with range.

- **Using variadic functions with fixed parameters:** You can combine fixed parameters with a variadic parameter in the same function. However, the variadic parameter must always be the last parameter in the function signature.
  - **Example:**

```
func greetAll(greeting string, names ...string) {
    for _, name := range names {
        fmt.Println(greeting, name)
    }
}

greetAll("Hello", "Shubham", "Venkatesh", "Raj")
// Output:
// Hello Shubham
// Hello Venkatesh
// Hello Raj
```

  - **In this example:**
    - **greeting** is a fixed parameter, and **names** is a variadic parameter.
    - The function outputs a greeting message for each name passed.

- **Passing a slice to a variadic function:** If you already have a slice and want to pass it to a variadic function, you can use the `...` operator to unpack the slice and pass each element as an individual argument.
  - **Example:**

```
func sum(numbers ...int) int {
    total := 0
    for _, number := range numbers {
        total += number
    }
    return total
}
values := []int{1, 2, 3, 4, 5}
fmt.Println(sum(values...)) // Output: 15
```

  In this example, the **`values`** slice is unpacked with values`...`, so each element in **`values`** is passed as an individual argument to the **`sum`** function.

- **Variadic functions with no arguments:** A variadic parameter can also handle cases where no arguments are passed. When this happens, the variadic parameter is an empty slice, so you can still use it safely without causing errors.
  - **Example:**

```
func displayNumbers(numbers ...int) {
    if len(numbers) == 0 {
        fmt.Println("No numbers provided.")
        return
    }
    for _, number := range numbers {
        fmt.Println(number)
    }
}
displayNumbers()          // Output: No numbers provided.
displayNumbers(5, 10, 15) // Output: 5, 10, 15
```

- **Variadic functions with multiple return values:** Variadic functions can also have multiple return values. This feature is useful for operations like calculations that need to return both a result and an error message.
  - **Example:**

```
func average(numbers ...float64) (float64, error) {
    if len(numbers) == 0 {
        return 0, fmt.Errorf("no numbers provided")
    }
    total := 0.0
    for _, number := range numbers {
        total += number
    }
    return total / float64(len(numbers)), nil
}
result, err := average(2.0, 4.0, 6.0)
if err != nil {
```

```
        fmt.Println("Error:", err)
    } else {
        fmt.Println("Average:", result) // Output: Average: 4
    }
```

- **In this example**:
    - If no numbers are provided, the function returns an error.
    - Otherwise, it calculates and returns the average.

- **Using variadic functions for flexible input types:** Although variadic parameters must be of a single specified type, you can still create flexible functions that accept different types of input by using the **`interface{}`** type, which can hold any data type.
    - **Example of using interface{}:**

```
func printDetails(details ...interface{}) {
    for _, detail := range details {
        fmt.Println(detail)
    }
}
printDetails("Venkatesh", 35, true)
// Output:
// Venkatesh
// 35
// true
```

- **In this example:**
    - **`details`** is a variadic parameter of type **`interface{}`**, allowing it to accept arguments of any type.
    - The function prints each detail, whether it is a **`string`**, **`int`**, or **`bool`**.

- **Common use cases for variadic functions:** Variadic functions are widely used in Go. Here are some common scenarios where variadic functions are especially helpful:
    - **Aggregation functions**: Functions like **`sum`**, **`max`**, or **`average`** often benefit from variadic parameters because they operate on a collection of values.

```
func max(numbers ...int) int {
    if len(numbers) == 0 {
        return 0 // or handle as needed
    }
    maxVal := numbers[0]
    for _, num := range numbers {
        if num > maxVal {
            maxVal = num
        }
    }
    return maxVal
}
```

- **Formatted output**: Functions like **`fmt.Printf`** uses variadic parameters to accept multiple arguments for dynamic string formatting.

```
fmt.Printf("Name: %s, Age: %d\n", "Venkatesh", 35)
```

- **Error logging**: Logging functions that log messages with variable-length details.

```
func logError(message string, details ...interface{}) {
    fmt.Print("Error: ", message)
    for _, detail := range details {
        fmt.Print(" - ", detail)
    }
    fmt.Println()
}
logError("File not found", "filename.txt", "attempt 3", 404)
```

Anonymous functions

In this section, we will be discussing anonymous functions. The details are as follows:

- **Definition:** An anonymous function is a function without a name. Unlike named functions, anonymous functions are often used as temporary or short-lived functions and are particularly useful when a function is only needed once or is embedded within another function. Anonymous functions can be assigned to variables, passed as arguments, or even returned from other functions.
- **Syntax of an anonymous function:** In Go, you define an anonymous function by simply omitting the name, writing **func** followed by the parameter list, and then the function body. You can immediately call the function or assign it to a variable.
  - **Basic syntax:**

```
func(parameterList) returnType {
    // function body
}
```

- **Immediate execution of anonymous functions:** You can define and immediately execute an anonymous function by adding parentheses after the function definition.
  - **Example:**

```
func() {
    fmt.Println("This is an anonymous function executed immediately.")
}()[
```

  - In this example, the anonymous function prints a message and is immediately executed with **()**.
- **Assigning anonymous functions to variables:** You can store an anonymous function in a variable, which allows you to call it multiple times by referencing the variable.
  - **Example**:

```
package main

import (
 "fmt"
)

func main() {
 // Assigning an anonymous function to a variable
 add := func(x, y int) int {
```

```
    return x + y
    }

    // Using the function assigned to the variable
    result := add(10, 5)
    fmt.Println("Addition Result:", result) // Output: Addition Result: 15

    // Another anonymous function assigned to a variable
    greet := func(name string) {
     fmt.Printf("Hello, %s!\n", name)
    }

    // Using the function assigned to the variable
    greet("Venkatesh") // Output: Hello, Venkatesh!
}
```

- **In this example:**
    - The **add** variable is assigned an anonymous function that takes two integers, adds them, and returns the result. This allows add to act as a function, so you can call **add(10, 5)** to get the sum.
    - The **greet** variable holds another anonymous function that takes a string argument and prints a greeting. Calling **greet("Venkatesh")** prints the greeting.

- **Anonymous functions with parameters and return types:** Just like named functions, anonymous functions can accept parameters and return values. This makes them flexible and capable of performing complex operations.
    - **Example**:

```
add := func(a int, b int) int {
    return a + b
}
result := add(3, 5)
fmt.Println("Result:", result)  // Output: Result: 8
```

- **In this example:**
    - The anonymous function takes two integers as parameters and returns their sum.
    - **add** is a variable that stores the anonymous function, allowing it to be called as needed.

- **Passing anonymous functions as arguments:** Anonymous functions are often used as arguments to other functions, allowing you to provide custom behavior without defining a separate named function.
    - **Example**:

```
func applyOperation(a, b int, operation func(int, int) int) int {
    return operation(a, b)
}
result := applyOperation(5, 3, func(x, y int) int {
    return x * y
})
fmt.Println("Result:", result)  // Output: Result: 15
```

- **In this example:**
  - **applyOperation** accepts a function as its third parameter (**operation**).
  - An anonymous function is defined and passed to **applyOperation**, which multiplies the two numbers.

- **Returning anonymous functions from functions:** Functions in Go can also return anonymous functions, making them higher-order functions. This can be useful when you want to generate a function with specific behavior based on some input.
  - **Example:**

```
func multiplier(factor int) func(int) int {
    return func(x int) int {
        return x * factor
    }
}
double := multiplier(2)
fmt.Println(double(5)) // Output: 10
```

  - **In this example:**
    - **multiplier** returns an anonymous function that multiplies its input by **factor**.
    - **double** becomes a function that doubles its argument, thanks to the **multiplier** function.

- **Closures in Go:** An important concept related to anonymous functions is a **closure**. A closure is an anonymous function that captures variables from its surrounding scope, allowing it to use those variables even when the surrounding function has finished execution.
  - **Example of closure:**

```
func counter() func() int {
    count := 0
    return func() int {
        count++
        return count
    }
}
increment := counter()
fmt.Println(increment()) // Output: 1
fmt.Println(increment()) // Output: 2
fmt.Println(increment()) // Output: 3
```

  - **In this example:**
    - The anonymous function returned by **counter** captures the **count** variable.
    - Each time **increment** is called, it has access to **count**, which retains its value across calls.

- **Practical use cases for anonymous functions:** Anonymous functions are versatile and can be used in various practical scenarios. Here are a few common use cases:
  - **Inline short-lived functions:** Anonymous functions are ideal for operations that do not need a named function, such as sorting with custom logic or filtering elements in a slice.

```
numbers := []int{5, 2, 6, 3, 1}
sort.Slice(numbers, func(i, j int) bool {
```

```
    return numbers[i] < numbers[j]
})
fmt.Println(numbers) // Output: [1 2 3 5 6]
```

- **Deferred function execution:** Anonymous functions are commonly used with defer to execute code after a function completes. This is useful for cleanup tasks, such as closing a file or unlocking a mutex.

```
func processFile(filename string) {
    file, err := os.Open(filename)
    if err != nil {
        log.Fatal(err)
    }
    defer func() {
        fmt.Println("Closing the file.")
        file.Close()
    }()
    fmt.Println("Processing the file:", filename)
}
```

In this example, the deferred anonymous function ensures the file is closed after **processFile** completes, regardless of errors.

- **Event handlers and callbacks:** Anonymous functions are often used as event handlers or callbacks, such as when handling button clicks in a GUI or when defining custom behavior in concurrent operations.

```
doTask := func(taskName string, callback func()) {
    fmt.Println("Starting:", taskName)
    callback()
    fmt.Println("Finished:", taskName)
}
doTask("Task 1", func() {
    fmt.Println("Executing callback...")
})
```

In this example, the anonymous function passed as a callback provides specific functionality that is executed as part of **doTask**.

- **Anonymous functions and goroutines:** Anonymous functions can be used directly with goroutines for concurrent tasks. This is useful for tasks that run in the background or need to execute concurrently without defining a separate function.

  - **Example**:

```
go func() {
    fmt.Println("Running in a goroutine")
}()
```

  In this example, the anonymous function runs concurrently as a goroutine.

  - **Another example with parameters**:

```
numbers := []int{1, 2, 3}
for _, num := range numbers {
    go func(n int) {
        fmt.Println(n)
```

```
        }(num)
    }
```

Here, the anonymous function takes num as a parameter, so each goroutine prints a unique value from the numbers.

> **Note: A goroutine is a lightweight way to run a function concurrently in Go. Think of it as a simple, efficient way to start a new task that runs alongside other tasks. We will cover goroutines in the coming chapters.**

- **Limitations of anonymous functions:** While anonymous functions are versatile, they have certain limitations:
    - **Code readability**: The overuse of anonymous functions, especially nested ones, can make code harder to read.
    - **Lack of named recursion**: Anonymous functions cannot refer to themselves by name, so recursive anonymous functions need to be assigned to variables or use named functions.
    - **Debugging complexity**: Debugging can be challenging since anonymous functions do not have descriptive names.
- **Deferred functions:** Deferred functions are functions whose execution is delayed until the surrounding function completes. They are useful for cleanup actions, like closing a file.
    - **Example**:

```
func readFile(filename string) {
    file, err := os.Open(filename)
    if err != nil {
        fmt.Println("Error opening file:", err)
        return
    }
    defer file.Close()  // Ensure the file is closed when readFile completes

    // Perform file operations
}
```

The **`defer`** keyword schedules **`file.Close()`** to run after **`readFile`** finishes, even if an error occurs.

Understanding and handling errors in Go

This section will take us through an in-depth understanding of how to handle errors in Go. The details are as follows:

- **Philosophy of error handling in Go:** Go's approach to error handling emphasizes simplicity and readability. Instead of exceptions (as in languages like Java or Python), Go uses a more explicit model, where functions typically return an error value alongside the main result. This approach ensures that errors are always part of the flow, leading to more transparent and manageable code.
    - **In Go**:
        - Errors are values that follow the error interface.
        - Every error check is explicit, making the code easy to follow and inspect.
        - Error handling is considered a core part of program logic rather than an afterthought.

- **Error types in Go**: The error type in Go is an interface with a single method, **`Error()`**, which returns a string.
  - **Definition**:

```
type error interface {
    Error() string
}
```

Any type that implements the **`Error()`** method in this way is considered to be of type error. This allows developers to create custom error types, giving more context to error values.

- **Basic error handling pattern:** Most functions in Go return two values:
  - The main result (or nil if there is no result).
  - An error value, which will be nil if no error occurred.
  - **Basic example**:

```
func divide(a, b float64) (float64, error) {
    if b == 0 {
        return 0, fmt.Errorf("cannot divide by zero")
    }
    return a / b, nil
}
result, err := divide(10, 0)
if err != nil {
    fmt.Println("Error:", err)
} else {
    fmt.Println("Result:", result)
}
```

  - **In this example**:
    - **`divide`** checks if **`b`** is zero, returning an error if true.
    - **`fmt.Errorf`** is used to create a formatted error message.
    - The caller checks the **`err`** value to see if it has an error value or **`nil`** and decides what to do next.
- **Creating errors with errors.New and fmt.Errorf:** Go's standard library provides two main ways to create errors:
  - **errors.New:** Creates a simple error with a given message.
  - **fmt.Errorf**: Allows formatted error messages, often incorporating variable values for clarity.
  - **Example with errors.New:**

```
import "errors"

var errNotFound = errors.New("item not found")

func findItem(id int) (string, error) {
    if id != 123 {
        return "", errNotFound
    }
```

```go
        return "Item123", nil
    }
```

- **Example with fmt.Errorf:**

```go
import "fmt"

func findItem(id int) (string, error) {
    if id != 123 {
        return "", fmt.Errorf("item with id %d not found", id)
    }
    return "Item123", nil
}
```

- **Checking and handling errors:** After a function returns, the returned error should be checked. In Go, it is common to see this pattern repeated:

```go
result, err := someFunction()
if err != nil {
    // handle the error
    return
}
// proceed with result if no error
```

This approach ensures that errors are handled as soon as they occur, helping to prevent unexpected behavior later in the code.

- **Error wrapping in Go:** Starting with Go 1.13, you can wrap errors with additional context, making debugging easier while preserving the original error. This is particularly useful for creating a stack of errors that point back to the root cause.

  - **Wrapping with fmt.Errorf:**

```go
import "fmt"

func readFile(filename string) error {
    return fmt.Errorf("failed to open file %s: %w", filename, err)
}
```

- **Common error handling patterns:**

  - **Early returns**: It is common to return early when an error occurs, rather than nesting code in multiple levels of **if** statements.

```go
func processFile(filename string) error {
    file, err := os.Open(filename)
    if err != nil {
        return err
    }
    defer file.Close()
    // Process the file
    return nil
}
```

  - **Sentinel errors:** Sentinel errors are predefined errors you can use to check specific conditions, like a missing resource.

```go
var ErrNotFound = errors.New("not found")

func findResource(id int) error {
    return ErrNotFound
}
```

- **Returning errors vs. logging and exiting:** Decide whether an error should be logged and returned to the caller, or if it is severe enough to warrant immediate program termination. Generally:
    - Return errors for issues the caller might handle.
    - Log and exit for unrecoverable errors, often in the main function.

```go
func main() {
    err := runApplication()
    if err != nil {
        log.Fatal("Application failed:", err)
    }
}
```

- **Best practices for error handling in Go:**
    - Check errors immediately after a function returns, especially for critical operations like opening files or reading data.
    - Add context to errors. Use **`fmt.Errorf`** with **`%w`** to wrap and annotate errors as needed.
    - Use custom errors when more detail is helpful, especially in libraries where consumers might need to inspect error types.
    - Avoid ignoring errors by omitting them in code. While Go allows _ to discard unused return values, it is best to handle errors to prevent silent failures.
    - Define sentinel errors for common error conditions, making checks more readable and consistent across the codebase.
    - **Example of good error handling:**

```go
func fetchData(id int) (Data, error) {
    data, err := fetchFromDatabase(id)
    if err != nil {
        return nil, fmt.Errorf("fetchData failed: %w", err)
    }
    return data, nil
}

data, err := fetchData(10)
if err != nil {
    log.Println("Error fetching data:", err)
}
```

- **In this example:**
    - **`fetchData`** adds context to the error from **`fetchFromDatabase`**.
    - The **`main`** function logs the error with a clear message if **`fetchData`** fails.

Creating and handling custom errors

We will be looking at how to create and handle custom errors in this section:

- **Why use custom errors:** Go's error interface is simple and powerful, but in larger applications, custom errors can provide additional context, making error handling more effective. Custom errors:
    - o Give more specific details about errors.
    - o Help categorize errors for conditional handling.
    - o Make error checking easier and clearer, especially for complex applications.
- **The error interface recap:** Go's error interface requires only one method, `Error()`, which returns a string. Any type implementing this method automatically satisfies the error interface.

```
type error interface {
    Error() string
}
```

- **Creating basic custom errors:** To create a custom error, define a new struct type and implement the `Error()` method to return an appropriate error message.
    - o **Example**: Custom error for validation:

```
package main

import (
    "fmt"
)

// ValidationError defines a custom error for input validation.
type ValidationError struct {
    Field   string
    Problem string
}

// Error method implementation for ValidationError.
func (e *ValidationError) Error() string {
    return fmt.Sprintf("validation error: field %s - %s", e.Field, e.Problem)
}

func validateAge(age int) error {
    if age < 18 {
        return &ValidationError{
            Field:   "Age",
            Problem: "must be at least 18",
        }
    }
    return nil
}

func main() {
```

```
    err := validateAge(15)
    if err != nil {
        fmt.Println("Error:", err)
    }
}
```

- In this example:
  - **ValidationError** is a struct representing a custom error.
  - **Error()** returns a detailed message that includes the field and problem.
  - **validateAge** returns a **ValidationError** if the age is below 18.

Note:

- **The `*ValidationError` in the method signature `func (e *ValidationError) Error() string` is a pointer receiver.**
- **The `&` operator in `return &ValidationError{...}` creates a pointer to a `ValidationError` instance, which is returned from `validateAge` as an error.**

Let us have a deeper look at pointers in the forthcoming chapters.

- **Adding context with fields:** Custom errors allow you to include context directly in the struct fields, making the error information richer and more specific. This is especially useful in applications that handle complex data or require detailed error logs.
  - **Example**: Custom error with detailed context:

```
type DatabaseError struct {
    Query string
    Err   error
}

func (e *DatabaseError) Error() string {
    return fmt.Sprintf("database error on query %s: %v", e.Query, e.Err)
}

func fetchData() error {
    err := someDatabaseOperation()
    if err != nil {
        return &DatabaseError{
            Query: "SELECT * FROM users",
            Err:   err,
        }
    }
    return nil
}
```

  - **In this example:**
    - **DatabaseError** includes both the query string and the underlying error.
    - The error message is contextualized, showing both the query and the underlying issue, making it easier to trace.

- **Error wrapping with %w:** Starting with Go 1.13, `fmt.Errorf` supports wrapping errors with the `%w` verb, which allows errors to be unwrapped later. Wrapping errors are useful when you need to propagate the original error with additional context.
    - **Example**: Wrapping errors with `%w`:

```
import (
	"fmt"
	"errors"
)

type FileError struct {
	FileName string
	Err      error
}

func (e *FileError) Error() string {
	return fmt.Sprintf("file error on %s: %v", e.FileName, e.Err)
}

func openFile(filename string) error {
	err := someFileOperation()
	if err != nil {
		return fmt.Errorf("failed to open file %s: %w",
filename, &FileError{FileName: filename, Err: err})
	}
	return nil
}
```

    - **In this example:**
        - The original error (`err`) is wrapped with `%w` to enable further unwrapping.
        - `FileError` provides context on which file caused the error.

Note: **In this program, the * (asterisk) symbol has two main uses:**

- **Defining a pointer receiver in the `Error` method of the `FileError` struct.**
- **Creating a pointer to a `FileError` when returning an error from `openFile`.**

Let us see pointers extensively in the forthcoming chapters.

- **Handling custom errors with errors.As and errors.Is:** Go provides two main functions in the errors package for working with wrapped or custom errors:
    - **errors.Is**: Checks if an error matches a specific error.
        - **Example**: Checking with `errors.Is`

```
import (
	"errors"
	"fmt"
)
```

```
var ErrNotFound = errors.New("resource not found")

func findResource(id int) error {
    if id != 123 {
        return ErrNotFound
    }
    return nil
}

func main() {
    err := findResource(999)
    if errors.Is(err, ErrNotFound) {
        fmt.Println("The resource was not found.")
    }
}
```

- In this example, **`errors.Is`** is used to compare err with **`ErrNotFound`**. This approach works well with sentinel errors and wrapped errors.

- **errors.As**: Checks if an error is of a specific type and extracts it.
  - **Example**: Type assertion with **`errors.As`**

    In Go, **`errors.As`** lets you check if an error belongs to a specific type and extract it for further inspection. This is useful when you need to access custom fields or methods of the error type. By casting the error, you can handle different error types uniquely. It simplifies error management by allowing more detailed checks. This approach makes your error handling code cleaner and more precise.

    The code is as follows:

```
import (
    "errors"
    "fmt"
)

func main() {
    err := fetchData() // Assume fetchData returns a DatabaseError.
    var dbErr *DatabaseError
    if errors.As(err, &dbErr) {
        fmt.Printf("Database error on query: %s\n", dbErr.Query)
    } else {
        fmt.Println("General error:", err)
    }
}
```

- In this example **`errors.As`** allows checking and extracting the **`DatabaseError`**. You can then access the **`Query`** field for detailed handling.

- **Aggregating multiple errors with errors.Join:** Go 1.20 introduced **`errors.Join`**, which lets you combine multiple errors into a single error. This can be useful when multiple operations need to be checked, such as a batch process where each item could produce an error.

- **Example**: Using **`errors.Join`**:

```
import (
    "errors"
    "fmt"
)

func validateFields(name string, age int) error {
    var errs []error
    if name == "" {
        errs = append(errs, errors.New("name is required"))
    }
    if age < 18 {
        errs = append(errs, errors.New("age must be at least 18"))
    }
    return errors.Join(errs...)
}

func main() {
    err := validateFields("", 15)
    if err != nil {
        fmt.Println("Validation errors:", err)
    }
}
```

  - **In this example:**
    - **`validateFields`** accumulates validation errors and joins them using **`errors.Join`**.
    - This approach is useful for applications requiring multiple validations or batch processing.

- **Best practices for custom error handling:**
  - **Define custom error types for important context**: Use custom error types for errors that require additional context or special handling.
  - **Use sentinel errors sparingly**: Sentinel errors are useful for well-known conditions, like *not found* or *already exists*. Avoid overusing them, as too many sentinel errors can make code confusing.
  - **Use fmt.Errorf with %w**: Wrap errors with additional context, but preserve the original error for traceability.
  - **Use errors.Is for comparison**: When you need to check for a specific error value, use **`errors.Is`**.
  - **Use errors.As for type-specific errors**: If you need to handle a specific custom error type, **`errors.As`** is the way to go. It lets you extract the error and access additional fields.
  - **Avoid masking errors**: Avoid using return **`errors.New("some error occurred")`** when wrapping errors, as it loses context. Instead, wrap errors using **`%w`**.
  - **Document custom errors**: If you are designing a package with custom errors, document them thoroughly so that other developers understand how to use them effectively.
  - **Aggregate multiple errors if needed**: If a function might encounter multiple errors, aggregate them with **`errors.Join`** to provide complete error information to the caller.

Best practices for error handling

Here are some best practices when handling errors in Go:

- **Check errors explicitly**: Always check for errors after a function call and handle them appropriately.
- **Use defer for cleanup**: Use defer to ensure resources are released properly.
- **Return errors instead of logging**: Functions should return errors to the caller instead of logging, letting the caller decide how to handle them.
- **Use fmt.Errorf for wrapping**: If adding context to errors, use `fmt.Errorf` to wrap errors with additional information.
- **Create custom errors judiciously**: Define custom error types only when additional context is needed for specific error conditions.

Conclusion

Mastering functions and error handling in Go is crucial for developing resilient software. With its straightforward function structure and emphasis on clear error handling, Go empowers developers to write code that is both efficient and easy to debug. By understanding these concepts thoroughly, developers can create modular, reusable functions and manage errors effectively, leading to more robust and maintainable applications.

In the next chapter, we will explore how to define and use structs in Go for organizing complex data efficiently. We will cover methods in Go, focusing on both pointer receivers and value receivers to modify or access struct data effectively. Additionally, we will deep dive into embedding and composition techniques to create reusable and maintainable code. The chapter will also explain how to compare and copy structs safely. Finally, we will discuss best practices for struct design to write clean, efficient, and idiomatic Go code.

Questions

1. What is the syntax of a basic function in Go, and how are parameters and return types declared? Provide an example.
2. Explain the concept of functions as first-class citizens in Go. How can you assign a function to a variable or pass it as an argument?
3. What are variadic functions in Go? How do they differ from regular functions, and how is a slice passed to them?
4. Describe the difference between passing parameters by value and by reference in Go. How can a function modify the original variable?
5. How do anonymous functions and closures work in Go? Give an example of a closure that maintains state across function calls.
6. What is the philosophy of error handling in Go? How does it differ from languages that use exception handling?
7. How do you create and handle custom errors in Go using structs? Illustrate with an example of a custom ValidationError.
8. What is the purpose of using fmt.Errorf with the %w verb, and how does it help in wrapping errors?
9. Explain the difference between errors.Is and errors.As in Go. When would you use each, and what problem do they solve?
10. What is errors.Join, introduced in Go 1.20, and how does it help with aggregating multiple errors? Provide a use-case example.

CHAPTER 4
Structs and Methods

Introduction

In this chapter, we will look at the core concepts of structs and methods in Go, which form the backbone of organizing and manipulating complex data. Understanding structs is essential for grouping related data fields efficiently, while methods enable you to define behaviors and operations associated with these data types. Additionally, we will explore the differences and applications of pointer receivers and value receivers for methods, helping you choose the right approach based on your use case. The chapter will also cover advanced struct design techniques, such as embedding and composition, to enhance code reusability and maintainability. Furthermore, we will discuss how to compare and copy structs effectively, along with best practices for struct design to write clean, idiomatic Go code.

Structure

The chapter covers the following topics:

- Defining structs
- Methods in Go
- Pointers to structs
- Embedding and composition
- Comparing and copying structs

Objectives

By the end of this chapter, you will have a solid understanding of how to define and work with structs in Go, enabling you to organize related data fields efficiently. You will learn how to create and use methods to extend the functionality of structs, making your code more modular and maintainable. The chapter will clarify the differences between pointer receivers and value receivers, helping you decide when to use each based on factors like memory efficiency and mutability requirements. Additionally, you will explore embedding and composition techniques to build complex data types through simpler components, avoiding the pitfalls of traditional inheritance. Understanding how to compare and copy structs accurately will equip you to handle data integrity and duplication scenarios effectively. This chapter will present best practices as we explore the various topics, ensuring that your Go code remains both efficient and idiomatic.

Defining structs

A struct in Go is a composite data type that groups together variables (fields) under a single type name. Each field can be of a different type, allowing for the creation of more complex data types that represent real-world objects.

Use case: Structs are ideal for representing any entity, like people, products, or geometric shapes, etc., where you need to store multiple related attributes.

The details about structs are as follows:

- **Basic syntax of structs**: In Go, you define a struct using the **`type`** keyword, followed by the struct's name and the **`struct`** keyword. A struct is a custom data type that can hold multiple fields of different types. For example, the **type Person struct** creates a struct named **Person** to store related information. Each field in the struct has a name and a type, such as **Name string** or **Age int**. This syntax helps organize and manage complex data efficiently.

```
type StructName struct {
    FieldName1 FieldType1
    FieldName2 FieldType2
}
```

Example:

```
type Person struct {
    Name    string
    Age     int
    Address string
}
```

Explanation: The **Person struct** has three fields: **Name** (**string**), **Age** (**int**), and **Address** (**string**).

- **Declaring and initializing structs:**
    - **Declaration without initialization:** When you declare a struct without initializing it, its fields are set to their zero values (e.g., **0** for integers, **""** for strings, **nil** for pointers):

      ```
      var p Person // Fields: Name="", Age=0, Address=""
      ```

    - **Declaration with initialization:** You can initialize a struct using a composite literal:

      ```
      p := Person{
          Name:    "Venkatesh",
          Age:     30,
          Address: "Bangalore",
      }
      ```

    - **Field order in initialization:** Fields can be initialized in the order they are defined or by specifying field names.

      ```
      p := Person{"Shubham", 25, "Bangalore"} // Field
      order must match struct definition
      ```

    - **Best practice:** Always use named field initialization for better readability and to avoid potential errors if the struct definition changes.
- **Accessing and modifying struct fields:** You can access and modify struct fields using the dot **.** operator.

  Example:

  ```
  p := Person{Name: "Shubham", Age: 28, Address: "Bangalore"}
  fmt.Println("Name:", p.Name) // Accessing a field

  p.Age = 29 // Modifying a field
  fmt.Println("Updated Age:", p.Age)
  ```

  Explanation: The **Name** and **Age** fields of the **Person struct** are accessed and printed, while the **Age** is modified using the **.** operator.
- **Zero values of struct fields:**
    - If a struct is declared without initializing its fields, Go assigns each field its type's zero value:
        - **Numeric fields: 0**

- **Boolean fields**: **`false`**
- **String fields**: **`""`** (empty string)
- **Pointers, slices, maps, interfaces**: **`nil`**

Example:

```
var defaultPerson Person
fmt.Println("Default Person:", defaultPerson)
// Output: Default Person: { 0 }
```

Explanation: In this example, **`Name`** is an empty **`string`**, **`Age`** is **`0`**, and **`Address`** is an empty string by default.

- **Anonymous structs**:
  - **Definition**: Anonymous structs are structs defined without a name. They are useful for one-time use or when a full type definition is not needed.

Example:

```
student := struct {
    FirstName string
    LastName  string
    Grade     int
}{
    FirstName: "Venkatesh",
    LastName:  "R",
    Grade:     10,
}

fmt.Println("Student:", student)
```

Explanation: The **`struct student`** is defined and initialized on the fly, making it ideal for temporary data structures.

- **Nested structs**:
  - **Definition**: A struct can contain other structs as fields, allowing for complex and hierarchical data structures.

Example:

```
type Address struct {
    Street string
    City   string
    Zip    int
}

type Employee struct {
    Name    string
    Age     int
    Address Address // Nested struct
}

func main() {
```

```
    emp := Employee{
        Name: "Shubham",
        Age:  35,
        Address: Address{
            Street: "1st street",
            City:   "Bangalore",
            Zip:    560001,
        },
    }
    fmt.Println("Employee Details:", emp)
    fmt.Println("City:", emp.Address.City) // Accessing nested struct field
}
```

Explanation: The **`Employee struct`** has an **`Address`** field, which is itself a struct. This nesting helps to model data more effectively.

- **Struct tags**:
  - **Definition**: Struct tags are metadata added to struct fields to provide additional information, often used for encoding and decoding data formats like JSON or XML.

    Syntax:

```
type User struct {
    Username string 'json:"username"'
    Email    string 'json:"email"'
}
```

Example with JSON encoding:

```
import (
    "encoding/json"
    "fmt"
)

type User struct {
    Username string 'json:"username"'
    Email    string 'json:"email"'
}

func main() {
    u := User{Username: "venkatesh", Email: "venkatesh@gmail.com"}
    jsonData, _ := json.Marshal(u)
    fmt.Println(string(jsonData)) // Output: {"username":"venkatesh","email":"
venkatesh@gmail.com"}
}
```

Explanation: The **`json struct`** tag specifies how field names should be encoded in JSON format. This is useful when you need to control the field names in output or input formats.

- **Struct field visibility**:
  - **Exported versus unexported fields**:

- Fields that start with an uppercase letter are exported (public) and accessible outside the package.
- Fields that start with a lowercase letter are unexported (private) and accessible only within the package.

  Example:

```
type Product struct {
    Name  string  // Exported field
    price float64 // Unexported field
}

func main() {
    prod := Product{Name: "Laptop", price: 129999.99}
    fmt.Println("Product Name:", prod.Name)
    // fmt.Println("Product Price:", prod.
price) // This would cause a compilation error
}
```

  Explanation: The **Name** field is accessible in the **main** function, but **price** is not because it is unexported.

- **Adding behavior with helper functions**: While methods are used to add behavior directly to structs, you can also create standalone functions that operate on struct instances.

  Example:

```
type Circle struct {
    Radius float64
}

func CalculateDiameter(c Circle) float64 {
    return c.Radius * 2
}

func main() {
    circle := Circle{Radius: 5}
    diameter := CalculateDiameter(circle)
    fmt.Println("Diameter of the circle:", diameter)
}
```

  Explanation: The **CalculateDiameter** function is a standalone function that takes a **Circle** struct as an argument and calculates its diameter.

Methods in Go

Method in Go is a function that is associated with a specific type, allowing you to define behaviors for data structures such as structs. Methods enable you to encapsulate functionality related to a type, improving code organization and readability, as follows:

- **Difference from functions**: While both methods and functions perform operations, a method is bound to a type, while a function is standalone. Methods offer object-like behavior, bringing the function closer to the data it operates on. Methods allow you to operate directly on an instance of a type. Functions are independent and not associated with any type.

Use case: Methods are useful when you need to attach specific behavior or operations to data structures, such as calculating an area for a **`Rectangle`** type.

- **Method syntax and declaration**: To define a method, Go extends the function syntax by adding a receiver in the function signature. The receiver acts like an implicit parameter representing the instance the method operates on.

  Syntax:

  ```
  func (receiverType ReceiverName) MethodName(parameters) returnType {
      // Method body
  }
  ```

  - **ReceiverType**: The type that the method is associated with. It defines which data structure the method belongs to, such as a struct like **`Circle`** or **`Rectangle`**. It tells the compiler that this method belongs to that type and can be invoked on its instances.

    Refer to the following table for usage guidelines on selecting the appropriate receiver type for Go methods:

Receiver type	When to use
Value	No changes to the struct are needed; the struct is small and copying is efficient.
Pointer	The struct needs to be modified; the struct is large, so copying would be inefficient.

    ***Table 4.1**: Receiver types in Go methods*

  - **ReceiverName**: A name that represents an instance of ReceiverType.
  - **MethodName**: The name of the method.
  - **Parameters**: Input parameters for the method (optional).
  - **returnType**: The type of value the method returns (optional).

  Example:

  ```
  type Circle struct {
      Radius float64
  }

  // Method to calculate the area of the circle
  func (c Circle) Area() float64 {
      return 3.14159 * c.Radius * c.Radius
  }

  func main() {
      circle := Circle{Radius: 5}
      fmt.Println("Area of the circle:", circle.Area())
  }
  ```

  Explanation: The **`Area`** method is bound to the **`Circle`** type, enabling any instance of **`Circle`** to call the **`Area`** method using the dot notation (e.g., **`circle.Area()`**).

- **Receivers in methods**:
  - **Types of receivers**:

- **Value receiver**: The receiver type is passed by value, meaning that the method works on a copy of the original data. This is suitable for methods that do not modify the instance's data.
- **Syntax**:

```
func (r Rectangle) Perimeter() float64 {
    return 2 * (r.Width + r.Height)
}
```

Example:

```
type Rectangle struct {
    Width, Height float64
}

func (r Rectangle) Perimeter() float64 {
    return 2 * (r.Width + r.Height)
}

func main() {
    rect := Rectangle{Width: 10, Height: 5}
    fmt.Println("Perimeter of the rectangle:", rect.Perimeter())
}
```

Explanation: The `Perimeter` method operates on a copy of `rect`, so the original `rect` remains unchanged.

- **Choosing between value and pointer receivers**:
  - Use value receivers when the method does not need to modify the instance's data or when the data structure is small, and copying is inexpensive.
  - Use pointer receivers when the method modifies the instance's data or when the data structure is large, and copying would be costly.

- **Method chaining**:
  - **Definition**: Method chaining is the practice of calling multiple methods on the same instance in a single line. It allows for more readable and fluent code.

Example:

```
type Account struct {
    Balance float64
}

func (a *Account) Deposit(amount float64) *Account {
    a.Balance += amount
    return a
}

func (a *Account) Withdraw(amount float64) *Account {
    if a.Balance >= amount {
        a.Balance -= amount
    } else {
```

```
        fmt.Println("Insufficient funds")
    }
    return a
}

func main() {
    acc := &Account{Balance: 100}
    acc.Deposit(50).Withdraw(30).Deposit(20)
    fmt.Println("Final Balance:", acc.Balance)
}
```

Explanation: Each method returns the pointer to the instance, enabling a sequence of method calls on the same object.

- **Method naming and conventions**:
  - **Use descriptive names**: Methods should have clear, descriptive names that indicate their purpose (e.g., **`CalculateArea`**, **`GetDetails`**).
  - **Naming style**: Follow the camelCase convention for method names (e.g., **`calculateVolume`**, **`processOrder`**).

    Example:

```
type Book struct {
    Title  string
    Author string
}

func (b Book) GetSummary() string {
    return fmt.Sprintf("%s by %s", b.Title, b.Author)
}
```

- **Method overloading in Go**:
  - **Explanation**: Unlike some programming languages, Go does not support method overloading (i.e., having multiple methods with the same name but different parameters). Each method name within a type must be unique.
  - **Workaround**: You can create methods with different names that handle different parameter types or numbers.

    Example:

```
type Math struct{}

func (m Math) Add(a int, b int) int {
    return a + b
}

func (m Math) AddThree(a int, b int, c int) int {
    return a + b + c
}
```

- **Anonymous methods**:

- **Definition**: Go supports anonymous functions, but you can use them in combination with methods to create more flexible code structures.

  Example:

```
type Processor struct {
    Data string
}

func (p Processor) Process(f func(string) string) string {
    return f(p.Data)
}

func main() {
    proc := Processor{Data: "Hello, Go!"}
    result := proc.Process(func(input string) string {
        return input + " - Processed"
    })
    fmt.Println(result)
}
```

  Explanation: The `Process` method takes an anonymous function as an argument, which allows for customizable processing logic.

- **Best practices for using methods**:
  - **Keep methods focused**: Each method should perform one clear task. This makes methods easier to understand, test, and maintain.
  - **Limit method length**: Keep methods concise to improve readability. If a method becomes too long, consider breaking it into smaller, helper methods.
  - **Use descriptive receivers**: For single-letter receiver names, use meaningful ones related to the type (e.g., `c` for `Circle`, `p` for `Person`). Avoid overly generic names like x unless it is conventional.
  - **Consistency in receivers**: To avoid confusion, ensure that the receiver type (value or pointer) is consistent for all methods attached to the same structure.

Pointers to structs

Let us understand the basics of pointers:

- **Definition**: A pointer is a variable that stores the memory address of another variable. In the context of structs, pointers are used to reference the memory location where a struct is stored, enabling direct modification of the struct's data.

  Use case: Pointers to structs are commonly used when you need to modify the original struct data or when passing large structs to functions to avoid copying large amounts of data.

  Note: We will have a dedicated session on pointers; for an in-depth study, refer to Chapter 6, Pointers.

- **Declaring pointers to structs**: Go provides a simple syntax to declare pointers to structs, allowing easy referencing and manipulation of struct data.

  Syntax:

```
var ptr *StructType
```

Example:

```
type Person struct {
    Name string
    Age  int
}

func main() {
    p := Person{Name: "Shubham", Age: 28}
    ptr := &p // Get the pointer to the struct

    fmt.Println("Pointer address:", ptr)
    fmt.Println("Name through pointer:", ptr.Name)
}
```

Explanation: The `&` operator is used to get the address of `p`, creating a pointer `ptr` that references the **`Person struct`**. You can access struct fields through the pointer using **`ptr.Name`**, as Go automatically dereferences the pointer.

- **Accessing and modifying structs via pointers**:
  - **Direct field access**: Go allows you to use the dot **.** operator on pointers to structs without explicitly dereferencing them.

    Example:

    ```
    type Car struct {
        Make  string
        Model string
        Year  int
    }

    func updateYear(c *Car, newYear int) {
        c.Year = newYear // Modify the Year field directly through the pointer
    }

    func main() {
        myCar := Car{Make: "Toyota", Model: "Corolla", Year: 2020}
        fmt.Println("Original Year:", myCar.Year)

        updateYear(&myCar, 2023) // Pass the pointer to the struct
        fmt.Println("Updated Year:", myCar.Year)
    }
    ```

    Explanation: The **`updateYear`** function accepts a pointer to a **`Car struct`** and modifies its **`Year`** field directly. The changes are reflected in **`myCar`** because the function works with the actual struct in memory.

- **Creating structs with pointers**: You can create a struct and obtain a pointer to it directly.

  Syntax:

  ```
  ptr := &StructType{Field1: value1, Field2: value2}
  ```

Example:

```
type Book struct {
    Title  string
    Author string
    Pages  int
}

func main() {
    bookPtr := &Book{Title: "Go in Action", Author: "William Kennedy",
Pages: 300}
    fmt.Println("Book pointer:", bookPtr)
    fmt.Println("Book title through pointer:", bookPtr.Title)
}
```

Explanation: The **`&Book{}`** creates a new **`Book struct`** and returns a pointer to it, allowing you to work with the struct via the **`bookPtr`**. Note that when using **`&Book{}`** to create a new **`Book struct`** and return a pointer, Go automatically handles memory allocation, eliminating the need for **`new()`** in most cases, as shown in the example.

- **Passing struct pointers to functions**:
  - **Benefits**:
    - **Memory efficiency**: Passing pointers to large structs avoids copying data, making the function call more efficient.
    - **Direct modification**: Allows functions to modify the original struct's data.

      Example:

      ```
      type Rectangle struct {
          Width, Height float64
      }

      func scaleRectangle(r *Rectangle, scale float64) {
          r.Width *= scale
          r.Height *= scale
      }

      func main() {
          rect := Rectangle{Width: 4, Height: 3}
          fmt.Println("Before scaling:", rect)

          scaleRectangle(&rect, 2) // Passing the pointer
          fmt.Println("After scaling:", rect)
      }
      ```

      Explanation: The **`scaleRectangle`** function accepts a pointer to **`Rectangle`**, allowing it to modify the **`Width`** and **`Height`** of **`rect`** directly.

- **Pointer receivers in methods**:
  - **Definition**: Methods can use pointer receivers to modify the struct's data. If a method is defined with a pointer receiver, it operates on the original struct, not a copy.

Example:

```go
type Counter struct {
    Value int
}

func (c *Counter) Increment() {
    c.Value++
}

func main() {
    count := Counter{Value: 0}
    count.Increment() // Method modifies the original struct
    fmt.Println("Counter value after increment:", count.Value)
}
```

Explanation: The `Increment` method uses a pointer receiver `*Counter`, so it can change the `Value` field of the `Counter struct` directly.

- **Best practices for using pointers with structs**:
  - **Use pointers when modifying data**: If your method or function needs to modify a struct, use a pointer receiver or pass the struct by pointer.
  - **Use pointers for large structs**: For large structs, use pointers to avoid performance issues due to copying large amounts of data.
  - **Avoid unnecessary pointers**: If a function or method does not need to modify a struct, pass the struct by value to improve readability and avoid potential issues with memory management.
  - **Consistency in method receivers**: Ensure consistency in receiver types (either all pointer receivers or all value receivers) for a given struct to avoid confusion.
- **Common pitfalls and considerations**:
  - **Nil pointers**: Dereferencing a `nil` pointer will result in a runtime panic.

    Example:

    ```go
    var p *Person
    fmt.Println(p.Name) // Runtime error: panic: runtime error:
    invalid memory address or nil pointer dereference
    ```
  - **Best practice**: Always check if a pointer is `nil` before dereferencing:

    ```go
    if p != nil {
        fmt.Println(p.Name)
    } else {
        fmt.Println("Pointer is nil")
    }
    ```
  - **Pointer aliasing**: Multiple pointers can point to the same struct, meaning changes made through one pointer will affect all references.

    Example:

    ```go
    p1 := &Person{Name: "Shubham", Age: 30}
    p2 := p1 // p2 also points to the same Person as p1
    ```

```
p2.Age = 35
fmt.Println("Age through p1:", p1.Age) // Output: 35
fmt.Println("Age through p2:", p2.Age) // Output: 35
```

- **Examples of real-world applications**:
  - **Data modifiers**: Functions that modify data structures (e.g., updating user information in a database or scaling dimensions in a graphics program) often use struct pointers.
  - **Performance optimization**: Struct pointers are widely used in applications requiring frequent function calls with large structs (e.g., processing large data records or game objects).

Embedding and composition

Embedding and composition in Go are techniques used to achieve code reuse and relationships between different types. Unlike traditional inheritance in object-oriented programming, Go promotes a more straightforward approach where types can embed other types to extend their functionality.

These techniques help in structuring programs with better modularity and code maintainability by composing complex types out of simpler ones:

- **Embedding in Go**:
  - **Definition**: Embedding in Go allows a struct to include another struct as an anonymous field. The fields and methods of the embedded struct become part of the parent struct and can be accessed directly.

    Syntax:

```
type InnerStruct struct {
    Field1 string
    Field2 int
}

type OuterStruct struct {
    InnerStruct // Embedded struct
    AdditionalField float64
}
```

Example:

```
type Engine struct {
    Horsepower int
    Type       string
}

type Car struct {
    Make   string
    Model  string
    Engine // Embedding the Engine struct
}

func main() {
    myCar := Car{
```

```
            Make:   "Ford",
            Model: "Mustang",
            Engine: Engine{
                Horsepower: 450,
                Type:       "V8",
            },
        }

        // Accessing embedded struct fields directly
        fmt.Println("Car details:", myCar)
        fmt.Println("Horsepower:", myCar.Horsepower)
    }
```

Explanation: The `Car struct` embeds `Engine`, so the fields of `Engine` are promoted to `Car` and can be accessed directly (e.g., `myCar.Horsepower`).

- **Behavior inheritance through embedding**:
  - **Method promotion**: When a struct embeds another struct, methods defined on the embedded struct are promoted to the parent struct. This means the parent struct can use the methods of the embedded struct as if they were its own.

    Example:

```
type Printer struct{}

func (p Printer) PrintMessage() {
    fmt.Println("Printing a message.")
}

type Document struct {
    Title   string
    Printer // Embedded struct
}

func main() {
    doc := Document{Title: "Golang Guide"}
    doc.PrintMessage() // Calls the PrintMessage method from Printer
}
```

    Explanation: The `Document struct` embeds `Printer`, which has a method `PrintMessage()`. This method is promoted, allowing `doc.PrintMessage()` to work seamlessly.

- **Composition in Go**:
  - **Definition**: Composition involves creating complex types by combining simpler ones. Unlike embedding, where the fields and methods of the embedded struct are promoted, composition explicitly defines fields within a struct.

    Syntax:

```
type Address struct {
    Street string
    City   string
```

```
    Zip    int
}

type Person struct {
    Name    string
    Age     int
    Address Address // Composition: Address is not embedded but
included as a field
}
```

Example:

```
type Author struct {
    Name  string
    Email string
}

type Book struct {
    Title  string
    Author Author // Composition: Author as a part of Book
}

func main() {
    myBook := Book{
        Title: "Go Crash Course",
        Author: Author{
            Name:  "Venkatesh",
            Email: "venkatesh@gmail.com",
        },
    }

    fmt.Println("Book title:", myBook.Title)
    fmt.Println("Author name:", myBook.Author.Name)
}
```

Explanation: In the **`Book struct`**, **`Author`** is composed as a field, allowing explicit access through **`myBook.Author.Name`**.

- **Differences between embedding and composition**:
    - **Field promotion**:
        - **Embedding**: Fields and methods of the embedded struct are promoted to the parent struct, enabling direct access.
        - **Composition**: Fields are not promoted; they must be accessed through their field names (e.g., **`myBook.Author.Name`**).
    - **Visibility**:
        - **Embedding**: Promotes a *has-a* relationship with easy access to embedded struct fields and methods.
        - **Composition**: Provides a *contains-a* relationship where fields are accessed explicitly.

- **Use cases**:
  - **Embedding**: Use when you want to promote the fields and methods of another struct for easier access.
  - **Composition**: Use when you need clear ownership and modular structures where field names are kept separate.

- **Method overriding in embedded structs**:
  - **Method overriding**: When a struct embeds another struct, the parent struct can define a method with the same name as the embedded struct, effectively overriding it.

    Example:

```
type Speaker struct{}

func (s Speaker) Speak() {
    fmt.Println("Speaking from Speaker.")
}

type Robot struct {
    Speaker // Embedded struct
}

// Method overriding
func (r Robot) Speak() {
    fmt.Println("Speaking from Robot.")
}

func main() {
    r := Robot{}
    r.Speak() // Calls the overridden method in Robot, not the
method in Speaker
}
```

    Explanation: The `Robot struct` has its own `Speak()` method, which overrides the `Speak()` method from the embedded `Speaker` struct.

- **Practical applications of embedding and composition**:
  - **Code reuse**: Embedding and composition allow for reusable, modular code by composing complex types from simpler ones.
  - **Inheritance-like behavior**: Embedding provides a way to mimic inheritance without the complexity of class hierarchies.
  - **Clearer code organization**: Using composition makes relationships between types explicit, helping developers understand the structure of complex data types.

    Example application:

```
type Dimensions struct {
    Width, Height float64
}
```

```go
type Window struct {
    Title      string
    Dimensions // Embedded struct
}

type Door struct {
    Material   string
    Dimensions // Embedded struct
}

func main() {
    win := Window{Title: "Living Room", Dimensions:
Dimensions{Width: 120, Height: 100}}
    door := Door{Material: "Wood", Dimensions:
Dimensions{Width: 80, Height: 200}}

    fmt.Println("Window width:", win.Width) // Accesses Width from Dimensions
    fmt.Println("Door height:", door.Height) // Accesses Height from Dimensions
}
```

Explanation: Both **`Window`** and **`Door`** embed **`Dimensions`**, allowing them to share common behavior and fields.

- **Best practices for embedding and composition**:
    - **Choose embedding for simplicity**: Use embedding when you want to promote the fields and methods of another struct for easier access and shared behavior.
    - **Use composition for explicit relationships**: Use composition when clear ownership and explicit field access are preferred for better code readability and maintenance.
    - **Avoid ambiguity**: Ensure that embedded fields do not introduce naming conflicts, especially when multiple structs are embedded.
    - **Leverage method promotion wisely**: Be cautious when promoting methods, as it can lead to unintentional overrides or unexpected behavior.
- **Common pitfalls**:
    - **Field conflicts**: If two embedded structs have fields or methods with the same name, accessing these fields may require explicit type qualification.
    - **Overusing embedding**: Embedding can lead to confusing code if used excessively or without a clear intent. Use it thoughtfully to keep the code readable.

      Example of field conflict:

```go
type A struct {
    Value int
}

type B struct {
    Value int
}
```

```
type C struct {
    A
    B
}

func main() {
    c := C{}
    c.A.Value = 10
    c.B.Value = 20

    // Access requires specifying the embedded struct to avoid ambiguity
    fmt.Println("Value from A:", c.A.Value)
    fmt.Println("Value from B:", c.B.Value)
}
```

Comparing and copying structs

Structs are user-defined composite data types that group together variables under a single type. Comparing and copying structs are common operations when working with Go programs, and it is important to understand how Go handles these processes.

Knowing how to compare and copy structs is crucial for writing clean, effective, and efficient Go code that handles data integrity, checks for equality, and performs shallow or deep copies, when necessary, as follows:

- **Comparing structs**: In Go, comparing structs is straightforward when they consist of simple, comparable types, i.e., in Go, you can directly compare two structs to see if they are the same. This works if all parts of the struct, like numbers and text fields, can be compared easily. However, if a struct has more complex parts like lists or maps, you cannot compare them directly and need to write extra code to do it. Knowing when and how to compare structs helps you avoid errors and keeps your code working smoothly.
    - **Direct comparison**: In Go, structs can be compared using the `==` and `!=` operators, provided all the fields within the struct are of types that support comparison (e.g., integers, floats, strings, and other comparable types).

      Syntax:

      ```
      struct1 == struct2 // Returns true if all fields are equal
      struct1 != struct2 // Returns true if any field is different
      ```

      Example:

      ```
      type Point struct {
          X int
          Y int
      }

      func main() {
          p1 := Point{X: 10, Y: 20}
          p2 := Point{X: 10, Y: 20}
          p3 := Point{X: 15, Y: 25}

          fmt.Println("p1 == p2:", p1 == p2) // true
      ```

```
    fmt.Println("p1 == p3:", p1 == p3) // false
}
```

Explanation: The comparison checks each corresponding field in **p1**, **p2**, and **p3** for equality. If all fields match, the structs are considered equal.

- **Limitations of struct comparison**:
  - **Non-comparable fields**:
    - Structs that contain non-comparable fields (e.g., slices, maps, functions) cannot be directly compared using == or !=.

      Example:

```
type Data struct {
    ID   int
    Info []string // Slices are not comparable
}

func main() {
    d1 := Data{ID: 1, Info: []string{"Go", "Lang"}}
    d2 := Data{ID: 1, Info: []string{"Go", "Lang"}}

    // fmt.Println(d1 == d2) // Compilation
error: slice can only be compared to nil
}
```

  - **Workaround**: For structs with non-comparable fields, you need to manually implement a comparison function or use a loop to compare individual elements:

```
func areSlicesEqual(a, b []string) bool {
    if len(a) != len(b) {
        return false
    }
    for i := range a {
        if a[i] != b[i] {
            return false
        }
    }
    return true
}
```

- **Copying structs**:
  - **Direct assignment**:
    - In Go, assigning one struct to another creates a shallow copy. This means the new struct will have the same values in its fields as the original, but it is a separate instance.

      Example:

```
type User struct {
    Name string
    Age  int
}
```

```
func main() {
    user1 := User{Name: "Shubham", Age: 30}
    user2 := user1 // Copy of user1

    user2.Name = "Venkatesh"

    fmt.Println("User 1:", user1) // Output: User 1: {Shubham 30}
    fmt.Println("User 2:", user2) // Output: User 2: {Venkatesh 30}
}
```

Explanation: Changing **user2** does not affect **user1** because **user2** is a separate copy with its own memory.

- **Shallow copy versus deep copy**:
  - **Shallow copy**: A shallow copy duplicates the struct but does not copy the underlying data referenced by pointers, slices, or maps within the struct. Changes to these underlying data structures affect both the original and the copied struct.
  - **Deep copy**: A deep copy duplicates the struct and all the data it references, creating a truly independent copy. Implementing a deep copy requires custom code to recursively copy all referenced data.

  Example of shallow copy:

```
type Profile struct {
    Username string
    Tags     []string // Slice field
}

func main() {
    p1 := Profile{Username: "Venkatesh", Tags: []string{"golang", "coding"}}
    p2 := p1 // Shallow copy

    p2.Tags[0] = "java" // Modifies the shared slice
    fmt.Println("Profile 1 Tags:", p1.Tags) // Output: [java coding]
    fmt.Println("Profile 2 Tags:", p2.Tags) // Output: [java coding]
}
```

  Explanation: The **Tags** slice is referenced by both **p1** and **p2**, so modifying it in **p2** also affects **p1**.

- **Implementing a deep copy**:
  - **Manual deep copy**: To create a deep copy, you need to manually copy each field and ensure that referenced data structures (e.g., slices, maps) are copied individually.

  Example:

```
type Profile struct {
    Username string
    Tags     []string
}

func deepCopyProfile(p Profile) Profile {
```

```
    copiedTags := make([]string, len(p.Tags))
    copy(copiedTags, p.Tags)
    return Profile{
        Username: p.Username,
        Tags:     copiedTags,
    }
}

func main() {
    p1 := Profile{Username: "Venkatesh", Tags: []string{"golang", "coding"}}
    p2 := deepCopyProfile(p1)

    p2.Tags[0] = "python"
    fmt.Println("Profile 1 Tags:", p1.Tags) // Output: [golang coding]
    fmt.Println("Profile 2 Tags:", p2.Tags) // Output: [python coding]
}
```

Explanation: The `deepCopyProfile` function creates a new `Profile struct` and copies the `Tags` slice independently, ensuring `p1` and `p2` have separate data.

- **Best practices for comparing and copying structs**:
    - **Avoid direct comparison with non-comparable fields**: Implement custom comparison logic for structs with slices, maps, or other non-comparable types.
    - **Use shallow copy for simple structs**: When the struct contains only primitive types or comparable fields, a shallow copy is sufficient.
    - **Implement deep copy for complex structs**: For structs with slices, maps, or other references, create custom functions to perform a deep copy to avoid shared data issues.
    - **Document copying and comparison**: Clearly document whether your functions perform shallow or deep copies to set correct expectations for the code's behavior.
- **Common pitfalls**:
    - **Unexpected shared references**: Be cautious with structs that contain slices, maps, or pointers. A shallow copy means these references are shared between the original and copied structs.
    - **Nil pointers**: Ensure that your deep copy functions check for nil pointers to avoid runtime errors.

      Example:

```
type Data struct {
    Info *string
}

func main() {
    var info *string
    data := Data{Info: info}

    if data.Info != nil {
        fmt.Println("Data contains info")
    } else {
```

```
            fmt.Println("Data.Info is nil")
        }
    }
```

Conclusion

In summary, this chapter provided a comprehensive guide to using structs and methods in Go, covering essential concepts such as pointer and value receivers, embedding and composition, and best practices for struct design. You now have the tools to create and manage complex data structures efficiently, implement methods to extend their functionality, and follow best practices for writing clean and maintainable code. Mastering these topics will serve as a strong foundation for building scalable and efficient Go applications.

In the next chapter, we will explore how to manage collections of data in Go using arrays, slices, and maps. You will learn the basics of arrays and how to work efficiently with slices for flexible data handling. We will cover creating and modifying maps to store key-value pairs and dive into multidimensional arrays and slices for managing complex datasets. Additionally, you will discover techniques for iterating over maps and slices effectively and learn about JSON encoding and decoding for data exchange. We will discuss best practices to ensure your use of arrays, slices, and maps is both efficient and idiomatic in Go.

Questions

1. What is a struct in Go? How do you declare and initialize a struct using named fields versus positional fields? Give examples.
2. Differentiate between exported and unexported struct fields in Go. How does this affect visibility across packages?
3. What are anonymous structs in Go and when would you use them over named structs? Illustrate with a use case.
4. What is the difference between a function and a method in Go? Explain with an example how to declare a method using a receiver.
5. Compare value receivers and pointer receivers in Go methods. When should each be used and why?
6. Explain the concept of method chaining in Go. How does returning a pointer receiver enable this pattern?
7. How does embedding differ from composition in Go structs? What are the benefits and potential naming conflicts of embedding?
8. Can methods of an embedded struct be accessed directly from the embedding struct? What happens when you override such a method?
9. How are structs compared in Go? What are the limitations of comparing structs with non-comparable fields like slices or maps?
10. What is the difference between shallow copy and deep copy of a struct in Go? Provide an example where shallow copy causes unintended side effects.

CHAPTER 5
Arrays, Slices, and Maps

Introduction

Efficient data handling is a crucial aspect of software development, and Go provides a range of built-in data structures, including arrays, slices, and maps, to manage collections of data effectively. These data structures allow developers to store, manipulate, and retrieve data efficiently, making Go applications highly optimized for performance and scalability.

Arrays in Go provide a fixed-length collection of elements, useful when working with a known data size. However, for dynamic resizing scenarios, Go introduces slices, which offer a flexible and efficient way to handle variable-length data. Additionally, maps serve as key-value stores, enabling rapid lookups and modifications, making them ideal for associative data structures.

This chapter deeply explores these data structures, covering array operations, slice manipulation, map creation and modification, multidimensional arrays, iteration techniques, and JSON handling. By mastering these concepts, you will be able to structure and process data effectively in Go, improving the efficiency and performance of your applications.

Structure

The chapter covers the following topics:

- Arrays in Go
- Working with slices
- Creating and modifying maps
- Multidimensional arrays and slices
- Iterating over maps and slices
- JSON in Go

Objectives

By the end of this chapter, you will have a solid understanding of arrays, slices, and maps in Go, enabling you to store, manipulate, and retrieve data efficiently. You will learn how to declare, initialize, and modify arrays, gaining insight into their fixed-length nature and their use in structured data storage. Additionally, you will explore slices, understanding how they provide a more flexible and dynamic approach to handling collections, including techniques for resizing and optimizing memory usage. The chapter will also cover maps, which are key-value stores that allow for fast lookups and efficient data modifications, making them a powerful tool in data-driven applications. Furthermore, you will delve into multidimensional arrays and slices, which are useful for managing complex and nested data structures. You will also learn efficient techniques for iterating over maps and slices, improving performance when processing large datasets. Finally, the chapter will introduce JSON handling in Go, enabling you to parse, serialize, and manipulate structured data for API communications and data exchange. By mastering these concepts, you will be well-equipped to handle structured data effectively, ensuring that your Go applications are both optimized and scalable.

Arrays in Go

An array in Go is a fixed-size collection of elements of the same type. Arrays provide a way to store multiple values under one variable name, where each value can be accessed using an index.

The key features are as follows:

- **Fixed size**: The size of an array is determined at the time of declaration and cannot be changed.
- **Homogeneous**: All elements in an array must be of the same type.
- **Value type**: Assigning one array to another creates a copy.

The details of the arrays are as follows:

- **Declaring arrays**:
  - **Syntax**:
    ```
    var arrayName [size]Type
    ```
  - **Examples**:
    - **Declaring an array of integers**:
      ```
      var numbers [5]int
      ```
    - **Declaring and initializing an array**:
      ```
      var names = [3]string{"Venkatesh", "Shubham", "Dinesh"}
      ```
    - **Using short declaration syntax**:
      ```
      scores := [4]int{10, 20, 30, 40}
      ```
  - **Size inference**:
    - You can omit the size and let Go infer it from the initialization:
      ```
      primes := [...]int{2, 3, 5, 7, 11}
      fmt.Println(primes) // Output: [2 3 5 7 11]
      ```
- **Accessing and modifying elements**:
  - **Accessing elements**: Array elements can be accessed using their index, starting from 0.
    ```
    numbers := [3]int{10, 20, 30}
    fmt.Println(numbers[0]) // Output: 10
    ```
  - **Modifying elements**: You can modify an array element by assigning a new value to its index.
    ```
    numbers[1] = 50
    fmt.Println(numbers) // Output: [10 50 30]
    ```
- **Default values in arrays**:
  - If an array is declared without initialization, its elements are set to the zero value of the element type:
    - **Zero value for integers**: `0`
    - **Zero value for strings**: `""`
    - **Zero value for Booleans**: `false`
  - **Example**:
    ```
    var uninitializedArray [4]int
    fmt.Println(uninitializedArray) // Output: [0 0 0 0]
    ```

- **Copying arrays**:
  - In Go, arrays are value types, meaning that assigning one array to another creates a copy of the entire array. This behavior ensures that the original array and the copy are completely independent of each other. Changes made to the copy do not affect the original array.
  - **Example**:

```
original := [3]int{1, 2, 3}
copy := original
copy[0] = 99
fmt.Println("Original:", original) // Output: [1 2 3]
fmt.Println("Copy:", copy)         // Output: [99 2 3]
```

  - **Explanation**: The **`original`** and the **`copy`** are separate arrays, so modifying the **`copy`** does not affect **`original`**.
- **Array length**:
  - In Go, **`len`** is a built-in function used to determine the length (size) of various data types. When used with arrays, it provides the number of elements in the array
  - **Example**:

```
arr := [5]int{10, 20, 30, 40, 50}
fmt.Println("Length of array:", len(arr)) // Output: 5
```

- **Working with constant arrays**: Arrays can be declared with constant values, useful for fixed data sets.
  - **Example**:

```
constSize := 5
constArray := [constSize]int{1, 2, 3, 4, 5}
fmt.Println(constArray) // Output: [1 2 3 4 5]
```

- **Comparing arrays**: Arrays in Go can be compared using the == operator if:
  - Both arrays have the same type.
  - Both arrays have the same size.
  - **Example**:

```
arr1 := [3]int{1, 2, 3}
arr2 := [3]int{1, 2, 3}
arr3 := [3]int{4, 5, 6}
fmt.Println(arr1 == arr2) // Output: true
fmt.Println(arr1 == arr3) // Output: false
```

- **Arrays as function arguments**: Arrays can be passed to functions by value. This means the function gets a copy of the array, and changes within the function do not affect the original array.
  - **Example**:

```
func modifyArray(arr [3]int) {
    arr[0] = 100
    fmt.Println("Inside function:", arr) // Output: [100 2 3]
}

func main() {
    original := [3]int{1, 2, 3}
```

```go
    modifyArray(original)
    fmt.Println("Outside function:", original) // Output: [1 2 3]
}
```

  - **Explanation**: The `modifyArray` function works on a copy of the array, so the original array remains unchanged.
- **Practical applications of arrays**:
  - **Static datasets**: Arrays are ideal for fixed-size data like days of the week, months of the year, or predefined constants.
  - **Grid-based data**: Arrays can represent 2D grids, such as images (pixels), game boards, or matrices in mathematical computations.
- **Limitations of arrays**:
  - **Fixed size**: Arrays have a fixed size, which makes them less flexible compared to slices.
  - **Memory overhead**: Assigning arrays to functions or other variables creates copies, which can be memory-intensive for large arrays.
  - **Rarely used directly**: Due to their fixed size and lack of flexibility, arrays are not as commonly used in Go as slices.

Working with slices

This section will discuss how to work with slices. The details are as follows:

- **What is a slice**:
  - **Definition**: A slice in Go is a dynamically sized, flexible view of an underlying array. Unlike arrays, slices do not have a fixed size and can grow or shrink as needed.
  - **Key features**:
    - Slices are references to an array.
    - They provide a convenient and powerful way to work with sequences of data.
- **Creating slices**:
  - **From arrays**:
    - Slices can be created from arrays by specifying a range.
    - **Syntax**:

```go
slice := array[start:end]
```

    - **Example**:

```go
arr := [5]int{10, 20, 30, 40, 50}
slice := arr[1:4] // Includes elements at index 1, 2, and 3
fmt.Println(slice) // Output: [20 30 40]
```

  - **Using slice literals**:
    - Slices can be declared directly without an array.
    - **Syntax**:

```go
slice := []Type{value1, value2, ...}
```

  - **Example**:
    ```
    slice := []int{1, 2, 3, 4, 5}
    fmt.Println(slice) // Output: [1 2 3 4 5]
    ```
- **Using make**:
  - The make function creates a slice with a specified length and capacity.
  - **Syntax**:
    ```
    slice := make([]Type, length, capacity)
    ```
  - **Example**:
    ```
    slice := make([]int, 3, 5)
    fmt.Println(slice)      // Output: [0 0 0]
    fmt.Println(len(slice)) // Output: 3
    fmt.Println(cap(slice)) // Output: 5
    ```

- **Appending to slices**:
  - **Appending elements**: In Go, the **append** function is a built-in utility used to add elements to a slice. Slices are dynamic data structures, unlike arrays, and append allows you to increase their size by adding new elements.
  - **Syntax**:
    ```
    slice = append(slice, elements...)
    ```
  - **Example**:
    ```
    slice := []int{1, 2, 3}
    slice = append(slice, 4, 5)
    fmt.Println(slice) // Output: [1 2 3 4 5]
    ```
  - **Automatic resizing**: If the slice capacity is exceeded, Go creates a new underlying array with increased capacity and copies the elements.
    - **Example**:
      ```
      slice := []int{1, 2}
      fmt.Println(cap(slice)) // Output: 2
      slice = append(slice, 3, 4, 5)
      fmt.Println(cap(slice)) // Output: 6 (capacity increases)
      ```
- **Length and capacity of slices**:
  - **Length**:
    - The number of elements in the slice.
    - Use **len(slice)** to get the length.
  - **Capacity**:
    - The maximum number of elements the slice can hold without resizing.
    - In Go, the **cap** function is a built-in utility that returns the capacity of a slice, array, or channel. When used with slices, it provides the total number of elements the underlying array can hold without requiring a resize. Understanding **cap** is crucial when working with slices in performance-sensitive or memory-efficient applications.
  - **Example**:
    ```
    slice := make([]int, 3, 5)
    ```

```
fmt.Println("Length:", len(slice)) // Output: 3
fmt.Println("Capacity:", cap(slice)) // Output: 5
```

- **Slicing slices**: A slice can be sliced further to create a new slice.
  - **Syntax**:

    ```
    newSlice := slice[start:end]
    ```

  - **Example**:

    ```
    original := []int{1, 2, 3, 4, 5}
    subSlice := original[1:4] // Elements at index 1, 2, and 3
    fmt.Println(subSlice)       // Output: [2 3 4]
    ```

  - **Modifying the subSlice**: Changes made to the **subSlice** affect the original slice since both reference the same underlying array.

    ```
    subSlice[0] = 99
    fmt.Println(original) // Output: [1 99 3 4 5]
    ```

- **Copying slices**: Use the copy function to create a duplicate slice with independent underlying data.
  - **Syntax**:

    ```
    copy(destination, source)
    ```

  - **Example**:

    ```
    original := []int{1, 2, 3}
    duplicate := make([]int, len(original))
    copy(duplicate, original)
    duplicate[0] = 99
    fmt.Println(original)  // Output: [1 2 3]
    fmt.Println(duplicate) // Output: [99 2 3]
    ```

- **Truncating slices**: You can truncate a slice by reslicing it to a smaller range.
  - **Example**:

    ```
    slice := []int{10, 20, 30, 40, 50}
    slice = slice[:3]
    fmt.Println(slice) // Output: [10 20 30]
    ```

- **Using nil slices**: A nil slice has no underlying array and a length and capacity of 0.
  - **Example**:

    ```
    var nilSlice []int
    fmt.Println(nilSlice == nil) // Output: true
    fmt.Println(len(nilSlice))   // Output: 0
    fmt.Println(cap(nilSlice))   // Output: 0
    ```

  - **Creating empty slices**: Use make to create an empty slice with a length and capacity of 0.

    ```
    emptySlice := make([]int, 0)
    fmt.Println(emptySlice == nil) // Output: false
    ```

- **Common slice pitfalls**:
  - **Capacity confusion**: When appending to a slice in Go, the **append** function may create a new underlying array if the current array lacks capacity to accommodate new elements. A slice is a lightweight view over an array, pointing to its memory. If append creates a new array, the appended slice references the new array, while the original slice continues to reference the old array. This results in the two slices

becoming independent, meaning changes to one will not affect the other. However, if no new array is created (because capacity suffices), both slices share the same underlying array, and changes in one slice can affect the other.

```
slice := []int{1, 2, 3}
appended := append(slice, 4)
appended[0] = 99
fmt.Println(slice)    // Output: [1 2 3]
fmt.Println(appended) // Output: [99 2 3 4]
```

- **Index out of range**: Accessing an index outside the slice's range causes a runtime panic.

```
slice := []int{1, 2, 3}
// fmt.Println(slice[5]) // This will cause a panic
```

- **Practical applications of slices**:
  - **Dynamic data storage**: Slices are ideal for storing data whose size is not known at compile time.

```
func collectInput(inputs ...int) []int {
    return append([]int{}, inputs...)
}

func main() {
    result := collectInput(10, 20, 30)
    fmt.Println(result) // Output: [10 20 30]
}
```

  - **Filtering and transforming data**: Slices are often used for filtering or transforming data.

```
func filterEvens(slice []int) []int {
    result :- []int{}
    for _, value := range slice {
        if value%2 == 0 {
            result = append(result, value)
        }
    }
    return result
}

func main() {
    numbers := []int{1, 2, 3, 4, 5, 6}
    evens := filterEvens(numbers)
    fmt.Println(evens) // Output: [2 4 6]
}
```

Creating and modifying maps

In this section, we will look at creating and modifying maps. The details are as follows:

- **What is a map**: A **map** in Go is a built-in data structure that stores key-value pairs, where keys are unique and are used to retrieve the corresponding values.

- **Key features**:
  - Keys must be of a comparable type (e.g., strings, integers, or custom types that can be compared).
  - Values can be of any type.
  - Maps are dynamically sized, and their size can grow as needed.

- **Creating maps**:
  - **Declaration without initialization**: Declaring a **map** without initializing it results in a nil map. A nil map cannot store any data.
  - **Syntax**:

```
var mapName map[KeyType]ValueType
```

  - **Example**:

```
var students map[string]int
fmt.Println(students == nil) // Output: true
```

  - **Initializing maps**: To use a **map**, you must initialize it with **make** or a **map** literal.
    - **Using make**: The **make** function creates an empty map.
    - **Syntax**:

```
mapName := make(map[KeyType]ValueType)
```

    - **Example**:

```
students := make(map[string]int)
students["Venkatesh"] = 85
fmt.Println(students) // Output: map[Venkatesh:85]
```

    - **Using a map literal**: A **map** literal allows initializing a **map** with predefined key-value pairs.
    - **Syntax**:

```
mapName := map[KeyType]ValueType{
    key1: value1,
    key2: value2,
}
```

    - **Example**:

```
scores := map[string]int{
    "Venkatesh": 90,
    "Shubham":   80,
}
fmt.Println(scores) // Output: map[Venkatesh:90 Shubham:80]
```

- **Adding key-value pairs**: To add data to a **map**, use the assignment syntax:

```
mapName[key] = value
```

  - **Example**:

```
products := make(map[string]float64)
products["Laptop"] = 129999.99
products["Phone"] = 79999.49
fmt.Println(products) // Output: map[Laptop:129999.99 Phone:79999.49]
```

- **Accessing map elements**:
  - **Syntax**:
    ```
    value := mapName[key]
    ```
  - If the key does not exist, the zero value of the value type is returned.
  - **Example**:
    ```
    scores := map[string]int{"Venkatesh": 90, "Shubham": 85}
    fmt.Println(scores["Venkatesh"]) // Output: 90
    fmt.Println(scores["Aditya"])   // Output: 0 (default zero
    value for int)
    ```
- **Checking for key existence**: To check if a key exists in a `map`, use the second return value of the `map` lookup.
  - **Syntax**:
    ```
    value, exists := mapName[key]
    ```
  - **Example**:
    ```
    scores := map[string]int{"Venkatesh": 90, "Shubham": 85}
    if value, exists := scores["Aditya"]; exists {
        fmt.Println("Aditya's score:", value)
    } else {
        fmt.Println("Aditya not found")
    }
    ```
- **Modifying values**: To modify a value in a `map`, simply assign a new value to an existing key.
  - **Example**:
    ```
    scores := map[string]int{"Venkatesh": 90, "Shubham": 85}
    scores["Shubham"] = 95
    fmt.Println(scores) // Output: map[Venkatesh:90 Shubham:95]
    ```
- **Deleting keys**: Use the `delete` function to remove a key-value pair from a `map`.
  - **Syntax**:
    ```
    delete(mapName, key)
    ```
  - **Example**:
    ```
    scores := map[string]int{"Venkatesh": 90, "Shubham": 85}
    delete(scores, "Venkatesh")
    fmt.Println(scores) // Output: map[Shubham:85]
    ```
- **Length of a map**: Use the `len` function to get the number of key-value pairs in a `map`.
  - **Example**:
    ```
    scores := map[string]int{"Venkatesh": 90, "Shubham": 85}
    fmt.Println("Number of entries:", len(scores)) // Output: 2
    ```
- **Copying maps**: Maps are reference types in Go. Assigning one `map` to another creates a reference to the same underlying data.
  - **Example**:
    ```
    original := map[string]int{"Venkatesh": 90}
    copy := original
    copy["Shubham"] = 85
    ```

```go
fmt.Println("Original:", original) // Output: map[Venkatesh:90 Shubham:85]
fmt.Println("Copy:", copy)         // Output: map[Venkatesh:90 Shubham:85]
```

  - **Explanation**: Modifying the copy also modifies the original because both variables reference the same map.

- **Maps with structs**: In Go, a `map` is a built-in data structure used to associate keys with values. You can use almost any type as a value in a `map`, including structs. However, the rules for keys are more restrictive: keys must be of types that are comparable.
  - **What does comparable mean**:
    - A type is considered comparable if values of that type can be compared using the `==` and `!=` operators. This comparison checks whether two values are equal or not. Comparable types include:
      - Basic types like integers, floats, strings, and Booleans.
      - Pointers, channels, and interfaces (if their dynamic types are comparable).
      - Structs (if all their fields are of comparable types).
      - Arrays (if their elements are of comparable types).
  - **Why the restriction**: Maps in Go rely on hashing for their implementation. For keys to work in a hash map, they need a consistent and deterministic way to compare equality, which is why only comparable types are allowed.
  - **Structs as values**:
    - **Example**:

```go
type Product struct {
    Name  string
    Price float64
}

func main() {
    inventory := map[string]Product{
        "Laptop": {Name: "Laptop", Price: 129999.99},
        "Phone":  {Name: "Phone", Price: 79999.49},
    }
    fmt.Println(inventory["Laptop"]) // Output: {Laptop 129999.99}
}
```

  - **Structs as keys**:
    - **Example**:

```go
type Point struct {
    X, Y int
}

func main() {
    grid := map[Point]string{
        {X: 1, Y: 2}: "Start",
        {X: 3, Y: 4}: "End",
```

```
        }
        fmt.Println(grid) // Output: map[{1 2}:Start {3 4}:End]
            }
```

- **Practical applications of maps**:
  - **Counting occurrences**:

    ```
    func countWords(words []string) map[string]int {
        wordCount := make(map[string]int)
        for _, word := range words {
            wordCount[word]++
        }
        return wordCount
    }

    func main() {
        words := []string{"go", "python", "go", "java", "go", "python"}
        fmt.Println(countWords(words)) // Output: map[go:3 python:2 java:1]
    }
    ```

  - **Storing configuration settings**:

    ```
    config := map[string]string{
        "host": "localhost",
        "port": "8080",
    }
    fmt.Println("Host:", config["host"])
    ```

- **Common pitfalls**:
  - **Accessing non-existent keys**: Accessing a key that does not exist returns the zero value for the value type.

    ```
    scores := map[string]int{"Venkatesh": 90}
    fmt.Println(scores["Shubham"]) // Output: 0
    ```

  - **Unintentional key overwriting**: Ensure keys are unique to avoid unintentional overwriting.
  - **Shared references**: Be cautious when assigning maps to avoid unexpected modifications due to shared references.

Multidimensional arrays and slices

This section deals with multidimensional arrays and slices. The details are as follows:

- **Multidimensional arrays in Go**: A multidimensional array is an array of arrays, where each element is itself an array.
  - **Syntax**:

    ```
    var arrayName [dim1][dim2]Type
    ```

    - **dim1**: Number of rows.
    - **dim2**: Number of columns.
  - **Creating and initializing multidimensional arrays**:
    - **Declaring without initialization**:

```
var matrix [3][3]int
```

This creates a 3x3 array with all elements initialized to their zero value (0 for integers).

- **Declaring with initialization**:

```
matrix := [2][3]int{
    {1, 2, 3},
    {4, 5, 6},
}
```

This creates a 2x3 matrix with the specified values.

- **Accessing elements**:
  - **Use two indices to access an element:**

```
matrix := [2][2]int{
    {1, 2},
    {3, 4},
}
fmt.Println(matrix[1][1]) // Output: 4
```

  - **Modifying elements**:

```
matrix[0][1] = 99
fmt.Println(matrix) // Output: [[1 99] [3 4]]
```

- **Length of multidimensional arrays**:
  - **Use the len function to get the size of the outer array and inner arrays:**

```
matrix := [3][4]int{}
fmt.Println("Rows:", len(matrix))         // Output: 3
fmt.Println("Columns:", len(matrix[0])) // Output: 4
```

- **Multidimensional slices in Go**: A multidimensional slice is a slice of slices, where each inner slice can have a different length. This makes slices more flexible than arrays.
  - **Creating multidimensional slices**:
    - **Using slice literals**:

```
grid := [][]int{
    {1, 2, 3},
    {4, 5},
    {6},
}
fmt.Println(grid) // Output: [[1 2 3] [4 5] [6]]
```

Here, each inner slice can have a different length.

- **Using make**: First, create the outer slice and then initialize each inner slice:

```
rows := 3
cols := 4
grid := make([][]int, rows)
for i := range grid {
    grid[i] = make([]int, cols)
}
fmt.Println(grid) // Output: [[0 0 0 0] [0 0 0 0] [0 0 0 0]]
```

- **Accessing and modifying elements**:
  - **Access elements using two indices**:

```
grid := [][]int{
    {1, 2, 3},
    {4, 5, 6},
}
fmt.Println(grid[1][2]) // Output: 6
```

  - **Modify an element**:

```
grid[1][2] = 99
fmt.Println(grid) // Output: [[1 2 3] [4 5 99]]
```

- **Adding rows to multidimensional slices**:
  - **Use the append function to add rows**:

```
grid := [][]int{
    {1, 2},
    {3, 4},
}
newRow := []int{5, 6}
grid = append(grid, newRow)
fmt.Println(grid) // Output: [[1 2] [3 4] [5 6]]
```

- **Removing rows from multidimensional slices**:
  - **To remove a row, use slicing**:

```
grid := [][]int{
    {1, 2},
    {3, 4},
    {5, 6},
}
grid = append(grid[:1], grid[2:]...)
fmt.Println(grid) // Output: [[1 2] [5 6]]
```

- **Key differences between multidimensional arrays and slices**:
  - **Fixed vs. dynamic size**: Arrays have a fixed size, while slices are dynamically resizable.
  - **Memory efficiency**: Multidimensional slices can be more memory-efficient as they allow inner slices to have different lengths.
  - **Flexibility**: Slices are more flexible because you can append, remove, or resize them easily.
- **Practical applications of multidimensional arrays and slices**:
  - **Matrix representation**:
    - **Use case**: Representing a matrix for mathematical computations.

```
func matrixAddition(a, b [2][2]int) [2][2]int {
    var result [2][2]int
    for i := 0; i < 2; i++ {
        for j := 0; j < 2; j++ {
            result[i][j] = a[i][j] + b[i][j]
        }
```

```
    }
    return result
}

func main() {
    matrix1 := [2][2]int{{1, 2}, {3, 4}}
    matrix2 := [2][2]int{{5, 6}, {7, 8}}
    result := matrixAddition(matrix1, matrix2)
    fmt.Println(result) // Output: [[6 8] [10 12]]
}
```

- **Dynamic grids**:
  - **Use case**: Creating a dynamic grid for a game or data representation.

```
func createGrid(rows, cols int) [][]int {
    grid := make([][]int, rows)
    for i := range grid {
        grid[i] = make([]int, cols)
    }
        return grid
    }

    func main() {
        grid := createGrid(3, 3)
        grid[1][1] = 9
        fmt.Println(grid) // Output: [[0 0 0] [0 9 0] [0 0 0]]
    }
```

- **Best practices for multidimensional arrays and slices**:
  - **Use arrays for fixed-size data**: If the size of the grid is known and constant, use arrays for better performance and simplicity.
  - **Prefer slices for dynamic data**: For grids or matrices that need resizing or dynamic memory allocation, use slices.
  - **Initialize inner slices properly**: Ensure inner slices are initialized before accessing them to avoid runtime panics.
  - **Avoid large multidimensional arrays in function arguments**: Pass large multidimensional arrays or slices by reference to save memory.

Iterating over maps and slices

We will discuss iterating over maps and slices. The details are as follows:

- **Iterating over slices**:
  - **Using the for loop with range**:
    - The `range` keyword iterates over a slice, providing both the `index` and the `value` of each element.
    - **Syntax**:

```
for index, value := range slice {
    // Process each element
}
```

- **Example**:

```
fruits := []string{"Apple", "Banana", "Cherry"}
for index, value := range fruits {
    fmt.Printf("Index: %d, Value: %s\n", index, value)
}
```

- **Output**:

```
Index: 0, Value: Apple
Index: 1, Value: Banana
Index: 2, Value: Cherry
```

- **Ignoring the index or value**:
  - **If you only need the value:**

```
for _, value := range slice {
    fmt.Println("Value:", value)
}

//If you only need the index:
for index := range slice {
    fmt.Println("Index:", index)
}
```

- **Modifying elements during iteration**: Modifying elements in the slice requires direct access using the `index`.
  - **Example**:

```
numbers := []int{1, 2, 3}
for index := range numbers {
    numbers[index] *= 2 // Double each element
}
fmt.Println(numbers) // Output: [2 4 6]
```

- **Exiting early from a loop**: Use the `break` statement to exit the loop prematurely.
  - **Example**:

```
numbers := []int{10, 20, 30, 40}
for index, value := range numbers {
    if value == 30 {
        fmt.Println("Found at index:", index)
        break
    }
}
```

- **Skipping iterations**: Use the `continue` statement to skip the current iteration.
  - **Example**:

```
numbers := []int{1, 2, 3, 4, 5}
for _, value := range numbers {
    if value%2 == 0 {
        continue // Skip even numbers
    }
```

```
        fmt.Println("Odd number:", value)
    }
```

- **Iterating over maps**:
    - **Using the for loop with range**: When iterating over a map, range provides both the key and the value.
        - **Syntax**:

```
for key, value := range map {
    // Process each key-value pair
}
```

        - **Example**:

```
scores := map[string]int{"Venkatesh": 90, "Shubham": 85, "Dinesh": 95}
for key, value := range scores {
    fmt.Printf("Key: %s, Value: %d\n", key, value)
}
```

        - **Output**:

```
Key: Venkatesh, Value: 90
Key: Shubham, Value: 85
Key: Dinesh, Value: 95
```

    - **Order of iteration**: The order of iteration over a map in Go is not guaranteed and may vary from one run to another.
        - **Example**:

```
cities := map[string]string{"India": "Delhi", "USA":
"Washington", "Japan": "Tokyo"}
for key, value := range cities {
    fmt.Printf("Country: %s, Capital: %s\n", key, value)
}
```

        The output order may differ on each run.

    - **Iterating only keys or values**:
        - **To iterate only over the keys:**

```
for key := range map {
    fmt.Println("Key:", key)
}
```

        - **To iterate only over the values:**

```
for _, value := range map {
    fmt.Println("Value:", value)
}
```

    - **Checking key existence during iteration**: Use conditional logic to process specific keys or values during iteration.
        - **Example**:

```
scores := map[string]int{"Venkatesh": 90, "Shubham": 85, "Dinesh": 95}
for key, value := range scores {
    if value > 90 {
        fmt.Printf("%s has an excellent score: %d\n", key, value)
```

```
        }
    }
```

- **Deleting keys during iteration**:
    - Avoid modifying the map (e.g., deleting keys) during iteration, as it can lead to unpredictable behavior.
    - To safely delete keys, collect them in a separate slice and delete them after the iteration.
    - **Example**:

```
scores := map[string]int{"Venkatesh": 90, "Shubham": 85, "Dinesh": 95}
var toDelete []string
for key, value := range scores {
    if value < 90 {
        toDelete = append(toDelete, key)
    }
}
for _, key := range toDelete {
    delete(scores, key)
}
fmt.Println(scores) // Output: map[Venkatesh:90 Dinesh:95]
```

- **Combining iteration with other logic**:
    - **Filtering slices**:
        - **Example**: Extract elements greater than a threshold.

```
numbers := []int{10, 20, 30, 40, 50}
var filtered []int
for _, value := range numbers {
    if value > 25 {
        filtered = append(filtered, value)
    }
}
fmt.Println(filtered) // Output: [30 40 50]
```

- **Mapping values in slices**:
    - **Example**: Create a new slice with modified values.

```
numbers := []int{1, 2, 3}
var doubled []int
for _, value := range numbers {
    doubled = append(doubled, value*2)
}
fmt.Println(doubled) // Output: [2 4 6]
```

- **Building reverse maps**:
    - **Example**: Reverse key-value pairs in a `map`.

```
original := map[string]int{"Venkatesh": 90, "Shubham": 85}
reversed := make(map[int]string)
for key, value := range original {
```

```
        reversed[value] = key
    }
    fmt.Println(reversed) // Output: map[90:Venkatesh 85:Shubham]
```

- **Best practices for iteration**:
    - **Avoid changing the collection during iteration**: Modifying maps or slices while iterating can lead to unexpected behavior. Plan such changes outside the loop.
    - **Optimize nested loops**: Minimize nested loops over large slices or maps to avoid performance issues.
    - **Use range for readability**: Prefer range over traditional indexed loops for cleaner and more readable code.
    - **Handle missing keys gracefully**: When iterating over maps, ensure the code handles cases where expected keys might not exist.

JSON in Go

JavaScript Object Notation (JSON) is a lightweight data interchange format that is easy for humans to read and write and easy for machines to parse and generate.

Further details are as follows:

- **Why use JSON in Go**:
    - JSON is widely used in APIs and configuration files.
    - Go provides built-in support for JSON encoding (marshaling) and decoding (unmarshaling) through the **`encoding/json`** package.
- **Encoding data into JSON (Marshaling)**:
    - **Marshaling**: The process of converting Go data types into JSON format.
    - **Function**: **`json.Marshal`**
    - **Encoding structs**:
        - **Example**:

```
package main

import (
    "encoding/json"
    "fmt"
)

type User struct {
    Name  string 'json:"name"'
    Email string 'json:"email"'
    Age   int    'json:"age"'
}

func main() {
    user := User{Name: "Venkatesh", Email: "venkatesh@gmail.com", Age: 35}
    jsonData, err := json.Marshal(user)
    if err != nil {
```

```
        fmt.Println("Error encoding JSON:", err)
    } else {
        fmt.Println(string(jsonData)) // Output: {"name":
"Venkatesh","email":"venkatesh@gmail.com","age":35}
    }
}
```

- **Explanation**:
  - The `json:"field_name"` tag maps Go struct fields to JSON keys.
  - The `Marshal` function returns a byte slice, which needs to be converted to a string for display.
- **Encoding maps**:
  - **Example**:

```
func main() {
    data := map[string]int{"A": 1, "B": 2}
    jsonData, err := json.Marshal(data)
    if err != nil {
        fmt.Println("Error encoding JSON:", err)
    } else {
        fmt.Println(string(jsonData)) // Output: {"A":1,"B":2}
    }
}
```

- **Pretty printing JSON**: Use `json.MarshalIndent` for human-readable JSON output.
  - **Example**:

```
func main() {
    user := map[string]interface{}{
        "name":  "Venkatesh",
        "email": "venkatesh@gmail.com",
        "age":   35,
    }
    jsonData, err := json.MarshalIndent(user, "", "  ")
    if err != nil {
        fmt.Println("Error encoding JSON:", err)
    } else {
        fmt.Println(string(jsonData))
    }
}
```

  - **Output**:

```
{
  "name": "Venkatesh",
  "email": "venkatesh@gmail.com",
  "age": 35
}
```

- **Decoding JSON into Go data (Unmarshaling)**:
  - **Unmarshaling**: The process of converting JSON data into Go data types.

- **Function**: `json.Unmarshal`
- **Decoding into structs**:
  - **Example**:

```
func main() {
    jsonData := '{"name":"Venkatesh","email":"venkatesh@gmail.com","age":35}'
    var user struct {
        Name  string 'json:"name"'
        Email string 'json:"email"'
        Age   int    'json:"age"'
    }
    err := json.Unmarshal([]byte(jsonData), &user)
    if err != nil {
        fmt.Println("Error decoding JSON:", err)
    } else {
        fmt.Printf("Decoded Struct: %+v\n", user) // Output:
Decoded Struct: {Name:Venkatesh Email:venkatesh@gmail.com Age:35}
    }
}
```

- **Decoding into maps**: Use maps for dynamic JSON data where the structure is unknown.
  - **Example**:

```
func main() {
    jsonData := '{"name":"Venkatesh","age":35}'
    var data map[string]interface{}
    err := json.Unmarshal([]byte(jsonData), &data)
    if err != nil {
        fmt.Println("Error decoding JSON:", err)
    } else {
        fmt.Println(data) // Output: map[age:35 name:Venkatesh]
    }
}
```

- **Handling nested JSON**:
  - **Example**:

```
func main() {
    jsonData := '{"person":{"name":"Venkatesh","age":35},"status":"active"}'
    var result map[string]interface{}
    err := json.Unmarshal([]byte(jsonData), &result)
    if err != nil {
        fmt.Println("Error decoding JSON:", err)
    } else {
        person := result["person"].(map[string]interface{})
        fmt.Println("Name:", person["name"]) // Output: Name: Venkatesh
        fmt.Println("Age:", person["age"])   // Output: Age: 35
    }
}
```

- **Working with custom JSON tags**:
  - **Using field tags**:
    - The **json** tag defines the key name in the JSON output.
    - **Example**:

```
type User struct {
    Name      string 'json:"name"'
    Email     string 'json:"email"'
    IsActive  bool   'json:"is_active"'
    OmitField string 'json:"-"' // This field will not appear in the JSON
}

func main() {
    user := User{Name: "Shubham", Email: "shubham@gmail.com", IsActive: true}
    jsonData, _ := json.Marshal(user)
    fmt.Println(string(jsonData)) // Output: {"name":"Shubham","email":"shubham@
gmail.com","is_active":true}
}
```

- **Handling JSON encoding/decoding errors**: Always check for errors during marshaling or unmarshaling to ensure proper handling of invalid or malformed JSON.
  - **Example**:

```
func main() {
    invalidJSON := '{"name":"Venkatesh","age":}'
    var data map[string]interface{}
    err := json.Unmarshal([]byte(invalidJSON), &data)
    if err != nil {
        fmt.Println("Error decoding JSON:", err) // Output: Error decoding JSON:
invalid character '}' looking for beginning of value
    }
}
```

- **Streaming JSON encoding and decoding**: The **json** package provides encoder and decoder types for streaming large JSON data.
  - **Streaming encoding**:
    - **Example**:

```
import (
    "encoding/json"
    "os"
)

func main() {
    user := map[string]string{"name": "Venkatesh", "email": "venkatesh@gmail.
com"}
    encoder := json.NewEncoder(os.Stdout)
    encoder.SetIndent("", "  ") // Pretty printing
```

```
        encoder.Encode(user)
    }
```

- **Streaming decoding**:
  - **Example**:

```
import (
    "encoding/json"
    "strings"
)

func main() {
    jsonStream := '{"name":"Venkatesh","age":35}'
    decoder := json.NewDecoder(strings.NewReader(jsonStream))

    var data map[string]interface{}
    decoder.Decode(&data)
    fmt.Println(data) // Output: map[name:Venkatesh age:35]
}
```

- **Best practices for JSON handling in Go**:
  - **Use structs for known data**: Structs provide type safety and are easier to work with compared to maps.
  - **Validate JSON input**: Always validate JSON input to handle errors gracefully and prevent crashes.
  - **Omit empty fields**: Use the `omitempty` tag to exclude fields with zero values.
    - **Example**:

```
type User struct {
    Name  string 'json:"name"'
    Email string 'json:"email,omitempty"'
}
user := User{Name: "Venkatesh"}
jsonData, _ := json.Marshal(user)
fmt.Println(string(jsonData)) // Output: {"name":"Venkatesh"}
```

  - **Pretty print for debugging**: Use `MarshalIndent` or `Encoder.SetIndent` for human-readable output during development.

Conclusion

In this chapter, we explored Go's core data structures like arrays, slices, and maps, along with their multidimensional variants. Arrays offer fixed-size, type-safe collections ideal for scenarios where the data size is known at compile time. While arrays are efficient and predictable in terms of memory layout, they are limited in flexibility. Slices, in contrast, provide a dynamic and resizable abstraction over arrays, making them the preferred choice for most Go programs. They allow for convenient operations like appending, slicing, and passing to functions with minimal overhead. Maps in Go serve as efficient key-value stores, enabling quick data lookups and updates. They are particularly useful for storing configuration data, counting occurrences, or associating keys with structured values. We also examined multidimensional arrays and slices for representing tabular or grid-like data and discussed how slices of slices provide the flexibility to represent jagged data structures. Practical examples and common pitfalls, such as memory sharing in slices and key overwrites in maps, were addressed to strengthen your understanding. Finally, we looked into JSON handling in Go, a vital skill for building APIs and working with structured data across systems.

In the next chapter, we turn our attention to pointers in Go. You will learn about the concept of memory references, how to declare and use pointers, and how pointer receiver methods can be used to mutate struct state efficiently. Understanding pointers is fundamental to mastering Go's performance characteristics and memory-safe design, making the upcoming chapter a critical milestone in your learning journey.

Questions

1. What is the difference between arrays and slices in Go, and when should each be used?
2. Explain how memory allocation and resizing work when using the append() function on slices.
3. How are maps initialized in Go? What happens if you try to add elements to a nil map?
4. What is the significance of the json:"field_name" tag in Go structs when working with JSON?
5. Describe the key differences between multidimensional arrays and slices of slices. What are the trade-offs?
6. Write a Go program that initializes a map of student names to their scores and prints out only those with scores above 90.
7. Given an array [5]int{1, 2, 3, 4, 5}, write Go code to create a slice that excludes the first and last elements.
8. Write a function that takes a slice of integers and returns a new slice containing only the even numbers.
9. Create a two-dimensional slice representing a 3x3 grid, initialize all elements to 0, and then set the center element to 1. Print the grid.
10. Demonstrate with code how changes to a subslice affect the original slice. Include comments to explain why this happens.

Join our Discord space

Join our Discord workspace for latest updates, offers, tech happenings around the world, new releases, and sessions with the authors:

https://discord.bpbonline.com

CHAPTER 6
Pointers

Introduction

In Go programming, pointers provide a powerful mechanism for referencing and manipulating memory directly. Unlike value types that hold data directly, pointers hold the address of a variable, enabling developers to write more efficient and flexible programs. This chapter introduces the fundamental concept of pointers in Go and walks through their declaration, usage, dereferencing, and practical applications. It also covers how pointers work with functions, structs, slices, arrays, and how Go manages memory safely through garbage collection. By understanding pointers, learners will gain deeper insights into memory efficiency, reference-based data handling, and foundational constructs used in advanced data structures and systems programming.

Structure

The chapter covers the following topics:

- Introduction to pointers
- Working with pointers in Go
- Pointer receiver methods in Go

Objectives

By the end of this chapter, students will be able to understand and effectively use pointers in Go. They will learn how to declare, assign, and dereference pointers, and understand their impact on memory and performance. Learners will also explore how pointers enhance function parameter handling, enable dynamic memory management, and allow direct manipulation of complex data structures. This chapter further builds competency in writing pointer receiver methods, distinguishing between pointer and value receivers, and applying pointers safely using Go's memory model. Overall, this chapter equips students with practical knowledge to write efficient, memory-aware, and modular Go programs.

Introduction to pointers

A pointer is a variable that stores the memory address of another variable. Instead of holding a direct value, it points to the memory location where the value resides.

Pointers enable efficient manipulation of data by referencing it directly in memory rather than copying it. Further details about pointers are provided as follows:

- **Key characteristics of pointers**:
    - **Memory efficiency**: Pointers allow functions and methods to operate on the actual data, avoiding unnecessary copying of large data structures.
    - **Direct memory access**: Pointers provide direct access to the memory address of a variable, which can be crucial for low-level programming and performance optimization.
    - **Flexibility**: Pointers can dynamically refer to different variables during runtime, providing flexibility in program design.

- **Use of pointers**:
  - o **Pass by reference**: Pointers allow functions to modify variables directly by passing their memory address rather than a copy of their value.
  - o **Efficient memory management**: Pointers enable efficient handling of large data structures like arrays, structs, and slices, as only the memory address is passed rather than duplicating the entire data.
  - o **Dynamic data structures**: Pointers are essential for creating and managing dynamic data structures like linked lists, trees, and graphs.
  - o **Low-level programming**: Pointers provide fine-grained control over memory, which is critical for systems programming and interfacing with hardware.

Example of memory address:

```
func main() {
    x := 42
    fmt.Println("Value of x:", x)   // Output: 42
    fmt.Println("Address of x:", &x) // Output: Memory address of x (e.g., 0xc0000100e0)
}
```

- **Explanation:**
  - o **&x** retrieves the memory address of the variable **x**.
  - o This address can be assigned to a pointer for further operations.
- **Declaration of a pointer**: A pointer is declared using the * symbol followed by the type of data it will point to.

```
var ptr *int // Declares a pointer to an integer
```

- **Assigning a pointer**: Use the **&** operator to assign the memory address of a variable to a pointer.

```
x := 10
var ptr *int = &x // ptr now stores the address of x
```

- **Pointer dereferencing**: Dereferencing a pointer means accessing or modifying the value stored at the memory address the pointer holds. This is done using the * operator.

```
x := 10
ptr := &x
fmt.Println(*ptr) // Output: 10 (value at the address)
*ptr = 20
fmt.Println(x)     // Output: 20 (value of x updated via pointer)
```

- **Nil pointer**: The zero value of a pointer in Go is **nil**, meaning it does not point to any valid memory address.

  Example:

```
var ptr *int
fmt.Println(ptr == nil) // Output: true
```

Attempting to dereference a **nil** pointer causes a runtime panic. Always check if a pointer is **nil** before dereferencing it.

```
var ptr *int
if ptr != nil {
    fmt.Println(*ptr) // Safe dereferencing
} else {
```

```
        fmt.Println("Pointer is nil")
    }
```

- **Pointer vs. value:**
    - **Value variables**:
        - **Definition**: Value variables hold the actual data directly in memory.
        - **Behavior**: When you perform operations on a value variable, it works on a copy of the data. The original variable remains unaffected.
        - **Use case**: Value variables are suitable for small data types or when you do not need to modify the original data.
    - **Pointer variables**:
        - **Definition**: Pointer variables store the memory address of a value variable. Instead of holding the actual data, they point to the location where the data is stored.
        - **Behavior**: Operations performed using pointers directly affect the original data because they operate on the memory address of the variable.
        - **Use case**: Pointers are ideal for large data structures, shared data between functions, or when modifications to the original variable are required.

Some key differences between value and pointer variables are presented in the following table:

Feature	Value variables	Pointer variables
What they store	The actual data	The memory address of the data
Modification	Changes affect only the local copy	Changes directly affect the original data
Efficiency	May involve copying large amounts of data	Works efficiently by referencing memory
Use case	Small, immutable data or local operations	Shared, large, or modifiable data

***Table 6.1**: Value variables vs. pointer variables*

Example: **Value vs. pointer behavior:**

```
func modifyValue(val int) {
    val = 20
}

func modifyPointer(ptr *int) {
    *ptr = 20
}

func main() {
    x := 10
    modifyValue(x)
    fmt.Println("After modifyValue:", x) // Output: 10 (unchanged)

    modifyPointer(&x)
    fmt.Println("After modifyPointer:", x) // Output: 20 (changed via pointer)
}
```

- **Practical use cases of pointers:**
    - **Efficient parameter passing**: Passing large data structures like arrays or structs to functions can be inefficient as they are copied. Pointers solve this by passing the memory address.

      Example:

```go
type Person struct {
    Name string
    Age  int
}

func updateAge(p *Person, newAge int) {
    p.Age = newAge
}

func main() {
    person := Person{Name: "Venkatesh", Age: 35}
    updateAge(&person, 40)
    fmt.Println(person.Age) // Output: 40
}
```

    - **Dynamic data structures**: Dynamic data structures like linked lists, trees, and graphs rely heavily on pointers to manage relationships between nodes efficiently. Pointers allow these structures to dynamically allocate and deallocate memory, enabling flexibility in size and structure. For example, in a linked list, each node contains a pointer to the next node, creating a chain of elements. Similarly, trees use pointers to establish parent-child relationships, and graphs use them to represent connections between nodes. This dynamic nature makes pointers indispensable for creating and managing these data structures.
    - **Interfacing with C libraries**: Go's **cgo** package uses pointers to interact with C code and libraries.
        - **Go manages pointers using a safe and efficient memory model**: Go has a garbage collector that automatically frees memory no longer referenced by pointers, reducing the risk of memory leaks.
        - **Pointer safety**: Unlike languages like C, Go does not support pointer arithmetic, ensuring pointer usage remains safe and avoids accidental memory corruption.

Working with pointers in Go

Working with pointers in Go involves tasks like obtaining memory addresses, dereferencing pointers, modifying values through pointers, and leveraging pointers for efficiency in functions and struct manipulation.

This section provides a comprehensive guide to mastering these operations with practical examples.

- **Pointers with functions**:
    - **Passing pointers to functions**: Functions can accept pointers as parameters to modify the original variables or avoid copying large data structures.

      Example: Modifying variables:

```go
func increment(num *int) {
    *num += 1 // Increment the value at the pointer
}
```

```go
func main() {
    x := 10
    increment(&x)
    fmt.Println("Incremented value:", x) // Output: 11
}
```

- **Returning pointers from functions**: Functions can return pointers to enable efficient data manipulation.

  Example: Returning a pointer

```go
func newCounter(initial int) *int {
    counter := initial
    return &counter
}

func main() {
    ptr := newCounter(5)
    fmt.Println("Counter value:", *ptr) // Output: 5
}
```

In Go, the **`newCounter`** creates a local variable counter and returns its memory address as a pointer. While this might seem risky since local variables typically cease to exist after a function exits, Go ensures safety through escape analysis. The compiler detects that counter's address escapes the function scope and allocates it on the heap instead of the stack. This heap allocation, managed by Go's garbage collector, keeps counter valid as long as the pointer is referenced, avoiding dangling pointer issues common in languages like C.

- **Pointers and structs**:
  - **Pointers to structs**: Pointers to structs allow you to modify the struct's fields without creating a copy.

    Example: Modifying struct fields:

```go
type Person struct {
    Name string
    Age  int
}

func updateName(p *Person, newName string) {
    p.Name = newName
}

func main() {
    person := Person{Name: "Venkatesh", Age: 30}
    updateName(&person, "Shubham")
    fmt.Println("Updated Name:", person.Name) // Output: Shubham
}
```

  - **Creating structs with pointers**: You can create a struct and obtain a pointer to it directly.

    Example: In Go, you can use the **&** operator with a struct literal to create a pointer to a newly created struct instance. This is a concise and common way to initialize and work with pointers to structs:

```go
func main() {
    person := &Person{Name: "Venkatesh", Age: 35}
```

```
    fmt.Println("Name:", person.Name) // Access fields directly through the pointer
}
```

- **Dereferencing struct pointers**: Go allows you to access struct fields directly through a pointer without explicit dereferencing.

  Example:

```
type Rectangle struct {
    Width, Height float64
}

func main() {
    rect := &Rectangle{Width: 10, Height: 20}
    rect.Width = 30 // No need for explicit dereferencing (*rect).Width
    fmt.Println("Updated Width:", rect.Width) // Output: 30
}
```

- **Pointers and slices**: Slices are reference types in Go and already point to an underlying array, meaning changes to a slice's elements within a function are reflected outside without needing a pointer. This is because a slice contains a pointer to the underlying array, a length, and a capacity, and passing a slice to a function passes a copy of this descriptor, but the underlying array remains shared. Therefore, you rarely need to use pointers with slices.

  Example: Passing slices to functions:

```
func doubleValues(slice []int) {
    for i := range slice {
        slice[i] *= 2
    }
}

func main() {
    numbers := []int{1, 2, 3}
    doubleValues(numbers)
    fmt.Println(numbers) // Output: [2 4 6]
}
```

- **Pointers and arrays**: Arrays are value types in Go, so passing them to functions creates a copy. Pointers to arrays allow efficient modification without copying.

  Example: Modifying arrays via pointers:

```
func modifyArray(arr *[3]int) {
    for i := range arr {
        arr[i] *= 2
    }
}

func main() {
    nums := [3]int{1, 2, 3}
    modifyArray(&nums)
    fmt.Println(nums) // Output: [2 4 6]
}
```

- **Pointers to pointers**: Go supports multiple levels of indirection through pointers to pointers. Using a pointer to a pointer is an advanced technique that is less frequently used but valuable for scenarios like modifying deeply nested references or managing shared configuration pointers across functions.

  Example: Using pointers to pointers:

```
func setTo100(ptr **int) {
    **ptr = 100
}

func main() {
    x := 10
    ptr := &x
    ptrPtr := &ptr
    setTo100(ptrPtr)
    fmt.Println("Updated value of x:", x) // Output: 100
}
```

- **Working with new and make:**
  - **Using new**: The **new** function allocates memory and returns a pointer to the zero value of the specified type.

    Example: Allocating with **new**:

```
func main() {
    ptr := new(int)  // Allocates memory for an int and returns a pointer
    fmt.Println(*ptr) // Output: 0 (zero value of int)
    *ptr = 42
    fmt.Println(*ptr) // Output: 42
}
```

  - **Using make**: The **make** function is used to create slices, maps, and channels. Unlike new, it initializes the data structure and does not return a pointer.

    Example: Difference between **new** and **make**

```
func main() {
    slice := make([]int, 5) // Initializes a slice
    fmt.Println(slice)      // Output: [0 0 0 0 0]

    ptr := new([]int)       // Creates a pointer to a slice
    fmt.Println(ptr)        // Output: &[]
}
```

- **Common pointer operations:**
  - **Swapping values using pointers**: Pointers are ideal for implementing operations like swapping values.

    Example: Swapping two variables:

```
func swap(a, b *int) {
    *a, *b = *b, *a
}
```

```go
func main() {
    x, y := 5, 10
    swap(&x, &y)
    fmt.Println("x:", x, "y:", y) // Output: x: 10 y: 5
}
```

- **Dynamic memory allocation**: Pointers can be used for dynamic memory allocation, allowing efficient management of resources.

  Example: Creating dynamic values:

```go
func createPointer(value int) *int {
    return &value
}

func main() {
    ptr := createPointer(42)
    fmt.Println("Value at pointer:", *ptr) // Output: 42
}
```

Best practices for working with pointers are as follows:

- **Avoid dereferencing nil pointers**: Always check for `nil` before dereferencing a pointer to avoid runtime panics.

```go
if ptr != nil {
    fmt.Println(*ptr)
} else {
    fmt.Println("Pointer is nil")
}
```

- **Use pointers for efficiency**: Use pointers when passing large structs or arrays to functions to avoid unnecessary copying.
- **Minimize pointer complexity**: Avoid excessive pointer usage (e.g., multiple levels of indirection) as it can make the code harder to read and debug.
- **Prefer struct methods for pointer manipulation**: Encapsulate pointer logic within methods to improve readability and maintainability.

While pointers are powerful and enable efficient memory usage, they must be used carefully. The following are some common pitfalls developers should be aware of:

- **Nil dereferencing**: Dereferencing a nil pointer causes runtime panics.
- **Unintended modifications**: Changes made through a pointer affect the original value, which may lead to unexpected side effects.
- **Overusing pointers**: Excessive pointer usage can lead to complicated and less maintainable code.

Pointer receiver methods in Go

In Go, methods can be defined with either value receivers or pointer receivers. Using pointer receiver methods allows the method to modify the original value the receiver points to, rather than working on a copy. This is particularly useful when dealing with large structs or when mutations are required within the method.

Pointer receiver methods

A pointer receiver method in Go is a method where the receiver is a pointer to a type. It allows the method to modify the actual instance of the struct it is called on, as opposed to working on a copy.

Pointer receiver methods are especially useful when:

- You need to modify the struct fields.
- Avoid copying large structs during method calls, improving efficiency.

Syntax of pointer receiver methods

The receiver is declared as a pointer to the type using the * symbol.

General syntax:

```
func (receiverType *ReceiverName) MethodName(params) returnType {
    // Method implementation
}
```

Example:

```
type Rectangle struct {
    Width, Height float64
}

// Pointer receiver method to modify the dimensions
func (r *Rectangle) Scale(factor float64) {
    r.Width *= factor
    r.Height *= factor
}
```

Let us look at the details:

- **Defining and using pointer receiver methods:**
  - **Defining a pointer receiver method**: Pointer receiver methods allow modifications to the original struct.

    ```
    type Counter struct {
        Value int
    }

    // Increment increases the value by 1
    func (c *Counter) Increment() {
        c.Value++
    }
    ```

  - **Calling a pointer receiver method**: Use the method with a struct instance. Go automatically handles the dereferencing for pointer receivers.

    ```
    func main() {
        count := Counter{Value: 10}
        count.Increment()
        fmt.Println("Updated Value:", count.Value) // Output: 11
    }
    ```

- **Pointer receiver vs. value receiver:**
  - **Value receiver:**
    - A value receiver operates on a copy of the struct.
    - Changes made inside the method do not affect the original struct.

Example: Value receiver:

```
type Rectangle struct {
    Width, Height float64
}

func (r Rectangle) Scale(factor float64) {
    r.Width *= factor
    r.Height *= factor
}

func main() {
    rect := Rectangle{Width: 10, Height: 5}
    rect.Scale(2)
    fmt.Println(rect) // Output: {10 5} (unchanged)
}
```

  - **Pointer receiver**: A pointer receiver modifies the actual struct.

Example: Pointer receiver:

```
type Rectangle struct {
    Width, Height float64
}

func (r *Rectangle) Scale(factor float64) {
    r.Width *= factor
    r.Height *= factor
}

func main() {
    rect := Rectangle{Width: 10, Height: 5}
    rect.Scale(2)
    fmt.Println(rect) // Output: {20 10} (modified)
}
```

The following table presents some key differences between value and pointer receivers:

Feature	Value receiver	Pointer receiver
Behavior	Operates on a copy of the struct.	Operates on the actual struct instance.
Memory usage	Creates a new copy for the method call.	Avoids copying, especially for large structs.
Modifications	Does not affect the original struct.	Directly modifies the original struct.
Use case	For read-only operations or small structs.	When modifications are required or for large structs.

Table 6.2: Value variables vs. pointer variables

Advantages of pointer receiver methods

The advantages of the pointer receiver method are as follows:

- **Modifying struct fields**: Pointer receiver methods allow direct modification of the struct's fields, enabling behavior that updates the state of the instance.

  Example:

```
type BankAccount struct {
    Balance float64
}

func (b *BankAccount) Deposit(amount float64) {
    b.Balance += amount
}

func (b *BankAccount) Withdraw(amount float64) bool {
    if b.Balance >= amount {
        b.Balance -= amount
        return true
    }
    return false
}
```

- **Efficiency**: Pointer receiver methods avoid copying the struct during method calls. This is especially useful for large structs.

  Example:

```
type BigStruct struct {
    Data [1000]int
}

func (b *BigStruct) Process() {
    b.Data[0] = 1
}
```

- **Method chaining**: Returning a pointer from a method allows method chaining, enabling a more fluent API design.

  Example:

```
type Account struct {
    Balance float64
}

func (a *Account) Deposit(amount float64) *Account {
    a.Balance += amount
    return a
}

func (a *Account) Withdraw(amount float64) *Account {
```

```
    if a.Balance >= amount {
        a.Balance -= amount
    }
    return a
}

func main() {
    acc := &Account{Balance: 100}
    acc.Deposit(50).Withdraw(30).Deposit(20)
    fmt.Println("Final Balance:", acc.Balance) // Output: 140
}
```

- **Practical applications of pointer receiver methods:**
    - **Modifying internal state**: Pointer receiver methods are widely used in data structures like stacks, queues, and linked lists.

      Example: Stack implementation:

```
type Stack struct {
    Elements []int
}

func (s *Stack) Push(value int) {
    s.Elements = append(s.Elements, value)
}

func (s *Stack) Pop() int {
    if len(s.Elements) == 0 {
        return -1 // Indicate empty stack
    }
    value := s.Elements[len(s.Elements)-1]
    s.Elements = s.Elements[:len(s.Elements)-1]
    return value
}

func main() {
    stack := &Stack{}
    stack.Push(10)
    stack.Push(20)
    fmt.Println(stack.Pop()) // Output: 20
    fmt.Println(stack.Pop()) // Output: 10
}
```

    - **Managing complex behavior**: Pointer receiver methods are ideal for encapsulating complex logic within a struct, such as scaling, resizing, or updating fields based on specific rules.

      Example: Resizing a rectangle:

```
type Rectangle struct {
    Width, Height float64
```

```
}

func (r *Rectangle) Resize(newWidth, newHeight float64) {
    r.Width = newWidth
    r.Height = newHeight
}

func main() {
    rect := Rectangle{Width: 10, Height: 5}
    rect.Resize(20, 10)
    fmt.Println("Resized Rectangle:", rect) // Output: {20 10}
}
```

While pointer receiver methods offer flexibility and performance benefits, incorrect usage can lead to subtle bugs and unexpected behavior.

The following are some common pitfalls developers should be mindful of:

- **Using value receivers instead of pointer receivers**: Forgetting to use a pointer receiver when modifications are required can lead to unexpected behavior.

```
type Counter struct {
    Value int
}

func (c Counter) Increment() {
    c.Value++
}

func main() {
    count := Counter{Value: 10}
    count.Increment()
    fmt.Println(count.Value) // Output: 10 (unchanged)
}
```

- **Dereferencing nil pointers**: Ensure that methods handle cases where the receiver is nil to avoid runtime panics.

```
type Node struct {
    Value int
    Next  *Node
}

func (n *Node) AddNext(value int) {
    if n == nil {
        fmt.Println("Cannot add to a nil node")
        return
    }
    n.Next = &Node{Value: value}
}
```

The best practices for pointer receiver methods are as follows:

- **Use for modifications**: Use pointer receivers for methods that need to update struct fields or manage state.
- **Be consistent**: For a given struct, use either pointer or value receivers consistently across all methods to avoid confusion.
- **Avoid using pointer receivers for small structs**: For small structs that do not require modifications, prefer value receivers for simplicity and performance.
- **Document method behavior**: Clearly document whether a method modifies the receiver or not to avoid misuse.

Conclusion

In this chapter, we explored the concept of pointers in Go and how they enable direct memory referencing, efficient data manipulation, and deeper control over variable behavior. We learned how to declare, assign, and dereference pointers, as well as how they interact with structs, slices, functions, and method receivers. Through practical examples, we also highlighted common pitfalls and best practices to ensure safe and effective pointer usage in Go programs.

The next chapter will introduce interfaces in Go, a powerful feature that allows you to design flexible, modular, and decoupled applications. You will learn how interfaces define behavior, how Go's implicit implementation model works, and how to leverage interfaces for polymorphism and extensibility in your code.

Questions

1. What is a pointer in Go, and how does it differ from a regular value variable?
2. Explain the role of the * and & operators when working with pointers in Go. Provide examples.
3. Why are pointer receiver methods preferred over value receivers when modifying struct fields?
4. What are some of the key advantages and disadvantages of using pointers in Go programs?
5. How does Go ensure memory safety while still supporting pointers? Mention at least two mechanisms.
6. Write a Go function swap(a, b *int) that swaps the values of two integers using pointers.
7. Given a struct Person with fields Name and Age, write a method with a pointer receiver that updates the Age field.
8. Demonstrate how a nil pointer can lead to a runtime panic and how to prevent it safely.
9. Implement a simple stack using a struct and pointer receiver methods Push() and Pop() as shown in the chapter.
10. What is the difference between the new and make functions in Go? Provide a code snippet to illustrate their usage.

CHAPTER 7
Interfaces in Go

Introduction

Interfaces in Go are a foundational concept that enables flexible, modular, and reusable code. By defining method sets without specifying implementation, interfaces allow different types to be used interchangeably, based purely on behavior. This powerful abstraction enables polymorphism, loose coupling, and clean software design. Go's unique approach to implicit interface satisfaction, where a type implements an interface just by defining its methods and removes the need for boilerplate code and encourages design simplicity. This chapter discusses how interfaces work, how they are defined and implemented, and how they enable advanced concepts like polymorphism, composition, testing, and modular architecture in Go.

Structure

This chapter covers the following topics:

- Interface
- Defining and implementing interfaces in Go
- Embedding interfaces in Go
- Interface satisfaction
- Type assertions and type switches in Go
- Empty interface and dynamic types in Go
- Best practices for using interfaces in Go

Objectives

By the end of this chapter, readers will have a thorough understanding of how interfaces enable abstraction, polymorphism, and reusability in Go programming. You will learn how to define and implement interfaces, how to use them effectively for structuring flexible code, and how to leverage them for modular design. This chapter will also help you appreciate the role of interfaces in the Go standard library and how they contribute to idiomatic Go programming. Furthermore, readers will become comfortable with advanced patterns such as interface embedding, type assertions, and the use of the empty interface (**`interface{}`**), equipping them to write scalable and maintainable Go applications.

Interface

An interface in Go is defined as an abstract type that specifies a set of methods. Any type that implements these methods is said to satisfy the interface. Interfaces define behavior, not data, allowing different types to be used interchangeably as long as they implement the required methods. Interfaces are a cornerstone of polymorphism in Go, enabling flexible and modular code design.

Look at the following example to understand:

```
type Shape interface {
    Area() float64
```

```
    Perimeter() float64
}
```

Here, `Shape` is an interface. Any type that provides implementations for the `Area` and `Perimeter` methods satisfies this interface.

Some more details are as follows:

- **Purpose of interfaces in Go:**
  - **Abstraction:** Interfaces define behavior without tying the code to specific implementations.
  - **Polymorphism:** Multiple types can satisfy the same interface, enabling them to be used interchangeably.
  - **Code reusability:** Functions and methods can operate on any type that satisfies an interface, reducing duplication.
  - **Flexibility:** Interfaces decouple the implementation from its usage, making code more flexible and testable.
- **Common use cases for interfaces:**
  - **Function parameters:** Functions can accept parameters of any type that satisfy a specific interface.
    - **Example:**

```
func PrintShapeDetails(s Shape) {
    fmt.Println("Area:", s.Area())
    fmt.Println("Perimeter:", s.Perimeter())
}

type Rectangle struct {
    Width, Height float64
}

func (r Rectangle) Area() float64 {
    return r.Width * r.Height
}

func (r Rectangle) Perimeter() float64 {
    return 2 * (r.Width + r.Height)
}

func main() {
    rect := Rectangle{Width: 10, Height: 5}
    PrintShapeDetails(rect)
}
```

  - **Returning an interface:** Functions can return an interface to hide the actual implementation details.
    - **Example:**

```
func NewRectangle(width, height float64) Shape {
    return Rectangle{Width: width, Height: height}
}
```

```go
func main() {
    shape := NewRectangle(10, 5)
    fmt.Println("Area:", shape.Area()) // Output: Area: 50
}
```

- **Mocking for testing:** Interfaces enable the creation of mock implementations for testing purposes.
  - **Example:**

```go
type Logger interface {
    Log(message string)
}

type MockLogger struct {
    Messages []string
}

func (m *MockLogger) Log(message string) {
    m.Messages = append(m.Messages, message)
}

func main() {
    logger := &MockLogger{}
    logger.Log("Test message")
    fmt.Println(logger.Messages) // Output: [Test message]
}
```

Understanding interfaces in Go

The interface types in Go are as follows:

- **Concrete type behind the Interface:** Interface is implemented as a pair consisting of:
  - The actual value stored in the interface.
  - The type of that value.

  This design allows an interface to represent any value of any type, as long as that type satisfies the methods defined by the interface. The value and its type are dynamically determined at runtime, enabling Go's interfaces to achieve polymorphism.

  When a value is assigned to an interface, Go internally records:
    - The concrete type of the value.
    - The actual value itself.

  When the interface is used, the stored type and value determine how the method calls, or operations, are executed.

  Example:

```go
type Greeter interface {
    Greet()
}
```

```go
type Person struct {
    Name string
}

func (p Person) Greet() {
    fmt.Println("Hello,", p.Name)
}

func main() {
    var g Greeter = Person{Name: "Venkatesh"}
    fmt.Printf("Type: %T\n", g) // Output: Type: main.Person
}
```

- **Interface variables:** An interface variable can hold any value of a type that satisfies the interface.

  Example:

```go
var s Shape
s = Rectangle{Width: 10, Height: 5} // s now holds a Rectangle
fmt.Println(s.Area())               // Output: 50
```

- **Interfaces and polymorphism:**
  - Polymorphism is the ability to use different types through a common interface.
  - Interfaces enable polymorphism by allowing different types to be treated uniformly based on shared behavior.

    Example: Polymorphism with interfaces

```go
type Shape interface {
    Area() float64
}

type Circle struct {
    Radius float64
}

func (c Circle) Area() float64 {
    return 3.14 * c.Radius * c.Radius
}

type Rectangle struct {
    Width, Height float64
}

func (r Rectangle) Area() float64 {
    return r.Width * r.Height
}

func PrintArea(s Shape) {
    fmt.Println("Area:", s.Area())
```

```go
}

func main() {
    c := Circle{Radius: 5}
    r := Rectangle{Width: 10, Height: 5}

    PrintArea(c) // Output: Area: 78.5
    PrintArea(r) // Output: Area: 50
}
```

- **Interfaces in the standard library:** Many Go standard library packages make extensive use of interfaces, enabling flexible and reusable code.

  Examples from the standard library:

  - **io.Reader and io.Writer**: Used for reading and writing streams of data.

    Example:

    ```go
    var reader io.Reader = strings.NewReader("Hello, World!")
    data := make([]byte, 5)
    reader.Read(data)
    fmt.Println(string(data)) // Output: Hello
    ```

    The **`strings.NewReader`** function in Go creates a **`Reader`** that allows you to read from a string as if it were a file or a stream.

- **fmt.Stringer:** Allows custom types to define their string representation.

  Example:

  ```go
  type Person struct {
      Name string
  }

  func (p Person) String() string {
      return fmt.Sprintf("Person(Name: %s)", p.Name)
  }

  func main() {
      p := Person{Name: "Venkatesh"}
      fmt.Println(p) // Output: Person(Name: Venkatesh)
  }
  ```

Key characteristics

The key characteristics of Go interfaces are presented in the following table:

Feature	Explanation
Implicit implementation	A type satisfies an interface simply by implementing its methods.
Behavioral abstraction	Interfaces focus on the methods (behavior) a type must implement, not its data structure.
Dynamic typing in interfaces	An interface can hold values of any type that satisfy it, enabling dynamic behavior.

Feature	Explanation
Single responsibility	Interfaces are often designed narrowly to represent a single behavior or responsibility.
Composition	Interfaces can be composed of other interfaces to build more complex abstractions.

Table 7.1: Characteristics of Go interfaces

The advantages of interfaces are as follows:

- **Modularity:** Interfaces promote modular design by decoupling implementations from their usage.
- **Code reusability:** Functions and methods can be written to work with interfaces, making them reusable for any type that satisfies the interface.
- **Flexibility:** Interfaces allow types with different implementations to be treated uniformly.
- **Improved testing:** Interfaces make it easier to mock dependencies for unit testing.

Defining and implementing interfaces in Go

As we know, the interfaces in Go provide a way to specify the behavior of an object. They are a cornerstone of Go's type system and are particularly useful for achieving polymorphism, where different types can be used interchangeably if they implement the same interface.

The details are as follows:

- **Defining interfaces:**
  - **Syntax:** An interface is defined using the **`type`** keyword followed by the interface name and the **`interface`** keyword.

    ```
    type InterfaceName interface {
        MethodName(parameters) returnType
    }AZ
    ```

    Example:

    ```
    type Shape interface {
        Area() float64
        Perimeter() float64
    }
    ```

  Here, **`Shape`** is an interface that requires two methods: **`Area`** and **`Perimeter`**.

- **Implementing interfaces:**
  - **Implicit implementation:** A type satisfies an interface if it implements all the methods specified in the interface. There is no explicit declaration of implementation.

    Example: Implementing an interface:

    ```
    type Rectangle struct {
        Width, Height float64
    }

    // Implementing the Area method
    func (r Rectangle) Area() float64 {
        return r.Width * r.Height
    }
    ```

```go
// Implementing the Perimeter method
func (r Rectangle) Perimeter() float64 {
    return 2 * (r.Width + r.Height)
}

func main() {
    var s Shape // Declare a variable of type Shape
    s = Rectangle{Width: 10, Height: 5} // Rectangle satisfies Shape
    fmt.Println("Area:", s.Area())       // Output: Area: 50
    fmt.Println("Perimeter:", s.Perimeter()) // Output: Perimeter: 30
}
```

The key characteristics of defining and implementing interfaces are as follows:

- **Method signatures:** Interfaces only include method signatures, not their implementations.

  Example:

  ```go
  type Printer interface {
      Print(message string)
  }
  ```

  Any type with a **Print(string)** method satisfies the **Printer** interface.

- **Implicit satisfaction:** Go automatically determines whether a type satisfies an interface. There is no need for **implements** or **extends** keywords.

  Example:

  ```go
  type Logger interface {
      Log(message string)
  }

  type ConsoleLogger struct{}

  func (c ConsoleLogger) Log(message string) {
      fmt.Println("Log:", message)
  }

  func main() {
      var l Logger = ConsoleLogger{} // Implicit implementation
      l.Log("Hello, World!")         // Output: Log: Hello, World!
  }
  ```

- **Narrow interfaces:** Go encourages defining narrow interfaces with a small number of methods to focus on specific behaviors.

  Example:

  ```go
  type Reader interface {
      Read(p []byte) (n int, err error)
  }
  ```

```
type Writer interface {
    Write(p []byte) (n int, err error)
}
```

Instead of combining **Read** and **Write** into a single interface, Go provides separate **Reader** and **Writer** interfaces.

- **Zero value of an interface:** The zero value of an interface is **nil**, meaning it does not hold any type or value.

  Example:

```
var s Shape
fmt.Println(s == nil) // Output: true
```

- **Interfaces are satisfied by methods:** A type satisfies an interface if it implements all the methods specified in the interface. Partial implementations are not allowed.
- **Multiple implementations for the same interface**: This clarifies that multiple distinct types (like **Circle** and **Square**) can implement the same interface (**Shape**), each providing their own method logic.

  Example:

```
type Shape interface {
    Area() float64
}

type Circle struct {
    Radius float64
}

func (c Circle) Area() float64 {
    return 3.14 * c.Radius * c.Radius
}

type Square struct {
    Side float64
}

func (s Square) Area() float64 {
    return s.Side * s.Side
}

func main() {
    var shapes []Shape
    shapes = append(shapes, Circle{Radius: 5}, Square{Side: 4})

    for _, shape := range shapes {
        fmt.Println("Area:", shape.Area())
    }
    // Output:
    // Area: 78.5
    // Area: 16
```

```
}
```

The **Shape** interface is implemented by both **Circle** and **Square**.

- **Interfaces with no methods:** An interface with no methods is called an empty interface (**interface{}**). This allows any type to satisfy it, effectively making it a type-agnostic container.

  Example:

```
func PrintAnything(i interface{}) {
    fmt.Println(i)
}

func main() {
    PrintAnything(42)
    PrintAnything("Hello")
    PrintAnything([]int{1, 2, 3})
}
// Output:
// 42
// Hello
// [1 2 3]
```

- **Combining interfaces with struct composition:**

  Example:

```
type Printer interface {
    Print()
}

type Scanner interface {
    Scan()
}

type MultiFunctionDevice interface {
    Printer
    Scanner
}

type OfficeMachine struct{}

func (o OfficeMachine) Print() {
    fmt.Println("Printing...")
}

func (o OfficeMachine) Scan() {
    fmt.Println("Scanning...")
}

func main() {
```

```
        var device MultiFunctionDevice = OfficeMachine{}
        device.Print() // Output: Printing...
        device.Scan()  // Output: Scanning...
    }
}
```

Embedding interfaces in Go

The details of embedding interfaces in Go are covered in the following subsections.

Interface embedding

Interface embedding in Go allows one interface to include the methods of another interface by embedding it within its definition. This promotes composition over inheritance, enabling the creation of complex interfaces by combining smaller, simpler ones.

The details are as follows:

- **Purpose:**
  - Enables modular design by combining reusable, smaller interfaces.
  - Simplifies code by inheriting method sets from embedded interfaces.
  - Supports polymorphism by treating a type as satisfying multiple behaviors.

The key characteristics of interface embedding are as follows:

- **Composition over inheritance:**
  - Unlike traditional inheritance in object-oriented languages, Go uses composition to combine behaviors from multiple interfaces.
  - Embedded interfaces contribute their methods to the embedding interface.
- **Flat method set:** When an interface embeds another interface, it inherits all methods of the embedded interface as if they were defined in the outer interface.
- **Implicit implementation:**
  - In Go, implicit implementation means that a type automatically satisfies an interface if it implements all the methods required by that interface, without explicitly declaring it. This principle extends to embedded interfaces as well.
  - When an interface embeds another interface, it inherits the methods of the embedded interface. Any type that implements the methods of the embedded interface (and any additional methods defined in the embedding interface) automatically satisfies the embedding interface.
- **Defining embedded interfaces:**
  - **Syntax**:
    - Embed an interface by specifying its name within another interface's definition.
    - Embedding interface only has embedded interfaces and none of its own methods:

```
type InterfaceA interface {
    MethodA()
}

type InterfaceB interface {
    InterfaceA // Embedding InterfaceA
```

```
        MethodB()
    }
```

- **Examples of interface embedding:**
  - **Basic interface embedding**:

    ```
    type Reader interface {
        Read(p []byte) (n int, err error)
    }

    type Writer interface {
        Write(p []byte) (n int, err error)
    }

    type ReadWriter interface {
        Reader // Embedding Reader
        Writer // Embedding Writer
    }
    ```

  - **Explanation:**
    - **ReadWriter** inherits the **Read** method from **Reader** and the **Write** method from **Writer**.
    - Any type that implements both **Read** and **Write** automatically satisfies **ReadWriter**.
- **Implementing the embedded interface:**

  ```
  type MyFile struct{}

  func (f MyFile) Read(p []byte) (n int, err error) {
      fmt.Println("Reading...")
      return 0, nil
  }

  func (f MyFile) Write(p []byte) (n int, err error) {
      fmt.Println("Writing...")
      return len(p), nil
  }

  func main() {
      var rw ReadWriter = MyFile{}
      rw.Read(nil)  // Output: Reading...
      rw.Write(nil) // Output: Writing...
  }
  ```

- **Interface embedding and struct composition:**
  - Interface embedding complements struct composition, allowing structs to embed interfaces for modular behavior.

    Example: Struct embedding with interface embedding

    ```
    type Printer interface {
        Print()
    ```

```
}

type Scanner interface {
    Scan()
}

type MultiFunctionDevice interface {
    Printer
    Scanner
}

type OfficeMachine struct{}

func (o OfficeMachine) Print() {
    fmt.Println("Printing...")
}

func (o OfficeMachine) Scan() {
    fmt.Println("Scanning...")
}

func main() {
    var mfd MultiFunctionDevice = OfficeMachine{}
    mfd.Print() // Output: Printing...
    mfd.Scan()  // Output: Scanning...
}
```

Some key differences between interface embedding and struct embedding are presented in the following table:

Feature	Interface embedding	Struct embedding
Purpose	Combines behaviors (methods) of multiple interfaces.	Combines data fields and behaviors (methods) of structs.
Composition	Achieves modularity by method composition.	Achieves modularity by combining data and behavior.
Polymorphism	Allows polymorphism across types that satisfy the interface.	Does not inherently provide polymorphism.
Inheritance-like	Inherits only methods, not fields.	Can inherit both fields and methods of an embedded struct.

Table 7.2: Interface embedding vs. struct embedding

- **Nested interface embedding:** Interfaces can embed other interfaces that themselves embed additional interfaces, creating a hierarchy of method sets.

  Example: Nested embedding:

```
type A interface {
    MethodA()
}
```

```
type B interface {
    A
    MethodB()
}

type C interface {
    B
    MethodC()
}

type MyType struct{}

func (m MyType) MethodA() {
    fmt.Println("MethodA")
}

func (m MyType) MethodB() {
    fmt.Println("MethodB")
}

func (m MyType) MethodC() {
    fmt.Println("MethodC")
}

func main() {
    var c C = MyType{}
    c.MethodA() // Output: MethodA
    c.MethodB() // Output: MethodB
    c.MethodC() // Output: MethodC
}
```

Advantages of interface embedding are as follows:

- **Modular design:** Encourages designing interfaces that focus on specific behaviors and combine them when needed.
- **Reusability:** Embedded interfaces can be reused across different interfaces without redefining methods.
- **Flexibility:** A type implementing embedded interface methods automatically satisfies all embedding interfaces.
- **Readability:** Combines smaller interfaces into a logical grouping, making the code easier to understand.

The limitations of interface embedding are as follows:

- **Potential for method conflicts:** If two embedded interfaces define methods with the same name and signature, it can lead to conflicts.
- **Excessive embedding:** Embedding too many interfaces can make the resulting interface unwieldy and harder to implement.

Interface satisfaction

Interface satisfaction refers to how a type fulfills the requirements of an interface by implementing its methods. Go uses implicit interface satisfaction, meaning a type automatically satisfies an interface if it implements all the required methods. This contrasts with languages like Java or C#, which use explicit declaration (e.g., implements or extends).

Implicit interface satisfaction in Go

The key characteristics are as follows:

- **No explicit declaration:** Types do not need to explicitly state that they implement an interface. The Go compiler automatically determines if a type satisfies an interface.
- **Focus on behavior:** Interface satisfaction is purely behavioral. A type is defined by what it does, not by what it claims to implement.
- **Loose coupling:** Types and interfaces remain loosely coupled, leading to more flexible and reusable code.

Example: Implicit satisfaction:

```
type Printer interface {
    Print()
}

type Document struct {
    Content string
}

// Document implements the Print method, satisfying Printer
func (d Document) Print() {
    fmt.Println(d.Content)
}

func main() {
    var p Printer
    doc := Document{Content: "Hello, World!"}
    p = doc // Implicit satisfaction
    p.Print() // Output: Hello, World!
}
```

Explanation: The **`Document`** type satisfies the **`Printer`** interface because it implements the **`Print`** method. No explicit declaration is needed.

Explicit interface satisfaction in other languages

In languages like Java or C#, a type must explicitly declare that it implements an interface using keywords like implements or extends.

Example in Java:

```
interface Printer {
    void print();
}
```

```
class Document implements Printer {
    @Override
    public void print() {
        System.out.println("Hello, World!");
    }
}
```

The comparison with Go is presented in the following table:

Feature	Implicit (Go)	Explicit (Java/C#)
Declaration	Automatic; no keywords required.	Requires explicit declaration (e.g., implements).
Focus	Behavioral: determined by method implementation.	Structural: tied to explicit declaration.
Code coupling	Loosely coupled; interfaces and types are independent.	More tightly coupled; interfaces dictate structure.
Ease of use	Simpler to implement and refactor.	Requires more boilerplate and adherence to syntax.

Table 7.3: *Go interfaces vs. other language interfaces*

The benefits of implicit satisfaction are as follows:

- **Reduced boilerplate code:** Types do not need to declare interfaces explicitly, reducing redundancy.

  Example:

  ```
  type Logger interface {
      Log(message string)
  }

  type ConsoleLogger struct{}

  func (c ConsoleLogger) Log(message string) {
      fmt.Println("Log:", message)
  }
  // No need for 'implements Logger'
  ```

- **Improved flexibility:** Types can satisfy multiple interfaces without explicit declarations, making it easier to adapt existing types to new interfaces.
- **Decoupling**: Interfaces remain independent of type definitions, promoting modular design.
- **Encourages focus on behavior**: Developers are encouraged to design interfaces that define behaviors rather than enforce structural constraints.

The potential challenges with implicit satisfaction are as follows:

- **Accidental implementation:** A type may unintentionally satisfy an interface if it implements the required methods, leading to logical errors.

  Example:

  ```
  type Logger interface {
      Log(message string)
  ```

```
}

type Counter struct {
    Value int
}

// Counter unintentionally satisfies Logger due to the Log method
func (c Counter) Log(message string) {
    fmt.Println("Counter:", c.Value, "Message:", message)
}
```

- **Discoverability**:
  - It can be harder to determine which types satisfy an interface, as there is no explicit declaration.
  - The solution is to use tools like Go documentation (**godoc**) or linters to analyze interface implementations.
- **Error messages:** Go compiler errors may be less descriptive when a type partially satisfies an interface.

  Example:

```
type Printer interface {
    Print()
    Scan()
}

type SimplePrinter struct{}

func (s SimplePrinter) Print() {
    fmt.Println("Printing...")
}

// Error: SimplePrinter does not satisfy Printer (missing Scan method)
```

Interface satisfaction across multiple Interfaces

A single type in Go can satisfy multiple interfaces by implementing all the required methods from each. This allows the type to be used in different contexts based on the behavior it supports. Go's implicit interface system makes this seamless without needing explicit declarations.

Let us see them in detail:

- **Single type, multiple interfaces:** A type can satisfy multiple interfaces by implementing their respective methods.

```
type Reader interface {
    Read(p []byte) (n int, err error)
}

type Writer interface {
    Write(p []byte) (n int, err error)
}
```

```
type File struct{}

func (f File) Read(p []byte) (n int, err error) {
    return 0, nil
}

func (f File) Write(p []byte) (n int, err error) {
    return len(p), nil
}

func main() {
    var r Reader = File{}
    var w Writer = File{}

    fmt.Println(r.Read(nil))  // Output: 0 <nil>
    fmt.Println(w.Write(nil)) // Output: 0 <nil>
}
```

- **Combining interfaces:** Interfaces can embed other interfaces, and types satisfying the embedded interfaces automatically satisfy the combined interface.

```
type ReadWriter interface {
    Reader
    Writer
}

func Process(rw ReadWriter) {
    rw.Read(nil)
    rw.Write(nil)
}
```

Type assertions and type switches in Go

Go's interfaces allow for polymorphism by enabling types to be treated abstractly. However, there are cases when you need to work with the concrete type underlying an interface value.

Type assertions and type switches are tools provided by Go to extract and work with the concrete type stored in an interface variable. Their details are as follows:

- **Type assertions:**
    - **Definition:** A type assertion is used to explicitly retrieve the underlying value of an interface as a specific concrete type.
    - **It allows you to:**
        - Confirm that an interface value holds a specific type.
        - Retrieve the underlying value if the assertion is valid.
    - **Syntax:**

      ```
      value, ok := interfaceVar.(ConcreteType)
      ```

        - **interfaceVar:** The variable of interface type.

- **ConcreteType:** The type you expect the interface to hold.
- **ok:** A Boolean indicating whether the assertion was successful.

Example: Simple type assertion:

```
func main() {
    var i interface{} = "Hello, Go!"

    // Attempting a type assertion
    str, ok := i.(string)
    if ok {
        fmt.Println("String value:", str) // Output: String value: Hello, Go!
    } else {
        fmt.Println("Type assertion failed")
    }

    // Invalid assertion
    num, ok := i.(int)
    if !ok {
        fmt.Println("Type assertion failed for int") // Output: Type
assertion failed for int
    }
}
```

Example: Type assertion without `ok`

When you omit the `ok` value and the assertion fails, Go panics.

```
func main() {
    var i interface{} = 42

    // Correct assertion
    fmt.Println(i.(int)) // Output: 42

    // Incorrect assertion (causes a panic)
    fmt.Println(i.(string)) // Panic: interface conversion:
interface {} is int, not string
}
```

- **Type switches:**
  - **Definition:**
    - A type switch is a construct that tests the dynamic type of an interface value and performs actions based on the type.
    - It eliminates the need for multiple `if` statements with type assertions.
  - **Syntax:**

```
switch value := interfaceVar.(type) {
case ConcreteType1:
    // Handle ConcreteType1
case ConcreteType2:
```

```
    // Handle ConcreteType2
default:
    // Handle unknown types
}
```

The **special** keyword type is used to retrieve the dynamic type of the interface value.

Example: Simple type switch:

```
func main() {
    var i interface{} = 3.14

    switch v := i.(type) {
    case int:
        fmt.Println("Integer:", v)
    case float64:
        fmt.Println("Float:", v) // Output: Float: 3.14
    case string:
        fmt.Println("String:", v)
    default:
        fmt.Println("Unknown type")
    }
}
```

Example: Type switch with multiple cases:

```
func main() {
    var i interface{} = "GoLang"

    switch v := i.(type) {
    case int, float64:
        fmt.Println("Numeric type:", v)
    case string:
        fmt.Println("String type:", v) // Output: String type: GoLang
    default:
        fmt.Println("Unhandled type")
    }
}
```

The use cases for type switches are as follows:

- **Handling multiple types:** Process values of different types stored in an interface.
- **Error handling:** Determine the type of error returned by a function and respond accordingly.
- **Dynamic behavior:** Implement polymorphic behavior without knowing the exact type at compile time.

The key differences between type assertions and type switches are as follows:

Feature	Type assertions	Type switches
Purpose	Extract and work with a specific type from an interface.	Handle multiple possible types in a single construct.

Feature	Type assertions	Type switches
Complexity	Simpler but requires multiple if statements for many types.	Concise for handling multiple types.
Error handling	Can use ok to check for assertion failure.	Automatically includes a default case for unknown types.
Readability	Can become verbose for multiple types.	More readable for complex type checking.

Table 7.4: *Difference between type assertions and type switches*

A couple of practical examples are as follows:

- **Dynamic type logging**:

```
func LogValue(v interface{}) {
    switch v := v.(type) {
    case int:
        fmt.Println("Integer:", v)
    case float64:
        fmt.Println("Float:", v)
    case string:
        fmt.Println("String:", v)
    default:
        fmt.Println("Unknown type")
    }
}
```

- **Custom error handling**:

```
type NotFoundError struct {
    Resource string
}

func (e NotFoundError) Error() string {
    return fmt.Sprintf("Resource %s not found", e.Resource)
}

func HandleError(err error) {
    switch e := err.(type) {
    case NotFoundError:
        fmt.Println("Not Found:", e.Resource)
    default:
        fmt.Println("General error:", err)
    }
}
```

Empty interface and dynamic types in Go

Empty interface (`interface{}`) is a special interface in Go that does not specify any methods. It can hold a value of any type, making it the most general type in Go.

The details are as follows:

- **Purpose**:
  - To handle values of unknown or dynamic types.
  - To enable flexibility in scenarios like data serialization, logging, or generic programming.
- **Syntax:**

```
var x interface{}
```

The key characteristics of the empty interface are as follows:

- **Dynamic typing:** The empty interface can store values of any type, including built-in types (**`int`**, **`string`**), structs, slices, maps, and custom types.
- **No method constraints:** Since **`interface{}`** has no methods, any type automatically satisfies it.
- **Type-safe:** While **`interface{}`** is flexible, Go ensures type safety during type assertions or type switches when extracting values.

The examples of using **`interface{}`** are as follows:

- **Holding values of any type:**

```
func main() {
    var data interface{}

    data = 42
    fmt.Println(data) // Output: 42

    data = "Hello, Go!"
    fmt.Println(data) // Output: Hello, Go!

    data = []int{1, 2, 3}
    fmt.Println(data) // Output: [1 2 3]
}
```

- **Function parameters and return values:**
  - **Dynamic parameters:** Functions can accept **`interface{}`** as a parameter to handle dynamic input types.

```
func PrintValue(value interface{}) {
    fmt.Println("Value:", value)
}

func main() {
    PrintValue(42)          // Output: Value: 42
    PrintValue("Dynamic!") // Output: Value: Dynamic!
    PrintValue([]int{1, 2, 3}) // Output: Value: [1 2 3]
}
```

  - **Dynamic return values:** Functions can return **`interface{}`** when the return type is not fixed.

```
func DynamicResult() interface{} {
    return "This could be anything!"
}
```

```
func main() {
    result := DynamicResult()
    fmt.Println(result) // Output: This could be anything!
}
```

- **Dynamic types in Go:**
  - **Definition:** Dynamic types refer to values that can take on various types during runtime and are often handled using **interface{}**.
  - **Working with dynamic types:**
    - **Type assertions:** Extract specific types from an **interface{}**.

```
var i interface{} = "Hello"

str, ok := i.(string)
if ok {
    fmt.Println("String:", str)
}
```

    - **Type switches:** Handle multiple dynamic types in a structured way.

```
func Process(value interface{}) {
    switch v := value.(type) {
    case int:
        fmt.Println("Integer:", v)
    case string:
        fmt.Println("String:", v)
    case []int:
        fmt.Println("Slice of int:", v)
    default:
        fmt.Println("Unknown type")
    }
}

func main() {
    Process(42)
    Process("Dynamic")
    Process([]int{1, 2, 3})
}
```

The challenges and pitfalls of using **interface{}** are as follows:

- **Type safety:** Using **interface{}** sacrifices compile-time type checking, increasing the risk of runtime errors.

  Example:

```
var i interface{} = 42
fmt.Println(i.(string)) // Panic: interface conversion: interface {} is int, not string
```

- **Readability and maintenance:** Excessive use of **interface{}** can make code harder to understand and maintain.

- **Performance overhead:** Storing and extracting values from `interface{}` incurs runtime type checks, which can impact performance in critical paths.

The use cases in the Go standard library are as follows:

- **fmt.Println and fmt.Sprintf:** These functions accept `interface{}` to handle arguments of any type.

  ```
  fmt.Println(42, "Dynamic", []int{1, 2, 3})
  ```

- **json.Unmarshal:** Decodes JSON into a map or slice using `interface{}` for dynamic type handling.
- **reflect package:** Works with dynamic types at runtime using `interface{}`.

Best practices for using interfaces in Go

Interfaces in Go are a powerful tool for achieving abstraction, polymorphism, and modular design. To maximize their utility while maintaining clean and efficient code, it is essential to follow these best practices:

- **Keep interfaces small and focused:** Define interfaces with a narrow scope, representing a single behavior or responsibility. Smaller interfaces are easier to implement, mock, and test.

  Example:

  ```
  type Reader interface {
      Read(p []byte) (n int, err error)
  }

  type Writer interface {
      Write(p []byte) (n int, err error)
  }
  ```

  Avoid combining multiple unrelated methods into a single interface. Instead, compose interfaces when needed.

- **Use descriptive names:** Interfaces should clearly describe the behavior they represent. Avoid vague names like Doer or Handler. For example, use `Notifier` for an interface with a `Notify` method.
- **Design for implicit satisfaction:** Let types naturally satisfy interfaces without requiring explicit modifications. This aligns with Go's implicit implementation philosophy.

  Example:

  ```
  type Printer interface {
      Print()
  }

  type Document struct {
      Content string
  }

  func (d Document) Print() {
      fmt.Println(d.Content)
  }
  ```

- **Use interfaces for dependencies:** Define dependencies in terms of interfaces rather than concrete types. This decouples your code and improves flexibility.

Example:

```
type Logger interface {
    Log(message string)
}

func ProcessData(logger Logger) {
    logger.Log("Processing started")
}
```

- **Avoid overusing interface{}:** The empty interface (`interface{}`) can hold any type, but it sacrifices type safety and readability. Use specific interfaces or generics (if applicable) instead.

  Example:

```
func Add(a, b interface{}) interface{} {
    return a.(int) + b.(int)
}
```

- **Combine interfaces with care:** Use interface embedding to build composite interfaces, combining smaller ones as needed. Ensure embedded interfaces complement each other logically.

  Example:

```
type ReadWriter interface {
    Reader
    Writer
}
```

- **Always handle unknown types:** When working with interfaces dynamically, use type switches or ok checks to handle unexpected types gracefully.

  Example:

```
func Process(value interface{}) {
    switch v := value.(type) {
    case int:
        fmt.Println("Integer:", v)
    case string:
        fmt.Println("String:", v)
    default:
        fmt.Println("Unknown type")
    }
}
```

- **Document interface behavior:** Clearly document what an interface represents and the purpose of its methods. This ensures readability and reduces confusion.
- **Minimize redundancy:** Avoid creating interfaces that duplicate existing functionality in the standard library or your codebase. Reuse existing interfaces wherever possible.
- **Test with mock implementations:** Leverage interfaces to create mock implementations for unit tests. This improves test coverage and isolates functionality.

Conclusion

Interfaces in Go are more than just a way to group method signatures. They are a core enabler of Go's philosophy of simple, flexible, and clean code. Through this chapter, we learned how to define interfaces, implement them implicitly, and use them to unlock powerful design patterns such as polymorphism, loose coupling, and testable architecture. We have also explored their use in the standard library, best practices for design, and the differences between Go's interface model and that of other languages like Java or C#.

In the next chapter, we will explore packages in Go and how to organize your code into modular, reusable components. You will learn about importing, exporting, naming conventions, and building a proper package structure to support large-scale Go development.

Questions

1. What is meant by implicit interface satisfaction in Go, and how does it differ from explicit interface implementation in other languages?
2. Explain the use and significance of the empty interface (interface{}) in Go. What are its advantages and potential drawbacks?
3. Describe how interface embedding works in Go. How does it support modular and reusable interface design?
4. Compare interface embedding and struct embedding in Go. Highlight at least two key differences between them.
5. What are the best practices to follow while designing interfaces in Go? Give examples to support your answer.
6. How does Go enable polymorphism using interfaces? Describe with reference to multiple types implementing the same interface.
7. What are the benefits of defining narrow interfaces in Go? Why is this considered an idiomatic practice?
8. How can interfaces be leveraged in Go to improve unit testing and mock implementations?
9. Explain the purpose and use cases of type assertions and type switches in Go. How do they enhance working with interface values?
10. What are some of the common mistakes or pitfalls developers should avoid while using interfaces in Go? How can these be mitigated?

CHAPTER 8
Packages and Modules

Introduction

In Go, packages are fundamental units for organizing and reusing code. A package is a collection of related Go source files that are compiled together, promoting modular design and encapsulation. By grouping related functions and types, packages help developers manage complexity and improve code maintainability.

Go distinguishes between executable packages (with main) and library packages meant for reuse. The standard library offers a rich set of packages for tasks like I/O, HTTP handling, and JSON parsing. Additionally, Go's module system introduced in version 1.11 adds support for versioning and dependency management.

This chapter explores how to create, use, and manage packages and modules effectively, helping you write clean, organized, and scalable Go applications.

Structure

In this chapter, we will cover the following topics:

- Creating and using packages in Go
- Organizing code with modules in Go
- Importing external libraries
- Best practices for importing external libraries

Objectives

By the end of this chapter, you will be able to understand and apply the principles of package management in Go. You will learn how to structure your code using packages and modules, create reusable functions, manage internal and external dependencies, and follow best practices for package naming and design. You will also be able to distinguish between exported and unexported identifiers, utilize Go's module system for dependency management, and avoid common pitfalls such as cyclic imports and improper initialization. These skills are fundamental for writing clean, efficient, and scalable Go applications suitable for both individual and collaborative development environments.

Creating and using packages in Go

In Go, a package is a collection of related Go source files that are compiled together. Packages promote modularity and code reuse, enabling developers to organize their codebase effectively. The package keyword at the beginning of a Go source file defines the package it belongs to.

Structure of a package

In Go, a package provides a way to organize and encapsulate related source code files. All files within the same directory that declare the same package name are considered part of the same package. This structure allows developers to build modular applications where functionality is grouped logically and can be easily reused.

At the core of every Go package is the package declaration, which appears at the top of each **.go** file. This declaration defines the package to which the file belongs.

Package declaration

The details are as follows:

- Every Go source file starts with a package declaration, specifying the package name.
- **Syntax**:

```
package packageName
```

The package types are as follows:

- **Executable packages**: Packages with the name **main** that produce an executable binary.

  Example:

```
package main

import "fmt"

func main() {
    fmt.Println("Hello, World!")
}
```

- **Library packages**: All other packages that are designed to be imported and reused.

  Example:

```
package utils

func Add(a, b int) int {
    return a + b
}
```

Creating a package

The steps are as follows:

1. **Create a directory**: Each package is represented by a directory. The directory name is typically the package name.

   Example:

```
project/
I--main.go
I--mathutils/
    I--operations.go
```

2. **Add Go files**:
   a. Place **.go** files in the package directory.
   b. Ensure all files in the same directory have the same package name.
3. **Define functions**: Functions, variables, and constants starting with an uppercase letter are exported and accessible outside the package. Lowercase identifiers are unexported and private to the package.

   Example: Creating a math package:

   File: **mathutils/operations.go**

```
package mathutils
```

```
// Add is an exported function
func Add(a, b int) int {
    return a + b
}

// subtract is an unexported function
func subtract(a, b int) int {
    return a - b
}
```

Using a package

The details are as follows:

- **Importing a package**: Use the import statement to include a package in your code.
- **Syntax**:

  ```
  import "path/to/package"
  ```

  Example: Using the **mathutils** package

  File: **main.go**

  ```
  package main

  import (
      "fmt"
      "project/mathutils"
  )

  func main() {
      sum := mathutils.Add(3, 5)
      fmt.Println("Sum:", sum) // Output: Sum: 8
  ```

Special cases

Let us look at some of the special cases:

- **Import with an Alias**: Assign an alias to a package to simplify its usage.

  Example:

  ```
  import mu "project/mathutils"
  func main() {
      fmt.Println(mu.Add(3, 5))
  }
  ```

- **Blank import (_)**: Used to execute the **init** function of a package without directly referencing it.

  Example:

  ```
  import _ "project/config"
  ```

The key functions in packages are as follows:

1. **Exported functions**: Functions starting with an uppercase letter can be accessed from other packages.

Example:

```
package greet

func Hello() string {
    return "Hello, World!"
}
```

2. **Unexported functions**: Functions starting with a lowercase letter are private to the package.

   Example:

```
package greet

func hello() string {
return "hello"
}
```

3. **The init function**: The **init** function is a special function that runs automatically when the package is imported.

   Example:

```
package config

import "fmt"

func init() {
    fmt.Println("Initializing configuration...")
}
```

4. **Standard library packages**:

   Go's standard library provides a rich set of packages for common tasks:

   a. **fmt**: Formatting and printing.
   b. **os**: Operating system functions.
   c. **io**: Input and output utilities.
   d. **net/http**: HTTP server and client.
   e. **encoding/json**: JSON encoding and decoding.

   Example: Using standard library packages

```
package main

import (
    "encoding/json"
    "fmt"
)

func main() {
    data := map[string]string{"Name": "Shubham", "City": "Bengaluru"}
    jsonData, _ := json.Marshal(data)
    fmt.Println(string(jsonData))
}
```

5. **Package initialization**:

   Packages are initialized in two ways:

   a. **Global variables**: Global variables are initialized first.

   b. **init function**: Executes before any other code in the package.

   Example: Package initialization

   File: **config/config.go**

```
package config

import "fmt"

var AppName string

func init() {
    AppName = "MyApp"
    fmt.Println("App initialized:", AppName)
}
```

   File: **main.go**

```
package main

import (
    "fmt"
    "project/config"
)

func main() {
    fmt.Println("Using App:", config.AppName)
}
```

The common pitfalls when using packages are as follows:

- **Cyclic imports**:
  - Packages cannot import each other in a cycle.
  - **Solution**: Refactor common code into a shared package.
- **Unused imports**:
  - Go does not allow unused imports, which ensures cleaner code.

  Example of error:

```
import "fmt" // Error: "fmt" imported but not used
```

- **Improper exporting**: Forgetting to capitalize the first letter of exported identifiers leads to access issues.

Advantages of using packages are as follows:

- **Code reusability**: Packages enable you to write reusable functions and structures.
- **Modularity**: Code is better organized and easier to maintain.
- **Encapsulation**: Packages allow you to control access to functionality using exported and unexported identifiers.
- **Team collaboration**: Packages simplify working in teams by dividing work into separate modules.

Organizing code with modules in Go

A module is a collection of related Go packages, with a defined dependency management system. It serves as the primary unit of code organization and versioning in Go. The details are as follows:

- Modules allow developers to group packages logically, manage dependencies, and share code across projects efficiently.
- Introduced in Go 1.11, modules replaced the earlier GOPATH-based dependency management.

The key features of Go modules are as follows:

- **Versioning**: Modules include semantic versioning (e.g., v1.2.3) to manage changes and compatibility.
- **Dependency management**: Automatically downloads, updates, and tracks dependencies.
- **Reproducible builds**: The `go.sum` file ensures consistent builds by locking dependency versions.
- **Independence from GOPATH**: Modules allow code to be placed anywhere on the filesystem, not constrained by the GOPATH.

Structure of a Go module

The details are as follows:

- **Typical layout:**

```
project/
I-- go.mod
I--  go.sum
I--  main.go
I--  utils/
        I--  helpers.go
I-- mathutils/
        I-- operations.go
```

- **Files and directories**
    - **go.mod**:
        - The `go.mod` file is the core of a Go module.
        - **Purpose**:
            - Specifies the module's name.
            - Declares dependencies and their versions.
            - Tracks the Go language version used.

    Example of a `go.mod` file:

```
module github.com/user/myproject

go 1.20

require (
    github.com/pkg/errors v0.9.1
    golang.org/x/text v0.3.6
)
```

    - **go.sum**:
        - Ensures reproducible builds by storing checksums of dependency versions.

    - Contains cryptographic hashes to verify the integrity of dependencies.
    - Ensures reproducible builds by locking exact dependency versions.

  Example of a **go.sum** file:

```
github.com/pkg/errors v0.9.1 h1:W4qWtDbAzGFsVv7fr5ZMgHQNOEBaNqiQ9Ef2Gf3D9gw=
github.com/pkg/errors v0.9.1/go.mod h1:WIgbDmJ0VAlCm3Ju1+SOPBTPcyYZuqJMBWqpHGUpiMY=
```

- **Packages**: Each directory (e.g., **utils**, **mathutils**) represents a package.

Let us create a new module. The step-by-step guide is as follows:

1. **Initialize the module**:
   a. Use **go mod init** to create a **go.mod** file.
   b. **Command**:
   ```
   go mod init module_name
   ```
   Example:
   ```
   go mod init github.com/username/project
   ```
2. **Write your code**: Create the necessary directories and Go files.
3. **Add dependencies**:
   a. Run go get to add external libraries.
   b. **Command**:
   ```
   go get github.com/pkg/errors
   ```
4. **Run and build the code**: Use **go run** command to execute the module and **go build** command to compile the module.

   Example: Initializing a module
   ```
   mkdir myproject
   cd myproject
   go mod init github.com/user/myproject
   ```
   Generated go.mod:
   ```
   module github.com/user/myproject
   ```
5. **Using a module**:
   a. **Importing packages from the same module**: Packages within the module can be imported using the module name and package path.
   ```
   import "github.com/user/myproject/utils"
   ```
   b. **Running code**: Use **go run** or **go build** to execute or compile the **main** package.
   ```
   go run main.go
   ```
   c. **Adding and updating dependencies:** Add a dependency.
   ```
   go get example.com/library
   ```
   d. **Update a dependency to the latest version:**
   ```
   go get -u example.com/library
   ```
6. **Managing dependencies**:

   Key commands are as follows:

   a. **go mod tidy**: Cleans up unused dependencies and adds missing ones.

b. **go list -m all**: Lists all the modules in use.

c. **go mod vendor**: Creates a **`vendor/`** directory in your project, containing a copy of all the module dependencies used in your project. This allows your project to use these dependencies locally without needing to fetch them from external sources. It is useful for environments with restricted network access or to ensure build consistency. The **`vendor/`** directory can also be committed to version control for reproducible builds.

7. **Organizing code in a module**:

a. **Split functionality into packages**: Splitting functionality into packages helps organize your code by grouping related functionalities together. Each package should focus on a specific area, like **`mathutils`** for mathematical operations or **`stringutils`** for string manipulation. This improves code readability, maintainability, and reusability across projects. By logically separating code, you can avoid clutter and make each package easier to understand and test independently.

Example:

```
plaintext
Copy code
project/
I---main.go
I---mathutils/
I   I--- add.go
I   I---subtract.go
I   I---multiply.go
I--- stringutils/
    I--- concat.go
    I---split.go
```

b. **Use meaningful package names**:

i. Choose descriptive names that reflect the purpose of the package.

ii. **Good examples**: **`mathutils`**, **`stringutils`**

iii. **Bad examples**: **`pkg1`**, **`lib`**

c. Avoid deep nesting.

d. Keep the package hierarchy flat to avoid complexity.

8. **Publishing a module**:

The steps to publish are as follows:

a. **Push code to a public repository**: Use platforms like GitHub, GitLab, or Bitbucket.

b. **Tag a version**: Create a version tag using semantic versioning.

Command:

```
git tag v1.0.0
git push origin v1.0.0
```

c. **Use in other projects**: Import the module in other Go projects.

Example:

```
import "github.com/username/myproject"
```

The common pitfalls are as follows:

- **Forgetting to initialize the module**: Always run go mod init to create the **go.mod** file.
- **Neglecting to use go mod tidy**: Forgetting to clean up dependencies can bloat the project.
- **Not pinning dependency versions**: Avoid using go get without specifying a version to prevent unintentional upgrades.
- **Circular dependencies**: Ensure packages do not depend on each other cyclically.

The benefits of organizing code with modules are as follows:

- **Encapsulation**: Modules provide a clear boundary for code and dependencies.
- **Reusability**: Modules can be imported and reused across projects.
- **Version control**: Semantic versioning ensures compatibility and reproducible builds.
- **Decoupled development**: Teams can develop modules independently.

Importing external libraries in Go

External libraries in Go are reusable packages written by others and made available for public use. Importing and managing these libraries is a core feature of Go's module system. Go uses the module system to fetch, version, and integrate these libraries into your project.

The reasons to import external libraries are as follows:

- **Code reusability**: Avoid reinventing the wheel by leveraging existing libraries.
- **Enhanced functionality**: Add capabilities like logging, data parsing, or HTTP handling without writing everything from scratch.
- **Community support**: Use libraries maintained by the Go community for well-tested and optimized solutions.

Importing external libraries

The steps are as follows:

1. **Initialize a Go module**: Before importing any external library, ensure your project is a Go module.

   Command:

   ```
   go mod init module_name
   ```

   Example:

   ```
   go mod init github.com/user/myproject
   ```

2. **Add the external library**: Use **go get** to fetch the desired library and add it to your **go.mod** file.

   Command:

   ```
   go get library_path@version
   ```

   Example:

   To fetch the **github.com/pkg/errors** library:

   ```
   go get github.com/pkg/errors@v0.9.1
   ```

   If no version is specified, the latest version is fetched.

3. **Import the library**: After adding the library, you can import it into your Go code.

   Syntax:

   ```
   import "library_path"
   ```

Example:

```
import (
    "fmt"
    "github.com/pkg/errors"
)
```

4. **Use the library**: Use the library functions in your code as needed.

   Example: Using **github.com/pkg/errors**:

```
package main

import (
    "fmt"
    "github.com/pkg/errors"
)

func main() {
    err := errors.New("an error occurred")
    fmt.Println(err)
}
```

5. **Managing external libraries:**

   a. **Viewing dependencies**: List all the libraries your project depends on.

      Command:

```
go list -m all
```

   b. **Updating dependencies**: Use **go get -u** to update a library to its latest compatible version.

      Command:

```
go get -u library_path
```

   c. **Removing unused dependencies**: Use **go mod tidy** to clean up unused dependencies.

      Command:

```
go mod tidy
```

   d. **Locking dependency versions**: The **go.sum** file locks the exact versions of dependencies to ensure reproducibility.

6. **Version constraints:**

   a. **Specifying a version**: Use **@version** to specify an exact version.

      Example:

```
go get github.com/pkg/errors@v0.9.1
```

   b. **Updating to the latest version**: Use **go get -u**.

      Example:

```
go get -u github.com/pkg/errors
```

   c. **Rolling back to an older version**: Specify the desired version explicitly.

      Example:

```
go get github.com/pkg/errors@v0.8.0
```

d. **Using pre-releases or pseudo-versions**: Fetch a development version if no stable release is available.

Example:

```
go get github.com/user/library@v1.2.3-20240315080000-abcd1234
```

The best practices for importing external libraries are as follows:

- **Choose well-maintained libraries**:

  Look for:

  - Active development
  - Community support
  - Regular updates and documentation
- **Avoid overloading with dependencies**: Use only necessary libraries to keep your project lightweight and maintainable.
- **Specify exact versions**: Pin exact versions in **go.mod** to ensure consistent builds.
- **Use Go tools for dependency management**:

  Regularly run:

  - **go mod tidy** to clean up unused dependencies.
  - **go list -m** all to review all dependencies.
- **Review licenses**: Ensure the libraries comply with your project's licensing requirements.

The common issues while importing external libraries are as follows:

- **Dependency conflicts**:
  - Occurs when multiple libraries require incompatible versions of the same dependency.
  - **Solution**: Use **go mod tidy** and review the dependency tree.
- **Network restrictions**:
  - Some environments block external access to dependency repositories.
  - **Solutions**:
    - Use a local proxy like **GOPROXY**.
    - **Command**:

      ```
      export GOPROXY=https://proxy.golang.org
      ```
- **Cyclic dependencies**: Avoid importing packages that depend on each other cyclically.
- **Breaking changes in updates**:
  - Updating libraries without reviewing release notes can introduce breaking changes.
  - **Solution**: Update carefully and run tests.

7. **Example workflow**: Importing and using a library

   Scenario: Import and use the **github.com/sirupsen/logrus** logging library.

   a. **Initialize the module:**

   ```
   go mod init github.com/user/myproject
   ```

   b. **Add the library:**

   ```
   go get github.com/sirupsen/logrus@v1.8.1
   ```

c. **Import the library:**

File: `main.go`

```
package main

import (
    "github.com/sirupsen/logrus"
)

func main() {
    logrus.Info("This is a log message")
}
```

d. **Run the application:**

```
go run main.go
```

The advantages of using external libraries are as follows:

- **Saves development time**: Leverage pre-built solutions for common tasks.
- **Enhances functionality**: Add advanced features like JSON parsing, HTTP handling, and logging.
- **Community collaboration**: Use libraries maintained by experienced developers and communities.
- **Standardized practices**: Adopt industry-standard approaches to common problems.

Best practices for importing external libraries

The best practices for package design in Go are as follows:

- **Package naming**:
    - **Use descriptive names**: Choose names that clearly describe the purpose of the package.
        - **Good examples:** `mathutils`, `stringutils`, `config`
        - **Bad examples:** `pkg1`, `misc`
- **Avoid redundancy**: Avoid repeating the package name in its identifiers.

  Example:

```
// Good
package mathutils

func Add(a, b int) int {
    return a + b
}

// Bad
package mathutils

func MathutilsAdd(a, b int) int {
    return a + b
}
```

- **Keep it lowercase**: Package names should always be lowercase and avoid underscores or special characters.

- **Control access with exported and unexported identifiers**:

  Export only what is necessary.

  - Export only the functions, variables, or types that are intended for use outside the package.
  - Start exported identifiers with an uppercase letter.

- **Keep implementation details unexported**:

  - Keep helper functions or variables unexported by starting their names with a lowercase letter.

    Example:

```go
package stringutils

// Exported function
func ToUpper(s string) string {
    return toUpperHelper(s)
}

// Unexported helper function
func toUpperHelper(s string) string {
    return strings.ToUpper(s)
}
```

- **Single responsibility principle**: A package should focus on a single responsibility or domain.

  - **Good example**:
    - `mathutils` for mathematical operations.
    - `httpserver` for handling HTTP requests.
  - **Bad example**: A `utils` package with unrelated functions like `Add()`, `ConnectToDB()`, and `ToUpper()`.

- **Package organization**:

  - **Group related functionality**: Group similar functionality into the same package to improve cohesion.

```
plaintext
Copy code
project/
├── main.go
├── mathutils/
│   ├── add.go
│   ├── subtract.go
│   └── multiply.go
└── stringutils/
    ├── concat.go
    └── split.go
```

- **Avoid deep nesting**: Keep the directory structure flat to improve readability and avoid complexity.

  Bad example:

```
plaintext
Copy code
project/
```

```
└── src/
    └── core/
        └── utils/
            └── string/
                └── concat.go
```

- **API design**:
  - **Keep APIs simple**: Design the package interface to be intuitive and easy to use. Avoid exposing unnecessary details.
  - **Consistent naming**: Use consistent naming conventions across the package to reduce confusion.

    Example: If using `Add()` for `mathutils`, avoid `Plus()` or `Combine()` for similar operations.
  - **Return errors for exceptional cases**: Avoid panics in your package. Instead, return errors for the caller to handle.

    Example:

```go
package config

import "errors"

func Load(file string) (Config, error) {
    if file == "" {
        return Config{}, errors.New("file path cannot be empty")
    }
    // Load configuration Logic
    return Config{}, nil
}
```

Note: We will see APIs more clearly in the upcoming chapters.

- **Avoid overloading a package**: Keep packages small and focused. If a package becomes too large, split it into multiple smaller packages.

  Example:

```
project/
I-- database/
        I--  connection.go
        I-- queries.go
I-- logging/
        I--  logger.go
I--  config/
        I-- loader.go
```

- **Document your package**:
  - Use comments for exported functions.
  - Provide clear comments for all exported functions, types, and variables.
  - Start comments with the function or type name.

  Example:

```go
// Add adds two integers and returns the result.
```

```go
func Add(a, b int) int {
    return a + b
}
```

- **Include a package-level comment**: Add a comment at the beginning of the file to describe the package's purpose.

  Example:

  ```go
  // Package mathutils provides utility functions for mathematical operations.
  package mathutils
  ```

- **Test your package**:
  - **Write unit tests**: Create a **`_test.go`** file in the same package directory and write test cases for exported functions.

    Example:

    ```go
    package mathutils

    import "testing"

    func TestAdd(t *testing.T) {
        result := Add(2, 3)
        if result != 5 {
            t.Errorf("Expected 5, got %d", result)
        }
    }
    ```

  - **Cover edge cases**: Ensure your tests cover typical, edge, and invalid input scenarios.
  - **Use benchmarks for performance**: Write benchmark tests to measure the performance of critical functions.

    Example:

    ```go
    func BenchmarkAdd(b *testing.B) {
        for i := 0; i < b.N; i++ {
            Add(2, 3)
        }
    }
    ```

- **Avoid circular dependencies**: Packages should not depend on each other in a cyclic manner. Use shared packages for common functionality.
  - **Bad example**: **`packageA -> packageB -> packageA`**
  - **Solution**: Create a common package for shared code.
- **Minimize use of init**: Avoid using the init function for package initialization. Instead, provide explicit initialization functions.
  - **Bad practice**:

    ```go
    func init() {
        fmt.Println("Initializing package")
    }
    ```

- **Good practice**:

```
func Initialize() {
    fmt.Println("Initializing package")
}
```

- **Version your package**:
  - For reusable packages, maintain versions using semantic versioning (`vMAJOR.MINOR.PATCH`).
  - Publish tagged versions to repositories like GitHub for easy use with Go modules.
- **Follow go conventions**:
  - Adhere to Go idiomatic practices, such as:
    - Returning multiple values (value, error).
    - Using descriptive and consistent variable names.
    - Avoiding global state unless absolutely necessary.

Conclusion

Packages in Go are essential for building well-structured, maintainable, and reusable code. By grouping related functionality and enforcing clear access rules through exported and unexported identifiers, packages help keep codebases clean and modular. Go's support for modules further enhances this by enabling version control and dependency management, making collaboration and code sharing much more effective.

Throughout this chapter, you have learned how to create packages, import them, use Go modules, manage dependencies, and follow best practices for package design. Mastering these concepts lays a solid foundation for developing scalable applications in Go.

In the next chapter, we will explore Go concurrency, one of Go's most powerful features. You will learn how to write programs that perform multiple tasks simultaneously using goroutines, channels, and other concurrency primitives, paving the way for building highly performant and responsive applications.

Questions

1. What are the two main types of packages in Go, and how do they differ in terms of purpose and usage?
2. Explain the significance of the init function in Go packages. When is it executed and what is it commonly used for?
3. How does Go distinguish between exported and unexported identifiers within a package? What rules determine their visibility?
4. What is a Go module and how does it differ from a package? Mention at least two benefits of using modules.
5. Describe the structure and purpose of the go.mod and go.sum files in Go module management.
6. What are the common pitfalls to avoid when creating or importing Go packages? Give examples to support your answer.
7. Outline the steps to publish a Go module and make it available for use in other projects.
8. Why is it recommended to keep package names descriptive and avoid deep directory nesting? What are the consequences of ignoring this advice?
9. How can Go developers manage external dependencies effectively using module commands? Name at least three useful commands.
10. What are the best practices for designing Go packages to ensure modularity, readability, and maintainability in large-scale applications?

CHAPTER 9
Introduction to Go Concurrency

Introduction

In today's software landscape, building efficient, responsive, and scalable systems is essential and concurrency plays a critical role in achieving this. Go was designed with concurrency as a core feature, offering built-in support that makes managing multiple tasks both powerful and developer friendly. Unlike traditional threading models that are often complex and resource-intensive, Go introduces lightweight goroutines and channels for seamless task execution and coordination. This chapter explores the fundamentals of concurrency, its practical significance in real-world systems, and how Go simplifies its implementation. Readers will gain a solid understanding of key concepts such as goroutines, wait groups, and error handling in concurrent programs. By examining use cases, performance comparisons, and concurrency models, this chapter equips developers with the knowledge to harness Go's concurrency model effectively. It forms the foundation for subsequent discussions on communication and synchronization using channels, paving the way for building highly concurrent applications.

Structure

In this chapter, we will cover the following topics:

- Concurrency
- Goroutines
- Performance comparison between goroutines and threads
- Concurrency patterns in Go

Objectives

By the end of this chapter, learners will be able to implement concurrency effectively in Go using goroutines and channels. They will understand the difference between concurrency and parallelism and apply this knowledge to improve system responsiveness and efficiency. Students will gain practical skills in launching and managing goroutines, synchronizing them using wait groups, and handling errors using channels. They will also be able to differentiate Go's concurrency model from traditional threading approaches and recognize its performance benefits. Additionally, learners will apply best practices to avoid race conditions and manage goroutine lifecycle, making their applications more robust and scalable. This chapter lays the groundwork for mastering Go's concurrency primitives, preparing learners for advanced topics like synchronization, communication patterns, and concurrent system design in upcoming chapters.

Concurrency

Concurrency is the ability of a program to perform multiple tasks simultaneously by overlapping their execution.

Concurrency is not the same as parallelism:

- **Concurrency**: Managing multiple tasks at the same time (not necessarily executing them simultaneously).
- **Parallelism**: Running multiple tasks at the exact same time on different processors.

Concurrency in Go is a fundamental feature designed to handle tasks that can run independently, such as network requests, file processing, or background computations.

Importance of concurrency

Concurrency enhances software performance by utilizing multiple CPU cores, improving responsiveness, and simplifying problem decomposition. It allows systems to handle multiple tasks at once, keeping applications responsive under load. For example, while one task waits for input or output, others can proceed independently. In real-time systems like IoT or gaming, concurrency ensures timely execution. Overall, it enables efficient, scalable, and maintainable application design.

Let us see some of them in detail:

- **Efficient use of system resources**: Modern systems have multiple CPU cores. Concurrency allows programs to utilize these cores efficiently by dividing tasks into smaller independent units. For example, while one goroutine waits for a network response, another can continue processing data.
- **Responsiveness**: Concurrency ensures that applications remain responsive, even under heavy workloads. For example, a web server can handle multiple client requests simultaneously without blocking other users.
- **Simplified problem decomposition**: Concurrency simplifies the decomposition of complex problems into smaller, manageable tasks. For example, a search engine can divide the task of indexing files into separate concurrent tasks for faster execution.
- **Real-time systems**: Many applications, like games or IoT systems, require real-time responsiveness. Concurrency ensures that time-sensitive tasks meet deadlines.

Real-world scenarios where concurrency matters

Concurrency is vital in web servers, data processing, microservices, and real-time systems to handle multiple tasks efficiently. For instance, Go-based servers spawn goroutines for each request, and ML pipelines preprocess data chunks in parallel. Microservices use concurrency for handling API calls and database access simultaneously. Real-time messaging apps and event-driven systems rely on it to stay responsive under continuous user or sensor interactions.

Let us see some of them in detail:

- **Web servers**: Handle thousands of simultaneous client requests without slowing down. For example, a Go-based web server can start a new goroutine for each HTTP request.
- **Data processing**: Concurrently process large datasets by splitting the workload. For example, a machine learning pipeline that concurrently preprocesses data chunks.
- **Microservices**: In distributed systems, microservices handle concurrent tasks, such as database queries, inter-service API calls, and event processing across independent services.
- **Real-time messaging**: Chat applications and messaging platforms need to handle multiple active users and conversations concurrently.
- **Event-driven architectures**: Concurrency is essential for handling asynchronous events, such as user inputs or sensor readings.

Challenges without concurrency

Without concurrency, applications can suffer from inefficiency and blocked execution, leading to poor performance and responsiveness. Sequential processing leaves CPU cores idle during I/O waits and blocking operations can freeze entire programs.

Let us see some of them in detail:

- **Inefficiency**: Sequential processing often results in idle CPU cores, wasting computational power. For example, a file upload application waiting for disk I/O could leave the CPU underutilized.
- **Blocked execution**: Without concurrency, a blocking operation (e.g., waiting for a network response) can halt the entire program.
- **Complex code for simulated concurrency**: Simulating concurrency without built-in language support often results in complex, error-prone code.

Advantages of concurrency in Go

Go simplifies concurrent programming with built-in features like goroutines and channels. Its lightweight concurrency model allows thousands of tasks to run efficiently, making it ideal for scalable, high-performance applications. Channels further ease task coordination without the pitfalls of shared memory.

Let us see some of them in detail:

- **Built-in support**: Go provides native concurrency features like goroutines and channels, making it easier to implement concurrency compared to traditional threading models.
- **Lightweight concurrency**: Goroutines are extremely lightweight compared to operating system threads, enabling the execution of thousands or even millions of concurrent tasks.
- **Simplified communication**: Channels provide a straightforward way to communicate between concurrent tasks, avoiding the complexity of traditional shared memory models.
- **Scalability**: Concurrency in Go scales well with increasing workloads and system resources, making it ideal for high-performance applications.

Common misconceptions about concurrency

Concurrency is not the same as parallelism; tasks may progress independently without running simultaneously. Also, more concurrency does not always mean better performance due to overheads like context switching and contention:

- **Concurrency equals parallelism**: Concurrency is about dealing with multiple tasks at the same time, while parallelism is about doing multiple tasks simultaneously. For example, a concurrent program can run on a single core by switching between tasks, but a parallel program requires multiple cores.
- **More concurrency always means better performance**: Excessive concurrency can lead to overheads like context switching or resource contention.

Go makes concurrency easier

Go uses goroutines and channels to simplify concurrent programming, enabling efficient task execution and safe communication. It is a built-in scheduler that handles goroutine management automatically, ensuring optimal performance with minimal developer effort:

- **Goroutines**: Lightweight threads managed by the Go runtime. It also enables efficient task execution with minimal resource usage.
- **Channels**: Provide a structured way to communicate between goroutines, ensuring data safety without explicit locking mechanisms.

- **Scheduler**: The Go runtime includes a built-in scheduler that maps goroutines to operating system threads, optimizing resource allocation automatically.

Comparing concurrency models

Different programming languages handle concurrency in unique ways, each with its own trade-offs in terms of performance, complexity, and resource usage. Let us compare:

- **Threads in traditional programming**:
  - **Heavyweight**: Each thread consumes significant memory (often several MB).
  - **Complexity**: Requires explicit locking mechanisms to prevent race conditions.
  - **Example**: Java threads or pthreads in C/C++.
- **Goroutines in Go**:
  - **Lightweight**: Each goroutine consumes a few KB of memory.
  - **Simplified communication**: Avoids explicit locks by using channels.
  - **Example**:

```
go func() {
    fmt.Println("Running in a goroutine")
}()
```

Use cases demonstrating the need for concurrency

Concurrency is essential for building responsive and high-performance applications that handle multiple tasks simultaneously. It helps reduce execution time, improve throughput, and deliver real-time experiences.

Here are some practical scenarios:

- **Concurrent file downloads**: A download manager can concurrently fetch multiple files from different URLs, significantly reducing overall download time.

  Example:

```
package main

import (
 "fmt"
 "sync"
)

func download(url string, wg *sync.WaitGroup) {
 defer wg.Done() // Decrement the counter when the goroutine completes
 fmt.Printf("Downloading from %s\n", url)
}

func main() {
 urls := []string{"http://example.com/file1", "http://example.com/file2"}

 var wg sync.WaitGroup // Create a WaitGroup
```

```
    for _, url := range urls {
     wg.Add(1) // Increment the counter for each goroutine
     go download(url, &wg)
    }

    wg.Wait() // Wait for all Goroutines to complete
    fmt.Println("All downloads completed.")
   }
```

- **Concurrent data aggregation**: Aggregating data from multiple APIs or databases concurrently improves efficiency.

```
func fetchData(api string, ch chan string) {
    ch <- fmt.Sprintf("Data from %s", api)
}

func main() {
    apis := []string{"API1", "API2"}
    ch := make(chan string)

    for _, api := range apis {
        go fetchData(api, ch)
    }

    for range apis {
        fmt.Println(<-ch)
    }
}
```

Real-time user notifications are as follows:

- Notify multiple users simultaneously when an event occurs, ensuring immediate delivery of messages or alerts.
- Concurrency allows sending messages to multiple users in parallel, without waiting for one to finish before starting another.
- This is critical for applications like chat systems, stock trading platforms, or emergency alert systems where timely communication is essential.

Goroutines

A goroutine is a lightweight, Go-managed thread for concurrent task execution. It enables concurrent execution of tasks with minimal overhead.

The reasons to use goroutines are as follows:

- Goroutines are much more efficient than traditional operating system threads.
- The Go runtime can manage thousands of goroutines on a single operating system thread using its scheduler.

The key characteristics are as follows:

- Goroutines are initiated using the **go** keyword.

- They run independently in the same memory space, making context switching fast and lightweight.

Creating goroutines

To create a goroutine, prefix a function call with the go keyword. The following is the basic syntax:

```
go functionName(parameters)
```

Example: Running a function as a goroutine

```
package main

import (
    "fmt"
    "time"
)

func sayHello() {
    fmt.Println("Hello from goroutine!")
}

func main() {
    go sayHello() // Start a goroutine
    time.Sleep(time.Second) // Allow goroutine to complete
    fmt.Println("Main function completed")
}
```

The following output will be generated:

```
Hello from goroutine!
Main function completed
```

Anonymous functions with goroutines

You can use anonymous functions to directly pass logic to a goroutine:

```
go func() {
    fmt.Println("Hello from an anonymous goroutine!")
}()
```

Example with parameters:

```
package main

import (
    "fmt"
    "time"
)

func main() {
    go func(message string) {
        fmt.Println(message)
    }("Hello, Go!")
```

```
    time.Sleep(time.Second)
}
```

Managing goroutines

To fully harness the power of concurrency in Go, it is important to manage goroutines properly, especially ensuring they complete their tasks before the main program exits. Go provides synchronization tools to coordinate and control the execution of multiple goroutines effectively, as follows:

- **Wait for completion**:
    - Since goroutines run asynchronously, Go uses **`sync.WaitGroup`** to ensure the main function waits for all goroutines to complete before **`exiting.Goroutines`** execute asynchronously, meaning the main program may terminate before goroutines finish.
    - A **`WaitGroup`** is a counter that tracks the number of goroutines that need to finish before the program continues.
    - It helps coordinate the execution of multiple goroutines.
    - Use **`sync.WaitGroup`** to wait for goroutines to complete.

The key methods are as follows:

- **Add(delta int)**: Adds or subtracts a value to/from the **`WaitGroup`** counter.
- **Done()**: Decrements the counter by 1 (equivalent to **`Add(-1)`**).
- **Wait()**: Blocks the calling goroutine until the counter becomes zero.

Example: Using **`sync.WaitGroup`**

```go
package main

import (
    "fmt"
    "sync"
)

func worker(id int, wg *sync.WaitGroup) {
    defer wg.Done() // Mark the goroutine as done
    fmt.Printf("Worker %d starting\n", id)
    fmt.Printf("Worker %d completed\n", id)
}

func main() {
    var wg sync.WaitGroup
    for i := 1; i <= 3; i++ {
        wg.Add(1) // Increment the counter
        go worker(i, &wg)
    }
    wg.Wait() // Wait for all goroutines to complete
    fmt.Println("All workers completed")
}
```

The following outputs will be generated:

- `Worker 1 starting`
- `Worker 2 starting`
- `Worker 3 starting`
- `Worker 1 completed`
- `Worker 2 completed`
- `Worker 3 completed`
- `All workers completed`

Reasons for passing by pointer instead of value in the previous program are as follows:

- **Shared state across goroutines**:
  - **Reason**: If you pass the `WaitGroup` by value, each goroutine would get a copy of the `WaitGroup`.
  - **Problem**: Each copy would maintain its own independent counter, leading to incorrect synchronization.
  - **Solution**: Passing by pointer ensures that all goroutines operate on the same `WaitGroup` instance, modifying the shared counter correctly.
- **Efficient memory usage**:
  - **Reason**: Passing a pointer avoids copying the `WaitGroup` structure, which can save memory, especially for larger structures.
  - **Problem**: Copying large structures can introduce unnecessary overhead.
  - **Solution**: Passing by pointer is more efficient as it involves only a memory address, regardless of the structure size.
- **Ensuring thread-safe modifications**:
  - **Reason**: The `sync.WaitGroup` is designed to work with concurrent goroutines.
  - **Problem**: Copies of the `WaitGroup` would break the thread-safety guarantees since each goroutine would be modifying its own copy.
  - **Solution**: A single shared instance ensures the internal state remains consistent and thread safe.

Note: Passing data to goroutines: Data can be passed to goroutines through function arguments.

Example:

```go
package main

import (
    "fmt"
    "time"
)

func printMessage(msg string) {
    fmt.Println(msg)
}

func main() {
    messages := []string{"Hello", "Concurrency", "Goroutines"}
    for _, msg := range messages {
```

```
        go printMessage(msg)
    }
    time.Sleep(time.Second)
}
```

Error handling in goroutines

Goroutines do not return errors directly. To handle errors, you can use channels to capture errors from goroutines.

Note: Channels in Go are a mechanism for communication between goroutines, allowing them to share data safely and efficiently. They provide a way to send and receive values of a specified type, synchronizing goroutines.

Channels can be unbuffered (blocking until data is sent or received) or buffered (allowing limited storage of values). The make function creates channels, and the **<-** operator is used for sending and receiving data. Channels are essential for implementing concurrency patterns and avoiding race conditions in Go programs.

Syntax for declaration:

```
var channelName chan valueType
```

- **channelName**: The name of the channel.
- **chan**: Keyword indicating a channel.
- **valueType**: The type of values the channel will send and receive.

  Example:

  ```
  var ch chan int // A channel for integers
  ```

Syntax for creation:

- Use the **make** function to initialize a channel.

  ```
  channelName := make(chan valueType)
  ```

  Example:

  ```
  ch := make(chan int) // Creates an integer channel
  ```

  Pass a channel to the goroutine, allowing it to send error messages.

  Example:

  ```
  package main

  import (
      "fmt"
      "time"
  )

  func worker(id int, errChan chan error) {
      if id%2 == 0 {
          errChan <- fmt.Errorf("Worker %d encountered an error", id)
      } else {
          errChan <- nil
      }
  }
  ```

```
func main() {
    errChan := make(chan error, 3)
    for i := 1; i <= 3; i++ {
        go worker(i, errChan)
    }
    time.Sleep(time.Second)
    for i := 1; i <= 3; i++ {
        if err := <-errChan; err != nil {
            fmt.Println(err)
        } else {
            fmt.Println("Worker completed successfully")
        }
    }
}
```

Goroutines vs. functions

Some key differences between goroutines and functions are highlighted in the following table:

Feature	Function	Goroutine
Execution	Runs synchronously in the caller's context.	Runs concurrently, managed by the Go runtime.
Blocking	Blocks the caller until it completes.	Non-blocking; main thread continues execution.
Overhead	Minimal overhead.	Slightly more overhead but highly efficient.
Control	Simple to debug and trace.	Requires careful management to avoid race conditions.

***Table 9.1**: Goroutines vs. functions*

Goroutines in practical applications

The applications are as follows:

- **Web servers**: Handle multiple client requests concurrently.

  Example:

```
package main

import (
    "fmt"
    "net/http"
)

func handler(w http.ResponseWriter, r *http.Request) {
    fmt.Fprintf(w, "Hello, %s!", r.URL.Path[1:])
}

func main() {
    http.HandleFunc("/", handler)
    go http.ListenAndServe(":8080", nil) // Start the server in a goroutine
```

```
        select {} // Block main from exiting
    }
```

- **File processing**: Process multiple files concurrently.

  Example:

```
package main

import (
    "fmt"
    "sync"
)

func processFile(filename string, wg *sync.WaitGroup) {
    defer wg.Done()
    fmt.Printf("Processing file: %s\n", filename)
}

func main() {
    files := []string{"file1.txt", "file2.txt", "file3.txt"}
    var wg sync.WaitGroup
    for _, file := range files {
        wg.Add(1)
        go processFile(file, &wg)
    }
    wg.Wait()
    fmt.Println("All files processed")
}
```

The best practices for using goroutines are as follows:

- **Avoid too many goroutines**: Excessive goroutines can cause memory overhead and CPU contention.
- **Use channels for communication**: Avoid shared memory and use channels to synchronize goroutines.
- **Manage goroutine lifecycle**: Ensure goroutines complete or are terminated gracefully to avoid memory leaks.
- **Use sync.WaitGroup for coordination**: Always wait for goroutines to finish, especially in short-lived programs.
- **Handle errors explicitly**: Capture and handle errors from goroutines using channels or logging mechanisms.
- **Be aware of race conditions**: Use synchronization primitives like `sync.Mutex` when accessing shared data.

Performance comparison between goroutines and threads

Goroutines are more lightweight and efficient than traditional threads, enabling higher concurrency with lower memory and scheduling overhead.

Concurrency in programming often involves using threads or similar abstractions to handle multiple tasks simultaneously. In Go, goroutines provide an efficient and lightweight mechanism for concurrency, designed as an alternative to traditional threads.

This section compares goroutines and threads across multiple dimensions, including performance, resource utilization, ease of use, and scalability.

Threads

Threads are the smallest units of execution in a process, managed by the operating system. Each thread operates in its own context but shares the process's resources (e.g., memory).

The key characteristics of threads are as follows:

- **Heavyweight**: Each thread requires significant memory and kernel resources.
- **Managed by OS**: The operating system is responsible for creating, scheduling, and destroying threads.
- **Context switching**: Switching between threads involves saving and restoring CPU registers, which can be expensive.

Use cases: Threads are commonly used in high-performance applications like database servers, video processing, and real-time systems.

Goroutines

Goroutines are lightweight, user-level threads managed by the Go runtime instead of the operating system.

The key characteristics of goroutines are as follows:

- **Lightweight**: Goroutines start with a small amount of stack memory (2 KB) and grow dynamically.
- **Managed by Go runtime**: The Go runtime handles scheduling and execution.
- **Efficient scheduling**: Go's scheduler multiplexes thousands of goroutines onto a small number of OS threads.

Use cases: Ideal for applications requiring thousands of concurrent tasks, such as web servers, chat applications, or real-time analytics.

Goroutines and threads

The key differences between goroutines and threads are as follows:

Aspect	Goroutines	Threads
Memory usage	Start with 2 KB and grow dynamically.	Requires several MB of memory per thread.
Creation overhead	Very low; created in microseconds.	Higher; involves OS-level resource allocation.
Scheduling	Managed by Go's runtime scheduler.	Managed by the OS kernel.
Context switching	Extremely fast due to Go's runtime.	Slower due to OS-level context switching.
Concurrency level	Can handle millions of goroutines.	Limited by system resources (thousands at best).
Communication	Simplified with Go's channels.	Requires explicit synchronization mechanisms.
Error handling	Requires channels or external mechanisms.	Errors are local to the thread and need handling.

Table 9.2: *Difference between goroutines and threads*

Performance metrics

The following are the performance metrics:

- **Memory consumption**: Goroutines are far more memory-efficient compared to threads.

  Example:
  - **Goroutine**: Starts with 2 KB stack memory.
  - **Thread**: Requires at least 1 MB stack memory by default.
- **Scalability**: Goroutines can scale to millions of concurrent tasks, while threads are limited to thousands due to their heavyweight nature.
- **Context switching overhead**: Switching between goroutines is faster as it is managed by the Go runtime, while threads rely on OS kernel context switching, which involves significant overhead.

Benchmarks and examples

Example 1: Creating 10,000 goroutines

```
package main

import (
    "fmt"
    "time"
)

func worker(id int) {
    fmt.Printf("Worker %d started\n", id)
    time.Sleep(time.Second)
    fmt.Printf("Worker %d completed\n", id)
}

func main() {
    for i := 0; i < 10000; i++ {
        go worker(i)
    }
    time.Sleep(2 * time.Second) // Allow all goroutines to finish
    fmt.Println("All workers completed")
}
```

Result: Successfully runs 10,000 concurrent tasks with minimal memory overhead.

Example 2: Threads in C

Creating 10,000 threads in C would likely cause significant resource consumption or failure due to memory limitations.

```
#include <stdio.h>
#include <pthread.h>
#include <unistd.h>

void* worker(void* arg) {
    int id = *(int*)arg;
    printf("Worker %d started\n", id);
    sleep(1);
```

```
    printf("Worker %d completed\n", id);
    return NULL;
}

int main() {
    pthread_t threads[10000];
    for (int i = 0; i < 10000; i++) {
        if (pthread_create(&threads[i], NULL, worker, &i) != 0) {
            printf("Failed to create thread %d\n", i);
            return 1;
        }
    }
    for (int i = 0; i < 10000; i++) {
        pthread_join(threads[i], NULL);
    }
    return 0;
}
```

Result: Likely fails due to memory limitations or thread count limits imposed by the OS.

Note: **Do not use the sleep syntax in production systems (unless the use case seriously demands), it is only for the learning process.**

Scheduler differences

The following are the key differences:

- **Goroutines scheduler (M:N model)**:
  - **Model**: Maps M goroutines onto N OS threads.
  - **Key features**:
    - Handles scheduling at the user level.
    - Minimizes context switching by reusing threads.
    - Automatically balances workload across threads.
- **Threads scheduler (1:1 model)**
  - **Model**: Each thread is mapped directly to an OS thread.
  - **Limitations**:
    - Relies heavily on the OS for scheduling.
    - Higher overhead due to frequent context switches.

Let us understand when to use goroutines and threads.

Use goroutines when:

- **High concurrency**: Applications need to handle thousands or millions of concurrent tasks.
- **Asynchronous workloads**: Tasks like handling HTTP requests, database queries, or message processing.
- **Resource constraints**: Environments with limited memory or processing power.

Use threads when:

- **Low-level control**: Applications require direct interaction with hardware or OS-level features.
- **Interfacing with non-go libraries**: Some C or system libraries might require OS threads for integration.
- **Real-time systems**: Where predictable timing is critical, and OS scheduling guarantees are needed.

If you absolutely need to use pthreads, you can call C functions using Go's cgo. For example, you can write C code to create pthreads and call those functions from Go. However, this is highly discouraged because it could interfere with the Go runtime's scheduling.

The advantages of goroutines over threads are as follows:

- **Lightweight**: Goroutines use minimal memory and grow stacks dynamically, making them ideal for high-concurrency tasks.
- **Simplified communication**: Channels provide a safe and idiomatic way to communicate between goroutines, reducing synchronization complexity.
- **Efficient scheduling**: The Go runtime scheduler is optimized for running goroutines efficiently across multiple cores.

The challenges with goroutines are as follows:

- **Race conditions**: Concurrent access to shared resources requires synchronization mechanisms like **`sync.Mutex`**.
- **Unmanaged growth**: Excessive goroutines can lead to resource contention if not monitored or limited.
- **Debugging complexity**: Debugging concurrent programs can be challenging due to the non-deterministic nature of execution.

The challenges with threads are as follows:

- **High memory usage**: Each thread consumes significant memory, limiting the number of concurrent threads.
- **Complex synchronization**: Threads often require explicit locking mechanisms to manage shared resources.
- **Expensive context switching**: Frequent context switching can degrade performance.

Summary

The following table highlights the summary of this section:

Aspect	Goroutines	Threads
Memory efficiency	Lightweight, starts with 2 KB stack.	Heavy, requires ~1 MB per thread.
Scalability	Handles millions of tasks easily.	Limited to thousands of threads.
Management	Managed by Go runtime (user-level).	Managed by OS (kernel-level).
Communication	Simplified with channels.	Requires manual synchronization.

***Table 9.3**: Tabular summarization*

Concurrency patterns in Go

Concurrency patterns are established techniques for structuring and managing concurrent programs. Go's built-in support for concurrency through goroutines and channels makes it uniquely suited for implementing these patterns. This section explores key concurrency patterns in Go, their implementation, and practical applications. We will see most of the patterns in detail in the coming subsections and this section will be a quick eye-opener.

Fan-out/fan-in pattern

Fan-out is defined as a pattern where tasks are distributed (fanned out) to multiple workers running in separate goroutines. The purpose is to utilize multiple CPU cores and distribute workload across multiple goroutines for parallel processing.

Fan-in is defined as a pattern where multiple results from concurrent tasks are collected into a single channel. The purpose is to aggregate outputs from multiple workers and simplify result collection.

Example: Fan-out/Fan-in

```
package main

import (
    "fmt"
    "sync"
)

func worker(id int, jobs <-chan int, results chan<- int, wg *sync.WaitGroup) {
    defer wg.Done()
    for job := range jobs {
        fmt.Printf("Worker %d processing job %d\n", id, job)
        results <- job * 2
    }
}

func main() {
    const numWorkers = 3
    jobs := make(chan int, 10)
    results := make(chan int, 10)

    var wg sync.WaitGroup

    // Fan-out: Start workers
    for i := 1; i <= numWorkers; i++ {
        wg.Add(1)
        go worker(i, jobs, results, &wg)
    }

    // Send jobs
    for j := 1; j <= 10; j++ {
        jobs <- j
    }
    close(jobs)

    // Wait for all workers to complete
    wg.Wait()
    close(results)
```

```
    // Fan-in: Collect results
    for result := range results {
        fmt.Println("Result:", result)
    }
}
```

The following output will be generated:

- `Worker 3 processing job 1`
- `Worker 3 processing job 4`
- `Worker 3 processing job 5`
- `Worker 3 processing job 6`
- `Worker 3 processing job 7`
- `Worker 3 processing job 8`
- `Worker 3 processing job 9`
- `Worker 3 processing job 10`
- `Worker 2 processing job 3`
- `Worker 1 processing job 2`
- `Result: 2`
- `Result: 8`
- `Result: 10`
- `Result: 12`
- `Result: 14`
- `Result: 16`
- `Result: 18`
- `Result: 20`
- `Result: 6`
- `Result: 4`

Note: **The `close` function in Go is used to close a channel to signal that no more values will be sent on it. Once a channel is closed, it cannot accept any more data, but it can still be read until all buffered data has been received.**

Pipeline pattern

A pipeline is a series of connected stages where data flows sequentially. Each stage is represented by a goroutine that processes data and sends it to the next stage via channels.

The purpose is to process data in stages with different processing requirements. Break down complex tasks into smaller, manageable units.

Example: Pipeline pattern

```
package main

import "fmt"

func generator(numbers ...int) <-chan int {
    out := make(chan int)
    go func() {
        for _, num := range numbers {
```

```
            out <- num
        }
        close(out)
    }()
    return out
}

func square(input <-chan int) <-chan int {
    out := make(chan int)
    go func() {
        for num := range input {
            out <- num * num
        }
        close(out)
    }()
    return out
}

func main() {
    nums := generator(1, 2, 3, 4, 5)
    results := square(nums)

    for result := range results {
        fmt.Println(result)
    }
}
```

The following output is generated:

- 1
- 4
- 9
- 16
- 25

Worker pool pattern

The worker pool pattern in Go is a concurrency design where multiple goroutines (workers) process tasks from a shared queue, distributing the workload efficiently. A channel is typically used to queue tasks, and each worker goroutine fetches tasks from the channel to execute. This pattern helps manage resource usage by limiting the number of active goroutines and balancing the load among workers. It is ideal for scenarios involving high-throughput processing, such as handling HTTP requests or processing large datasets.

The purpose is to limit the number of active goroutines to manage resource usage and balance workload among multiple workers.

Example: Worker pool

```
package main

import (
    "fmt"
```

```
    "sync"
)

func worker(id int, tasks <-chan int, wg *sync.WaitGroup) {
    defer wg.Done()
    for task := range tasks {
        fmt.Printf("Worker %d processing task %d\n", id, task)
    }
}

func main() {
    const numWorkers = 3
    tasks := make(chan int, 10)
    var wg sync.WaitGroup

    // Start workers
    for i := 1; i <= numWorkers; i++ {
        wg.Add(1)
        go worker(i, tasks, &wg)
    }

    // Send tasks
    for t := 1; t <= 10; t++ {
        tasks <- t
    }
    close(tasks)

    wg.Wait()
}
```

The following output will be generated:

- **`Worker 3 processing task 1`**
- **`Worker 3 processing task 3`**
- **`Worker 3 processing task 5`**
- **`Worker 3 processing task 6`**
- **`Worker 3 processing task 7`**
- **`Worker 3 processing task 8`**
- **`Worker 1 processing task 2`**
- **`Worker 1 processing task 10`**
- **`Worker 3 processing task 9`**
- **`Worker 2 processing task 4`**

Publish-subscribe pattern

A pattern where one or more publishers send messages to multiple subscribers through channels. The purpose is to enable multiple subscribers to listen to the same data source and decouple producers and consumers.

Example: Publish-subscribe

```
package main

import "fmt"

func publish(data string, subscribers ...chan string) {
    for _, sub := range subscribers {
        sub <- data
    }
}

func main() {
    sub1 := make(chan string)
    sub2 := make(chan string)

    go func() {
        for msg := range sub1 {
            fmt.Println("Subscriber 1 received:", msg)
        }
    }()

    go func() {
        for msg := range sub2 {
            fmt.Println("Subscriber 2 received:", msg)
        }
    }()

    publish("Hello, Go!", sub1, sub2)

    close(sub1)
    close(sub2)
}
```

Select pattern

The select pattern in Go allows a program to handle multiple channel operations simultaneously using the select statement. It listens to multiple channels and performs the corresponding action for the first one that becomes ready. This is useful for implementing timeouts, multiplexing, or non-blocking operations. Each case in the select handles a specific channel operation, while a default case provides non-blocking behavior. It simplifies concurrent code by managing multiple communication paths efficiently.

The purpose is to react to data from multiple channels and handle timeouts and non-blocking operations.

Example: Select pattern

```
package main

import (
    "fmt"
```

```
    "time"
)

func producer(ch chan string, msg string) {
    for {
        ch <- msg
        time.Sleep(time.Second)
    }
}

func main() {
    ch1 := make(chan string)
    ch2 := make(chan string)

    go producer(ch1, "Message from ch1")
    go producer(ch2, "Message from ch2")

    for i := 0; i < 5; i++ {
        select {
        case msg := <-ch1:
            fmt.Println(msg)
        case msg := <-ch2:
            fmt.Println(msg)
        case <-time.After(2 * time.Second):
            fmt.Println("Timeout!")
        }
    }
}
```

The following output will be generated:

```
Message from ch1
Message from ch2
Message from ch1
Message from ch2
Message from ch1
```

Cancellation with context

The context package in Go is used to propagate cancellation signals and deadlines across multiple goroutines, enabling coordinated shutdowns or task cancellations. By passing a context. Context object to goroutines, you can signal them to stop working when the task is no longer needed. This prevents resource wastage and ensures graceful termination of background processes. Commonly used methods include context. **`WithCancel`**, **`context.WithTimeout`**, and **`context.WithDeadline`**. It is particularly useful in applications with time-sensitive or interdependent tasks, such as HTTP servers or database queries.

The purpose is to gracefully terminate goroutines when tasks are no longer needed.

Example: Cancellation with context

```
package main
```

```
import (
    "context"
    "fmt"
    "time"
)

func worker(ctx context.Context, id int) {
    for {
        select {
        case <-ctx.Done():
            fmt.Printf("Worker %d stopping\n", id)
            return
        default:
            fmt.Printf("Worker %d working\n", id)
            time.Sleep(time.Second)
        }
    }
}

func main() {
    ctx, cancel := context.WithTimeout(context.Background(), 3*time.Second)
    defer cancel()

    for i := 1; i <= 3; i++ {
        go worker(ctx, i)
    }

    time.Sleep(5 * time.Second)
    fmt.Println("Main function exiting")
}
```

The following output will be generated:

- `Worker 1 working`
- `Worker 3 working`
- `Worker 2 working`
- `Worker 2 working`
- `Worker 3 working`
- `Worker 1 working`
- `Worker 1 working`
- `Worker 2 working`
- `Worker 3 working`
- `Worker 2 stopping`
- `Worker 1 stopping`
- `Worker 3 stopping`
- `Main function exiting`

Rate limiting pattern

It is defined as a pattern to control the rate at which tasks or requests are processed. The purpose is to prevent resource exhaustion by limiting concurrency.

Example: Rate limiting

```
package main

import (
    "fmt"
    "time"
)

func main() {
    limiter := time.Tick(500 * time.Millisecond)
    for i := 1; i <= 5; i++ {
        <-limiter
        fmt.Printf("Processing task %d\n", i)
    }
}
```

The following output will be generated:

- **Processing task 1**
- **Processing task 2**
- **Processing task 3**
- **Processing task 4**
- **Processing task 5**

Conclusion

Concurrency is a core strength of Go, empowering developers to write scalable, efficient, and responsive programs. By understanding why concurrency is essential, developers can identify scenarios where concurrent execution improves performance and user experience. Go's lightweight goroutines offer a distinct advantage over traditional threads, enabling massive concurrency with minimal resource overhead. Moreover, mastering concurrency patterns equips developers with the tools to tackle real-world challenges like task distribution, synchronization, and communication between components effectively. This chapter lays a solid foundation for leveraging Go's powerful concurrency model, setting the stage for exploring advanced techniques and best practices in subsequent chapters.

In the upcoming chapter, we will explore how goroutines communicate and coordinate safely using Go's channel mechanism. Channels play a critical role in synchronizing concurrent tasks and avoiding data races. You will learn how to send, receive, and manage data across goroutines using unbuffered and buffered channels. This chapter will build the foundation for designing robust, concurrent programs using Go's idiomatic patterns.

Questions

1. What is the difference between concurrency and parallelism in the context of Go, and why is it important to distinguish between the two?
2. How do goroutines differ from traditional threads in terms of memory usage, scheduling, and performance?
3. Explain the purpose and typical use of sync.WaitGroup in managing goroutines. Why should it be passed by pointer?

4. What are channels in Go, and how do they help avoid shared memory issues in concurrent programming?
5. Describe a real-world scenario where the fan-out/fan-in concurrency pattern would be beneficial.
6. What are some best practices for launching and managing goroutines in large-scale applications?
7. Explain how the pipeline pattern works in Go and what types of applications benefit most from it.
8. What are the advantages and limitations of using Go's select statement in handling multiple channels?
9. How does the context package help in canceling goroutines, and why is it considered a best practice in concurrent system design?
10. Compare and contrast the worker pool and publish-subscribe concurrency patterns. In what scenarios is each pattern most effective?

CHAPTER 10
Channels and Synchronization

Introduction

Concurrency in Go is elegantly managed through goroutines and channels, with channels serving as the key building blocks for safe and efficient inter-goroutine communication. Channels allow data to be passed synchronously or asynchronously without the need for explicit locking, ensuring data integrity and ease of reasoning in concurrent systems. This chapter explores the design, usage, and best practices of channels in Go, providing a comprehensive guide to both buffered and unbuffered channels, directional channels, and synchronization techniques. Through illustrative examples and practical insights, you will learn how channels behave under various conditions, how blocking occurs, how to avoid deadlocks, and how to coordinate tasks effectively. Whether you are building a simple producer-consumer pattern or orchestrating complex workflows, mastering Go's channels is essential for writing robust, scalable concurrent programs.

Structure

In this chapter, we cover the following topics:

- Introduction to channels
- Unbuffered and buffered channels in Go
- Sending and receiving data from channels in Go
- Channel direction in Go
- Go channel synchronization overview

Objectives

By the end of this chapter, learners will be able to confidently implement Go channels for safe and efficient concurrency. You will understand the differences between buffered and unbuffered channels and be equipped to use them appropriately in real-world scenarios. You will gain skills to avoid deadlocks, leverage non-blocking operations using select, and improve communication between goroutines using directional channels. Additionally, you will learn best practices for closing channels, handling errors during send or receive, and integrating sync.WaitGroup for complete task coordination. These foundational skills are crucial for writing performant, maintainable, and concurrent Go applications.

Introduction to channels

Channels in Go are a powerful concurrency primitive that enable communication between goroutines. They provide a safe and structured way to share data between multiple concurrent tasks, eliminating the need for explicit locking mechanisms.

A channel is a path through which goroutines can send and receive values of a specific type.

Channels synchronize communication between goroutines, ensuring data consistency and avoiding race conditions.

The key features of channels are as follows:

- **Type-safe**: Channels are strongly typed, meaning they can only send and receive values of a specific type.

  Example:

  ```
  var ch chan int // Channel for integers
  ```

- **Concurrency-safe**: Channels provide built-in synchronization, making them safe for concurrent use.
- **Two-way communication**: Data can flow in both directions: sending (<-) and receiving (->).
- **Blocking behavior**: A send operation blocks until another goroutine is ready to receive the value, and vice versa.
- **Supports buffered and unbuffered modes**: Channels can be buffered (allowing limited storage) or unbuffered (direct handoff between goroutines).

Creating and initializing channels

Let us create and initialize channels as follows:

- **Declaration**: Channels are declared using the `chan` keyword.

  ```
  var ch chan int // A channel for integers
  ```

- **Initialization**: Use the `make` function to initialize a channel.

  ```
  ch := make(chan int) // Unbuffered channel
  ```

Reasons to use channels

Channels are a fundamental part of Go's concurrency model, designed to facilitate communication and synchronization between goroutines in a safe and expressive manner. Instead of relying on shared memory and complex locking mechanisms, channels offer a simple and elegant way to send and receive data, ensuring thread-safe operations and enhancing program clarity, as follows:

- **Safe communication**: Channels enable goroutines to communicate without shared memory, reducing the risk of race conditions.
- **Simplifies coordination**: Channels eliminate the complexity of manually managing locks or condition variables.
- **Improves readability**: Channels provide a clear and structured way to express communication between goroutines.
- **Supports concurrency patterns**: Many Go concurrency patterns, like worker pools or pipelines, rely on channels.

Anatomy of a channel

Understanding how channels work at a fundamental level is essential to writing effective concurrent programs in Go. Channels have a simple yet powerful interface that supports sending, receiving, and closing operations. These operations form the backbone of inter-goroutine communication and are designed to be intuitive, safe, and expressive. Let us look at the details:

- **Send operation**:
  - **Syntax**: `channel <- value`
  - Sends value into the channel.

- **Receive operation**:
  - **Syntax**: `value := <-channel`
  - Receives a value from the channel.
- **Closing a channel**:
  - **Syntax**: `close(channel)`
  - Signals that no more values will be sent into the channel.

Best practices

The best practices for using channels are as follows:

- **Close channels when done**: Use close to signal that no more values will be sent.
- **Avoid closing from receivers**: Only the sender should close the channel to avoid runtime panic.
- **Buffer appropriately**: Use buffered channels when the producer is faster than the consumer.
- **Avoid excessive channels**: Limit the use of channels to where they are necessary for clear communication.
- **Handle blocking**: Be mindful of blocking operations when sending or receiving data.

Common mistakes

The common mistakes with channels are as follows:

- **Deadlocks**: They occur when a channel sends / receives blocks indefinitely because there is no corresponding operation.
- **Sending to a closed channel**: It causes panic. Ensure that the channels are only closed once.
- **Unnecessary use of channels**: Avoid using channels when simple data sharing or mutexes suffice.
- **Ignoring buffered capacity**: Misconfiguring buffer size can lead to unexpected blocking behavior.

Unbuffered and buffered channels in Go

Channels in Go can be either unbuffered or buffered, which determines their behavior when sending and receiving data. Choosing the appropriate type of channel depends on the specific requirements of your application.

Unbuffered channels

An unbuffered channel does not have storage capacity. It requires both the sender and receiver to be ready at the same time for data transfer to occur. This type of channel facilitates direct communication between goroutines.

The characteristics are as follows:

- **Blocking behavior**:
  - **Sender**: Blocks until a receiver is ready to receive the data.
  - **Receiver**: Blocks until a sender sends data.
- **One-to-one synchronization**: It ensures that data is immediately handed off between the sender and receiver.

Use cases

The use cases are as follows:

- When you want to synchronize goroutines directly.

- When immediate processing of sent data is required.

  Example: Unbuffered channel:

```go
package main

import "fmt"

func sendData(ch chan string) {
    ch <- "Hello, Unbuffered Channel!"
    fmt.Println("Data sent")
}

func main() {
    ch := make(chan string)

    go sendData(ch)

    msg := <-ch // Receives data
    fmt.Println("Received:", msg)
}
```

Output:

```
Data sent
Received: Hello, Unbuffered Channel!
```

Explanation is as follows:

- The **sendData** function sends a message to the channel.
- The sender blocks until the main function receives the message.

Buffered channels

A buffered channel has a predefined capacity to store data. The sender does not block until the buffer is full, and the receiver does not block until the buffer is empty.

The characteristics are as follows:

- **Non-blocking behavior**:
  - **Sender**: Blocks only when the buffer is full.
  - **Receiver**: Blocks only when the buffer is empty.
- **Decoupling**: Sender and receiver operations can happen at different times.
- **Capacity**: The size of the buffer is defined when creating the channel.

Syntax:

```go
ch := make(chan type, capacity)
```

Use cases

The use cases are as follows:

- When you want to decouple the sender and receiver.
- When you need to handle bursts of data without immediate processing.

Example: Buffered channel:

```
package main

import "fmt"

func main() {
    ch := make(chan string, 3) // Buffered channel with capacity 3

    ch <- "Message 1"
    ch <- "Message 2"
    ch <- "Message 3"

    fmt.Println(<-ch) // Receives "Message 1"
    fmt.Println(<-ch) // Receives "Message 2"
    fmt.Println(<-ch) // Receives "Message 3"
}
```

Output:

```
Message 1
Message 2
Message 3
```

Explanation:

- The buffered channel allows the sender to enqueue three messages without waiting for a receiver.
- The receiver retrieves the messages one by one from the buffer.

Comparing unbuffered and buffered channels

The following table shows the key differences between unbuffered and buffered channels:

Aspect	Unbuffered channel	Buffered channel
Storage capacity	No storage; requires simultaneous send/receive.	Stores up to a defined capacity.
Blocking behavior	Sender and receiver block until the other is ready.	Sender blocks only when the buffer is full.
Decoupling	No decoupling; tightly synchronizes goroutines.	Decouples sender and receiver.
Use cases	Immediate handoff, synchronization.	Burst handling, decoupled processing.
Performance	Slower if synchronization is not needed.	Faster when bursts of data need temporary storage.

***Table 10.1**: Unbuffered channel vs. buffered channel*

Let us look at some advanced examples.

Handling bursts of data with buffered channels:

```
package main

import (
    "fmt"
    "time"
```

```
)

func producer(ch chan int) {
    for i := 1; i <= 5; i++ {
        fmt.Printf("Produced: %d\n", i)
        ch <- i
        time.Sleep(500 * time.Millisecond)
    }
    close(ch)
}

func consumer(ch chan int) {
    for data := range ch {
        fmt.Printf("Consumed: %d\n", data)
        time.Sleep(time.Second)
    }
}

func main() {
    ch := make(chan int, 3)

    go producer(ch)
    consumer(ch)
}
```

Output:

```
Produced: 1
Produced: 2
Produced: 3
Consumed: 1
Produced: 4
Consumed: 2
Produced: 5
Consumed: 3
Consumed: 4
Consumed: 5
```

Explanation: The buffered channel temporarily stores data, allowing the producer to continue generating values even when the consumer is slower.

Let us understand deadlocks in channels.

Deadlock with unbuffered channel

A deadlock occurs when neither the sender nor the receiver can proceed:

```
package main

func main() {
```

```
    ch := make(chan int)
    ch <- 42 // Deadlock: No receiver to accept the value
}
```

Deadlock with buffered channel

A deadlock can also occur when the buffer is full:

```
package main

func main() {
    ch := make(chan int, 1)
    ch <- 42
    ch <- 43 // Deadlock: Buffer is full, no receiver to consume values
}
```

The following solutions will be generated:

- Always have corresponding senders and receivers.
- Use close to indicate no more data will be sent.

Best practices

The best practices for choosing channel types are as follows:

- **Use unbuffered channels when**:
    - You need immediate synchronization between sender and receiver.
    - Data must be processed as soon as it is produced.
- **Use buffered channels when**:
    - You want to decouple the sender and receiver.
    - The producer generates bursts of data, and the consumer processes it at a slower pace.
- **Avoid excessive buffer sizes**: Choose an appropriate buffer size to balance performance and memory usage.

Sending and receiving data from channels in Go

In Go, channels serve as the conduit for safely passing data between goroutines. Mastering how to send and receive data through channels is essential to building robust concurrent applications. This section explores the core mechanisms, behaviors, and best practices for working with channels, ensuring seamless synchronization and communication in your Go programs.

Channels in Go facilitate communication between goroutines by allowing the transfer of data in a type-safe manner. Sending and receiving operations are core to working with channels and are critical for implementing concurrency patterns effectively.

Sending data to a channel

Channels enable safe communication between goroutines by allowing one routine to send data while another receives it. Sending data to a channel helps synchronize concurrent operations and prevents race conditions. This mechanism forms the foundation of Go's concurrency model, promoting structured and reliable parallel execution.

Syntax:

```
channelName <- value
```

- The **<-** operator sends the value into the specified channel.
- The sender blocks until another goroutine is ready to receive the value if the channel is unbuffered or the buffer is full.

Example: Sending data:

```
package main

import "fmt"

func sender(ch chan int) {
    ch <- 42 // Send data into the channel
    fmt.Println("Data sent to the channel")
}

func main() {
    ch := make(chan int)
    go sender(ch)

    data := <-ch // Receive the data
    fmt.Println("Data received:", data)
}
```

Output:

```
Data sent to the channel
Data received: 42
```

Receiving data from a channel

Let us look at the details:

Syntax:

```
value := <-channelName
```

- The <- operator receives a value from the channel.
- The receiver blocks until data is available in the channel.

Example: Receiving data:

```
package main

import "fmt"

func receiver(ch chan string) {
    data := <-ch // Receive data from the channel
    fmt.Println("Data received:", data)
}

func main() {
```

```
    ch := make(chan string)
    go receiver(ch)

    ch <- "Hello, Go!" // Send data to the channel
    fmt.Println("Data sent to the channel")
}
```

Output:

```
Data received: Hello, Go!
Data sent to the channel
```

Blocking nature of send and receive

One of the defining features of Go channels is their synchronous, blocking behavior. Unlike other communication mechanisms, channel operations wait for a corresponding send or receive, making them powerful for coordinating goroutine execution.

Understanding how and when blocking occurs is crucial to writing predictable and deadlock-free concurrent programs, as follows:

- **Sender blocks**: The sender blocks if no goroutine is ready to receive the value (for unbuffered channels) or if the channel buffer is full (for buffered channels).
- **Receiver blocks**: The receiver blocks if no data is available in the channel.

Example of blocking behavior:

```
package main

import "fmt"

func main() {
    ch := make(chan int)

    // This will block until a receiver is ready
    go func() {
        fmt.Println("Sending data...")
        ch <- 100
        fmt.Println("Data sent")
    }()

    fmt.Println("Receiving data...")
    data := <-ch // Blocks until data is received
    fmt.Println("Data received:", data)
}
```

Output:

```
Receiving data...
Sending data...
Data sent
Data received: 100
```

Non-blocking channel operations

Using select with a default case: The select statement with a default case allows non-blocking operations on channels.

Example: Non-blocking send:

```
package main

import "fmt"

func main() {
    ch := make(chan int)

    select {
    case ch <- 42:
        fmt.Println("Data sent successfully")
    default:
        fmt.Println("Channel is not ready for sending")
    }
}
```

Example: Non-blocking receives:

```
package main

import "fmt"

func main() {
    ch := make(chan int)

    select {
    case data := <-ch:
        fmt.Println("Data received:", data)
    default:
        fmt.Println("No data available in the channel")
    }
}
```

Using range to receive data: The **range** keyword iterates over values sent on a channel until the channel is closed.

Example: Iterating over a channel:

```
package main

import "fmt"

func sender(ch chan int) {
    for i := 1; i <= 5; i++ {
        ch <- i
    }
```

```
    close(ch) // Close the channel to signal no more data
}

func main() {
    ch := make(chan int)
    go sender(ch)

    for data := range ch {
        fmt.Println("Received:", data)
    }

    fmt.Println("Channel closed, no more data")
}
```

Output:

```
Received: 1
Received: 2
Received: 3
Received: 4
Received: 5
Channel closed, no more data
```

Error handling in send and receive

Checking if a channel is closed:

- When receiving data, you can use the comma-**ok** idiom to check if the channel is closed.

  `value, ok := <-channelName`
- **ok** is false if the channel is closed.

Example: Handling a closed channel:

```
package main

import "fmt"

func main() {
    ch := make(chan int)
    close(ch) // Close the channel

    value, ok := <-ch
    if !ok {
        fmt.Println("Channel is closed")
    } else {
        fmt.Println("Received:", value)
    }
}
```

Output:

```
Channel is closed
```

Deadlock scenarios

The scenarios are as follows:

- **Scenario 1**: **No receiver**: If no goroutine is ready to receive data, sending to an unbuffered channel will result in a deadlock.

```
package main

func main() {
    ch := make(chan int)
    ch <- 42 // Deadlock: No receiver is ready
}
```

- **Scenario 2**: **No sender**: If no goroutine sends data, receiving from an unbuffered channel will result in a deadlock.

```
package main

func main() {
    ch := make(chan int)
    data := <-ch // Deadlock: No sender is ready
    println(data)
}
```

Solution: Always ensure there is a corresponding sender or receiver.

Combine send and receive in real-world applications, as follows:

```
package main

import (
    "fmt"
    "time"
)

func producer(ch chan int) {
    for i := 1; i <= 5; i++ {
        fmt.Printf("Producing: %d\n", i)
        ch <- i
        time.Sleep(500 * time.Millisecond)
    }
    close(ch)
}

func consumer(ch chan int) {
    for data := range ch {
        fmt.Printf("Consuming: %d\n", data)
        time.Sleep(time.Second)
    }
}
```

```
func main() {
    ch := make(chan int, 2)

    go producer(ch)
    consumer(ch)
}
```

Output:

```
Producing: 1
Producing: 2
Consuming: 1
Producing: 3
Consuming: 2
Producing: 4
Consuming: 3
Consuming: 4
Consuming: 5
```

Best practices

The best practices for sending and receiving data are as follows:

- **Ensure corresponding operations**: Always have a sender and receiver to avoid deadlocks.
- **Use buffered channels for bursts**: For high-frequency data, use buffered channels to prevent blocking.
- **Close channels when done**: Signal the end of data transmission by closing the channel.
- **Handle blocking carefully**: Be mindful of blocking behavior in unbuffered channels.
- **Use range for iteration**: Iterate over channels using range for simplicity when receiving multiple values.

Channel direction in Go

In Go, channels can be restricted to a specific direction: send-only, receive-only, or bidirectional. By defining the direction of a channel, you can enforce clear communication patterns between goroutines, enhancing code clarity and preventing accidental misuse.

Types of channel directions

In Go, channels can be directionally constrained to enhance code safety and clarity. While the default channel is bidirectional, Go also supports send-only and receive-only channels, allowing developers to explicitly specify how a channel should be used in a function or goroutine. Understanding these types helps prevent unintended usage and improves the design of concurrent programs:

- **Bidirectional channels**:
  - A bidirectional channel allows both sending and receiving of data.
  - This is the default type of channel when declared and created.

  Syntax:

  ```
  var ch chan int
  ```

Example:

```
package main

import "fmt"

func main() {
    ch := make(chan string) // Bidirectional channel

    go func() {
        ch <- "Hello, Go!" // Sending data
    }()

    msg := <-ch // Receiving data
    fmt.Println("Message:", msg)
}
```

- **Send-only channels:**
  - A send-only channel restricts the channel to sending data.
  - Declared using the **`chan<- type`**.

Syntax:

```
var sendOnly chan<- int
```

Example:

```
package main

import "fmt"

func sendData(ch chan<- string) {
    ch <- "Sending to a send-only channel"
}

func main() {
    ch := make(chan string)

    go sendData(ch) // Pass the channel as send-only
    fmt.Println(<-ch) // Receive data
}
```

Output:

```
Sending to a send-only channel
```

- **Receive-only channels:**
  - A receive-only channel restricts the channel to receiving data.
  - Declared using the **`<-chan type`**.

Syntax:

```
var receiveOnly <-chan int
```

Example:

```
package main

import "fmt"

func receiveData(ch <-chan string) {
    fmt.Println("Received:", <-ch)
}

func main() {
    ch := make(chan string)

    go func() {
        ch <- "Hello from send goroutine"
    }()

    receiveData(ch) // Pass the channel as receive-only
}
```

Output:

```
Received: Hello from send goroutine
```

The benefits of using directional channels are as follows:

- **Improved code clarity**: Clearly indicates how a channel is intended to be used.
- **Prevents misuse**: Ensures channels are used only in their designated roles.
- **Encourages modularity**: Promotes separation of responsibilities in concurrent systems.

Converting bidirectional to directional

You can pass a bidirectional channel as either a send-only or receive-only channel to a function or goroutine.

Example:

```
package main

import "fmt"

func sender(ch chan<- int) {
    ch <- 42 // Send data
}

func receiver(ch <-chan int) {
    fmt.Println("Received:", <-ch) // Receive data
}

func main() {
    ch := make(chan int)
```

```
    go sender(ch)    // Pass as send-only
    go receiver(ch) // Pass as receive-only
}
```

Output:

```
Received: 42
```

Let us cover some of the common mistake with directional channels:

- **Misinterpreting directionality**:
  - Directionality applies only to the function parameter, not the channel itself.
  - **Example**:

    ```
    var ch chan int
    ch = (chan<- int)(ch) // Compile error: cannot convert
    ```

- **Attempting to use in both directions**: Directional channels cannot be used for both sending and receiving.

Combining directional channels with goroutines

Example: Producer-consumer with directional channels:

```
package main

import "fmt"

func producer(ch chan<- int) {
    for i := 1; i <= 5; i++ {
        ch <- i
        fmt.Println("Produced:", i)
    }
    close(ch)
}

func consumer(ch <-chan int) {
    for data := range ch {
        fmt.Println("Consumed:", data)
    }
}

func main() {
    ch := make(chan int)

    go producer(ch)
    consumer(ch)
}
```

Output:

```
Produced: 1
Consumed: 1
Produced: 2
```

```
Consumed: 2
Produced: 3
Consumed: 3
Produced: 4
Consumed: 4
Produced: 5
Consumed: 5
```

Best practices

The best practices for using directional channels are as follows:

- **Define direction in function parameters**: Specify channel direction in function signatures to enforce roles.
- **Avoid overuse**: Use directional channels only when roles are clearly distinct.
- **Combine with goroutines**: Leverage directional channels to ensure safe and predictable communication in concurrent applications.

Go channel synchronization overview

Synchronization and blocking operations are fundamental aspects of Go's concurrency model. Channels inherently provide synchronization between goroutines by blocking either the sender or receiver until the operation can proceed. Understanding these concepts is critical for building efficient, deadlock-free, and synchronized concurrent programs.

Synchronization

Synchronization ensures that multiple goroutines coordinate their execution to share resources or communicate data safely and predictably. Channels in Go are designed to synchronize communication between goroutines without requiring explicit locking mechanisms.

Synchronization through unbuffered channels

Unbuffered channels provide automatic synchronization between the sender and receiver because both operations must occur simultaneously.

Example: Synchronizing goroutines:

```
package main

import (
    "fmt"
    "time"
)

func worker(id int, ch chan int) {
    fmt.Printf("Worker %d waiting for task\n", id)
    task := <-ch // Waits for a task to be sent
    fmt.Printf("Worker %d processing task %d\n", id, task)
}

func main() {
```

```
    ch := make(chan int)

    for i := 1; i <= 3; i++ {
        go worker(i, ch)
    }

    for task := 1; task <= 3; task++ {
        fmt.Printf("Sending task %d\n", task)
        ch <- task // Sends tasks to workers
        time.Sleep(time.Second)
    }
}
```

Output:

```
Worker 1 waiting for task
Worker 2 waiting for task
Worker 3 waiting for task
Sending task 1
Worker 1 processing task 1
Sending task 2
Worker 2 processing task 2
Sending task 3
Worker 3 processing task 3
```

Synchronization through buffered channels

Buffered channels provide limited capacity to hold data, allowing senders to proceed without waiting for immediate receivers if the buffer is not full.

Example: Synchronizing with buffered channels:

```
package main

import (
    "fmt"
    "time"
)

func worker(ch chan int) {
    for task := range ch {
        fmt.Printf("Processing task %d\n", task)
        time.Sleep(time.Second) // Simulate work
    }
    fmt.Println("Worker completed")
}

func main() {
    ch := make(chan int, 2) // Buffered channel with capacity 2
```

```
    go worker(ch)

    for task := 1; task <= 5; task++ {
        fmt.Printf("Sending task %d\n", task)
        ch <- task
    }

    close(ch) // Close the channel to signal no more tasks
}
```

Output:

```
 Sending task 1
 Sending task 2
 Processing task 1
 Sending task 3
 Processing task 2
 Processing task 3
 Processing task 4
 Processing task 5
Worker completed
```

Explanation: The buffer allows the first two tasks to be sent without waiting for a receiver, while subsequent tasks block until the buffer has space.

Select for non-blocking synchronization

The select statement enables non-blocking operations by monitoring multiple channels.

Example: Non-blocking with select:

```
package main

import "fmt"

func main() {
    ch := make(chan int, 1)
    ch <- 42

    select {
    case data := <-ch:
        fmt.Println("Received:", data)
    default:
        fmt.Println("No data available")
    }
}
```

Output:

```
 Received: 42
```

Synchronization with close

Closing a channel is another way to synchronize goroutines, signaling that no more data will be sent.

Example: Using **`close`** for synchronization

```
package main

import "fmt"

func main() {
    ch := make(chan int)

    go func() {
        for i := 1; i <= 3; i++ {
            ch <- i
        }
        close(ch) // Close the channel
    }()

    for data := range ch { // Receive until the channel is closed
        fmt.Println("Received:", data)
    }

    fmt.Println("All data received")
}
```

Output:

```
Received: 1
Received: 2
Received: 3
All data received
```

Common synchronization scenarios

Goroutine coordination: Channels are often used with **`sync.WaitGroup`** for coordinating goroutines.

Example:

```
package main

import (
    "fmt"
    "sync"
)

func worker(id int, ch chan int, wg *sync.WaitGroup) {
    defer wg.Done() // Decrement counter when done
    for task := range ch {
```

```
        fmt.Printf("Worker %d processing task %d\n", id, task)
    }
}

func main() {
    var wg sync.WaitGroup
    ch := make(chan int)

    for i := 1; i <= 3; i++ {
        wg.Add(1)
        go worker(i, ch, &wg)
    }

    for task := 1; task <= 5; task++ {
        ch <- task
    }
    close(ch) // Close channel to signal no more tasks

    wg.Wait() // Wait for all workers to complete
    fmt.Println("All workers completed")
}
```

Best practices

The best practices for synchronization and blocking are as follows:

- **Avoid deadlocks**: Ensure there is a corresponding sender or receiver for every channel operation.
- **Use buffered channels wisely**: Choose buffer sizes based on expected workloads to avoid unnecessary blocking.
- **Leverage select**: Use select for handling multiple channels or adding timeouts.
- **Close channels properly**: Close channels to signal that no more data will be sent.
- **Combine with WaitGroup**: Use `sync.WaitGroup` alongside channels for better control of goroutine completion.

Conclusion

In this chapter, we explored the core concept of channels in Go and how they enable safe and structured communication between goroutines. We examined the differences between buffered and unbuffered channels, learned how to send and receive data, and understood the blocking nature of channel operations. We also looked into directional channels, synchronization strategies, and best practices to avoid common pitfalls like deadlocks and misuse of closed channels. With practical examples and detailed explanations, you are now equipped to leverage channels effectively for orchestrating concurrent workflows.

The next chapter introduces two powerful tools in Go's concurrency toolkit: select statements and timers. These constructs allow programs to wait on multiple channel operations simultaneously and manage time-based events, such as timeouts and scheduled execution. Building on your understanding of channels, you will now learn how to write more responsive, flexible, and time-aware concurrent applications using these advanced patterns.

Questions

1. What are the key differences between buffered and unbuffered channels in Go, and when should each be used?
2. How does Go's channel mechanism ensure safe and synchronized communication between goroutines?
3. Explain the blocking behavior of send and receive operations on both buffered and unbuffered channels.
4. What is a directional channel in Go, and how does it help improve safety and clarity in concurrent programs?
5. Describe a scenario that could lead to a deadlock in channel-based communication and suggest strategies to avoid it.
6. How can the range keyword be used to receive data from channels, and what role does channel closure play in this context?
7. What are the benefits of using the select statement with channels, especially in non-blocking operations?
8. What best practices should be followed when sending, receiving, and closing channels to avoid panics and synchronization issues?
9. How do Go channels help eliminate the need for explicit locking mechanisms like mutexes?
10. In what ways can sync.WaitGroup be combined with channels to manage synchronization of goroutines effectively?

Chapter 11
Select Statements and Timers

Introduction

In Go, building responsive and robust concurrent programs often requires monitoring multiple communication channels and reacting to time-based events. The select statement, along with timers and tickers from the time package, provides a clean and efficient way to manage such scenarios. Whether you are handling asynchronous messages, implementing timeouts, or performing periodic actions, these constructs allow your programs to remain non-blocking and well-structured. This chapter introduces the select statement, explores its use with channels, and demonstrates how to combine it with timers, tickers, and graceful shutdown techniques to create time-aware and resilient applications.

Structure

- Select statement for channels
- Timeouts and non-blocking operations in Go
- Timer and ticker functions in Go
- Graceful shutdowns using channels in Go

Objectives

By the end of this chapter, you will be able to use Go's select statement to manage multiple channel operations concurrently. You will learn how to implement timeouts using time. After, perform scheduled tasks with tickers, and build non-blocking logic using default cases. Additionally, you will gain practical skills in designing graceful shutdown mechanisms, handling OS signals, and preventing deadlocks, making their Go applications more reliable and production ready.

Select statement for channels

The **`select`** statement in Go provides an elegant solution for managing multiple channel operations within a single control structure. Whether you are receiving data from different sources, sending updates, or reacting to timeouts, select enables your program to remain responsive and organized. This feature is especially valuable in concurrent systems where multiple communication paths need to be monitored simultaneously.

Overview of the select statement

In Go, the **`select`** statement is a powerful construct that enables a goroutine to wait on multiple channel operations simultaneously. It allows the program to handle communication from multiple channels in a concise and non-blocking way. Similar to a **`switch`** statement for channels, **`select`** executes the first available case that is ready. The power of **`select`** lies in its ability to block until at least one of the specified channel operations can proceed. It enables a goroutine to listen to multiple channels without writing verbose if-else or switch-case constructs. The **select** block waits until one of its cases can run, and executes that case immediately, ensuring efficient synchronization and communication across goroutines.

Syntax of select

The basic syntax of the **select** statement is as follows:

```
select {
case value := <-channel1:
    // Handle data received from channel1
case channel2 <- value:
    // Send data to channel2
default:
    // Execute if no other case is ready
}
```

Before exploring examples, let us understand the structure of a **select** block and how different cases define the behavior for communication over channels:

- Each case represents a channel operation (send or receive).
- The default case executes immediately if none of the channels are ready, preventing blocking.

Characteristics of select

The **select** statement is packed with several key characteristics that make it a fundamental construct in concurrent programming with Go. These characteristics include:

- **Non-blocking**: Select blocks execution only if no channels are ready and there is no default case.
- **Randomized execution**: If multiple cases are ready, one is selected at random to prevent starvation.
- **Concurrent channel handling**: Enables efficient management of multiple channels, making it ideal for multiplexing.

Using select for multiple receives

One of the most common use cases for **select** is to receive messages from multiple channels. This helps in building responsive applications that deal with asynchronous data.

Example: Handling multiple channels:

```
package main

import (
    "fmt"
    "time"
)

func main() {
    ch1 := make(chan string)
    ch2 := make(chan string)

    // Simulate data being sent to channels
    go func() {
```

```
        time.Sleep(1 * time.Second)
        ch1 <- "Data from Channel 1"
    }()
    go func() {
        time.Sleep(2 * time.Second)
        ch2 <- "Data from Channel 2"
    }()

    for i := 0; i < 2; i++ {
        select {
        case msg1 := <-ch1:
            fmt.Println("Received:", msg1)
        case msg2 := <-ch2:
            fmt.Println("Received:", msg2)
        }
    }
}
```

Expected output:

- `Received: Data from Channel 1`
- `Received: Data from Channel 2`

Using select for send and receive operations

Select can handle both sending and receiving operations, making it useful for bidirectional communication.

Example: Send and receive:

```
package main

import "fmt"

func main() {
    ch1 := make(chan int, 1)
    ch2 := make(chan int, 1)

    select {
    case ch1 <- 42: // Send data to ch1
        fmt.Println("Sent data to ch1")
    case ch2 <- 84: // Send data to ch2
        fmt.Println("Sent data to ch2")
    case data := <-ch1: // Receive data from ch1
        fmt.Println("Received from ch1:", data)
    case data := <-ch2: // Receive data from ch2
        fmt.Println("Received from ch2:", data)
    default:
        fmt.Println("No channel ready")
    }
}
```

Following is the output:

- Sent data to ch1

Combining select for continuous monitoring

The **select** statement can be combined with a for loop to continuously monitor multiple channels.

Example: Continuous channel monitoring:

```
package main

import (
    "fmt"
    "time"
)

func main() {
    ch1 := make(chan string)
    ch2 := make(chan string)

    go func() {
        for {
            ch1 <- "Ping from Channel 1"
            time.Sleep(1 * time.Second)
        }
    }()

    go func() {
        for {
            ch2 <- "Ping from Channel 2"
            time.Sleep(2 * time.Second)
        }
    }()

    for {
        select {
        case msg1 := <-ch1:
            fmt.Println(msg1)
        case msg2 := <-ch2:
            fmt.Println(msg2)
        }
    }
}
```

Expected output:

- Ping from channel 1
- Ping from channel 1
- Ping from channel 2

- Ping from channel 1
- Ping from channel 1
- Ping from channel 2

Using select for channel multiplexing

Multiplexing refers to the ability to manage data from multiple channels simultaneously.

Example: Channel multiplexing:

```
package main

import (
    "fmt"
    "time"
)

func sender(id int, ch chan<- string) {
    for i := 0; i < 3; i++ {
        ch <- fmt.Sprintf("Message %d from Sender %d", i, id)
        time.Sleep(time.Second)
    }
}

func main() {
    ch1 := make(chan string)
    ch2 := make(chan string)

    go sender(1, ch1)
    go sender(2, ch2)

    for i := 0; i < 6; i++ {
        select {
        case msg1 := <-ch1:
            fmt.Println("Received:", msg1)
        case msg2 := <-ch2:
            fmt.Println("Received:", msg2)
        }
    }
}
```

Expected output:

- Received: Message 0 from sender 1
- Received: Message 0 from sender 2
- Received: Message 1 from sender 1
- Received: Message 1 from sender 2
- Received: Message 2 from sender 1
- Received: Message 2 from sender 2

Handling timeouts with select

The **select** statement can be combined with Go's **time.After** implementing timeouts for channel operations.

Example: Timeout handling:

```
package main

import (
    "fmt"
    "time"
)

func main() {
    ch := make(chan string)

    go func() {
        time.Sleep(2 * time.Second)
        ch <- "Data received after 2 seconds"
    }()

    select {
    case msg := <-ch:
        fmt.Println(msg)
    case <-time.After(1 * time.Second):
        fmt.Println("Timeout: No data received")
    }
}
```

Following is the output:

- `Timeout: No data received`

Advantages of select in channel operations

Go's **select** construct provides a number of advantages when handling concurrent communication between goroutines using channels.

Let us discuss some of them as follows:

- **Concurrent channel handling**: Allows efficient monitoring and interaction with multiple channels.
- **Prevents deadlocks**: With proper use of default and timeouts, it helps avoid blocking indefinitely.
- **Dynamic behavior**: Supports conditional execution based on channel readiness.
- **Simplifies complex logic**: Reduces the complexity of handling multiple channels in separate goroutines.

Best practices

While using **select**, adhering to best practices can help ensure that your concurrent programs remain robust, readable, and efficient. Let us see some of them as follows:

- **Use default for non-blocking logic**: Avoid blocking when immediate processing is required.
- **Combine with time.After for timeouts**: Ensure operations are bounded by time to prevent indefinite waiting.

- **Handle multiple channels carefully**: Prioritize channel handling based on application needs.
- **Monitor channel closures**: Use range loops or **ok** checks to handle closed channels gracefully.

Timeouts and non-blocking operations in Go

When designing responsive systems, Go's timeout and non-blocking capabilities become essential tools for handling delays and avoiding deadlocks in concurrent operations.

Overview

Timeouts and non-blocking operations are essential in concurrent programming to ensure responsiveness and prevent indefinite blocking. In Go, these can be efficiently implemented using channels, the select statement, and time-related functions from the time package. These allow developers to build responsive systems that do not freeze up while waiting for operations that may take too long or never complete. Whether waiting on user input, network I/O, or background tasks, timeouts and non-blocking operations ensure continued progress and safe fallback behavior. timeouts in Go.

Timeouts define a maximum duration a goroutine waits for a task to complete. If the operation exceeds this duration, the program executes alternative logic (for example, aborting the task or logging a timeout). Timeouts allow you to define how long your program should wait before moving on. This is particularly useful when interacting with external systems like APIs or databases that may be slow to respond.

Following are the use cases:

- **Network communication**: Abort a network request if the server does not respond within a specified time.
- **Task completion**: Enforce limits on long-running tasks to avoid resource blocking.
- **User interaction**: Set time limits for user responses in real-time applications.

Implementing timeouts using time.After

The **time.After** function returns a channel that sends the current time after a specified duration.

Following is a syntax:

```
time.After(duration)
```

Example: Timeout with select:

```
package main

import (
    "fmt"
    "time"
)

func main() {
    ch := make(chan string)

    go func() {
        time.Sleep(3 * time.Second)
        ch <- "Task completed"
    }()
```

```
    select {
    case msg := <-ch:
        fmt.Println(msg)
    case <-time.After(2 * time.Second):
        fmt.Println("Timeout: Task took too long")
    }
}
```

Following is the output:

- `Timeout: Task took too long`

Following are the explanations:

- The **`time.After`** channel sends a signal after 2 seconds.
- If the task takes more than 2 seconds, the timeout case executes.

Non-blocking operations with select

Non-blocking operations ensure that a program can proceed even if a channel operation cannot be completed immediately. Non-blocking operations are particularly helpful in applications that must keep running other logic without waiting for channel operations to end. With the default clause in a select block, Go enables a safe way to try channel communication without stalling the program.

Using select with default

The **`default`** case in a **`select`** statement is executed if no other case is ready.

Example: Non-blocking send:

```
package main

import "fmt"

func main() {
    ch := make(chan int)

    select {
    case ch <- 42:
        fmt.Println("Data sent")
    default:
        fmt.Println("Channel not ready for sending")
    }
}
```

Following is the output:

- `Channel not ready for sending`

Example: Non-blocking receive:

```
package main

import "fmt"
```

```
func main() {
    ch := make(chan int)

    select {
    case data := <-ch:
        fmt.Println("Data received:", data)
    default:
        fmt.Println("No data available in the channel")
    }
}
```

Following is the output:

- `No data available in the channel`

Combining timeouts with non-blocking operations

By combining **`select`**, **`default`**, and **`time.After`**, you can design flexible, time-sensitive logic.

Example: Timeout with default non-blocking case:

```
package main

import (
    "fmt"
    "time"
)

func main() {
    ch := make(chan string)

    go func() {
        time.Sleep(3 * time.Second)
        ch <- "Task completed"
    }()

    for {
        select {
        case msg := <-ch:
            fmt.Println("Received:", msg)
            return
        case <-time.After(1 * time.Second):
            fmt.Println("Still waiting...")
        default:
            fmt.Println("Processing other tasks...")
            time.Sleep(500 * time.Millisecond)
        }
    }
}
```

Expected output:

```
• Processing other tasks...
• Processing other tasks...
• Processing other tasks...
• Processing other tasks...
• Received task completed
```

Following are the explanations:

- The program processes other tasks while waiting for data.
- If the timeout elapses, it logs `Still waiting...`
- Once data is received, the program exits.

Advantages of timeouts and non-blocking operations

By incorporating timeouts and non-blocking logic, your application becomes more resilient and better equipped to handle uncertainty and delays in communication, as follows:

- **Prevents deadlocks**: Ensures that the program does not hang indefinitely waiting for data.
- **Improves responsiveness**: Non-blocking operations allow the program to perform other tasks while waiting.
- **Efficient resource utilization**: Releases resources promptly when a task exceeds its allocated time.
- **Error handling**: Provides a mechanism to gracefully handle delays or failures.

Real-world use cases

The following real-world scenarios illustrate how timeouts and non-blocking operations can be used to improve system behavior in practical applications:

- **Network request timeout**: Abort a network request if it takes too long to respond.

  Example: Simulating a network request:

```
package main

import (
    "fmt"
    "time"
)

func networkRequest(ch chan string) {
    time.Sleep(3 * time.Second) // Simulate delay
    ch <- "Response received"
}

func main() {
    ch := make(chan string)

    go networkRequest(ch)
```

```
    select {
    case res := <-ch:
        fmt.Println(res)
    case <-time.After(2 * time.Second):
        fmt.Println("Timeout: Request took too long")
    }
}
```

Following is the output:

- `Timeout: Request took too long`

- **Non-blocking queue processing**: Process tasks in a queue without waiting indefinitely for new tasks.

  Example: Task queue:

```
package main

import (
    "fmt"
    "time"
)

func main() {
    tasks := make(chan string, 3)
    tasks <- "Task 1"
    tasks <- "Task 2"

    for {
        select {
        case task := <-tasks:
            fmt.Println("Processing:", task)
        default:
            fmt.Println("No tasks available")
            time.Sleep(1 * time.Second)
        }
    }
}
```

Expected output:

- `Processing-task 1`
- `Processing-task 2`
- `No tasks available`
- `No tasks available`

Common pitfalls

While using timeouts and non-blocking operations improves program responsiveness, developers must be aware of common mistakes that can introduce subtle bugs or inefficiencies. Some of them are discussed as follows:

- **Overusing non-blocking logic**: Excessive use of default can lead to missed data if the channel is ready later.

- **Improper timeout handling**: Setting timeouts too short may cause premature termination of tasks.
- **Ignoring deadlocks**: Ensure there are sufficient senders and receivers for channel operations.

Best practices

Using timeouts and non-blocking logic effectively helps in writing robust concurrent programs. The following are key practices to follow when designing systems that rely on timely communication:

- **Combine timeouts and non-blocking logic**: Use both to create robust, responsive systems.
- **Set reasonable timeouts**: A balance between responsiveness and task completion.
- **Handle errors gracefully**: Log or retry operations when a timeout occurs.
- **Monitor channel states**: Use select and default to avoid indefinite blocking.

Timer and ticker functions in Go

Go offers built-in tools for executing code based on timing events using timers and tickers. These are invaluable when you need delays, scheduled execution, or repeated actions.

Overview of timer and ticker

The time package in Go provides timer and ticker functions to manage operations based on time. These functions are essential for implementing delays, scheduling tasks, or performing repeated operations in a controlled manner.

Timer functions

A timer represents a single event in the future. It waits for a specified duration and sends a signal on its channel when the time expires. Timers provide a way to schedule a one-time action after a delay, making them useful for delayed task execution, retries, and time-based control flows, as follows:

- **Creating a timer**: The **`time.NewTimer`** function creates a new timer that sends the current time on its channel after the specified duration.

  Following is the syntax:

  ```
  timer := time.NewTimer(duration)
  ```

  Example: Basic timer usage:

  ```
  package main

  import (
      "fmt"
      "time"
  )

  func main() {
      timer := time.NewTimer(3 * time.Second)
      fmt.Println("Timer started...")

      <-timer.C // Blocks until the timer fires
      fmt.Println("Timer expired")
  }
  ```

Following are the outputs:

- `Timer started`
- `Timer expired`

- **Using time.After**: **`time.After`** is a simplified alternative to **`NewTimer`**. It returns a channel that sends the current time after the specified duration.

  Example: Using **`time.After`**:

```
package main

import (
    "fmt"
    "time"
)

func main() {
    fmt.Println("Waiting for 2 seconds...")
    <-time.After(2 * time.Second)
    fmt.Println("2 seconds passed")
}
```

  Expected output:

  - `Waiting for 2 seconds`
  - `2 seconds passed`

  Following is the key difference:

  - **`NewTimer`** provides more control (for example, stopping or resetting the timer) than **`time.After`**.

- **Stopping a timer**: Timers can be stopped to prevent them from firing.

  Example: Stopping a timer:

```
package main

import (
 "fmt"
 "time"
)

func main() {
 timer := time.NewTimer(5 * time.Second)
 done := make(chan bool)

 go func() {
  time.Sleep(2 * time.Second)
  if timer.Stop() {
   fmt.Println("Timer stopped")
  }
  done <- true // Signal that the timer has been stopped
 }()
```

```
    select {
    case <-timer.C:
     fmt.Println("Timer expired")
    case <-done:
     fmt.Println("Timer was stopped before expiring")
    }
  }
```

Expected output:

- Timer stopped
- Timer was stopped before expiring

- **Resetting a timer**: A timer can be reset to change its duration.

  Example: Resetting a timer:

```
package main

import (
    "fmt"
    "time"
)

func main() {
    timer := time.NewTimer(3 * time.Second)
    fmt.Println("Timer set for 3 seconds")

    timer.Reset(1 * time.Second)
    fmt.Println("Timer reset to 1 second")

    <-timer.C
    fmt.Println("Timer expired")
}
```

Expected output:

- Timer set for 3 seconds
- Timer reset to 1 second
- Timer expired

Ticker functions

A ticker is used to repeatedly execute tasks at regular intervals. It sends the current time on its channel after every specified duration. Tickers enable periodic execution of tasks at fixed intervals. They are ideal for activities such as status polling, periodic data collection, or scheduled updates, as follows:

- **Creating a ticker**: The **`time.NewTicker`** function creates a new ticker that sends a value on its channel at regular intervals.

  Following is the syntax:

```
ticker := time.NewTicker(duration)
```

Example: Basic ticker usage:

```
package main

import (
    "fmt"
    "time"
)

func main() {
    ticker := time.NewTicker(1 * time.Second)
    defer ticker.Stop()

    for i := 0; i < 5; i++ {
        <-ticker.C
        fmt.Println("Ticker ticked:", time.Now())
    }
}
```

Expected output:

- **Ticker ticked: 2025-01-05 13:24:32.4329388 +0530 IST m=+1.000644301**
- **Ticker ticked: 2025-01-05 13:24:33.4327872 +0530 IST m=+2.000492701**
- **Ticker ticked: 2025-01-05 13:24:34.432647 +0530 IST m=+3.000352501**
- **Ticker ticked: 2025-01-05 13:24:35.4326667 +0530 IST m=+4.000372201**
- **Ticker ticked: 2025-01-05 13:24:36.4327723 +0530 IST m=+5.000477801**

- **Stopping a ticker**: A ticker can be stopped using the stop method to release resources and stop sending ticks.

  Example: Stopping a ticker:

```
package main

import (
 "fmt"
 "time"
)

func main() {
 ticker := time.NewTicker(1 * time.Second)
 done := make(chan bool)

 go func() {
  time.Sleep(3 * time.Second)
  ticker.Stop()
  fmt.Println("Ticker stopped")
  done <- true // Notify main routine that the ticker has stopped
 }()
```

```
  for {
   select {
   case tick := <-ticker.C:
    fmt.Println("Tick at:", tick)
   case <-done:
    fmt.Println("Exiting ticker loop")
    return
   }
  }
 }
```

Expected output:

```
o    Tick at: 2025-01-05 13:25:25.2519776 +0530 IST m=+1.000000001
o    Tick at: 2025-01-05 13:25:26.2519776 +0530 IST m=+2.000000001
o    Ticker stopped
```

Differences between timer and ticker

Let us compare timers and tickers to understand when to use each based on the nature of the task whether it is a single delay or a recurring operation, as shown:

Aspect	Timer	Ticker
Purpose	Triggers once after a set duration.	Repeats at regular intervals.
Use case	Delayed execution or timeout.	Periodic execution of tasks.
Stop method	`timer.Stop()`	`ticker.Stop()`
Reset method	`timer.Reset(newDuration)`	Not available for Ticker.

***Table 11.1**: Ticker vs. timer*

Ticker and timer use cases

Timers and tickers are widely used in real-world applications to execute code after delays, schedule periodic work, or ensure graceful exits.

Let us look at a few practical examples:

- **Delayed task execution with timer**: Timers in Go are perfect for scheduling future tasks. When a delay is required before executing an operation, such as retrying an action or deferring execution, a timer can be used to trigger the action after a specified interval.

  Use a timer to execute a task after a specific delay, as follows:

```
package main

import (
    "fmt"
    "time"
)

func main() {
    fmt.Println("Task scheduled...")
```

```
    time.AfterFunc(2*time.Second, func() {
        fmt.Println("Task executed after 2 seconds")
    })

    time.Sleep(3 * time.Second) // Wait to observe the timer execution
}
```

Expected output:

- `Task scheduled`
- `Task executed after 2 seconds`

- **Periodic task execution with ticker**: Tickers are useful when tasks need to be executed at regular intervals, such as polling services, updating dashboards, or generating periodic events in your application.

  Use a ticker to execute a task periodically, as follows:

```
package main

import (
    "fmt"
    "time"
)

func main() {
    ticker := time.NewTicker(1 * time.Second)
    defer ticker.Stop()

    for i := 0; i < 3; i++ {
        <-ticker.C
        fmt.Println("Task executed at:", time.Now())
    }
}
```

Expected output:

- `Task executed at: 2025-01-05 13:30:29.0482316 +0530 IST m=+1.001123701`
- `Task executed at: 2025-01-05 13:30:30.0474043 +0530 IST m=+2.000296401`
- `Task executed at: 2025-01-05 13:30:31.0475727 +0530 IST m=+3.000464801`

- **Graceful shutdown with timer**: Timers can also be leveraged for timeout-based shutdowns. When a task or service needs to finish within a certain time, a timer ensures that the system shuts down gracefully if the task takes too long.

  Use a timer to enforce a shutdown timeout, as follows:

```
package main

import (
    "fmt"
    "time"
)

func main() {
```

```
    done := make(chan bool)
    go func() {
        time.Sleep(3 * time.Second)
        done <- true
    }()

    select {
    case <-done:
        fmt.Println("Task completed within time")
    case <-time.After(2 * time.Second):
        fmt.Println("Timeout: Task took too long")
    }
}
```

Following is the output:

```
o   Timeout: Task took too long
```

Best practices for timer and timer functions

To make the most of Go's timing constructs, developers should follow best practices for managing resources, ensuring correctness, and avoiding leaks or unnecessary delays, as follows:

- **Stop timers and tickers**: Always call `Stop` to release resources when a timer or ticker is no longer needed. Long-running tasks triggered by timers or tickers must be designed carefully to avoid conflicts or missed intervals. The tips ensure clean and consistent behavior.
- **Handle long-running ticks**: Ensure the interval between ticks allows sufficient time for task execution.
- **Avoid overlapping tasks**: Use synchronization mechanisms to prevent multiple tick executions from overlapping.
- **Use defer for cleanup**: Ensure timers and tickers are stopped using defer to prevent leaks.

Graceful shutdowns using channels in Go

Graceful shutdowns are essential in applications that maintain long-lived connections or manage multiple concurrent operations. Channels provide a clean way to coordinate termination signals and ensure orderly exits.

Overview on graceful shutdown

Graceful shutdowns ensure that a program terminates cleanly, releasing resources, closing connections, and completing ongoing tasks without abrupt interruptions. In Go, channels play a crucial role in implementing graceful shutdowns by signaling goroutines to stop work and clean up resources.

Importance of graceful shutdowns

Graceful shutdowns are not just about cleaning up; they are critical for avoiding issues like resource leaks, data loss, and interrupted services.

The following points highlight their significance:

- **Prevent resource leaks**: Ensure that file handles, database connections, and other resources are properly closed.
- **Avoid data loss**: Complete pending tasks or flush buffered data before exiting.
- **Handling interrupt signals**: Respond to OS-level termination signals like SIGINT or SIGTERM.

Note: SIGINT and SIGTERM are two common operating system signals used to gracefully stop running processes.

Here is a quick explanation:

- **SIGINT (signal interrupt)**:
  - Triggered when the user presses *Ctrl+C* in the terminal.
  - Allows the program to perform cleanup before exiting (e.g., closing files, shutting down goroutines).
- **SIGTERM (signal terminate)**:
  - A termination signal sent by the operating system or another process using the kill command (e.g., `kill <pid>`).
  - It also requests the program to stop.
  - Minimize disruptions in systems with long running or critical tasks.

Using channels for graceful shutdowns

Go programs use channels to signal goroutines about shutdown events. This approach ensures all background tasks receive the signal and exit properly without abrupt interruption.

Shutdown signal channel

A dedicated channel can be used to signal goroutines to stop work and clean up.

Example: Basic shutdown mechanism:

```
package main

import (
    "fmt"
    "time"
)

func worker(shutdown chan bool) {
    for {
        select {
        case <-shutdown:
            fmt.Println("Worker shutting down")
            return
        default:
            fmt.Println("Worker is running...")
            time.Sleep(1 * time.Second)
        }
    }
}

func main() {
    shutdown := make(chan bool)

    go worker(shutdown)
```

```
    time.Sleep(5 * time.Second) // Simulate work
    fmt.Println("Sending shutdown signal")
    shutdown <- true // Signal the worker to stop
}
```

Expected output:

- Worker is running
- Worker is running
- Worker is running
- Worker is running
- Worker is running
- Sending shutdown signal
- Worker shutting down

Coordinating multiple goroutines

For programs with multiple goroutines, a broadcast mechanism using close ensures all goroutines receive the shutdown signal.

Example: Broadcast shutdown signal:

```
package main

import (
    "fmt"
    "sync"
    "time"
)

func worker(id int, shutdown chan struct{}, wg *sync.WaitGroup) {
    defer wg.Done()
    for {
        select {
        case <-shutdown:
            fmt.Printf("Worker %d shutting down\n", id)
            return
        default:
            fmt.Printf("Worker %d is running\n", id)
            time.Sleep(1 * time.Second)
        }
    }
}

func main() {
    var wg sync.WaitGroup
    shutdown := make(chan struct{}) // Signal channel
```

```
    for i := 1; i <= 3; i++ {
        wg.Add(1)
        go worker(i, shutdown, &wg)
    }

    time.Sleep(5 * time.Second) // Simulate work
    fmt.Println("Broadcasting shutdown signal")
    close(shutdown) // Signal all workers to stop

    wg.Wait()
    fmt.Println("All workers have stopped")
}
```

Expected output:

- **`Worker 1 is running`**
- **`Worker 2 is running`**
- **`Worker 3 is running`**
- **`Broadcasting shutdown signal`**
- **`Worker 1 shutting down`**
- **`Worker 2 shutting down`**
- **`Worker 3 shutting down`**
- **`All workers have stopped`**

Handling OS signals for shutdown

Go's os/signal package allows programs to handle OS-level termination signals like SIGINT (*Ctrl+C*) or SIGTERM. When you terminate the program manually with *Ctrl+C*, we get the following message: **`All workers have stopped`**, and the applications get gracefully terminated.

Example: Shutdown on OS signal:

```
package main

import (
    "fmt"
    "os"
    "os/signal"
    "sync"
    "syscall"
    "time"
)

func worker(id int, shutdown chan struct{}, wg *sync.WaitGroup) {
    defer wg.Done()
    for {
        select {
        case <-shutdown:
            fmt.Printf("Worker %d shutting down\n", id)
```

```
            return
        default:
            fmt.Printf("Worker %d is running\n", id)
            time.Sleep(1 * time.Second)
        }
    }
}

func main() {
    var wg sync.WaitGroup
    shutdown := make(chan struct{})

    for i := 1; i <= 2; i++ {
        wg.Add(1)
        go worker(i, shutdown, &wg)
    }

    // Handle OS signals
    sig := make(chan os.Signal, 1)
    signal.Notify(sig, syscall.SIGINT, syscall.SIGTERM)

    <-sig // Wait for termination signal
    fmt.Println("Received shutdown signal")
    close(shutdown) // Broadcast shutdown to workers

    wg.Wait()
    fmt.Println("All workers have stopped")
}
```

Expected output:

- `Worker 1 is running`
- `Worker 2 is running`
- `Worker 1 is running`
- `Worker 2 is running`
- `Received shutdown signal`
- `Worker 1 shutting down`
- `Worker 2 shutting down`
- `All workers have stopped`

Handling long-running tasks

Long-running tasks should regularly check the shutdown signal to ensure they terminate gracefully.

Example: Periodic check for shutdown signal:

```
package main

import (
```

```
 "fmt"
 "time"
)

func longTask(shutdown chan struct{}) {
 for i := 1; i <= 10; i++ {
  select {
  case <-shutdown:
   fmt.Println("Task interrupted, cleaning up")
   return
  case <-time.After(1 * time.Second): // Wait 1 second before the next step
   fmt.Printf("Processing step %d\n", i)
  }
 }
 fmt.Println("Task completed successfully")
}

func main() {
 shutdown := make(chan struct{})

 go longTask(shutdown)

 time.Sleep(5 * time.Second) // Simulate work
 fmt.Println("Sending shutdown signal")
 close(shutdown)

 // Allow some time for the cleanup message to print
 time.Sleep(1 * time.Second)
}
```

Expected output:

- **Processing step 1**
- **Processing step 2**
- **Processing step 3**
- **Processing step 4**
- **Sending shutdown signal**
- **Task interrupted, cleaning up**

Graceful shutdown in web servers

For web servers, gracefully shutting down includes closing active connections and completing in-flight requests.

Example: Web server graceful shutdown:

```
package main

import (
    "context"
```

```
	"fmt"
	"net/http"
	"os"
	"os/signal"
	"syscall"
	"time"
)

func main() {
	server := &http.Server{Addr: ":8080"}

	http.HandleFunc("/", func(w http.ResponseWriter, r *http.Request) {
		fmt.Fprintln(w, "Hello, World!")
	})

	go func() {
		if err := server.ListenAndServe(); err != http.ErrServerClosed {
			fmt.Printf("Server error: %v\n", err)
		}
	}()
	fmt.Println("Server started on port 8080")

	// Graceful shutdown on OS signals
	sig := make(chan os.Signal, 1)
	signal.Notify(sig, syscall.SIGINT, syscall.SIGTERM)

	<-sig
	fmt.Println("Received shutdown signal, shutting down server")

	ctx, cancel := context.WithTimeout(context.Background(), 5*time.Second)
	defer cancel()

	if err := server.Shutdown(ctx); err != nil {
		fmt.Printf("Error during shutdown: %v\n", err)
	}
	fmt.Println("Server gracefully stopped")
}
```

Expected output:

- **Server started on port 8080**
- **Received shutdown signal, shutting down server**
- **The server gracefully stopped**

Best practices for graceful shutdowns

When building concurrent applications, it is crucial to shut them down in a predictable and clean manner. Go provides tools like channels, signal handlers, timeouts, and WaitGroups to make this process safe and efficient.

The following best practices help ensure that resources are released properly, tasks are completed gracefully, and no goroutines are left hanging during application termination:

- **Use close for signal channels**: Closing a channel signal all listening goroutines.
- **Periodically check for signals**: Long-running tasks should periodically check the shutdown channel.
- **Handle OS signals**: Use `os/signal` for clean exits in response to SIGINT or SIGTERM.
- **Use sync.WaitGroup for coordination**: Ensure all goroutines complete before exiting.
- **Set timeouts**: Use timeouts to enforce deadlines during shutdown, especially for servers or tasks with external dependencies.

Conclusion

This chapter explored how Go's select statement, timers, and tickers enable efficient, responsive, and concurrent programming. By combining channel operations with timeout mechanisms and non-blocking constructs, developers can manage communication across goroutines while ensuring graceful shutdowns and robust error handling. We also examined real-world use cases, common pitfalls, and best practices to build reliable time-sensitive systems.

In the next chapter, we will build upon this foundation and dive into advanced concurrency patterns. You will learn powerful techniques such as worker pools, fan-in/fan-out architectures, pipeline patterns, and context-based cancellations to structure complex concurrent systems that are scalable and maintainable.

Questions

1. What is the purpose of the select statement in Go, and how does it differ from a regular switch statement?
2. Explain how the default case works in a select block. When should you use it?
3. Write a Go program using select that waits for messages from two channels and prints whichever message is received first.
4. How can you use time after selecting to implement a timeout in a concurrent program? Provide an example.
5. What are the benefits of using goroutines and channels for graceful shutdowns in Go? Explain with a brief use case.
6. What is the difference between time NewTimer and time after? When would you choose one over the other?
7. Describe a situation where using a ticker is more appropriate than a timer. Provide a short code snippet to illustrate.
8. What are some common pitfalls when using non-blocking channel operations with select? How can you avoid them?
9. Why is sync WaitGroup useful in coordinating goroutines during shutdown? Provide an example of its usage.
10. List and explain any three best practices for implementing graceful shutdowns in a Go application.

Join our Discord space

Join our Discord workspace for latest updates, offers, tech happenings around the world, new releases, and sessions with the authors:

https://discord.bpbonline.com

CHAPTER 12
Advanced Concurrency Patterns

Introduction

Go's concurrency model is one of its standout features, enabling developers to build fast, efficient, and scalable systems. While basic goroutines and channels offer powerful tools for concurrent execution, real-world applications often require more advanced patterns to manage complexity, performance, and correctness. This chapter explores such patterns as worker pools, pipelines, mutexes, condition variables, rate limiting, and throttling. These are essential for structuring scalable software, maintaining data integrity, and optimizing resource utilization. You will learn not only how these patterns work, but also when and why to use them. Through real-world examples, this chapter equips you with practical techniques to build concurrency-safe and high-performance applications.

Structure

In this chapter, we will cover the following topics:

- Worker pools and goroutine management in Go
- Pipelines and stream processing in Go
- Mutexes and race conditions in Go
- Condition variables and locks in Go
- Building concurrency-safe applications in Go
- Rate limiting and throttling in Go

Objectives

The objective of this chapter is to deepen your understanding of Go's concurrency model by introducing advanced patterns essential for building robust and scalable applications. You will learn how to implement and manage worker pools for controlled parallelism, design pipelines for efficient stream processing, and apply synchronization techniques using mutexes and condition variables to avoid race conditions and deadlocks. The chapter also covers practical approaches to ensure concurrency safety through atomic operations and context-based goroutine management. Additionally, you will explore how to implement rate limiting and throttling mechanisms to maintain system stability under varying loads. By mastering these concepts, you will be well-equipped to write high-performance Go programs that handle complex concurrency challenges with ease and precision.

Worker pools and goroutine management in Go

Worker pools are a foundational concurrency pattern that allows Go applications to manage a controlled number of goroutines for executing tasks in parallel. They help prevent system overload, improve throughput, and simplify error handling by decoupling task submission from execution.

Overview

Worker pools and goroutine management are critical patterns for implementing efficient and scalable concurrent systems in Go. A worker pool is a design pattern where multiple worker goroutines perform tasks from a shared queue, allowing for controlled parallelism and optimized resource usage. By using worker pools, developers can avoid launching unbounded goroutines, which could lead to excessive memory usage or CPU thrashing. Worker pools are ideal for handling a large number of similar tasks, such as processing jobs from a queue, serving HTTP requests, or executing file I/O.

Usage of worker pools

Worker pools bring structure and efficiency to concurrent task execution. The following are key reasons why they are preferred in scalable Go systems:

- **Controlled parallelism**: Limit the number of concurrent tasks to avoid overwhelming system resources.
- **Efficient resource utilization**: Balance workload across multiple workers, ensuring no single worker is overburdened.
- **Simplified goroutine management**: Centralize task distribution and worker coordination.
- **Scalability**: Easily scale up or down by adjusting the number of workers.

Basic components of a worker pool

A worker pool consists of several components working together to distribute tasks and coordinate their execution. Let us discuss them as follows:

- **Task queue**: A buffered channel where tasks are enqueued.
- **Workers**: Goroutines that process tasks from the queue.
- **Result collection**: A channel or mechanism to gather results from workers (optional).
- **Synchronization**: Use `sync.WaitGroup` to ensure all tasks are completed before exiting.

Example of basic worker pool implementation

Let us look at a simple implementation of a worker pool in Go, demonstrating how to distribute tasks among multiple worker goroutines.

Code example

In the following code, a set number of workers pull tasks from a shared channel and execute them concurrently, with a `WaitGroup` ensuring all tasks complete before program exit:

```
package main

import (
    "fmt"
    "sync"
    "time"
)

// Worker function
func worker(id int, tasks <-chan int, wg *sync.WaitGroup) {
    defer wg.Done()
```

```
    for task := range tasks {
        fmt.Printf("Worker %d processing task %d\n", id, task)
        time.Sleep(time.Second) // Simulate work
    }
}

func main() {
    const numWorkers = 3
    const numTasks = 10

    tasks := make(chan int, numTasks)
    var wg sync.WaitGroup

    // Start workers
    for i := 1; i <= numWorkers; i++ {
        wg.Add(1)
        go worker(i, tasks, &wg)
    }

    // Enqueue tasks
    for t := 1; t <= numTasks; t++ {
        tasks <- t
    }
    close(tasks) // Signal that no more tasks will be sent

    // Wait for all workers to finish
    wg.Wait()
    fmt.Println("All tasks completed")
}
```

Following are the outputs:

- `Worker 1 processing task 1`
- `Worker 2 processing task 2`
- `Worker 3 processing task 3`
- `Worker 1 processing task 4`
- `Worker 2 processing task 5`
- `Worker 3 processing task 6`
- `Worker 1 processing task 7`
- `Worker 2 processing task 8`
- `Worker 3 processing task 9`
- `Worker 1 processing task 10`
- `All tasks completed`

Advanced features of worker pools

Worker pools can be extended with features like result collection, dynamic resizing, and error reporting. These improvements enhance flexibility and control in large-scale concurrent systems.

Collecting results

Workers can send processed results to a results channel for further use.

Example: Result collection:

```
package main

import (
    "fmt"
    "sync"
    "time"
)

func worker(id int, tasks <-chan int, results chan<- int, wg *sync.WaitGroup) {
    defer wg.Done()
    for task := range tasks {
        fmt.Printf("Worker %d processing task %d\n", id, task)
        time.Sleep(time.Second)
        results <- task * 2 // Send result
    }
}

func main() {
    const numWorkers = 3
    const numTasks = 5

    tasks := make(chan int, numTasks)
    results := make(chan int, numTasks)
    var wg sync.WaitGroup

    // Start workers
    for i := 1; i <= numWorkers; i++ {
        wg.Add(1)
        go worker(i, tasks, results, &wg)
    }

    // Enqueue tasks
    for t := 1; t <= numTasks; t++ {
        tasks <- t
    }
    close(tasks)

    // Wait for workers and close results
    go func() {
        wg.Wait()
        close(results)
```

```
    }()

    // Collect results
    for result := range results {
        fmt.Println("Result:", result)
    }
}
```

Following are the outputs:

- `Worker 1 processing task 1`
- `Worker 3 processing task 3`
- `Worker 2 is processing task 2`
- `Worker 2 processing task 4`
- `Worker 1 processing task 5`
- `Result: 4`
- `Result: 2`
- `Result: 6`
- `Result: 10`
- `Result: 8`

Dynamic worker pools

Adjust the number of workers dynamically based on workload.

Example: Dynamic worker count:

```
package main

import (
    "fmt"
    "sync"
    "time"
)

func worker(id int, tasks <-chan int, wg *sync.WaitGroup) {
    defer wg.Done()
    for task := range tasks {
        fmt.Printf("Worker %d processing task %d\n", id, task)
        time.Sleep(time.Second)
    }
}

func main() {
    numWorkers := 5
    tasks := make(chan int, 10)
    var wg sync.WaitGroup

    // Dynamically adjust workers
```

```
    for i := 1; i <= numWorkers; i++ {
        wg.Add(1)
        go worker(i, tasks, &wg)
    }

    for i := 1; i <= 20; i++ {
        tasks <- i
    }
    close(tasks)

    wg.Wait()
    fmt.Println("All tasks completed")
}
```

Following are the outputs:

- Worker 5 processing task 1
- Worker 1 processing task 2
- Worker 2 processing task 3
- Worker 3 processing task 4
- Worker 4 processing task 5
- Worker 4 processing task 7
- Worker 1 processing task 6
- Worker 2 processing task 8
- Worker 5 processing task 9
- Worker 3 processing task 10
- Worker 1 processing task 11
- Worker 5 processing task 12
- Worker 2 processing task 13
- Worker 4 processing task 14
- Worker 3 processing task 15
- Worker 5 processing task 16
- Worker 3 processing task 17
- Worker 1 processing task 18
- Worker 2 processing task 19
- Worker 4 processing task 20
- All tasks completed

Handling errors in worker pools

Workers can return errors using an error channel.

Example: Error handling:

```
package main

import (
 "errors"
 "fmt"
```

```
  "sync"
)

func worker(id int, tasks <-chan int, errors chan<- error, wg *sync.WaitGroup) {
  defer wg.Done()
  for task := range tasks {
    if task%3 == 0 {
      errors <- fmt.Errorf("Worker %d failed on task %d", id, task)
    } else {
      fmt.Printf("Worker %d completed task %d\n", id, task)
    }
  }
}

func main() {
  const numWorkers = 3
  const numTasks = 10

  tasks := make(chan int, numTasks)
  errors := make(chan error, numTasks)
  var wg sync.WaitGroup

  // Start workers
  for i := 1; i <= numWorkers; i++ {
    wg.Add(1)
    go worker(i, tasks, errors, &wg)
  }

  // Send tasks to workers
  for t := 1; t <= numTasks; t++ {
    tasks <- t
  }
  close(tasks)

  // Close the errors channel once all workers are done
  go func() {
    wg.Wait()
    close(errors)
  }()

  // Process errors
  for err := range errors {
    fmt.Println("Error:", err)
  }
}
```

Following are the outputs:

```
•   Worker 2 completed task 2
•   Worker 2 completed task 4
•   Worker 2 completed task 5
•   Worker 1 completed task 1
•   Worker 1 completed task 8
•   Error: Worker 2 failed on task 6
•   Worker 2 completed task 7
•   Error: Worker 1 failed on task 9
•   Worker 1 completed task 10
•   Error: Worker 3 failed on task 3
```

Use cases for worker pools

Worker pools are highly effective in scenarios that require concurrent task processing with controlled resource usage. Some common use cases include:

- **Data processing pipelines**: Process large datasets in chunks using multiple workers.
- **Web crawlers**: Fetch multiple web pages concurrently.
- **Task scheduling**: Execute scheduled tasks in parallel with controlled concurrency.
- **File I/O operations**: Read/write files concurrently to optimize disk usage.
- **Microservices**: Distribute incoming API requests among multiple handlers.

Pipelines and stream processing in Go

Pipelines enable concurrent data processing in stages, where each stage performs a transformation and passes the result to the next. This model enhances scalability and separation of concerns.

Overview of pipelines and stream processing

Pipelines and stream processing are concurrency patterns used to handle continuous data flow through a series of stages, where each stage performs a specific transformation or operation on the data. In Go, these patterns leverage channels and goroutines to create efficient and scalable systems.

Pipelines

A pipeline is a sequence of connected stages, where:

- Data flows from one stage to the next through channels.
- Each stage is implemented as a goroutine, performing a specific task.
- The pipeline processes data in a streaming manner, enabling concurrency and scalability.

Components of a pipeline

Pipelines in Go are composed of source, stage, and sink components, each implemented as goroutines connected through channels. Let us discuss them as follows:

- **Source**: The entry point of the pipeline, generating or fetching data to be processed.
- **Stages**: Intermediate processing units, each performing a transformation or computation on the data.
- **Sink**: The endpoint of the pipeline where results are collected, stored, or displayed.

Basic pipeline example

Here is a basic example of a pipeline that takes a stream of integers, squares them, and outputs the result:

```
package main

import (
    "fmt"
    "time"
)

func source(data []int, out chan int) {
    for _, v := range data {
        out <- v
    }
    close(out)
}

func square(in, out chan int) {
    for v := range in {
        out <- v * v
    }
    close(out)
}

func sink(in chan int) {
    for result := range in {
        fmt.Println("Result:", result)
    }
}

func main() {
    data := []int{1, 2, 3, 4, 5}

    ch1 := make(chan int)
    ch2 := make(chan int)

    go source(data, ch1)
    go square(ch1, ch2)
    sink(ch2)
}
```

Following are the outputs:

- **Result: 1**
- **Result: 4**
- **Result: 9**
- **Result: 16**
- **Result: 25**

Advantages of pipelines

Pipelines promote clean, modular design and make it easier to process large streams of data efficiently:

- **Concurrency**: Each stage runs as a separate goroutine, enabling parallel processing.
- **Scalability**: Pipelines can handle large data streams by distributing the workload across stages.
- **Flexibility**: Stages can be easily added, removed, or modified without affecting the entire pipeline.
- **Separation of concerns**: Each stage focuses on a specific task, making the code more modular and maintainable.

Advanced pipeline example

More complex pipelines can involve multiple transformation stages running concurrently, with synchronization between stages.

Multi-stage pipeline with multiple goroutines

The following example shows a multi-stage pipeline where values are first doubled, then squared, using goroutines and channels to orchestrate the flow:

```
package main

import (
    "fmt"
    "sync"
    "time"
)

func source(data []int, out chan int) {
    for _, v := range data {
        out <- v
        time.Sleep(100 * time.Millisecond) // Simulate delay
    }
    close(out)
}

func double(in, out chan int, wg *sync.WaitGroup) {
    defer wg.Done()
    for v := range in {
        out <- v * 2
    }
}

func square(in, out chan int, wg *sync.WaitGroup) {
    defer wg.Done()
    for v := range in {
        out <- v * v
    }
```

```
}

func sink(in chan int) {
    for result := range in {
        fmt.Println("Processed result:", result)
    }
}

func main() {
    data := []int{1, 2, 3, 4, 5}
    ch1 := make(chan int)
    ch2 := make(chan int)
    ch3 := make(chan int)

    var wg sync.WaitGroup

    // Start source
    go source(data, ch1)

    // Start processing stages
    wg.Add(2)
    go double(ch1, ch2, &wg)
    go square(ch2, ch3, &wg)

    // Start sink in a separate goroutine
    go sink(ch3)

    wg.Wait()
    close(ch3) // Ensure the final channel is closed
}
```

Following are the outputs:

- **Processed result: 4**
- **Processed result: 16**
- **Processed result: 36**
- **Processed result: 64**
- **Processed result: 100**

Error handling in pipelines

Errors can be propagated through a dedicated error channel.

Example: Error handling:

```
package main

import (
    "fmt"
```

```
)

func process(in, out chan int, errChan chan error) {
    for v := range in {
        if v < 0 {
            errChan <- fmt.Errorf("negative value: %d", v)
            continue
        }
        out <- v * 2
    }
    close(out)
}

func main() {
    input := make(chan int)
    output := make(chan int)
    errors := make(chan error)

    go func() {
        input <- 1
        input <- -1 // Simulate error
        input <- 3
        close(input)
    }()

    go process(input, output, errors)

    for {
        select {
        case res, ok := <-output:
            if !ok {
                return
            }
            fmt.Println("Result:", res)
        case err := <-errors:
            fmt.Println("Error:", err)
        }
    }
}
```

Following are the outputs:

- **Result: 2**
- **Error: negative value is -1**
- **Result: 6**

Real-world applications

Pipelines are widely used in systems that require continuous, staged data processing. Some real-world applications include:

- **Data processing**: ETL pipelines for transforming and aggregating data.
- **Image processing**: Process large batches of images through multiple stages like resizing, watermarking, and compression.
- **Network data streams**: Process packets or events in real-time.
- **Web crawlers**: Crawl web pages through a series of stages, including fetching, parsing, and storing.

Mutexes and race conditions in Go

Managing shared state in concurrent programs requires careful synchronization to avoid race conditions. Mutexes offer a way to guard critical sections and ensure safe access.

Overview of mutexes and race conditions

In concurrent programming, a race condition arises when multiple goroutines access shared data at the same time, and the final result depends on the order or timing of their execution. To address this, mutexes, short for mutual exclusion, are used as synchronization tools. They ensure that only one goroutine can access a critical section of code at any given moment, effectively preventing race conditions.

Race conditions

Race conditions can lead to unpredictable results in concurrent programs. They occur when goroutines access and modify shared variables simultaneously without synchronization.

Definition

A race condition happens when the program's behavior is influenced by the unpredictable sequence in which concurrent goroutines are executed.

Following is an example of a race condition:

```
package main

import (
 "fmt"
 "time"
)

var counter int

func increment() {
 for i := 0; i < 1000000; i++ { // Increase iterations to increase overlap
  counter++
  time.Sleep(time.Nanosecond) // Add a small delay to force context switching
 }
}
```

```
func main() {
 go increment() // First goroutine
 go increment() // Second goroutine

 time.Sleep(2 * time.Second) // Allow time for both goroutines to finish
 fmt.Println("Final Counter:", counter)
}
```

Following are the example outputs:

- **Run 1:**
  - **Final counter: 1827**
- **Run 2:**
  - **Final counter: 1542**
- **Run 3:**
  - **Final counter: 1943**

Both goroutines access and modify the counter simultaneously, causing unpredictable results due to race conditions.

Detecting race conditions

Go provides a race detector to identify race conditions in your code. Race conditions are often subtle and hard to detect through manual testing. Go's built-in race detector provides a powerful tool to catch these issues during development. It reports conflicting accesses to memory, helping developers fix concurrency bugs early.

Usage of the race detector

Run your program with the **-race** flag:

```
go run -race main.go
```

Following are the output examples:

- **WARNING: DATA RACE**
- **Read by goroutine 6:**
  main.increment()
- **Write by goroutine 7:**
  main.increment()

Solving race conditions with mutexes

One of the most effective solutions to race conditions is the use of mutexes to ensure mutual exclusion. Go provides the **sync.Mutex** type to guard critical sections.

Mutex

A mutex is a synchronization tool designed to guarantee that only a single goroutine can enter and execute a critical section at any given moment.

Following are the key operations:

- **Lock**: Acquires the mutex, blocking other goroutines from entering the critical section.
- **Unlock**: Releases the mutex, allowing other goroutines to acquire it.

Using sync.Mutex in Go

Here is a practical example of using **`sync.Mutex`** to safely increment a shared counter from multiple goroutines:

```go
package main

import (
    "fmt"
    "sync"
)

var (
    counter int
    mu      sync.Mutex
)

func increment(wg *sync.WaitGroup) {
    defer wg.Done()
    for i := 0; i < 1000; i++ {
        mu.Lock()   // Lock the critical section
        counter++   // Modify shared resource
        mu.Unlock() // Unlock the critical section
    }
}

func main() {
    var wg sync.WaitGroup

    wg.Add(2)
    go increment(&wg)
    go increment(&wg)

    wg.Wait()
    fmt.Println("Final Counter:", counter)
}
```

Following is the output:

- **`Final counter: 2000`**

Following is the explanation:

- The **`sync.Mutex`** ensures that only one goroutine can modify the counter at a time.

Common mutex patterns

Several common concurrency patterns involve mutexes, especially where read-modify-write operations occur. The following are examples of such use cases:

- **Read-modify-write**: When a goroutine reads, modifies, and writes back to shared data, mutexes prevent race conditions.

Example: Read-modify-write:

```
package main

import (
    "fmt"
    "sync"
)

var (
    balance int
    mu      sync.Mutex
)

func deposit(amount int, wg *sync.WaitGroup) {
    defer wg.Done()
    mu.Lock()
    balance += amount
    mu.Unlock()
}

func withdraw(amount int, wg *sync.WaitGroup) {
    defer wg.Done()
    mu.Lock()
    balance -= amount
    mu.Unlock()
}

func main() {
    var wg sync.WaitGroup
    balance = 100

    wg.Add(2)
    go deposit(50, &wg)
    go withdraw(30, &wg)

    wg.Wait()
    fmt.Println("Final Balance:", balance)
}
```

Following is the output:

- `Final balance: 120`

- **Using sync.RWMutex**: `sync.RWMutex` allows multiple readers but only one writer.

  Example: RWMutex for reader-writer problem:

```
package main
```

```
import (
    "fmt"
    "sync"
    "time"
)

var (
    value int
    mu    sync.RWMutex
)

func readValue(id int, wg *sync.WaitGroup) {
    defer wg.Done()
    mu.RLock() // Acquire read lock
    fmt.Printf("Goroutine %d reads value: %d\n", id, value)
    time.Sleep(1 * time.Second)
    mu.RUnlock()
}

func writeValue(newValue int, wg *sync.WaitGroup) {
    defer wg.Done()
    mu.Lock() // Acquire write lock
    fmt.Printf("Writing value: %d\n", newValue)
    value = newValue
    time.Sleep(1 * time.Second)
    mu.Unlock()
}

func main() {
    var wg sync.WaitGroup
    value = 42

    wg.Add(3)
    go readValue(1, &wg)
    go readValue(2, &wg)
    go writeValue(100, &wg)

    wg.Wait()
}
```

Following are the outputs:

- **Goroutine 1 reads value: 42**
- **Goroutine 2 reads value: 42**
- **Writing value: 100**

Deadlocks and avoiding them

Deadlocks are serious issues where goroutines wait on each other indefinitely. Understanding their causes and how to avoid them is essential in concurrent programming.

Deadlock

A deadlock happens when two or more goroutines become stuck, each waiting for the other to release a resource, resulting in the program becoming unresponsive.

Example of a deadlock:

```
package main

import (
    "sync"
)

func main() {
    var mu sync.Mutex

    mu.Lock()
    mu.Lock() // Deadlock: Attempting to lock an already locked mutex
}
```

Following are the ways to avoid deadlocks:

- **Lock in a consistent order**: Always acquire locks in the same order across goroutines.
- **Use defer for unlocking**: Ensures the mutex is released even if an error occurs.
- **Minimize critical sections**: Keep the locked section as short as possible.

Mutex versus other synchronization techniques

While mutexes are useful, Go offers other synchronization tools for different concurrency needs. Here is a quick comparison of when to use each:

Technique	When to use
`sync.Mutex`	For exclusive access to shared resources.
`sync.RWMutex`	For scenarios with many readers and few writers.
Channels	When sharing data between goroutines, especially for producer-consumer patterns.
Atomic operations	For simple, low-overhead updates to shared variables (e.g., sync/atomic).

***Table 12.1**: Mutexes vs. other synchronization*

Real-world applications of mutexes

Mutexes are commonly used in scenarios where shared data must be accessed and modified safely by multiple goroutines:

- **Banking systems**: Ensuring consistent updates to account balances.
- **Cache management**: Synchronizing read/write operations on in-memory caches.

- **File I/O**: Preventing simultaneous writes to the same file.
- **Shared data structures**: Safely accessing maps, slices, or other data structures across goroutines.

Condition variables and locks in Go

In addition to basic locks, Go supports condition variables for advanced synchronization. These allow goroutines to wait until certain conditions are met.

Overview of condition variables and locks

Condition variables and locks are synchronization mechanisms used in concurrent programming to coordinate the execution of goroutines. Locks provide mutual exclusion by allowing only one goroutine to access a shared resource at a time, whereas condition variables enable goroutines to pause execution until certain conditions are satisfied before continuing. Condition variables, implemented via **`sync.Cond`**, are useful for scenarios like producer-consumer problems where one goroutine must wait for another to signal a condition before proceeding.

Locks

Locks, like **`sync.Mutex`** and **`sync.RWMutex`** is essential for synchronizing access to shared resources. They ensure that only a single goroutine can execute a critical section at any given time.

Following are the key operations of locks:

- **Lock**: Acquires the lock, blocking other goroutines from accessing the critical section.
- **Unlock**: Releases the lock, allowing other goroutines to acquire it.

Example: Using **`sync.Mutex`** for mutual exclusion:

```
package main

import (
    "fmt"
    "sync"
)

var counter int
var mu sync.Mutex

func increment(wg *sync.WaitGroup) {
    defer wg.Done()
    mu.Lock()
    counter++
    mu.Unlock()
}

func main() {
    var wg sync.WaitGroup
    wg.Add(2)

    go increment(&wg)
    go increment(&wg)
```

```
    wg.Wait()
    fmt.Println("Final Counter:", counter)
}
```

Following is the output:

- **Final counter: 2**

Condition variables

In Go, condition variables are implemented through **sync.Cond** enables goroutines to pause execution until certain conditions are satisfied. They are commonly used alongside locks to manage and coordinate access to shared resources effectively.

Following are the key methods of **sync.Cond**:

- **Wait**: Releases the associated lock and blocks the calling goroutine until the condition is signaled.
- **Signal**: Notifies one waiting goroutine to wake up and proceed.
- **Broadcast**: Notifies all waiting goroutines to wake up and continue execution.

Using sync.Cond for coordination

Condition variables are ideal for coordinating multiple goroutines. Let us look at how they are used to manage synchronization in concurrent applications.

Producer-consumer problem

In this classic problem, producers add data to a shared resource while consumers retrieve it. Condition variables can signal consumers when data is available.

Example: Producer-consumer with **sync.Cond**:

```
package main

import (
    "fmt"
    "sync"
)

type Queue struct {
    items []int
    cond  *sync.Cond
}

func (q *Queue) Enqueue(item int) {
    q.cond.L.Lock()
    q.items = append(q.items, item)
    fmt.Printf("Enqueued: %d\n", item)
    q.cond.Signal() // Notify a waiting consumer
    q.cond.L.Unlock()
}
```

```
func (q *Queue) Dequeue() int {
    q.cond.L.Lock()
    for len(q.items) == 0 {
        q.cond.Wait() // Wait for data to be available
    }
    item := q.items[0]
    q.items = q.items[1:]
    fmt.Printf("Dequeued: %d\n", item)
    q.cond.L.Unlock()
    return item
}

func main() {
    queue := &Queue{
        items: []int{},
        cond:  sync.NewCond(&sync.Mutex{}),
    }

    go func() {
        for i := 1; i <= 5; i++ {
            queue.Enqueue(i)
        }
    }()

    for i := 1; i <= 5; i++ {
        queue.Dequeue()
    }
}
```

Following are the outputs:

- **Enqueued: 1**
- **Dequeued: 1**
- **Enqueued: 2**
- **Dequeued: 2**
- **Enqueued: 3**
- **Dequeued: 3**
- **Enqueued: 4**
- **Dequeued: 4**
- **Enqueued: 5**
- **Dequeued: 5**

Combining condition variables with locks

Locks provide mutual exclusion, while condition variables enable waiting and signaling. Together, they form a powerful combination for synchronizing complex interactions.

Following is an example of a bounded buffer.

A bounded buffer limits the number of items it can hold, requiring coordination between producers and consumers. Condition variables often work alongside mutexes to build more complex synchronization patterns. One such example is the bounded buffer:

```
package main

import (
    "fmt"
    "sync"
)

type BoundedBuffer struct {
    items       []int
    maxSize     int
    cond        *sync.Cond
}

func NewBoundedBuffer(size int) *BoundedBuffer {
    return &BoundedBuffer{
        items:   make([]int, 0, size),
        maxSize: size,
        cond:    sync.NewCond(&sync.Mutex{}),
    }
}

func (b *BoundedBuffer) Produce(item int) {
    b.cond.L.Lock()
    for len(b.items) == b.maxSize {
        b.cond.Wait() // Wait for space
    }
    b.items = append(b.items, item)
    fmt.Printf("Produced: %d\n", item)
    b.cond.Broadcast() // Notify all consumers
    b.cond.L.Unlock()
}

func (b *BoundedBuffer) Consume() int {
    b.cond.L.Lock()
    for len(b.items) == 0 {
        b.cond.Wait() // Wait for data
    }
    item := b.items[0]
    b.items = b.items[1:]
    fmt.Printf("Consumed: %d\n", item)
    b.cond.Broadcast() // Notify all producers
```

```
    b.cond.L.Unlock()
    return item
}

func main() {
    buffer := NewBoundedBuffer(3)

    var wg sync.WaitGroup

    // Producer
    wg.Add(1)
    go func() {
        defer wg.Done()
        for i := 1; i <= 5; i++ {
            buffer.Produce(i)
        }
    }()

    // Consumer
    wg.Add(1)
    go func() {
        defer wg.Done()
        for i := 1; i <= 5; i++ {
            buffer.Consume()
        }
    }()

    wg.Wait()
}
```

Following are the outputs:

- **Produced: 1**
- **Consumed: 1**
- **Produced: 2**
- **Consumed: 2**
- **Produced: 3**
- **Consumed: 3**
- **Produced: 4**
- **Consumed: 4**
- **Produced: 5**
- **Consumed: 5**

Real-world applications

Condition variables are applied in many systems where communication between concurrent tasks must be coordinated. Examples include:

- **Producer-consumer systems**: Coordinate data production and consumption using bounded buffers.
- **Thread pools**: Manage a pool of workers waiting for tasks.
- **Resource allocation**: Synchronize access to limited resources (for example, database connections).
- **Event handling**: Notify waiting goroutines of events like file availability or completion of a task.

Building concurrency-safe applications in Go

Concurrency-safe applications are at the heart of robust systems that manage multiple tasks simultaneously. In this section, we explore the principles and techniques that help avoid common pitfalls like data races, deadlocks, and goroutine leaks when building reliable concurrent applications in Go.

Definition

Concurrency-safe applications ensure that multiple goroutines can execute without causing data corruption, race conditions, or undefined behavior. In Go, concurrency safety involves managing access to shared resources, synchronizing operations, and designing robust communication patterns.

Core principles of concurrency safety

Understanding the fundamental rules of concurrency safety is crucial for designing resilient systems. These principles help developers structure their programs in a way that avoids common concurrency bugs and ensures data integrity across goroutines:

- **Avoid race conditions**: Ensure that shared data is accessed and modified in a synchronized manner.
- **Minimize blocking**: Avoid bottlenecks by limiting long-running operations within critical sections.
- **Leverage Go's concurrency primitives**: Use channels, mutexes, and other synchronization tools effectively.
- **Design for scalability**: Ensure that the application can handle an increased workload without compromising safety.

Common concurrency issues

Before we can build safe concurrent programs, it is essential to recognize the issues that can arise from improper synchronization and goroutine management. This subsection outlines frequent pitfalls and their corresponding remedies:

- **Race conditions**: Occur when multiple goroutines access shared data at the same time, resulting in unpredictable and inconsistent behavior.

  Solution: Use mutexes, channels, or atomic operations to manage access.
- **Deadlocks**: Occur when goroutines are waiting indefinitely for each other to release resources.

  Solution: Avoid nested locks and ensure proper lock ordering.
- **Starvation**: Occurs when a goroutine is perpetually denied access to a resource due to unfair scheduling.

  Solution: Use fair locking mechanisms or condition variables.
- **Goroutine leaks**: Occur when goroutines are not terminated properly, leading to resource wastage.

  Solution: Use channels or context to signal goroutines to exit.

Techniques for building concurrency-safe applications

Go provides several built-in mechanisms that help enforce safe concurrent execution. This section demonstrates how to apply synchronization primitives and context management to maintain control over goroutine behavior and data access.

Synchronization with mutexes

Mutexes offer fine-grained control over critical sections of code. By locking and unlocking access to shared resources, we can avoid race conditions and ensure a consistent state.

Example: Synchronizing access to shared data:

```
package main

import (
    "fmt"
    "sync"
)

var (
    counter int
    mu      sync.Mutex
)

func increment(wg *sync.WaitGroup) {
    defer wg.Done()
    mu.Lock()
    counter++
    mu.Unlock()
}

func main() {
    var wg sync.WaitGroup
    wg.Add(2)

    go increment(&wg)
    go increment(&wg)

    wg.Wait()
    fmt.Println("Final Counter:", counter)
}
```

Following is the output:

- **Final counter: 2**

Using channels for safe communication

Channels are a first-class feature in Go that help synchronize data transfer between goroutines. When used correctly, they prevent race conditions and simplify pipeline-style communication.

Example: Producer-consumer model:

```
package main

import "fmt"
```

```
func producer(ch chan int) {
    for i := 1; i <= 5; i++ {
        ch <- i
        fmt.Println("Produced:", i)
    }
    close(ch)
}

func consumer(ch chan int) {
    for v := range ch {
        fmt.Println("Consumed:", v)
    }
}

func main() {
    ch := make(chan int)

    go producer(ch)
    consumer(ch)
}
```

Following is the output:

- makefile
- Copy code
- Produced: 1
- Consumed: 1
- Produced: 2
- Consumed: 2

Atomic operations

For lightweight concurrency-safe updates to numeric values, Go provides atomic operations. These are especially useful when performance is critical and full-blown mutex locks are unnecessary.

Example: Using sync/atomic:

```
package main

import (
    "fmt"
    "sync/atomic"
)

func main() {
    var counter int64

    go func() {
        atomic.AddInt64(&counter, 1)
```

```
    }()
    atomic.AddInt64(&counter, 1)

    fmt.Println("Final Counter:", atomic.LoadInt64(&counter))
}
```

Context for goroutine management

The context package in Go is essential for controlling the lifetime of goroutines, especially in long-running or cancelable operations. It is a structured way to propagate deadlines and cancellation signals.

Example: Using **`context.Context`**:

```
package main

import (
    "context"
    "fmt"
    "time"
)

func worker(ctx context.Context, id int) {
    for {
        select {
        case <-ctx.Done():
            fmt.Printf("Worker %d stopping\n", id)
            return
        default:
            fmt.Printf("Worker %d working\n", id)
            time.Sleep(1 * time.Second)
        }
    }
}

func main() {
    ctx, cancel := context.WithTimeout(context.Background(), 3*time.Second)
    defer cancel()

    go worker(ctx, 1)
    go worker(ctx, 2)

    time.Sleep(5 * time.Second)
}
```

Following are the outputs:

- **`Worker 1 working`**
- **`Worker 2 working`**
- **`Worker 1 stopping`**
- **`Worker 2 stopping`**

Testing and debugging concurrency

Testing concurrent code requires specialized tools to uncover hidden issues. Go offers the race flag and profiling tools like `pprof` to debug and optimize concurrent applications:

- **Use the race detector**: Run with `-race` to identify race conditions:

  ```
  go run -race main.go
  ```

- **Logging and tracing**: Use structured logs and tools like `pprof` to analyze goroutine behavior.

  Example: Basic logging:

  ```
  log.Printf("Worker %d started\n", id)
  ```

Real-world applications of concurrency-safe design

Concurrency safety is not just academic; it powers mission critical systems in production. From web servers to data pipelines, this section showcases where these concepts apply in the real world:

- **Web servers**: Handled multiple client requests concurrently while maintaining data consistency.
- **Database access**: Synchronize reads and writes to shared data structures or connections.
- **Task queues**: Distribute and process tasks efficiently using worker pools.
- **Event processing systems**: Process real-time streams of events, ensuring reliable delivery and order.
- **Microservices**: Implement concurrency-safe APIs for distributed systems.

Rate limiting and throttling in Go

Rate limiting and throttling are essential to prevent overloading systems, ensure fair usage, and maintain responsiveness. This section introduces techniques to implement these controls effectively in Go.

Overview of rate limiting

Rate limiting and throttling are techniques used to control the rate at which requests or operations are processed. They are essential for ensuring system stability, preventing resource overuse, and maintaining quality of service. In Go, these patterns can be efficiently implemented using channels, time-based tokens, and custom algorithms.

Usage of rate limiting and throttling

Unregulated access to system resources can lead to service degradation or failure. Rate limiting and throttling protect against such issues by controlling access and maintaining operational stability, as follows:

- **Protect system resources**: Prevent overloading servers, APIs, or databases.
- **Ensure fair usage**: Distribute resources equitably among multiple clients or tasks.
- **Prevent abuse**: Limit misuse of services by restricting request rates.
- **Improve stability**: Ensure the system remains responsive under heavy load.

Key concepts

The following are the key concepts:

- **Rate limiting**: Controls the number of operations over a fixed time window.

  For example, allow a maximum of ten requests per second.

- **Throttling**: Restricts the rate of operations at any given time to avoid spikes.

  For example, limit a process to execute only one request every 100 milliseconds.

Implementing rate limiting

This section explores two popular techniques for enforcing rate limits: fixed-window and token bucket algorithms. These patterns are ideal for regulating access to APIs, services, and internal resources, as follows:

- **Fixed-window rate limiter**: This approach tracks the count of operations within a fixed time window.

  Example: Simple fixed-window implementation:

```
package main

import (
    "fmt"
    "sync"
    "time"
)

type FixedWindowLimiter struct {
    maxRequests int
    count       int
    window      time.Duration
    mu          sync.Mutex
    resetTimer  *time.Timer
}

func NewFixedWindowLimiter(maxRequests int, window time.Duration) *FixedWindowLimiter {
    limiter := &FixedWindowLimiter{
        maxRequests: maxRequests,
        window:      window,
        resetTimer:  time.NewTimer(window),
    }
    go limiter.reset()
    return limiter
}

func (l *FixedWindowLimiter) reset() {
    for {
        <-l.resetTimer.C
        l.mu.Lock()
        l.count = 0
        l.mu.Unlock()
        l.resetTimer.Reset(l.window)
    }
}

func (l *FixedWindowLimiter) Allow() bool {
    l.mu.Lock()
    defer l.mu.Unlock()
```

```
    if l.count < l.maxRequests {
        l.count++
        return true
    }
    return false
}

func main() {
    limiter := NewFixedWindowLimiter(3, 2*time.Second)

    for i := 0; i < 10; i++ {
        if limiter.Allow() {
            fmt.Printf("Request %d allowed\n", i+1)
        } else {
            fmt.Printf("Request %d denied\n", i+1)
        }
        time.Sleep(500 * time.Millisecond)
    }
}
```

Following are the outputs:

- `Request 1 allowed`
- `Request 2 allowed`
- `Request 3 allowed`
- `Request 4 denied`
- `Request 5 denied`
- `Request 6 allowed`

- **Token bucket algorithm**: The token bucket algorithm allows a fixed number of tokens to accumulate over time, which can be spent on requests.

  Example: Token bucket implementation:

```
package main

import (
    "fmt"
    "time"
)

type TokenBucket struct {
    tokens        int
    maxTokens     int
    refillRate    int
    refillTicker *time.Ticker
    requestTicker *time.Ticker
}
```

```
func NewTokenBucket(maxTokens, refillRate int, refillInterval time.Duration) *TokenBucket {
    bucket := &TokenBucket{
        maxTokens:    maxTokens,
        refillRate:   refillRate,
        tokens:       maxTokens,
        refillTicker: time.NewTicker(refillInterval),
    }

    go bucket.refill()
    return bucket
}

func (tb *TokenBucket) refill() {
    for range tb.refillTicker.C {
        if tb.tokens < tb.maxTokens {
            tb.tokens += tb.refillRate
            if tb.tokens > tb.maxTokens {
                tb.tokens = tb.maxTokens
            }
        }
    }
}

func (tb *TokenBucket) Allow() bool {
    if tb.tokens > 0 {
        tb.tokens--
        return true
    }
    return false
}

func main() {
    bucket := NewTokenBucket(5, 1, 1*time.Second)

    for i := 0; i < 10; i++ {
        if bucket.Allow() {
            fmt.Printf("Request %d allowed\n", i+1)
        } else {
            fmt.Printf("Request %d denied\n", i+1)
        }
        time.Sleep(500 * time.Millisecond)
    }
}
```

Following are the outputs:

- `Request 1 allowed`
- `Request 2 allowed`
- `Request 3 allowed`
- `Request 4 allowed`
- `Request 5 allowed`
- `Request 6 denied`

Implementing throttling

Throttling focuses on smoothing out spikes in traffic by spacing out requests over time. Go's timing mechanisms, like ticker, help in crafting efficient throttling logic.

Time-based throttling

Throttling can be implemented using Go's **`time.Ticker`** to control the rate of requests.

Example: Time-based throttling:

```
package main

import (
    "fmt"
    "time"
)

func throttle(requests []int, interval time.Duration) {
    ticker := time.NewTicker(interval)
    defer ticker.Stop()

    for _, req := range requests {
        <-ticker.C
        fmt.Printf("Processing request: %d\n", req)
    }
}

func main() {
    requests := []int{1, 2, 3, 4, 5}
    throttle(requests, 500*time.Millisecond)
}
```

Following are the outputs:

- **`Processing requests: 1`**
- **`Processing requests: 2`**
- **`Processing requests: 3`**

Real-world applications

These concurrency control strategies are widely adopted in API management, job scheduling, and traffic shaping. Understanding their applications helps solidify their importance in production-grade systems:

- **API rate limiting**: Prevent application programming interface clients from overwhelming the server with excessive requests.
- **Database throttling**: Limit the rate of queries to prevent overloading the database.
- **Traffic shaping**: Control the flow of network packets to ensure fair bandwidth usage.
- **Job scheduling**: Restrict the rate of background job execution to optimize resource utilization.

Conclusion

Advanced concurrency patterns in Go provide the foundation for building scalable, efficient, and safe applications in real-world environments. From worker pools that manage task execution efficiently to pipelines that streamline data flow across processing stages, these patterns empower developers to harness the full potential of goroutines and channels. Additionally, synchronization tools like mutexes, condition variables, and atomic operations help prevent race conditions and ensure data integrity. Rate limiting and throttling strategies offer further control over resource consumption and system responsiveness. By mastering these patterns, you are now equipped to tackle complex concurrency challenges with confidence and clarity.

In the next chapter, we will explore how to manage errors gracefully in multi-goroutine environments. You will learn strategies for propagating, collecting, and recovering from errors without compromising application stability, which is an essential skill for building reliable concurrent systems.

Questions

1. What is a worker pool and how does it help in managing goroutines effectively in Go?
2. Explain the role of sync.WaitGroup in worker pool implementations. Why is it necessary?
3. How can results be collected from multiple workers in a concurrent Go application? Give an example.
4. Differentiate between a fixed number of workers and dynamic worker pool patterns. When would you use each?
5. What is a pipeline in Go? Describe its key components and benefits with an example.
6. How do you handle errors in pipelines or worker pools without blocking the main execution flow?
7. What is a race condition, and how can you detect it using Go's built-in tools? Provide a simple code snippet.
8. Explain the use of sync.Mutex and sync.RWMutex. When would you use one over the other?
9. What is the difference between rate limiting and throttling? How would you implement them in Go?
10. Describe a real-world use case where condition variables are better suited than basic mutexes or channels.

Join our Discord space

Join our Discord workspace for latest updates, offers, tech happenings around the world, new releases, and sessions with the authors:

https://discord.bpbonline.com

CHAPTER 13
Error Handling in Concurrency

Introduction

Concurrency introduces powerful capabilities in Go, but it also brings unique challenges, especially around error handling and program stability. This chapter explores best practices for handling errors, detecting and avoiding deadlocks, recovering from panics, and synchronizing state across goroutines. You will learn how to build resilient, fault-tolerant concurrent programs that can gracefully handle unexpected conditions without crashing. Practical examples and real-world applications illustrate the concepts, ensuring you can apply these skills effectively. Mastering these techniques will elevate your ability to design robust, maintainable concurrent Go applications suitable for production environments.

Structure

In this chapter, we will be covering the following topics:

- Best practices for handling errors in concurrency
- Deadlocks and their solutions
- Recovering from panics in concurrent programs
- Synchronizing state between goroutines
- Common pitfalls and solutions

Objectives

By the end of this chapter, you will be able to understand the importance of structured error handling in concurrent programs and identify common challenges such as error propagation, goroutine leaks, and race conditions. You will learn how to apply best practices like centralized error handling, using contexts, signaling errors through channels, and implementing graceful shutdowns. Additionally, you will be able to recognize and avoid deadlocks, implement panic recovery strategies to build robust concurrent applications, and synchronize shared state between goroutines safely and efficiently.

Best practices for handling errors in concurrency

Concurrent programs often deal with multiple goroutines executing simultaneously, which makes error management complex. Without proper handling, errors can lead to goroutine leaks, inconsistent program states, and unpredictable failures. This section explores techniques to make error handling reliable, scalable, and easier to debug.

Overview

Managing errors in concurrent programs is inherently more complex than in sequential ones, as it involves coordinating multiple goroutines and shared resources. To ensure the system remains reliable and easy to maintain, implementing a strong error management strategy is essential.

Importance of error handling in concurrency

Managing errors properly is essential for the stability and reliability of concurrent programs, where errors can cascade quickly if not controlled.

Let us see the importance of it as follows:

- **System stability**: Prevents cascading failures across goroutines.
- **Data integrity**: Ensures consistent states when errors occur in shared resources.
- **Debugging and monitoring**: Simplifies identifying and resolving issues in complex systems.
- **Graceful degradation**: Allows partial system functionality in case of errors.

Common challenges in concurrency error handling

Concurrency introduces complexities where errors can be lost, hidden, or cause side effects across unrelated parts of a system. Understanding the unique challenges of error communication, propagation, and goroutine management is essential to prevent elusive bugs and maintain system reliability, as follows:

- **Non-blocking errors**: Errors might go unnoticed if not explicitly communicated.
- **Error propagation**: Difficulty in propagating errors between goroutines.
- **Goroutine leaks**: Goroutines might continue running despite errors in other parts of the system.
- **Race conditions**: Errors might result in data corruption or undefined behavior due to unsynchronized access.

Best practices for handling errors

Applying structured error handling patterns such as centralized error reporting, context propagation, and clean shutdowns helps to maintain system stability and makes debugging easier. Following best practices improves the predictability and resilience of concurrent Go programs:

- **Centralize error handling**: Maintain a centralized mechanism for collecting and processing errors from multiple goroutines.

  Example: Centralized error channel:

```
package main

import (
    "fmt"
    "sync"
)

func worker(id int, tasks <-chan int, errors chan<- error, wg *sync.WaitGroup) {
    defer wg.Done()
    for task := range tasks {
        if task%2 == 0 {
            errors <- fmt.Errorf("worker %d: error processing task %d", id, task)
```

```
            } else {
                fmt.Printf("worker %d processed task %d\n", id, task)
            }
        }
    }

func main() {
    tasks := make(chan int, 5)
    errors := make(chan error, 5)
    var wg sync.WaitGroup

    for i := 1; i <= 3; i++ {
        wg.Add(1)
        go worker(i, tasks, errors, &wg)
    }

    for i := 1; i <= 10; i++ {
        tasks <- i
    }
    close(tasks)

    go func() {
        wg.Wait()
        close(errors)
    }()

    for err :- range errors {
        fmt.Println("Error:", err)
    }
}
```

Following are the outputs:

- `Worker 1: processed task 1`
- `Worker 2: processed task 3`
- `Error-worker 1: error processing task 2`
- `Error-worker 2: error processing task 4`

- **Propagate errors using context**: Use `context.Context` to manage error propagation and cancellation across goroutines.

  Example: Using context for error propagation:

```
package main

import (
    "context"
    "fmt"
    "sync"
    "time"
)
```

```
func worker(ctx context.Context, id int, wg *sync.WaitGroup) {
    defer wg.Done()
    for {
        select {
        case <-ctx.Done():
            fmt.Printf("worker %d stopped: %v\n", id, ctx.Err())
            return
        default:
            fmt.Printf("worker %d is working\n", id)
            time.Sleep(500 * time.Millisecond)
        }
    }
}

func main() {
    ctx, cancel := context.WithTimeout(context.Background(), 2*time.Second)
    var wg sync.WaitGroup

    for i := 1; i <= 3; i++ {
        wg.Add(1)
        go worker(ctx, i, &wg)
    }

    time.Sleep(3 * time.Second) // Simulate some work
    cancel()

    wg.Wait()
    fmt.Println("All workers stopped")
}
```

Following are the outputs:

- **Worker 1: is working**
- **Worker 2: is working**
- **Worker 3: is working**
- **Worker 1 stopped: context deadline exceeded**
- **Worker 2 stopped: context deadline exceeded**
- **Worker 3 stopped: context deadline exceeded**
- **All workers: stopped**

- **Use channels to signal errors**: Channels are a natural choice for propagating errors in Go's concurrency model.

  Example: Signaling errors with a dedicated channel:

```
package main

import (
    "fmt"
```

```
    "time"
)

func worker(id int, ch chan int, errCh chan error) {
    for task := range ch {
        if task%2 == 0 {
            errCh <- fmt.Errorf("worker %d failed on task %d", id, task)
        } else {
            fmt.Printf("worker %d completed task %d\n", id, task)
        }
    }
}

func main() {
    tasks := make(chan int, 5)
    errors := make(chan error)

    go worker(1, tasks, errors)
    go worker(2, tasks, errors)

    go func() {
        for i := 1; i <= 10; i++ {
            tasks <- i
        }
        close(tasks)
    }()

    go func() {
        for err := range errors {
            fmt.Println("Error:", err)
        }
    }()

    time.Sleep(2 * time.Second)
}
```

Following are the outputs:

- `Worker 1: completed task 1`
- `Worker 2: completed task 3`
- `Worker 2: completed task 5`
- `Error: worker 2 failed on task 2`
- `Error: worker 1 failed on task 4`
- `Error: worker 2 failed on task 6`
- `Worker 2: completed task 7`
- `Worker 2: completed task 9`
- `Error: worker 2 failed on task 8`

- `Error: worker 2 failed on task 10`

- **Graceful goroutine shutdown**: Always clean up resources and exit gracefully on errors.

  Example: Graceful shutdown with **`WaitGroup`**:

```
package main

import (
    "fmt"
    "sync"
)

func worker(id int, wg *sync.WaitGroup, ch <-chan int) {
    defer wg.Done()
    for task := range ch {
        if task < 0 {
            fmt.Printf("worker %d encountered error: negative task %d\n", id, task)
            return
        }
        fmt.Printf("worker %d processed task %d\n", id, task)
    }
}

func main() {
    var wg sync.WaitGroup
    tasks := make(chan int, 5)

    for i := 1; i <= 3; i++ {
        wg.Add(1)
        go worker(i, &wg, tasks)
    }

    for i := -1; i < 5; i++ {
        tasks <- i
    }
    close(tasks)

    wg.Wait()
    fmt.Println("All workers completed")
}
```

Following are the outputs:

- `Worker 3: processed task 1`
- `Worker 3: processed task 2`
- `Worker 3: processed task 3`
- `Worker 3: processed task 4`

- `Worker 1: encountered error, negative task -1`
- `worker 2: processed task 0`
- `All workers: completed`

Testing and debugging concurrency errors

Concurrency errors are often non-deterministic and hard to reproduce. Therefore, tools and strategies such as race detectors, detailed logging, and deliberate fault injection are critical. Regular testing under load and chaos testing also help ensure error handling mechanisms are robust and effective, as shown here:

- **Use the -race detector**: Run your program with the **`-race`** flag to detect race conditions.
- **Log errors verbosely**: Log errors with enough context to identify the source of the issue.
- **Simulated errors**: Test your error-handling mechanisms by deliberately introducing errors.

Best practices

Centralized error handling, context propagation, graceful goroutine shutdowns, avoiding silent failures, and designing for resilience are critical for stable concurrent programs, as follows:

- **Centralized error handling**: Use shared channels or contexts to aggregate errors.
- **Use contexts for propagation**: Pass **`context.Context`** across goroutines to handle timeouts and cancellations.
- **Gracefully handle errors**: Ensure goroutines exit cleanly and resources are released.
- **Avoid silent failures**: Always log or communicate errors to ensure visibility.
- **Design for resilience**: Allow partial functionality even when some components fail.

Deadlocks and their solutions

A deadlock arises when two or more goroutines are stuck waiting for each other to release resources, preventing any of them from making progress. Deadlocks can cause a program to hang indefinitely, leading to unresponsiveness and wasted resources.

Understanding the causes of deadlocks and implementing strategies to avoid them are critical for building robust concurrent applications in Go.

Deadlock

A deadlock arises when:

- Goroutines acquire resources in such a way that a circular dependency is formed.
- Each goroutine waits for another to release a resource it needs, creating a standstill.

Example of a deadlock

A simple deadlock happens when a single goroutine tries to acquire the same lock twice without releasing it in between. In more complex scenarios, multiple goroutines can create a cycle where each waits indefinitely for the others. Careful resource management and consistent locking strategies are crucial to avoid deadlocks.

Example: Simple deadlock:

```
package main

import (
```

```
    "sync"
)

func main() {
    var mu sync.Mutex

    mu.Lock()
    mu.Lock() // Deadlock: Second lock attempt blocks forever
}
```

Explanation:

The example demonstrates a simple deadlock in Go where a single goroutine attempts to lock the same **`sync.Mutex`** twice without unlocking it in between. The first **`mu.Lock()`** successfully locks the mutex, allowing the goroutine to proceed. However, the second **`mu.Lock()`** tries to acquire the same mutex again, and since it is already locked by the same goroutine and not yet unlocked, this call blocks indefinitely. This occurs because Go's **`sync.Mutex`** is non-reentrant, meaning a goroutine cannot acquire a lock it already holds until it releases it first. The goroutine waits for the mutex to be unlocked, but it cannot move past the second **`mu.Lock()`** to do so, resulting in a deadlock. Consequently, the program hangs, and no further execution occurs.

Common causes of deadlocks

Deadlocks typically arise from incorrect resource acquisition patterns, such as inconsistent lock ordering or forgotten unlock operations. Misusing channels by blocking senders and receivers without appropriate goroutines also leads to deadlocks. Recognizing these patterns early helps in avoiding serious production issues, as follows:

- **Double locking**: A goroutine attempts to acquire a lock it already holds.
- **Lock ordering**: Multiple goroutines acquire locks in an inconsistent order.
- **Circular wait**: Goroutines form a dependency cycle, waiting for each other to release resources.
- **Unreleased locks**: Locks are not released due to missing unlock calls, often caused by errors or panics.
- **Channel misuse**: Deadlocks occur when sending or receiving on a channel with no corresponding receiver or sender.

Identifying deadlocks

Deadlocks can be detected when a program hangs indefinitely or when Go runtime reports that all goroutines are asleep. Using the **`-race`** detector, runtime profiles (**`pprof`**), and debuggers like dlv can help analyze and resolve deadlocks during development or testing, as shown:

- **Runtime panic**: Go detects some deadlocks at runtime and panics with a message like the following:

  ```
  all goroutines are asleep - deadlock!
  ```

- **Using debugging tools**: Use Go's **`pprof`** or **`dlv`** debugger to analyze blocked goroutines.
- **Simulate high load**: Deadlocks often appear under specific conditions, such as high concurrency or heavy load.

Strategies to avoid deadlocks

Developers can prevent deadlocks by enforcing consistent lock acquisition order, using defer to ensure unlocks, avoiding nested locks, preferring channels over locks, and detecting deadlocks early with tools like the **`-race`** detector, as follows:

- **Consistent lock ordering**: Always acquire locks in the same order across goroutines to prevent circular wait conditions.

  Example: Correct lock ordering:

```
package main

import (
    "fmt"
    "sync"
)

func main() {
    var mu1, mu2 sync.Mutex

    go func() {
        mu1.Lock()
        mu2.Lock()
        fmt.Println("Goroutine 1")
        mu2.Unlock()
        mu1.Unlock()
    }()

    go func() {
        mu1.Lock()
        mu2.Lock()
        fmt.Println("Goroutine 2")
        mu2.Unlock()
        mu1.Unlock()
    }()
}
```

  Following is the explanation:

  - Both goroutines acquire locks in the same order (`mu1` → `mu2`), preventing deadlocks.

- **Use defer to ensure unlocking**: Always release locks using defer to prevent locks from being left unreleased due to errors or early returns.

  Example: Using defer:

```
package main

import (
    "fmt"
    "sync"
)

func safeIncrement(mu *sync.Mutex, counter *int) {
    mu.Lock()
    defer mu.Unlock()
```

```
        *counter++
        fmt.Println("Counter:", *counter)
    }

    func main() {
        var mu sync.Mutex
        counter := 0

        safeIncrement(&mu, &counter)
    }
```

Following is the output:

- o **Counter: 1**

- **Avoid nested locks**: Limit the use of nested locks, as they significantly raise the risk of deadlocks.

  Example: Nested locks:

```
package main

import (
    "fmt"
    "sync"
)

func main() {
    var mu1, mu2 sync.Mutex

    go func() {
        mu1.Lock()
        defer mu1.Unlock()

        mu2.Lock()
        defer mu2.Unlock()

        fmt.Println("Goroutine 1 completed")
    }()

    go func() {
        mu2.Lock()
        defer mu2.Unlock()

        mu1.Lock()
        defer mu1.Unlock()

        fmt.Println("Goroutine 2 completed")
    }()
}
```

- In the aforementioned code, we have two goroutines, each attempting to acquire two mutexes (**mu1** and **mu2**) in a nested fashion but in opposite order. goroutine 1 locks **mu1** first then tries to lock **mu2**, while goroutine 2 locks **mu2** first then tries to lock **mu1**. When both goroutines run concurrently, a deadlock occurs when goroutine 1 successfully acquires mu1 and goroutine 2 successfully acquires **mu2** at roughly the same time.
- Now goroutine 1 blocks waiting for **mu2**, which is held by goroutine 2, while goroutine 2 blocks waiting for **mu1**, which is held by goroutine 1, creating a circular dependency where neither can proceed and neither will ever release their held lock.
- This example demonstrates the potential for deadlocks due to nested locks. Avoiding such patterns or introducing consistent lock ordering resolves the issue.

• **Use channels instead of locks**: Channels provide a safer and more idiomatic way to synchronize goroutines, avoiding many common pitfalls of locks.

Example: Using channels:

```
package main

import (
    "fmt"
    "time"
)

func worker(id int, ch chan int) {
    for task := range ch {
        fmt.Printf("Worker %d processing task %d\n", id, task)
    }
}

func main() {
    ch := make(chan int, 3)

    go worker(1, ch)
    go worker(2, ch)

    for i := 1; i <= 5; i++ {
        ch <- i
    }
    close(ch)

    time.Sleep(1 * time.Second)
}
```

• **Detect deadlocks early**: Use tools and techniques to identify potential deadlocks during development and testing.

Use the **-race** detector:

```
go run -race main.go
```

• **Analyze goroutines**: Use **runtime.Stack** to dump stack traces and identify blocked goroutines.

Real-world applications

In real-world systems, concurrency error handling ensures robust database access, safe file I/O operations, resilient API servers, and stable distributed systems, as shown:

- **Database access**: Synchronize access to database connections to avoid deadlocks.
- **File I/O**: Prevent simultaneous writes to the same file.
- **API servers**: Manage access to shared resources like caches or session stores.
- **Distributed systems**: Ensure distributed locks do not lead to circular waits.

Recovering from panics in concurrent programs

In Go, a panic represents an unexpected condition that halts the normal flow of execution. While panics are useful for debugging during development, they can lead to catastrophic failures in production if not handled properly. Recovering from panics in concurrent programs ensures that a single goroutine's failure does not crash the entire application.

Panic

A panic is triggered when a program encounters an unrecoverable error, such as:

- Accessing a nil pointer.
- Out-of-bounds array access.
- Explicit call to `panic()`.

The following are the behaviors:

- Panics immediately stop the execution of the current function.
- Control propagates up the call stack until it encounters the `main` function or a `recover()` call.

Importance of recovering panics

Recovering from panics prevents crashes, allows graceful degradation of functionality, supports effective error reporting, and enhances application reliability even during unexpected failures, as shown:

- **Prevent application crashes**: A panic in one goroutine should not bring down the entire application.
- **Graceful degradation**: Recover gracefully and allow the application to continue functioning.
- **Error reporting**: Log and diagnose the cause of the panic for debugging and maintenance.

Using recover to handle panics

The recover function captures a panic and prevents it from propagating further. It must be called within a defer statement.

Example: Recover from a panic:

```
package main

import "fmt"

func safeFunction() {
    defer func() {
        if r := recover(); r != nil {
```

```
            fmt.Println("Recovered from panic:", r)
        }
    }()

    fmt.Println("Executing safeFunction")
    panic("something went wrong")
}

func main() {
    fmt.Println("Starting main")
    safeFunction()
    fmt.Println("Continuing execution in main")
}
```

The following are the outputs:

- **Starting main**
- **Executing safeFunction**
- **Recovered from panic; something went wrong**
- **Continuing execution in main**

Panics in concurrent programs

In concurrent programs, panics occurring in one goroutine do not directly affect other goroutines. However, if not recovered, they may crash the main goroutine.

Example: Panic in a goroutine:

```
package main

import (
    "fmt"
    "time"
)

func worker(id int) {
    defer func() {
        if r := recover(); r != nil {
            fmt.Printf("Worker %d recovered from panic: %v\n", id, r)
        }
    }()

    fmt.Printf("Worker %d starting\n", id)
    if id == 2 {
        panic(fmt.Sprintf("Worker %d encountered an error", id))
    }
    fmt.Printf("Worker %d completed\n", id)
}

func main() {
```

```
    for i := 1; i <= 3; i++ {
        go worker(i)
    }

    time.Sleep(1 * time.Second) // Allow goroutines to complete
    fmt.Println("Main function continues execution")
}
```

The following are the outputs:

- `Worker 1 starting`
- `Worker 2 starting`
- `Worker 3 starting`
- `Worker 2 recovered from panic; worker 2 encountered an error`
- `Worker 1 completed`
- `Worker 3 completed`
- `The main function continues execution`

Strategies for recovering panics in goroutines

Using centralized panic recovery, combining **`sync.WaitGroup`** with panic recovery, and logging stack traces ensure that individual goroutine failures do not cascade into application-wide failures, as follows:

- **Centralized panic recovery**: Encapsulate panic recovery in a reusable wrapper function.

  Example: Panic recovery wrapper:

```
package main

import "fmt"

func safeGo(fn func()) {
    go func() {
        defer func() {
            if r := recover(); r != nil {
                fmt.Println("Recovered from panic:", r)
            }
        }()
        fn()
    }()
}

func main() {
    safeGo(func() {
        fmt.Println("Goroutine 1 started")
        panic("unexpected error in Goroutine 1")
    })

    safeGo(func() {
        fmt.Println("Goroutine 2 started")
```

```
        // No panic
    })

    fmt.Println("Main function continues")
}
```

The following are the outputs:

- **`Main function continues`**
- **`Goroutine 2 started`**

- **Using sync.WaitGroup with panic recovery**: Combine **`sync.WaitGroup`** with recovery to ensure all goroutines complete gracefully.

  Example: Recover in goroutines with **`WaitGroup`**:

```
package main

import (
    "fmt"
    "sync"
)

func worker(id int, wg *sync.WaitGroup) {
    defer wg.Done()
    defer func() {
        if r := recover(); r != nil {
            fmt.Printf("Worker %d recovered from panic: %v\n", id, r)
        }
    }()

    fmt.Printf("Worker %d starting\n", id)
    if id == 2 {
        panic(fmt.Sprintf("Worker %d panicked", id))
    }
    fmt.Printf("Worker %d completed\n", id)
}

func main() {
    var wg sync.WaitGroup

    for i := 1; i <= 3; i++ {
        wg.Add(1)
        go worker(i, &wg)
    }

    wg.Wait()
    fmt.Println("All workers completed")
}
```

The following are the outputs:

```
o    Worker 1 starting
o    Worker 2 starting
o    Worker 3 starting
o    Worker 2 recovered from panic; worker 2 panicked
o    Worker 1 completed
o    Worker 3 completed
o    All workers completed
```

- **Logging panics**: Log panic information, including stack traces, to diagnose issues effectively.

  Example: Logging stack traces:

```go
package main

import (
    "fmt"
    "runtime"
)

func recoverAndLog() {
    if r := recover(); r != nil {
        buf := make([]byte, 1024)
        runtime.Stack(buf, false)
        fmt.Printf("Recovered from panic: %v\nStack trace:\n%s\n", r, buf)
    }
}

func worker() {
    defer recoverAndLog()
    panic("Worker panicked")
}

func main() {
    go worker()
    fmt.Println("Main function continues")
}
```

Best practices for panic recovery

Always recover panics inside goroutines, centralize recovery logic, log panics with stack traces for diagnosis, avoid overusing panics for normal errors, and rigorously test recovery mechanisms, as shown:

- **Recover in goroutines**: Always use recover in long-running goroutines to prevent application crashes.
- **Centralized recovery logic**: Encapsulate recovery in reusable functions or wrappers for consistency.
- **Log and monitor panics**: Record panic details for debugging and monitoring.
- **Avoid overusing panics**: Use panics only for truly exceptional conditions; prefer errors for expected failures.
- **Test recovery mechanisms**: Simulate panics during testing to ensure that recovery logic is robust.

Real-world applications

Panic recovery is critical in production web servers, worker pools, background services, and distributed systems to maintain stability and avoid large-scale outages, as follows:

- **Web servers**: Recover panics in request handlers to prevent server crashes.
- **Worker pools**: Use recovery in worker goroutines to handle task-specific errors.
- **Background services**: Ensure background tasks recover gracefully and continue execution.
- **Distributed systems**: Prevent a single node or process failure from affecting the entire system.

Synchronizing state between goroutines

In concurrent programming, sharing and synchronizing the state between goroutines is essential to ensure correctness and consistency. Improper synchronization can lead to issues like race conditions, data corruption, or deadlocks. Go provides several tools, such as channels, mutexes, and atomic operations, to synchronize state effectively.

Importance of synchronization

Correct synchronization prevents data races, ensures data consistency, coordinates goroutine activities, and maintains predictable system behavior, which is essential in concurrent applications as follows:

- **Avoid data races**: Ensure that shared resources are accessed in a thread-safe manner.
- **Preserve data integrity**: Prevent partial or inconsistent updates to shared state.
- **Coordinate goroutines**: Manage dependencies and execution order between goroutines.
- **Ensure predictable behavior**: Guarantee that program behavior remains consistent regardless of execution timing.

Techniques for synchronizing state

Mutexes, RWMutexes, channels, atomic operations, and condition variables provide powerful tools for synchronizing access to shared resources among goroutines, preventing data corruption and contention, as follows:

- **Using mutexes**: The **`sync.Mutex`** is utilized to synchronize access to shared resources, guaranteeing that only one goroutine can enter a critical section at a given time.

  Example: Synchronizing a shared counter:

```
package main

import (
    "fmt"
    "sync"
)

var counter int
var mu sync.Mutex

func increment(wg *sync.WaitGroup) {
    defer wg.Done()
    mu.Lock()
```

```
    counter++
    mu.Unlock()
}

func main() {
    var wg sync.WaitGroup

    for i := 0; i < 5; i++ {
        wg.Add(1)
        go increment(&wg)
    }

    wg.Wait()
    fmt.Println("Final Counter:", counter)
}
```

Following is the output:

- `Final counter: 5`

- **Using sync.RWMutex**: The `sync.RWMutex` permits multiple goroutines to read a resource concurrently while ensuring that only one goroutine can write to it at any given time.

  Example: Read-write synchronization:

```
package main

import (
    "fmt"
    "sync"
)

type SafeMap struct {
    mu    sync.RWMutex
    items map[string]int
}

func (s *SafeMap) Read(key string) int {
    s.mu.RLock()
    defer s.mu.RUnlock()
    return s.items[key]
}

func (s *SafeMap) Write(key string, value int) {
    s.mu.Lock()
    defer s.mu.Unlock()
    s.items[key] = value
}
```

```
func main() {
    sm := &SafeMap{items: make(map[string]int)}

    sm.Write("a", 1)
    fmt.Println("Value of 'a':", sm.Read("a"))
}
```

- **Using channels**: Channels are the idiomatic way to share state in Go. They allow goroutines to communicate safely without explicit locking.

  Example: State management with channels:

```
package main

import (
    "fmt"
)

func stateManager(ch chan int, done chan bool) {
    counter := 0
    for {
        select {
        case val := <-ch:
            counter += val
        case <-done:
            fmt.Println("Final Counter:", counter)
            return
        }
    }
}

func main() {
    ch := make(chan int)
    done := make(chan bool)

    go stateManager(ch, done)

    for i := 1; i <= 5; i++ {
        ch <- i
    }
    close(done)
}
```

- **Atomic operations**: The sync/atomic package offers low-level primitives for performing thread-safe operations on integers and pointers.

  Example: Using atomic operations:

```
package main
```

```
import (
    "fmt"
    "sync/atomic"
)

func main() {
    var counter int64

    for i := 0; i < 10; i++ {
        go atomic.AddInt64(&counter, 1)
    }

    atomic.StoreInt64(&counter, atomic.LoadInt64(&counter)+1)
    fmt.Println("Final Counter:", atomic.LoadInt64(&counter))
}
```

Following is the output:

- **Final counter: 7**

- **Using sync.Cond for condition synchronization**: **sync.Cond** allows goroutines to wait for specific conditions to be met before proceeding.

  Example: Using **sync.Cond**:

```
package main
import (
    "fmt"
    "sync"
)

func main() {
    var mu sync.Mutex
    cond := sync.NewCond(&mu)
    ready := false

    go func() {
        cond.L.Lock()
        for !ready {
            cond.Wait()
        }
        fmt.Println("Goroutine proceeding")
        cond.L.Unlock()
    }()

    cond.L.Lock()
    ready = true
    cond.Signal()
    cond.L.Unlock()
}
```

Comparing synchronization techniques

The following table shows the various synchronization techniques:

Technique	When to use
Mutex	To protect critical sections or shared resources.
RWMutex	For scenarios with many readers and few writers.
Channels	For sharing state through message-passing (idiomatic Go approach).
Atomic operations	For simple, fast, and low-level updates to shared variables.
Condition variables	For more complex coordination requiring waiting for specific conditions.

***Table 13.1**: Comparison of synchronization techniques*

Applications of Go synchronization

Synchronization techniques are widely used to protect shared caches, manage database connections, coordinate job scheduling, and process large-scale data streams concurrently. Let us look at the applications:

- **Web servers**: Synchronize access to shared caches or session data.
- **Database connections**: Manage a pool of connections safely.
- **Job scheduling**: Distribute tasks across worker goroutines while maintaining a consistent state.
- **Concurrent data processing**: Aggregate results from multiple goroutines processing data streams.

Common pitfalls and solutions

Go's concurrency feature comes with a ton of advantages. However, if not handled properly, it may lead to a couple of pitfalls.

Some of the pitfalls and the solutions are discussed as follows:

- **Pitfall race conditions**: Race conditions occur when multiple goroutines simultaneously access and modify shared state.

  Solution: Use mutexes, channels, or atomic operations to synchronize access.
- **Pitfall deadlocks**: Arise when goroutines wait indefinitely for each other to release locks.

  Solution: Avoid nested locks and maintain consistent lock order.
- **Pitfall goroutine leaks**: Occur when goroutines are blocked indefinitely.

  Solution: Use channels or `context.Context` to signal termination.

Best practices for Go synchronization

Prefer channels for synchronization, minimize shared state, leverage atomic operations for simple counters, keep locks short-lived, and always use the `-race` detector during testing for the following:

- **Prefer channels over locks**: Use Go's idiomatic message-passing approach for synchronization.
- **Minimize shared state**: Limit the amount of shared data to reduce complexity.
- **Use atomic operations for simplicity**: For single-value updates, prefer atomic operations to avoid locking overhead.
- **Avoid long lock durations**: Keep critical sections as short as possible to minimize contention.
- **Test with -race**: Use Go's race detector to identify race conditions during development.

Conclusion

Concurrency magnifies the challenges of error handling, deadlock avoidance, panic recovery, and shared state management. This chapter introduced you to best practices and practical strategies for building resilient and robust concurrent Go programs.

In the next chapter, we will explore how concurrent programming patterns extend into distributed systems, microservices designs, and cloud-native architectures, setting the foundation for large-scale, scalable systems.

Questions

1. What is the main challenge of error handling in concurrency?
2. Why should we use context in concurrent programs?
3. What causes a deadlock in Go programs?
4. How can you detect race conditions in Go?
5. What is the purpose of the recover function?
6. How does centralized error handling improve concurrent applications?
7. What is a goroutine leak?
8. Which Go synchronization primitive allows multiple readers but only one writer?
9. When should atomic operations be preferred over mutexes?
10. Why is logging panic stack traces important?

Join our Discord space

Join our Discord workspace for latest updates, offers, tech happenings around the world, new releases, and sessions with the authors:

https://discord.bpbonline.com

CHAPTER 14
Understanding Microservices Architecture

Introduction

In this chapter, we explore the world of microservices architecture, a modern approach to building scalable and flexible applications. You will learn about the fundamentals of microservices, their advantages over traditional monolithic applications, core components, challenges, real-world use cases, and best practices for deployment. We will also discuss why Go is an excellent choice for developing microservices. Whether you are new to the concept or looking to deepen your understanding, this chapter provides a comprehensive foundation to get you started with microservices.

Structure

In this chapter, we will discuss the following topics:

- Microservices
- Need for Go microservices
- Principles of designing microservices

Objectives

By the end of this chapter, you will understand the essential principles and benefits of microservices architecture. You will be able to differentiate between monolithic and microservices designs, identify key components and deployment strategies, and recognize challenges associated with microservices. Additionally, you will appreciate why Go is particularly suited for building scalable, high-performance microservices. You will also be equipped with design principles to create resilient, autonomous, and well-architected microservices, preparing you for hands-on development in subsequent chapters.

Microservices

Microservices are an architectural style where a software application is composed of many small, independent services. Each service handles a specific business capability, communicates over lightweight protocols (typically HTTP or messaging queues), and can be developed, deployed, and scaled independently. Microservices promote modularity, make applications easier to scale and maintain, and allow teams to work autonomously on different services using different technology stacks.

Overview

Microservices architecture is a contemporary design used in software development that organizes an application into a set of small, independently deployable services. Each service is designed to handle a distinct function and interacts with others through an application programming interface. This approach enhances scalability, flexibility, and ease of maintenance, making it well-suited for managing large and complex systems.

Understanding microservices architecture

Microservices is a design approach that breaks down an application into a collection of small, independent services that collaborate to achieve overall functionality. Each service operates autonomously and focuses on a specific task, ensuring modularity and flexibility in development.

The following are the key characteristics of microservices:

- **Independent deployment**: Each microservice can be built, deployed, and scaled separately without impacting others.
- **Adherence to the single responsibility principle (SRP)**: Every microservice is dedicated to a distinct business function.
- **Loose coupling**: Microservices communicate using lightweight protocols such as REST, gRPC, or messaging queues, ensuring minimal dependencies.
- **Technology flexibility**: Each service can be implemented using different programming languages, frameworks, and databases as needed.
- **Decentralized data management**: Microservices maintain their own databases, ensuring data autonomy and reducing dependencies.
- **Fault tolerance**: Failures in one microservice do not necessarily disrupt the complete system, enhancing resilience.

Monolithic vs. microservices architecture

A monolithic architecture is like a single big block where all functionalities are tightly coupled into one unit. If one module fails or needs updating, the entire application might need to be rebuilt or redeployed.

In contrast, a microservices architecture splits the application into multiple smaller services that can operate, deploy, and scale independently. This improves agility, fault tolerance, and scalability, as follows:

Aspect	Monolithic architecture	Microservices architecture
Structure	Single, tightly integrated application	Distributed, loosely coupled services
Scalability	Horizontal scaling is challenging	Services can be scaled independently
Technology stack	One technology stack for the entire application	Each service can use different technologies
Deployment	Uses a single-unit deployment approach	Each service is deployed independently
Maintenance	Becomes difficult to maintain as the codebase expands	Easier to manage and update individual services.
Fault tolerance	A single failure can collapse the entire system.	Failures in one service do not impact others, ensuring better resilience.

***Table 14.1**: Monolithic vs. microservices architecture*

The following are the example scenarios:

- **Monolithic application**: A traditional e-commerce application includes a user management module, an order management module, and a payment module within a single codebase.
- **Microservices approach**: Each of these modules is developed as an independent microservice, communicating via APIs.

Components of microservices architecture

There are various components that together form the Microservices Architecture. The components of microservices architecture are given as follows:

- **API gateway**: An API gateway serves as a point of entry for clients, managing authentication, request routing, and rate limiting. It acts as an intermediary between clients and microservices, ensuring security, load balancing, and efficient communication.
- **Service discovery**: Automatically detects and registers microservices to allow seamless communication.
- **Load balancer**: Distributes incoming requests among multiple instances of microservices to enhance performance.
- **Database per service**: Each microservice can manage its own database, reducing dependencies.
- **Communication mechanisms**: When building distributed systems, services need to communicate with each other. Communication can be categorized into two main types:
    - **Synchronous**: In synchronous communication, the sender waits for a response from the receiver before continuing. Examples: REST API, gRPC.
    - **Asynchronous**: In asynchronous communication, the sender does not wait for a response and continues processing other tasks. Messages are typically placed into a queue and handled separately.
    - **Examples**: Message brokers (Kafka, RabbitMQ).
- **Monitoring and logging**: Microservices demand comprehensive monitoring and logging solutions to ensure performance, reliability, and debugging efficiency. Tools like Prometheus (for metrics collection), Grafana (for visualization), and the **Elasticsearch, Logstash, and Kibana** (**ELK**) Stack (ELK for centralized logging) help in tracking system health, detecting anomalies, and diagnosing issues effectively.

Advantages of microservices

Microservices allow independent development and deployment of components, enabling faster delivery and scaling. They improve fault isolation, so failures in one service do not crash the whole system. Teams can choose the best technology stack suited for each service. Microservices enhance system resilience, flexibility, and make maintenance easier over time. Let us look at the advantages:

- **Scalability**: Microservices can be scaled individually, ensuring efficient resource usage and cost savings:
    - Each microservice can be scaled independently based on demand, giving optimal resource utilization and high system efficiency. This enables organizations to allocate computing power where needed, ensuring better performance and cost-effectiveness.
    - Enables efficient use of computing resources.
- **Faster development and deployment**: Teams can work independently, leading to faster releases and continuous deployment.
    - Teams can develop, test, and deploy microservices independently, enabling quicker release cycles and improved agility in software development.
    - Facilitates **continuous integration/continuous deployment** (**CI/CD**).
- **Flexibility in technology**: Each microservice can use different programming languages, frameworks, and databases.
- **Improved fault isolation**: A failure in one microservice does not impact the entire system.
- **Easier maintenance**: Smaller codebases make it easier to modify and refactor services.

Challenges of microservices

While microservices offer many benefits, they also introduce new challenges that teams must manage carefully. These challenges often revolve around system complexity, data management, security, and operational overhead, as follows:

- **Complexity**: Managing a distributed set of services significantly increases architectural complexity.
  - Services must be properly orchestrated and monitored.
  - Dependency management, versioning, and service discovery become critical tasks.
  - Requires specialized tools like Kubernetes, Istio, or service meshes for orchestration.
- **Network latency**: Microservices communicate over the network, leading to potential latency issues.
- **Data consistency**:
  - Maintaining consistent data across multiple services is difficult.
  - Traditional ACID transactions are hard to implement across services.
  - Systems often rely on eventual consistency through patterns like Sagas and distributed transactions.
  - Careful design is needed to maintain integrity without tightly coupling services.
- **Security concerns**: The distributed nature of microservices exposes more attack surfaces.
  - Each service's API becomes a potential vulnerability.
  - Strong authentication, authorization, and encryption mechanisms must be implemented.
  - Secure service-to-service communication (e.g., using mTLS) becomes important.
- **Deployment overhead**: Each microservice needs to be built, tested, and deployed separately.

Real-world use cases of microservices

Microservices architecture is widely adopted across industries to build scalable, resilient, and flexible applications. It enables businesses to independently develop, deploy, and scale different parts of their systems, improving efficiency and user experience.

The details are as follows:

- **E-commerce platforms**: Order processing, payment, and inventory management as separate microservices.
- **Streaming services**: Video encoding, recommendation engines, and content delivery run as independent services.
- **Financial systems**: Fraud detection, transaction processing, and user account management operate separately.
- **Social media applications**: News feeds, messaging, and notifications are handled by different microservices.

Microservices deployment strategies

Microservices must be packaged and deployed before they can start functioning. The following are some common strategies for deployment:

- **Containerization**:
  - Each microservice can be packaged into a lightweight Docker container along with its dependencies. This ensures consistent behavior across development, testing, and production environments. Kubernetes can orchestrate these containers for load balancing, scaling, and self-healing. Services are packaged into containers using Docker.

Docker is a containerization tool that enables developers to package the applications along with their dependencies into portable and lightweight containers. These containers ensure consistent execution across different environments, including development machines, test servers, and cloud platforms. Docker utilizes images as templates for creating containers, streamlining deployment, and enhancing reliability. By encapsulating everything an application requires, Docker eliminates compatibility issues and simplifies application management and scaling.

  - Kubernetes is used for orchestration and auto-scaling. Kubernetes is a system for managing and scaling containerized applications automatically. It helps deploy, run, and balance workloads across multiple machines, ensuring high availability and efficient resource use. Kubernetes organizes containers into groups called pods and manages them across a cluster of servers. It handles tasks like load balancing, scaling, and self-healing to keep applications running smoothly. With Kubernetes, developers can easily manage complex applications across different environments.

- **Serverless computing**: Services can be deployed as serverless functions using platforms like AWS Lambda and Google Cloud Functions, allowing automatic scaling, reduced operational overhead, and cost efficiency by running code only when needed

  Serverless functions, like AWS Lambda and Google Cloud Functions, let developers run code without managing servers. They automatically scale based on demand and only execute when triggered, reducing costs. These functions are event-driven, meaning they run in response to actions like HTTP requests or database changes. Since the cloud provider handles infrastructure, developers can focus on developing code instead of managing servers. Serverless computing simplifies deployment and is ideal for microservices, automation, and real-time processing.

- **CI/CD pipelines**: Automating deployment using Jenkins, GitHub Actions, GitLab CI/CD.
- **Service mesh**: Using tools like Istio for service-to-service communication, security, and observability.

  Istio is a service mesh that facilitates communication management between microservices in cloud-native applications. It offers traffic control, security, and observability without modifying the application code. By leveraging a sidecar proxy (such as Envoy), Istio efficiently handles service-to-service traffic, enabling features like load balancing, authentication, and monitoring. It simplifies the management of complex distributed systems, enhancing reliability, security, and performance in microservices architectures.

Usage of microservices

Some of the popular use cases of microservices are given as follows:

- **Suitable scenarios**: Microservices are ideal for applications requiring independent scalability, built by large teams working on different modules, systems with frequent feature updates, applications needing multiple database technologies, or where rapid deployments and iterations are critical.
  - Applications requiring scalability and high availability.
  - Large development teams working on different modules.
  - Systems with frequent updates and rapid deployment needs.
  - Applications needing multi-language and multi-database support.
- **When not to use microservices**: Avoid using microservices for simple, small-scale applications, projects with limited infrastructure budgets, or teams lacking experience with distributed system complexities, as the overhead may outweigh the benefits.
  - Small applications with low complexity.
  - Limited infrastructure resources.
  - Teams unfamiliar with microservices best practices.

Need for Go microservices

Go is an excellent choice for microservices due to its minimalistic design, fast execution, built-in concurrency support, simple deployment, strong networking libraries, small binary size, and seamless integration with cloud-native tools like Docker, Kubernetes, and gRPC.

Golang has emerged as one of the most famous programming languages for building microservices due to its simplicity, performance, concurrency model, and ease of deployment. Developed at Google, Go is designed for scalability, efficiency, and maintainability, making it an excellent choice for microservices architectures.

Key reasons for choosing Go for microservices

Go offers excellent performance with its lightweight runtime and fast execution speed, making it ideal for microservices. Its strong support for concurrency using goroutines helps efficiently handle multiple requests. The simplicity and clarity of Go's syntax speed up development and reduce bugs. Built-in features like a powerful standard library and easy deployment with static binaries make Go a practical choice.

Simplicity and readability

Go's clean and minimalistic syntax allows developers to quickly read, understand, and maintain code. Its design eliminates unnecessary complexities, enabling faster ramp-up for teams and supporting maintainable microservices development. Let us look at the details:

- **Minimalistic syntax**: Go has a clean and concise syntax, making it easier to read and maintain.
- **No unnecessary features**: Lacks unnecessary complexities such as explicit class-based inheritance, reducing cognitive load for developers.
- **Faster development**: New developers can quickly ramp up and start contributing.

Example: Simple Go web server:

```
package main

import (
    "fmt"
    "net/http"
)

func handler(w http.ResponseWriter, r *http.Request) {
    fmt.Fprintf(w, "Hello, Microservices with Go!")
}

func main() {
    http.HandleFunc("/", handler)
    http.ListenAndServe(":8080", nil)
}
```

Following is the output as shown in the following figure:

Figure 14.1: Output viewed in browser

This example demonstrates how quickly a microservice can be built in Go.

Note: There is no need to understand all the syntax now; we will discuss this in the coming chapters.

Concurrency model

Concurrency is at the heart of microservices since multiple requests, tasks, or processes need to be handled simultaneously:

- **Lightweight goroutines**: Instead of threads, Go uses goroutines, which are more efficient in terms of memory and execution.
- **Efficient communication**: Channels allow safe data exchange between goroutines without locks or mutexes.

Example: Using goroutines and channels:

```
package main

import (
    "fmt"
    "time"
)

func worker(id int, jobs <-chan int, results chan<- int) {
    for job := range jobs {
        fmt.Printf("Worker %d processing job %d\n", id, job)
        time.Sleep(time.Second)
        results <- job * 2
    }
}

func main() {
    jobs := make(chan int, 5)
    results := make(chan int, 5)

    for w := 1; w <= 3; w++ {
        go worker(w, jobs, results)
    }

    for j := 1; j <= 5; j++ {
        jobs <- j
    }
    close(jobs)

    for a := 1; a <= 5; a++ {
        <-results
    }
}
```

The following are the outputs:

- `Worker 3 processing job 1`
- `Worker 1 processing job 2`
- `Worker 2 processing job 3`
- `Worker 2 processing job 5`
- `Worker 1 processing job 4`

This example shows how microservices can efficiently process multiple tasks in parallel.

High performance

Go is a compiled language that translates source code directly into machine code, resulting in fast startup times, low memory usage, and efficient execution. These traits make Go ideal for building highly performant microservices that can handle heavy loads, as follows:

- **Compiled language**: Go is compiled directly into machine code, making execution faster than interpreted languages like Python or JavaScript.
- **Efficient memory management**: Go has a **garbage collector** (**GC**) optimized for low-latency applications.
- **Optimized HTTP handling**: The built-in **`net/http`** package provides highly optimized network performance.

Following is the benchmark of Go vs. other languages in microservices:

Feature	Go	Java	Python
Startup time	~Few ms	~500ms - 1s	~1s+
Memory usage	Low	High	Moderate
Concurrency	Goroutines	Threads	Async IO
Performance	High	High	Moderate

***Table 14.2**: Go's benchmark with other languages*

Native support for networking and HTTP

Go has built-in support for networking and HTTP, making it easier to develop RESTful APIs and gRPC-based microservices.

Example: Creating a REST API:

```
package main

import (
    "encoding/json"
    "net/http"
)

type Response struct {
    Message string 'json:"message"'
}

func helloHandler(w http.ResponseWriter, r *http.Request) {
    response := Response{Message: "Welcome to Microservices with Go!"}
```

```
    json.NewEncoder(w).Encode(response)
}

func main() {
    http.HandleFunc("/hello", helloHandler)
    http.ListenAndServe(":8080", nil)
}
```

Following is the output as shown in the following figure:

***Figure 14.2**: Output viewed in browser*

This API returns a JSON response without requiring any third-party libraries.

Note: There is no need to understand all the syntax now; we will discuss it in the coming chapters.

Small binary size

Go applications compile into a single small binary without external runtime dependencies. This reduces deployment complexity, improves start-up time, and minimizes resource consumption, making Go ideal for cloud-native and containerized environments:

- Go applications are compiled into a single standalone binary, reducing dependency management issues.
- Microservices built with Go require minimal runtime overhead, making them ideal for cloud environments.

Following table shows the comparison of executable sizes:

Language	Binary size (Hello World)
Go	~2MB
Java	~50MB (with JDK dependencies)
Python	Requires separate interpreter

***Table 14.3**: Size of executables*

Cloud-native and container-friendly

Go's design is inherently suited for building microservices that run inside containers. Its minimal memory footprint, fast boot-up time, and simple networking make it easy to integrate with Docker and Kubernetes for scalable cloud-native deployments. Let us look at the features:

- Go is lightweight and fast, making it a great choice for containerized microservices.
- Docker and Kubernetes integration is seamless.
- Go applications start quickly and consume fewer resources, which is ideal for serverless deployments.

Example: Dockerizing a Go microservice:

```
FROM golang:1.18 AS builder
WORKDIR /app
COPY . .
RUN go build -o main .
```

```
FROM alpine
WORKDIR /root/
COPY --from=builder /app/main .
CMD ["./main"]
```

This Dockerfile compiles and runs a Go microservice inside a lightweight Alpine Linux container.

gRPC support for high-performance communication

Go provides first-class support for gRPC, which is a high-performance, language-neutral, and platform-independent framework for **remote procedure calls** (**RPCs**).

Example: gRPC in Go:

```
package main

import (
    "context"
    "fmt"
    "google.golang.org/grpc"
    pb "example.com/microservice/proto"
)

func main() {
    conn, _ := grpc.Dial("localhost:50051", grpc.WithInsecure())
    defer conn.Close()

    client := pb.NewMicroserviceClient(conn)
    response, _ := client.SayHello(context.Background(), &pb.HelloRequest{Name: "Go Developer"})
    fmt.Println(response.Message)
}
```

gRPC enables efficient inter-service communication in a microservices environment.

Note: There is no need to understand this code as we will be covering it in the coming chapters and will not discuss it in GRPC. This code is not provided as part of the source code.

Easy deployment and CI/CD integration

Go supports cross-compilation, allowing you to build executables for different operating systems and architectures easily. It integrates well with CI/CD pipelines like Jenkins, GitHub Actions, or GitLab CI, facilitating automated testing, building, and deployment workflows:

- Go applications can be cross compiled for different platforms (Linux, Windows, macOS).
- Easily integrates with CI/CD pipelines for automated deployments.

Strong community and ecosystem

Go is supported by Google and a vibrant developer community. It boasts a rich ecosystem with mature libraries and frameworks such as Gin, Echo, and Fiber, extensive tooling for cloud-native development, and continuous enhancements for scalability and security:

- Backed by Google, with contributions from top cloud-native companies.
- Rich ecosystem with frameworks like Gin, Echo, Fiber for building APIs.
- Active developer community with continuous improvements.

Usage of Go for microservices

Use Go when you need high-performance, cloud-native, containerized microservices with low latency, rapid deployment cycles, and efficient concurrency handling, particularly in Kubernetes environments:

- High-performance, low latency microservices.
- Cloud-native applications are deployed in Kubernetes or Docker.
- Scalable, concurrent services with high request loads.
- CI/CD-driven development with fast deployment cycles.
- Cross-platform microservices that need small binaries.

Avoiding the use of Go for microservices

If the team lacks Go expertise, or if the application demands complex runtime behaviors, heavy metaprogramming, or dynamic features like those provided by Python or Ruby, Go might not be the best fit:

- If the team lacks, Go expertise (steep learning curve for complex projects).
- If microservices require extensive metaprogramming (Go has minimal reflection).
- If using frameworks requiring dynamic runtime behavior (for example, Django in Python).

Principles of designing microservices

Good microservices design follows principles like the single responsibility principle, loose coupling, autonomy, decentralized data management, API-first design, asynchronous communication, fault tolerance, observability, and security-first architecture to build resilient, maintainable, and scalable systems.

Designing microservices is more than just breaking a monolithic application into smaller services. A well-architected microservices system adheres to several fundamental principles to ensure scalability, maintainability, resilience, and independence. These principles help in building reliable, loosely coupled, and efficiently communicating services.

Key principles of microservices design

Key principles of microservices design include building small, independent, and loosely coupled services. Each service should own its data and be deployable independently for maximum flexibility. Services must communicate through lightweight protocols like REST, gRPC, or message queues. A strong focus on scalability, fault tolerance, and clear service boundaries is essential for success.

Let us discuss them in detail in the following subsections.

Single responsibility principle

Each microservice should be dedicated to a single, well-defined business capability, ensuring modularity, better maintainability, and improved scalability within the system.

The following is the importance of the SRP:

- Reducing complexity within each service.
- Makes debugging and maintenance easier.
- Improves separation of concerns.

For example, the e-commerce system. Instead of a single monolithic service handling all functions, break it down into the following:

- **User Service**: Manages user accounts and authentication.
- **Order Service**: Handles order processing.
- **Inventory Service**: Tracks stock levels.

Each service operates independently, making it easy to update or replace.

Loose coupling

Microservices should have minimal dependencies on each other. Changes in one service should not break another.

The following are the strategies for loose coupling:

- Use well-defined APIs (REST / gRPC) for communication.
- Avoid direct database sharing between microservices.
- Use asynchronous messaging (Kafka, RabbitMQ) instead of direct synchronous calls.

Following are the examples:

- **Bad practice**: Order Service directly queries the Inventory Service's database.
- **Good practice**: Order Service requests and inventory updates through a REST API.

Autonomy

Each microservice should be self-contained and deployable independently.

Following are the key aspects:

- Services should be independent in development, deployment, and scaling.
- Each service should manage its own data and logic.
- Deployment should not require coordination with other teams.

For example, the payment service can be updated and deployed without affecting the cart service.

Decentralized data management

Microservices should own their own data, eliminating shared databases that create dependencies.

The following are the usages of the database per microservice:

- Avoids tight coupling.
- Improves performance by optimizing for specific queries.
- Reducing contention and locking issues.

The following are the common patterns:

- Database per microservice (Preferred)
- Event sourcing (Changes are stored as a sequence of events)
- **Command Query Responsibility Segregation** (CQRS)

The following are the examples:

- User Service | PostgreSQL
- Order Service | MongoDB
- Inventory Service | Redis Cache

Each service manages its own database and does not depend on others.

API first communication

Microservices interact using APIs. A well-designed API ensures scalability and maintainability.

The following are the best practices:

- Use REST or gRPC for structured communication.
- Provide clear API documentation (Swagger, OpenAPI).
- Implement versioning (for example, **`/v1/orders`**).

The following is an example of a user service API could expose:

```
GET /users/{id}
{
    "id": 1,
    "name": "Venkatesh R",
    "email": "Venkateshjramesh@gmail.com"
}
```

This allows other services (for example, order service) to request user details without direct database access.

Asynchronous communication

Microservices should favor event-driven, asynchronous communication instead of direct synchronous calls.

The following are the reasons for asynchronous messaging:

- Reduces service-to-service dependencies.
- Increases fault tolerance.
- Allows microservices to process requests independently.

The following are the common messaging systems:

- Apache Kafka
- RabbitMQ
- Google Pub/Sub

The following are examples of order processing flow:

- Order Service places an order | Publishes an event (order_created).
- Inventory Service consumes the event | Updates stock levels.
- The Notification Service listens | Sends an email confirmation.

By using event-driven architecture, each service operates independently.

Fault tolerance and resilience

Microservices should be designed to handle failures gracefully.

The following are the best practices:

- Implement circuit breakers (for example, Netflix Hystrix).
- Use retry mechanisms for temporary failures.
- Implement timeouts for slow responses.
- Use bulkheads to isolate failures.

Example: Circuit breaker in Go:

```
package main

import (
    "fmt"
    "net/http"
    "time"

    "github.com/sony/gobreaker"
)

func main() {
    cb := gobreaker.NewCircuitBreaker(gobreaker.Settings{
        MaxRequests: 5,
        Timeout:     10 * time.Second,
    })

    for i := 0; i < 10; i++ {
        _, err := cb.Execute(func() (interface{}, error) {
            return http.Get("http://example.com")
        })

        if err != nil {
            fmt.Println("Request failed:", err)
        } else {
            fmt.Println("Request succeeded")
        }
    }
}
```

Note: If you face compiling issues for the following dependency, github.com/sony/gobreaker.

Run the following command:

```
go mod tidy
```

The following are the outputs:

- `Request succeeded`
- `Request succeeded`
- `Request succeeded`
- `Request succeeded`

The circuit breaker prevents excessive failures from affecting the system.

Note: There is no need to understand all the syntax now; we will discuss it in the coming chapters.

Observability and monitoring

To ensure system reliability, microservices need logging, monitoring, and tracing.

The following are the key observability tools:

- **Logging**: Use Logrus, Zap for structured logs.
- **Monitoring**: Prometheus and Grafana for real-time metrics.
- **Distributed tracing**: Jaeger, OpenTelemetry to trace requests across services.

Example: Logging in Go:

```
package main

import (
    "log"
    "os"
)

func main() {
    logger := log.New(os.Stdout, "INFO: ", log.Ldate|log.Ltime|log.Lshortfile)
    logger.Println("Microservice started")
}
```

Security first

Security should be an integral part of microservices design.

The following are the security best practices:

- **API authentication**: Use **JSON Web Tokens (JWT)** or OAuth 2.0.
- **Data encryption**: Secure sensitive data with **Transport Layer Security** (**TLS**) or **Secure Sockets Layer** (**SSL**).
- **Zero Trust**: Assume every request is untrusted and validate it.

Example: API authentication:

```
package main

import (
    "fmt"
    "github.com/dgrijalva/jwt-go"
    "time"
)

func generateJWT() (string, error) {
    token := jwt.NewWithClaims(jwt.SigningMethodHS256, jwt.MapClaims{
        "user": "admin",
        "exp":  time.Now().Add(time.Hour * 24).Unix(),
    })
    return token.SignedString([]byte("mysecret"))
}

func main() {
    token, _ := generateJWT()
    fmt.Println("JWT Token:", token)
}
```

Note: There is no need to understand all the syntax now; we will discuss it in the coming chapters.

Example of real-world microservices design

An e-commerce system is split into services like User Management, Order Processing, Inventory Management, Payment Handling, and Notifications. Each service maintains its own database, communicates via APIs or messaging, and is independently deployable, ensuring resilience and scalability.

E-commerce microservices architecture

The architecture is given as follows:

Microservice	Responsibilities	Database
User Service	Manages user accounts and authentication.	PostgreSQL
Order Service	Processes customer order history.	MongoDB
Inventory Service	Manages product stock levels.	Redis
Payment Service	Handles payments and transactions.	Stripe API
Notification Service	Sends emails and push notifications.	Firebase

Table 14.4: *E-commerce microservices architecture*

All services in a microservices architecture communicate through APIs or messaging systems. They use REST or gRPC APIs for synchronous, request-response communication between services. For asynchronous messaging, services rely on message brokers like Kafka to exchange information without waiting. This approach ensures flexibility, scalability, and better fault tolerance across the system. Each service is independently deployable and scalable.

Conclusion

This chapter provided a comprehensive introduction to microservices, covering their advantages, challenges, and architecture. You learned the principles of designing robust microservices and why Go is an ideal language for building them. Real-world examples illustrated how companies structure microservices effectively. Equipped with this foundational knowledge, you are now ready to start building actual microservices.

In the next chapter, we will take the first practical step by building a simple REST API using Go, which will lay the groundwork for more complex microservices applications.

Questions

1. What is a microservice?
2. List two key benefits of microservices over monolithic architecture.
3. Name two common communication mechanisms between microservices.
4. What component manages client requests in a microservices system?
5. Why is Go a good choice for microservices?
6. What is service discovery in microservices?
7. Give one real-world example where microservices are used.
8. What does the SRP mean in microservices?
9. Name a tool used for container orchestration in microservices.
10. When should you avoid using microservices?

CHAPTER 15
Building a Simple REST API in Go

Introduction

This chapter introduces the foundational concepts of building RESTful web APIs using Go. It begins by leveraging Go's powerful net/http package to create lightweight and efficient web servers without any third-party dependencies. The chapter then walks through setting up basic HTTP servers, serving static files, implementing graceful shutdowns, and adding middleware. Developers are also introduced to customizing server configurations and running web servers on multiple ports. This chapter equips you with the essential building blocks to get a web service running in Go, emphasizing simplicity, performance, and reliability.

Structure

The chapter covers the following topics:

- Setting up a web server in Go
- Handling HTTP requests and responses in Go
- Routing in Go web applications
- JSON encoding and decoding in Go
- Error handling in web APIs

Objectives

By the end of this chapter, you will be able to understand the role of the net/http package in building Go web servers and set up a basic HTTP server that can handle client requests effectively. You will learn how to serve static files such as HTML, CSS, and JavaScript using http.FileServer, and implement graceful shutdown techniques that respond to termination signals while allowing in-progress requests to complete safely. The chapter also equips you with the ability to use middleware for logging HTTP requests, enhancing server observability. Additionally, you will be able to configure key server parameters like ReadTimeout, WriteTimeout, and IdleTimeout to protect against slow or malicious clients. Running content on different ports and managing multiple server instances concurrently is also covered. Finally, you will apply best practices, including structured routing, middleware integration, and static asset handling, to build production-ready web servers. These objectives form a critical foundation for developing robust, secure, and scalable REST APIs in the upcoming chapters.

Setting up a web server in Go

This section will deal with setting up a web server with `net/http` in Go:

- **Overview**: Go's built-in `net/http` package provides a lightweight and efficient way to build web servers and handle HTTP requests. Unlike other frameworks that require additional dependencies, `net/http` is part of the Go standard library, making it a great choice for developing RESTful APIs and web applications.

- **Why use net/http for web servers**:
  - **Built-in support**: No external dependencies are required.
  - **Lightweight and fast**: Optimized for high-performance networking.
  - **Concurrency-ready**: Go's goroutines efficiently handle multiple requests.
  - **Extensible**: Can be integrated with frameworks like Gin or Echo if needed.
- **Setting up a basic HTTP server**:
  - **Minimal web server example**: To start a web server, we need to:
    1. Define a handler function.
    2. Register the handler with an HTTP route.
    3. Start the server using **`http.ListenAndServe`**.
  - **Example**: Basic web server:

```go
package main

import (
    "fmt"
    "net/http"
)

func handler(w http.ResponseWriter, r *http.Request) {
    fmt.Fprintf(w, "Go Web Server has started!")
}

func main() {
    http.HandleFunc("/", handler)
    fmt.Println("Server is running on default port 8080...")
    http.ListenAndServe(":8080", nil)
}
```

  - **Output**:

    Open **http://localhost:8080** in a browser. This displays **`Go Web Server has started!`**
  - **Explanation of key functions**: Let us look at the following table:

Function	Description
`http.HandleFunc(pattern, handler)`	Registers a route and associates it with a handler function.
`http.ResponseWriter`	Used to write responses to the client.
`http.Request`	Represents the incoming HTTP request.
`http.ListenAndServe(":8080", nil)`	Starts the HTTP server on the specified port.

***Table 15.1**: HTTP functions*

- **Serving static files**: Web applications often serve static files such as HTML, CSS, JS, and images.
  - **Serving static files using http.FileServer**:

```
package main

import (
    "net/http"
)

func main() {
    fs := http.FileServer(http.Dir("static"))
    http.Handle("/", fs)

    http.ListenAndServe(":8080", nil)
}
```

- **Directory structure**:

```
/static
    index.html
    style.css
    script.js
```

- **Sample index.html**:

```
<!DOCTYPE html>
<html lang="en">
<head>
    <title>Go Web Server Demo</title>
</head>
<body>
    <h1>Hello World</h1>
</body>
</html>
```

- Start the server, and open **http://localhost:8080/** | Serves **index.html**.

- **Graceful shutdown of web server**: When shutting down a web server, we must ensure all ongoing requests are completed gracefully.
  - **Graceful shutdown with http.Server**:

```
package main

import (
    "context"
    "fmt"
    "net/http"
    "os"
    "os/signal"
    "syscall"
    "time"
)

func handler(w http.ResponseWriter, r *http.Request) {
```

```
        fmt.Fprintf(w, "Server is shutting down gracefully...")
    }

    func main() {
        server := &http.Server{Addr: ":8080", Handler: http.HandlerFunc(handler)}

        go func() {
            fmt.Println("Server is running on port 8080...")
            if err := server.ListenAndServe(); err != http.ErrServerClosed {
                fmt.Println("Server error:", err)
            }
        }()

        // Graceful shutdown on Ctrl+C
        stop := make(chan os.Signal, 1)
        signal.Notify(stop, os.Interrupt, syscall.SIGTERM)

        <-stop // Wait for a termination signal
        fmt.Println("\nShutting down the go server...")

        ctx, cancel := context.WithTimeout(context.Background(), 5*time.Second)
        defer cancel()

        if err := server.Shutdown(ctx); err != nil {
            fmt.Println("Shutdown error:", err)
        }
        fmt.Println("Server stopped gracefully ")
    }
```

- **How it works**:
  - Runs the web server in a goroutine.
  - Listens for interrupt signals (*Ctrl+C*).
  - Uses **`context.WithTimeout`** to give 5 seconds for ongoing requests to complete.
  - Calls **`server.Shutdown(ctx)`** for graceful cleanup.

- **Adding middleware for logging requests**: Middleware functions allow us to modify requests/responses before they reach the main handler.
  - **Implementing a logging middleware**:

```
    package main

    import (
        "fmt"
        "net/http"
        "time"
    )
```

```
func loggingMiddleware(next http.Handler) http.Handler {
    return http.HandlerFunc(func(w http.ResponseWriter, r *http.Request) {
        start := time.Now()
        next.ServeHTTP(w, r)
        duration := time.Since(start)
        fmt.Printf("Request: %s %s - %v\n", r.Method, r.URL.Path, duration)
    })
}

func handler(w http.ResponseWriter, r *http.Request) {
    fmt.Fprintln(w, "Hello from Go Server!")
}

func main() {
    mux := http.NewServeMux()
    mux.HandleFunc("/", handler)

    loggedMux := loggingMiddleware(mux)
    http.ListenAndServe(":8080", loggedMux)
}
```

- **How it works:**
  - Logs each request's method, path, and duration.
  - Calls **`next.ServeHTTP(w, r)`** to pass the request to the next handler.
  - Useful for monitoring and debugging API requests.

- **Configuring the server with custom timeouts**: Setting timeouts prevents long-running requests from consuming resources.
  - **Setting read, write, and idle timeouts:**

```
package main

import (
    "fmt"
    "net/http"
    "time"
)

func handler(w http.ResponseWriter, r *http.Request) {
    fmt.Fprintln(w, "Request processed successfully!")
}

func main() {
    server := &http.Server{
        Addr:         ":8080",
        Handler:      http.HandlerFunc(handler),
```

```
        ReadTimeout:  5 * time.Second,
        WriteTimeout: 10 * time.Second,
        IdleTimeout:  15 * time.Second,
    }

    fmt.Println("Server running with timeouts...")
    server.ListenAndServe()
}
```

- **Explanation**:
  - **Read timeout**: Limits the time to read the request body.
  - **Write timeout**: Limits the time to write the response to the client.
  - **Idle timeout**: Closes idle connections after a period of inactivity.

- **Running the server on different ports**:
  - **Default port**: 8080
  - **Change port**: Modify `http.ListenAndServe(":9090", nil)`
  - **To run multiple servers**:

```
go http.ListenAndServe(":8080", nil)
go http.ListenAndServe(":9090", nil)
```

  This runs servers on 8080 and 9090 simultaneously.

- **Best practices for setting up a web server**:
  - Use middleware for logging and authentication.
  - Configure timeouts to prevent slow clients from consuming resources.
  - Use graceful shutdown to handle unexpected terminations.
  - Serve static files efficiently using `http.FileServer`.
  - Avoid using `nil` as a default handler; use structured routing instead.
- **Summary**: Setting up a web server with `net/http` in Go is straightforward and efficient. It provides:
  - A lightweight HTTP server with built-in support.
  - Static file serving for websites and assets.
  - Middleware support for logging and monitoring.
  - Graceful shutdown mechanisms for production readiness.

With this foundation, we can now move on to handling HTTP requests and responses, which will cover GET, POST, PUT, and DELETE methods, request headers, and query parameters.

Handling HTTP requests and responses in Go

In this section, we will be looking at handling HTTP requests and responses in Go:

- **Overview**: Handling HTTP requests and responses is a fundamental part of building REST APIs and web applications in Go. The `net/http` package provides powerful yet simple tools for processing different HTTP methods (GET, POST, PUT, DELETE), parsing request parameters, handling headers, and sending structured responses.

This section covers:

- Handling different HTTP request methods
- Extracting query parameters and form data
- Working with request headers
- Sending JSON responses
- Handling errors properly

- **Understanding HTTP handlers in Go**: In Go, an HTTP handler is a function that takes `http.ResponseWriter` and `http.Request` as parameters.
  - **Basic handler function:**
    ```
    func handler(w http.ResponseWriter, r *http.Request) {
        fmt.Fprintf(w, "Hello, this is a response from Go server!")
    }
    ```
  - **w http.ResponseWriter**: Writes the response to the client.
  - **r *http.Request**: Represents the incoming HTTP request.
- **Handling different HTTP methods**: HTTP defines multiple methods for interacting with resources. Let us handle GET, POST, PUT, and DELETE.
  - **Handling GET requests**: GET requests are used for retrieving data from the server.
    - **Example**: Handling a GET request:
      ```
      package main

      import (
          "fmt"
          "net/http"
      )

      func getHandler(w http.ResponseWriter, r *http.Request) {
          if r.Method != http.MethodGet {
              http.Error(w, "Invalid request method", http.StatusMethodNotAllowed)
              return
          }
          fmt.Fprintf(w, "Received a GET request!")
      }

      func main() {
          http.HandleFunc("/get", getHandler)
          fmt.Println("Server is running on port 8080")
          http.ListenAndServe(":8080", nil)
      }
      ```
    - Only allows GET requests.
    - Returns an error for other methods.
    - **Test it**: Open **http://localhost:8080/get** in a browser.
    - We can find the `Received a GET request` message.

- **Handling POST requests**: POST requests send data to the server.
  - **Example**: Handling a POST request:

```
package main

import (
    "fmt"
    "io/ioutil"
    "net/http"
)

func postHandler(w http.ResponseWriter, r *http.Request) {
    if r.Method != http.MethodPost {
        http.Error(w, "Invalid request method", http.StatusMethodNotAllowed)
        return
    }

    body, _ := ioutil.ReadAll(r.Body)
    fmt.Fprintf(w, "Received POST data: %s", string(body))
}

func main() {
    http.HandleFunc("/post", postHandler)
    fmt.Println("Server is running on port 8080")
    http.ListenAndServe(":8080", nil)
}
```

  - **Test it with curl**:

```
curl -X POST -d "name=Venkatesh&age=40" http://localhost:8080/post
```

  - **Output**: `Received POST data: name=Venkatesh&age=40`
  - Reads request body using `ioutil.ReadAll(r.Body)`.
  - Supports sending form data and JSON payloads.
- **Handling PUT requests**: PUT requests update existing data.
  - **Example**: Handling a PUT request:

```
package main

import (
    "fmt"
    "io/ioutil"
    "net/http"
)

func putHandler(w http.ResponseWriter, r *http.Request) {
    if r.Method != http.MethodPut {
        http.Error(w, "Invalid request method", http.StatusMethodNotAllowed)
```

```
        return
    }

    body, _ := ioutil.ReadAll(r.Body)
    fmt.Fprintf(w, "Updated data: %s", string(body))
}

func main() {
    http.HandleFunc("/put", putHandler)
    fmt.Println("Server is running on port 8080")
    http.ListenAndServe(":8080", nil)
}
```

- **Test it with curl**:

  `curl -X PUT -d "name=Venkat&role=admin" http://localhost:8080/put`

- **Output**: `Updated data: name=Venkat&role=admin`
- This is used for updating existing resources.

- **Handling DELETE requests**: DELETE requests remove a resource from the server.
  - **Example**: Handling a DELETE request:

```
package main

import (
    "fmt"
    "net/http"
)

func deleteHandler(w http.ResponseWriter, r *http.Request) {
    if r.Method != http.MethodDelete {
        http.Error(w, "Invalid request method", http.StatusMethodNotAllowed)
        return
    }

    // Extract input from query parameter (for example, 'id')
    query := r.URL.Query()
    item := query.Get("id")

    if item == "" {
        http.Error(w, "Missing 'id' parameter", http.StatusBadRequest)
        return
    }

    fmt.Fprintf(w, "Item with ID %s has been deleted", item)
}
```

```
func main() {
    http.HandleFunc("/delete", deleteHandler)
    fmt.Println("Server is running on port 8080")
    http.ListenAndServe(":8080", nil)
}
```

   - **Test it with curl:**

     ```
     curl -X DELETE "http://localhost:8080/delete?id=123"
     ```

   - Used to remove a resource from the server.
   - **Output**: `Item with ID 123 has been deleted`

- **Extracting query parameters**: Query parameters allow users to pass data via the URL.
  - **Example**: Extracting query parameters:

```
package main

import (
    "fmt"
    "net/http"
)

func queryHandler(w http.ResponseWriter, r *http.Request) {
    name := r.URL.Query().Get("name")
    age := r.URL.Query().Get("age")

    fmt.Fprintf(w, "Received: Name=%s, Age=%s", name, age)
}

func main() {
    http.HandleFunc("/query", queryHandler)
    fmt.Println("Server is running on port 8080")
    http.ListenAndServe(":8080", nil)
}
```

  - **Test it**: Open **http://localhost:8080/query?name=Venkatesh&age=40** in browser.
  - Parses query parameters using `r.URL.Query().Get(key)`.
  - **Output**:
    - `Received: Name=Venkatesh, Age=40`

- **Reading request headers**: Headers provide metadata about the request.
  - **Example**: Accessing request headers:

```
package main

import (
    "fmt"
    "net/http"
```

```
)

func headerHandler(w http.ResponseWriter, r *http.Request) {
    userAgent := r.Header.Get("User-Agent")
    fmt.Fprintf(w, "Your User-Agent: %s", userAgent)
}

func main() {
    http.HandleFunc("/headers", headerHandler)
    fmt.Println("Server is running on port 8080")
    http.ListenAndServe(":8080", nil)
}
```

- **Test it with curl:**

  ```
  curl -H "User-Agent: GoClient" http://localhost:8080/headers
  ```

- Reads request headers using **`r.Header.Get(User-Agent)`**.
- **Output**:
  - **`Your user-agent: GoClient`**

- **Sending JSON responses**: Microservices often return JSON responses.
  - **Example**: Sending JSON response:

```
package main

import (
    "encoding/json"
    "net/http"
)

type Response struct {
    Message string 'json:"message"'
}

func jsonHandler(w http.ResponseWriter, r *http.Request) {
    w.Header().Set("Content-Type", "application/json")

    response := Response{Message: "Welcome to the Go API"}
    json.NewEncoder(w).Encode(response)
}

func main() {
    http.HandleFunc("/json", jsonHandler)
    http.ListenAndServe(":8080", nil)
}
```

- **Test it:**

  ```
  http://localhost:8080/json
  ```

- Returns structured JSON data using **`json.NewEncoder(w).Encode(response)`**.
- **Output**: **`{"message":"Welcome to the Go API"}`**

- **Handling errors in responses**: Instead of raw errors, send structured JSON error messages.
  - **Example**: Structured error response:

```go
package main

import (
    "encoding/json"
    "net/http"
)

type ErrorResponse struct {
    Error   string 'json:"error"'
    Message string 'json:"message"'
}

func errorHandler(w http.ResponseWriter, r *http.Request) {
    w.WriteHeader(http.StatusBadRequest)

    response := ErrorResponse{
        Error:   "Bad Request",
        Message: "Invalid input provided",
    }
    json.NewEncoder(w).Encode(response)
}

func main() {
    http.HandleFunc("/error", errorHandler)
    http.ListenAndServe(":8080", nil)
}
```

  - **Test it:**

```
http://localhost:8080/error
```

  - Returns structured error responses.
  - **Output**: **`{"error":"Bad Request","message":"Invalid input provided"}`**

- **Summary**:
  - GET, POST, PUT, DELETE requests are supported natively.
  - Extract query parameters and headers for dynamic responses.
  - Handle JSON encoding and decoding efficiently.
  - Send structured error responses for better debugging.

Routing in Go web applications

This section discusses routing in Go web applications:

- **Overview**: Routing is the process of mapping URLs (routes) to their respective handler functions in a web application. Go's standard library (`net/http`) provides basic routing capabilities, but for more advanced features like dynamic routes, middleware, and parameter extraction, third-party routers like gorilla/mux and chi are commonly used.

  This section covers:

  - Basic routing with `net/http`
  - Dynamic route handling (path parameters)
  - Using third-party routers (Gorilla Mux, Chi)
  - Middleware in routing

- **Basic routing with net/http**: In Go's standard library, routes are defined using `http.HandleFunc()`, which associates a URL path with a handler function.

  - **Example**: Basic routing:

```go
package main

import (
    "fmt"
    "net/http"
)

func mainHandler(w http.ResponseWriter, r *http.Request) {
    fmt.Fprintln(w, "Welcome to the Main Page!")
}

func testHandler(w http.ResponseWriter, r *http.Request) {
    fmt.Fprintln(w, "This is the Test Page.")
}

func main() {
    http.HandleFunc("/", mainHandler)
    http.HandleFunc("/test", testHandler)

    fmt.Println("Server running on http://localhost:8080")
    http.ListenAndServe(":8080", nil)
}
```

  - **Test it in the browser:**
    - **http://localhost:8080/** gives `Welcome to the Main Page!`
    - **http://localhost:8080/test** gives `This is the Test Page`.
  - **Pros**: Simple and lightweight.
  - **Cons**: Lacks support for dynamic routes and middleware.

- **Handling dynamic routes (Path parameters)**: Dynamic routes allow extracting path parameters from the URL (e.g., `/user/{id}`).
    - **Manual path parameter extraction**: Since Go's standard library lacks built-in path parameter support, we must manually extract them.

```
package main

import (
    "fmt"
    "net/http"
    "strings"
)

func userHandler(w http.ResponseWriter, r *http.Request) {
    parts := strings.Split(r.URL.Path, "/")
    if len(parts) < 3 {
        http.Error(w, "Invalid user path", http.StatusBadRequest)
        return
    }
    userID := parts[2]
    fmt.Fprintf(w, "User ID: %s", userID)
}

func main() {
    http.HandleFunc("/user/", userHandler) // Matches /user/{id}

    fmt.Println("Server is running on http://localhost:8080")
    http.ListenAndServe(":8080", nil)
}
```

    - **Test it:**

      `http://localhost:8080/user/42`
    - Extracts **42** from **/user/42**.
    - **Limitation**: Manual parsing is tedious for large projects.
- **Advanced routing with gorilla/mux**: `gorilla/mux` is a powerful third-party router with support for:
    - Dynamic path parameters (`/{id}`)
    - Middleware
    - HTTP method restrictions
    - **Installing gorilla/mux**: Run:

      `go get -u github.com/gorilla/mux`
    - **Example**: Using `mux` for routing:

```
package main

import (
    "fmt"
```

```
    "net/http"

    "github.com/gorilla/mux"
)

func userHandler(w http.ResponseWriter, r *http.Request) {
    vars := mux.Vars(r)
    userID := vars["userId"]
    fmt.Fprintf(w, "User ID: %s", userID)
}

func main() {
    r := mux.NewRouter()
    r.HandleFunc("/user/{userId}", userHandler).Methods("GET")

    fmt.Println("Server running on http://localhost:8080")
    http.ListenAndServe(":8080", r)
}
```

  - **Test it:**

    ```
    http://localhost:8080/user/42
    ```

  - Easier path parameter extraction: **`mux.Vars(r)["id"]`**
  - Supports method-specific routes: **`.Methods("GET")`**

- **Routing with chi (lightweight alternative)**: chi is a lightweight and fast router optimized for RESTful APIs.
  - **Installing chi**: Run:

    ```
    go get -u github.com/go-chi/chi/v5
    ```

  - **Example**: Using **`chi`** for routing:

```
package main

import (
    "fmt"
    "net/http"

    "github.com/go-chi/chi/v5”
)

func userHandler(w http.ResponseWriter, r *http.Request) {
    userID := chi.URLParam(r, "userId”)
    fmt.Fprintf(w, "User ID: %s", userID)
}

func main() {
    r := chi.NewRouter()
```

```
    r.Get("/user/{userId}", userHandler)

    fmt.Println("Server is running on http://localhost:8080")
    http.ListenAndServe(":8080", r)
}
```

- **Test it:**

  ```
  http://localhost:8080/user/42
  ```

- Ultra-lightweight
- More readable than mux

* **Middleware in routing**: Middleware allows us to intercept and modify HTTP requests before they reach the handler.

  - **Logging middleware:**

```
package main

import (
    "fmt"
    "net/http"
    "time"

    "github.com/gorilla/mux"
)

func loggingMiddleware(next http.Handler) http.Handler {
    return http.HandlerFunc(func(w http.ResponseWriter, r *http.Request) {
        start := time.Now()
        next.ServeHTTP(w, r)
        fmt.Printf("Request: %s %s - %v\n", r.Method, r.URL.Path, time.Since(start))
    })
}

func homeHandler(w http.ResponseWriter, r *http.Request) {
    fmt.Fprintln(w, "Welcome to the Main Page!")
}

func main() {
    r := mux.NewRouter()
    r.HandleFunc("/", homeHandler)
    r.Use(loggingMiddleware) // Attach middleware

    fmt.Println("Server is running on http://localhost:8080")
    http.ListenAndServe(":8080", r)
}
```

- **Test it:**
  ```
  http://localhost:8080/
  ```
- Logs each request with method, path, and duration.

- **Route grouping**: For organizing large applications, routers allow the grouping of related routes.
  - **Route grouping in mux:**
    ```
    r := mux.NewRouter()

    userRouter := r.PathPrefix("/user").Subrouter()
    userRouter.HandleFunc("/{id}", userHandler).Methods("GET")
    userRouter.HandleFunc("/{id}", updateUserHandler).Methods("PUT")
    ```
  - Route grouping in chi:
    ```
    r := chi.NewRouter()

    r.Route("/user", func(r chi.Router) {
        r.Get("/{id}", userHandler)
        r.Put("/{id}", updateUserHandler)
    })
    ```
  - Better organization of related endpoints.
- **Error handling in routing**: Handling **`404 Not Found`** for undefined routes.
  - **Custom 404 handler:**
    ```
    r.NotFoundHandler = http.HandlerFunc(func(w http.ResponseWriter, r *http.Request) {
        http.Error(w, "Route not found", http.StatusNotFound)
    })
    ```
  - **Now http://localhost:8080/unknown returns**:
    ```
    Route not found
    ```
  - Improves user experience by handling undefined routes gracefully.
- **Best practices for routing**:
  - Use third-party routers (**`mux`** or **`chi`**) for better flexibility.
  - Use middleware for logging, authentication, and request validation.
  - Group related routes for cleaner code organization.
  - Return structured error responses instead of plain text.
  - Implement graceful shutdown to clean up resources on exit.
- **Summary**: Routing is essential for handling HTTP requests efficiently in web applications. While Go's **`net/http`** provides basic routing, libraries like **`gorilla/mux`** and **`chi`** offer better flexibility, path parameters, and middleware support.

JSON encoding and decoding in Go

Here, we will be discussing JSON encoding and decoding in Go:

- **Overview**: JSON is a widely used format for exchanging data between clients and servers. In Go, the encoding/json package provides built-in support for encoding (serializing) Go structs into JSON and decoding (deserializing) JSON into Go structs.

This section covers:

- Encoding Go structs to JSON
- Decoding JSON into Go structs
- Handling JSON requests in REST APIs
- Customizing JSON output with struct tags
- Error handling during encoding/decoding

- **Understanding JSON encoding and decoding**:
    - **Encoding (Serialization)**: Convert Go objects to JSON format.
    - **Decoding (Deserialization)**: Convert JSON format to Go objects.
    - **Example JSON object**:

```
{
    "id": 101,
    "name": "Venkatesh ramesh",
    "email": "venkateshjramesh@gmail.com"
}
```

    - We can encode this data from a Go struct.
    - We can decode this data into a Go struct.

- **Encoding Go structs to JSON**: Encoding means converting Go structs into JSON format using **`json.Marshal()`**.
    - Encoding example:

```
package main

import (
    "encoding/json"
    "fmt"
)

type User struct {
    ID    int    'json:"id"'
    Name  string 'json:"name"'
    Email string 'json:"email"'
}

func main() {
    user := User{ID: 101, Name: "Venkatesh R", Email: "venkateshjramesh@gmail.com"}

    jsonData, err := json.Marshal(user)
    if err != nil {
        fmt.Println("Error encoding JSON:", err)
        return
    }
```

```
    fmt.Println(string(jsonData))
}
```

- **Output**: `{"id":101,"name":"Venkatesh R","email":"venkateshjramesh@gmail.com"}`
- Uses **`json.Marshal()`** to encode data.
- Converts Go struct to JSON format.
- Uses struct tags (**`json:"field_name"`**) to map JSON keys.

• **Decoding JSON into Go structs**: Decoding means parsing JSON data into Go structs using **`json.Unmarshal()`**.

- **Decoding example:**

```
package main

import (
    "encoding/json"
    "fmt"
)

type User struct {
    ID    int    'json:"id"'
    Name  string 'json:"name"'
    Email string 'json:"email"'
}

func main() {
    jsonData := '{"id":101,"name":"Venkatesh R","email":"venkateshjramesh@gmail.com"}'

    var user User
    err := json.Unmarshal([]byte(jsonData), &user)
    if err != nil {
        fmt.Println("Error decoding JSON:", err)
        return
    }

    fmt.Printf("User ID: %d, Name: %s, Email: %s\n", user.ID, user.Name, user.Email)
}
```

- **Output**:
  - **`User ID: 101, Name: Venkatesh R, Email: venkateshjramesh@gmail.com`**
- Uses **`json.Unmarshal()`** to decode JSON into a Go struct.
- Converts JSON to Go struct using **`json:"field_name"`** tags.

• **Handling JSON requests in a REST API**:

- **Accepting JSON data in a REST API**: To enable seamless communication between clients and servers, a well-designed REST API must be capable of accepting and processing JSON data, which is one of the most widely used formats for transmitting structured information over HTTP. The code is as follows:

```
package main

import (
    "encoding/json"
    "fmt"
    "net/http"
)

type User struct {
    ID    int    'json:"id"'
    Name  string 'json:"name"'
    Email string 'json:"email"'
}

func createUserHandler(w http.ResponseWriter, r *http.Request) {
    var user User

    decoder := json.NewDecoder(r.Body)
    if err := decoder.Decode(&user); err != nil {
        http.Error(w, "Invalid JSON", http.StatusBadRequest)
        return
    }

    fmt.Fprintf(w, "User Created: ID=%d, Name=%s, Email=%s\n", user.ID, user.
Name, user.Email)
}

func main() {
    http.HandleFunc("/create", createUserHandler)
    fmt.Println("Server running on http://localhost:8080")
    http.ListenAndServe(":8080", nil)
}
```

- **Test with curl:**

```
curl -X POST -H "Content-Type: application/json" \
-d '{"id":101,"name":"Venkatesh R","email":"venkateshjramesh@gmail.com"}' \
http://localhost:8080/create
```

- Reads JSON request body using **`json.NewDecoder(r.Body)`**.
- Validates and decodes JSON into a Go struct.
- **Output**:
  - **`kUser created: ID=101, Name=Venkatesh R, Email=venkateshjramesh@gmail.com`**
- **Sending JSON response in REST API**: For consistency, interoperability, and ease of integration, a REST API should return responses in JSON format, allowing various REST clients to easily parse and utilize the data received. The code is as follows:

```
package main

import (
    "encoding/json"
    "net/http"
)

type Response struct {
    Status  string 'json:"status"'
    Message string 'json:"message"'
}

func jsonResponseHandler(w http.ResponseWriter, r *http.Request) {
    response := Response{Status: "success", Message: "Data processed successfully"}

    w.Header().Set("Content-Type", "application/json")
    json.NewEncoder(w).Encode(response)
}

func main() {
    http.HandleFunc("/response", jsonResponseHandler)
    http.ListenAndServe(":8080", nil)
}
```

  - **Test it:**

    http://localhost:8080/response
  - Sets response content-type: **`application/json`**
  - Uses **`json.NewEncoder(w).Encode(response)`** to send JSON data.
  - **Output**: **`{"status":"success","message":"Data processed successfully"}`**
- **Customizing JSON with struct tags**: Struct tags help control JSON encoding and decoding.
  - **Custom field names:**

```
type User struct {
    ID    int    'json:"user_id"'
    Name  string 'json:"full_name"'
    Email string 'json:"email_address"'
}
```

  - **JSON output**: **`{"user_id":101,"full_name":"Venkatesh R","email_address":"venkateshjramesh@gmail.com"}`**
  - **Omitting empty fields**: Use **`omitempty`** to skip empty fields.

```
type User struct {
    ID    int    'json:"id,omitempty"'
    Name  string 'json:"name,omitempty"'
}
```

If the **`Name`** is empty, it will not appear in JSON.

- **Handling errors in JSON processing**: Proper error handling prevents crashes in real-world applications.
  - **Handling invalid JSON:**

    ```
    decoder := json.NewDecoder(r.Body)
    if err := decoder.Decode(&user); err != nil {
        http.Error(w, "Invalid JSON format", http.StatusBadRequest)
        return
    }
    ```

  Returns **`400 Bad Request`** for malformed JSON input.
  - **Handling empty JSON response:**

    ```
    if user.ID == 0 {
        http.Error(w, "User not available", http.StatusNotFound)
        return
    }
    ```

  Returns **`404 Not Found`** when user data is missing.
- **JSON streaming for large data sets**: For large datasets, use streaming with **`json.Encoder`** instead of **`json.Marshal()`**.
  - **JSON streaming example:**

    ```
    func streamJSON(w http.ResponseWriter, r *http.Request) {
        w.Header().Set("Content-Type", "application/json")

        encoder := json.NewEncoder(w)
        users := []User{
            {ID: 1, Name: "Venkatesh", Email: "venkateshjramesh@gmail.com"},
            {ID: 2, Name: "Shubham", Email: "Shubham.raizada@gmail.com"},
        }

        encoder.Encode(users) // Stream JSON response
    }
    ```

  - Faster for large JSON responses.
  - Avoids memory overhead from **`json.Marshal()`**.
- **Best practices for JSON handling**:
  - Use **`json.Encoder`** for efficient streaming responses.
  - Always set content-type to **`application/json`**.
  - Handle empty fields with **`omitempty`**.
  - Validate JSON before decoding it.
  - Use meaningful struct tags (**`json:"field_name"`**) to control output.
- **Summary**: Go's encoding/json package makes encoding and decoding JSON easy. We covered:
  - **Encoding Go struct**: JSON (**`json.Marshal()`**)
  - **Decoding JSON**: Go structs (**`json.Unmarshal()`**)
  - Handling JSON requests in REST APIs
  - Customizing JSON output
  - Best practices for error handling and performance

Error handling in web APIs

This section deals with error handling in web APIs:

- **Overview**: Error handling in web APIs is crucial for providing clear, meaningful responses to clients. A well-structured error-handling mechanism ensures:
  - Proper HTTP status codes
  - Structured error messages
  - Logging for debugging
  - Prevention of system crashes

  This section covers:
  - Returning proper HTTP status codes
  - Sending structured JSON error responses
  - Handling client-side vs. server-side errors
  - Centralized error handling with middleware
  - Logging and debugging errors
- **HTTP status codes for error handling**: To ensure clarity and proper handling of issues, web APIs must return appropriate HTTP status codes that accurately reflect the nature of errors, enabling clients to respond effectively. The error codes are shown as follows:

Status code	Meaning	Example scenario
200 OK	Success response	Data retrieval (GET) successful
400 Bad Request	Invalid request input	Missing or malformed JSON
401 Unauthorized	Authentication required	Accessing protected resources
403 Forbidden	Access denied	Insufficient permissions
404 Not Found	Resource does not exist	Requested item is missing
500 Internal Server Error	Unexpected server issue	Database failure, crash

***Table 15.2**: HTTP error codes*

- **Returning structured JSON error responses**: Instead of sending plain text errors, APIs should return structured JSON error responses.
  - **Example**: Structuring error responses:

```
package main

import (
    "encoding/json"
    "net/http"
)

// Define an error response struct
type ErrorResponse struct {
    Error   string 'json:"error"'
    Message string 'json:"message"'
```

```
}

// Function to send JSON error responses
func sendErrorResponse(w http.ResponseWriter, statusCode int, errMsg string) {
    w.WriteHeader(statusCode)
    response := ErrorResponse{
        Error:    http.StatusText(statusCode),
        Message: errMsg,
    }
    json.NewEncoder(w).Encode(response)
}

func handler(w http.ResponseWriter, r *http.Request) {
    if r.Method != http.MethodGet {
        sendErrorResponse(w, http.
StatusMethodNotAllowed, "Only GET requests are allowed")
        return
    }

    sendErrorResponse(w, http.StatusNotFound, "Requested resource not found")
}

func main() {
    http.HandleFunc("/", handler)
    http.ListenAndServe(":8080", nil)
}
```

- **Test it:**

  http://localhost:8080/

- Sends structured error responses in JSON format.
- Uses **`sendErrorResponse()`** to maintain consistency.
- **Output**: **`{"error":"Not Found","message":"Requested resource not found"}`**

- **Handling client-side errors (4xx)**: Client-side errors occur when the request is incorrect.
  - **Handling 400 bad request (invalid input):**

```
func badRequestHandler(w http.ResponseWriter, r *http.Request) {
    if r.Method != http.MethodPost {
        sendErrorResponse(w, http.StatusBadRequest, "Invalid request method")
        return
    }

    if r.ContentLength == 0 {
        sendErrorResponse(w, http.StatusBadRequest, "Request body cannot be empty")
        return
    }
```

```
}
```

  - Ensures only POST requests are allowed.
  - `Returns 400 Bad Request` if no request body is provided.

- **Handling 401 unauthorized (authentication failure)**:

```
func authHandler(w http.ResponseWriter, r *http.Request) {
    apiKey := r.Header.Get("Authorization")
    if apiKey != "Bearer valid_token" {
        sendErrorResponse(w, http.StatusUnauthorized, "Invalid API token")
        return
    }

    w.Write([]byte("Access granted!"))
}
```

- **Test with curl:**

```
curl -H "Authorization: Bearer wrong_token" http://localhost:8080/auth
```

  - Checks API authentication before allowing access.
  - Returns **`401 Unauthorized`** if API key is missing or invalid.

- **Handling 404 not found (missing resource)**: If a requested resource does not exist, return **`404 Not Found`**.

```
func notFoundHandler(w http.ResponseWriter, r *http.Request) {
    sendErrorResponse(w, http.StatusNotFound, "Resource not found")
}

func main() {
    http.HandleFunc("/", notFoundHandler)
    http.ListenAndServe(":8080", nil)
}
```

- Now, accessing **http://localhost:8080/unknown** returns:

```
{
    "error": "Not Found",
    "message": "Resource not found"
}
```

Provides a meaningful error message for missing resources.

- **Handling server-side errors (5xx)**: Server-side errors indicate issues within the API itself.
  - **Handling 500 internal server error:**

```
func internalServerErrorHandler(w http.ResponseWriter, r *http.Request) {
    sendErrorResponse(w, http.StatusInternalServerError,
"Something went wrong, please try again later")
}
```

Use 500 only for unexpected failures (e.g., database issues).

- **Centralized error handling with middleware**: Instead of handling errors manually in each function, we can use middleware.

- **Middleware for error logging:**

```go
package main

import (
    "log"
    "net/http"
)

// Error logging middleware
func loggingMiddleware(next http.Handler) http.Handler {
    return http.HandlerFunc(func(w http.ResponseWriter, r *http.Request) {
        log.Printf("Request: %s %s", r.Method, r.URL.Path)
        next.ServeHTTP(w, r)
    })
}

func handler(w http.ResponseWriter, r *http.Request) {
    w.Write([]byte("Hello, API is working!"))
}

func main() {
    mux := http.NewServeMux()
    mux.HandleFunc("/", handler)

    loggedMux := loggingMiddleware(mux)
    http.ListenAndServe(":8080", loggedMux)
}
```

  - Logs each request before passing it to handlers.
  - Helps in debugging errors efficiently.

- **Debugging and logging errors**: Use logging for debugging errors.
  - **Using log for error logging**: Logs error messages instead of exposing internal errors to users.

```go
func dbHandler(w http.ResponseWriter, r *http.Request) {
    err := simulateDatabaseError()
    if err != nil {
        log.Println("Database error:", err)
        sendErrorResponse(w, http.
StatusInternalServerError, "Database is unavailable")
        return
    }
}

func simulateDatabaseError() error {
    return fmt.Errorf("Database connection failed")
}
```

- **Handling panics and graceful recovery**: If a panic occurs during request processing, the API should recover gracefully and respond with a HTTP status of 500 (Internal Server Error).

```
func recoverMiddleware(next http.Handler) http.Handler {
    return http.HandlerFunc(func(w http.ResponseWriter, r *http.Request) {
        defer func() {
            if err := recover(); err != nil {
                log.Println("Recovered from panic:", err)
                sendErrorResponse(w, http.
StatusInternalServerError, "Unexpected server error")
            }
        }()
        next.ServeHTTP(w, r)
    })
}
```

Prevents API crashes by catching unexpected panics.

- **Best practices for error handling**:
  - **Use meaningful HTTP status codes**: Ensure status codes reflect the nature of the error (e.g., 400, 404, 500).
  - **Return structured JSON error messages**: Provide clients with machine-readable error details.
  - **Log errors with relevant context**: Use structured logging to capture important details like request ID, error messages, and stack traces.
  - **Handle panics gracefully**: Use defer and **`recover()`** to prevent server crashes from panics.
  - **Provide useful error messages**: Clearly explain what went wrong and how to resolve it.
- **Summary**:
  - **Client-side errors (4xx)**: Handle invalid inputs, authentication failures, and missing resources.
  - **Server-side errors (5xx)**: Handle database failures and unexpected issues.
  - **Structured JSON error responses**: Improve API usability.
  - **Logging and debugging**: Capture errors effectively.
  - **Panic recovery**: Prevent crashes with middleware.

Conclusion

This chapter provided a solid foundation for building web servers using Go's net/http package. You learned how to initialize and configure a basic HTTP server, serve static files, implement graceful shutdowns, and incorporate middleware for enhanced logging and monitoring. You also explored timeout configurations and the setup of multiple concurrent server instances. These techniques ensure that your web services are lightweight, efficient, and production-ready. The skills gained here are crucial for building reliable and maintainable APIs.

In the upcoming chapter, we turn our focus on RESTFUL API best practices in Go. While writing clean and robust APIs is crucial, being able to observe and monitor their behavior in real time is equally important. You will learn how to implement structured logging using packages like logrus, track HTTP requests and responses with middleware, and monitor performance metrics using Prometheus and Grafana. We will also introduce distributed tracing using OpenTelemetry to provide end-to-end visibility across services. These tools and techniques are essential for debugging, maintaining SLAs, and ensuring long-term operational excellence in any production environment.

Questions

1. Why is Go's net/http package considered a strong foundation for building RESTful web servers?
2. What are the advantages of using graceful shutdowns in web servers, and how do they improve reliability?
3. How does middleware enhance the functionality of a Go web server? Provide some common use cases.
4. Why is it important to configure server parameters such as ReadTimeout, WriteTimeout, and IdleTimeout?
5. How can serving static files (HTML, CSS, JS) be integrated into Go web servers using http.FileServer?
6. What are the differences between handling GET, POST, PUT, and DELETE requests in REST APIs?
7. Why should APIs return structured JSON error messages instead of plain text errors?
8. How does using third-party routers like Gorilla Mux or Chi improve routing compared to the standard net/http package?
9. What are the benefits of using JSON encoding and decoding in REST APIs, and how do struct tags help?
10. What best practices should developers follow when setting up a web server in Go to ensure scalability and maintainability?

CHAPTER 16
Advanced RESTful API Design

Introduction

In today's microservices-driven architecture, building reliable and maintainable APIs is at the heart of successful software systems. This chapter explores best practices for designing and developing RESTful APIs using Go. Go is known for its simplicity, strong concurrency features, and performance, making it an excellent choice for web services. However, writing an API that merely works is not enough. Ensuring that it follows industry standards, covering aspects like proper HTTP method usage, meaningful status codes, consistent JSON structures, secure authentication, and effective logging, is crucial for scalability, security, and maintainability. Through practical examples and Go code snippets, this chapter provides a comprehensive guide to building robust application programming interfaces. It also covers advanced areas like rate limiting, caching, monitoring with Prometheus and Grafana, distributed tracing with OpenTelemetry, and generating interactive API documentation with Swagger. These practices collectively help deliver high-quality APIs that developers and clients can trust.

Structure

We will cover the following topics in this chapter:

- RESTful API best practices
- Logging and monitoring API requests in Go
- Implementing API versioning in Go
- API documentation in Go with Swagger
- Handling rate limiting and throttling in APIs
- Building Docker image and deploying to GKE

Objectives

By the end of this chapter, you will be equipped with a deep understanding of how to build high-quality RESTful APIs using Go, aligned with modern development standards. Specifically, you will learn to choose and implement the correct HTTP methods and status codes for your endpoints, design resource-oriented and predictable URLs, and structure JSON responses consistently across your API. You will explore critical security aspects such as token-based authentication and secure headers, along with techniques to mitigate abuse through rate limiting and caching. Furthermore, you will gain hands on knowledge of API versioning strategies and learn to document your APIs effectively using Swagger, ensuring clear communication with developers and clients. Altogether, these objectives prepare you to build professional grade APIs ready for production environments.

RESTful API best practices

The best practices for RESTful API are as follows:

- **Using HTTP methods correctly**: Use POST for creating, PUT for full updates, and PATCH for partial updates. The following table provides an overview of standard HTTP methods, the typical actions they perform in a RESTful API, and practical examples of their use cases. This serves as a quick guide for designing or consuming REST APIs effectively.

HTTP method	Action	Use case
GET	Retrieve a resource	Fetch user details (`/api/users/1`)
POST	Create a new resource	Add a new user (`/api/users`)
PUT	Update an existing resource	Update user info (`/api/users/1`)
PATCH	Partial update of a resource	Update user email (`/api/users/1/email`)
DELETE	Remove a resource	Delete user (`/api/users/1`)

***Table 16.1**: HTTP methods*

- **HTTP status codes**: Use appropriate status codes. Return clear and consistent status codes for every endpoint. The following table summarizes common HTTP status codes, their meanings, and typical use cases in RESTful APIs. This serves as a handy reference for understanding how various client-server interactions are communicated and what each response indicates.

Status code	Meaning	Use case
200 OK	Successful request	GET user details
201 Created	Resource created	POST a new user
204 No Content	Success with no body	DELETE a user
400 Bad Request	Invalid request data	Missing required fields
401 Unauthorized	Authentication failure	Invalid API key
404 Not Found	Resource not found	User ID does not exist
500 Internal Server Error	Server error	Database failure

***Table 16.2**: HTTP status codes*

- **Structuring RESTful URLs**: Ensure URLs are resource-based, hierarchical, and predictable. The URL design principles are as follows:
    - **Use nouns for resources**: `/api/users` instead of `/api/getUsers`.
    - **Use plural nouns**: `/api/products` instead of `/api/product`.
    - **Hierarchical relationships**: `/api/users/1/orders`.
    - **Avoid verbs**: Actions should be represented by HTTP methods, not in the URL.

  The following are the consistent URL examples:

Endpoint	Action
`/api/users`	GET all users
`/api/users/1`	GET a specific user
`/api/users/1/orders`	GET orders for a specific user
`/api/users?role=admin`	Filter users by role

***Table 16.3**: URL examples*

- **JSON responses**: When designing APIs, it is important to maintain a predictable and uniform JSON structure for all responses. This ensures easier integration and clearer communication with clients.
  - For maintaining a consistent JSON structure, refer to the following:
    - Use camelCase for JSON keys.
    - Include a status field in responses.
    - Use consistent error structures for failures.

    The following code is an example of a success response:

    ```
    {
        "status": "success",
        "data": {
            "id": 1,
            "name": "Venkatesh",
            "email": "Venkateshjramesh@gmail.com"
        }
    }
    ```

    The following code is an example of an error response:

    ```
    {
        "status": "error",
        "message": "User not found"
    }
    ```

  - **Returning paginated data**: For large datasets, use pagination with limit and offset. Implement pagination for large datasets to improve performance.

    The following code is an example of a paginated response:

    ```
    {
        "status": "success",
        "data": [
            {"id": 1, "name": "Venkatesh"},
            {"id": 2, "name": "Shubham"}
        ],
        "pagination": {
            "total": 100,
            "limit": 10,
            "offset": 0
        }
    }
    ```

- **Error handling**: Use structured error responses with clear codes and messages. The following are the ways for standardizing error responses:
  - Include error code and message fields.
  - Use meaningful error messages.

    The following is an example of a validation error:

    ```
    {
        "status": "error",
    ```

```
        "error": {
            "code": "VALIDATION_ERROR",
            "message": "Email is required"
        }
    }
```

- **Authentication and security**: To secure your APIs and verify user identity, implement token-based authentication mechanisms. This approach ensures that each request can be independently verified without maintaining server-side sessions.
    - **Token-based authentication**: Use Bearer tokens and validate them in middleware.
        - Use **JSON Web Tokens (JWT)** for authentication.

        Note: JWT is a compact, URL-safe token format that allows you to securely transmit information between parties. It is widely adopted for stateless authentication in modern web and mobile applications.

        - Include tokens in **`Authorization`** headers.

    The following code is an example of a secured endpoint:

```
func authMiddleware(next http.Handler) http.Handler {
    return http.HandlerFunc(func(w http.ResponseWriter, r *http.Request) {
        token := r.Header.Get("Authorization")
        if token != "Bearer valid-token" {
            http.Error(w, "Unauthorized", http.StatusUnauthorized)
            return
        }
        next.ServeHTTP(w, r)
    })
}
```

    - **Secure headers**: Enhance the security of your web applications by configuring essential HTTP headers. These headers protect against common vulnerabilities and enforce best practices for secure communication. The details are as follows:
        - **Cross-origin resource sharing (CORS)**: Prevent unauthorized domain access.
        - **HTTP strict transport security (HSTS)**: Enforce HTTPS.
        - **Content security policy**: Prevent XSS attacks.

    The following code is an example of setting secure headers:

```
func secureHeadersMiddleware(next http.Handler) http.Handler {
    return http.HandlerFunc(func(w http.ResponseWriter, r *http.Request) {
        w.Header().Set("Strict-Transport-Security", "max-
age=63072000; includeSubDomains")
        w.Header().Set("Content-Security-Policy", "default-src 'self'")
        next.ServeHTTP(w, r)
    })
}
```

Note: We will be covering this concept extensively in Chapter 17, Securing Microservices.

- **Rate limiting and throttling**: Implement rate limiting to prevent abuse. We would take the following steps to implement rate limiting:
  1. Limit the number of requests per IP address.
  2. Return **`429 Too Many Requests`** if the limit is exceeded.

  The following code is an example of rate-limiting middleware:

```
func rateLimitMiddleware(next http.Handler) http.Handler {
    var requests = make(map[string]int)
    return http.HandlerFunc(func(w http.ResponseWriter, r *http.Request) {
        ip := r.RemoteAddr
        requests[ip]++
        if requests[ip] > 100 {
            http.Error(w, "Too Many Requests", http.StatusTooManyRequests)
            return
        }
        next.ServeHTTP(w, r)
    })
}
```

- **Caching responses**: Use caching for faster responses and reduced server load. Cache-Control headers are used for the following:
  - Use cache-control for static responses.
  - Store frequently requested data in Redis or Memcached.

  The following is an example of a caching header:

```
w.Header().Set("Cache-Control", "max-age=3600")
```

The best practices can be summarized in the following table:

Best practice	Description
Use proper HTTP methods	GET, POST, PUT, DELETE for respective actions
Return appropriate status codes	200, 201, 400, 404, 500
Consistent JSON responses	Standardized structure for success and error
Secure endpoints	Authentication, rate limiting, HTTPS
Implement versioning	**`/api/v1/resource`** for backward compatibility
Document API with Swagger	Interactive API documentation for developers

***Table 16.4**: API best practices*

Building robust RESTful APIs in Go requires the following:

- Consistent HTTP methods and status codes.
- Clear and standardized JSON responses.
- Proper authentication and security practices.
- Efficient error handling and rate limiting.
- Well-structured and maintainable URLs.

Logging and monitoring API requests in Go

Logging and monitoring are crucial for ensuring the reliability, performance, and security of RESTful APIs. Effective logging helps in debugging errors, auditing user actions, and analyzing performance bottlenecks. Monitoring allows you to track API usage, response times, error rates, and resource utilization.

Effective logging is essential for monitoring application behavior, troubleshooting issues, and maintaining system health. Go offers several ways to implement logging, starting with its built-in standard library:

- **Using the standard log package**: The standard log package provides basic logging capabilities.

  The following code is an example of basic logging:

```
package main

import (
    "log"
    "net/http"
)

func handler(w http.ResponseWriter, r *http.Request) {
    log.Println("Received a request on /")
    w.Write([]byte("Hello, Go!"))
}

func main() {
    http.HandleFunc("/", handler)
    log.Println("Starting server on :8080")
    log.Fatal(http.ListenAndServe(":8080", nil))
}
```

  Output:

```
2025/03/09 12:00:00 Starting server on :8080
2025/03/09 12:00:05 Received a request on /
```

  The following are the best practices:

  - It is good to have logs with timestamps.
  - We should avoid logs that lack structured logging capabilities.

- **Structured logging with logrus**: Logrus is a popular structured logger for Go.

  To install **logrus**, refer to the following code:

```
go get github.com/sirupsen/logrus
```

  The following code is an example of structured logging:

```
package main

import (
    "github.com/sirupsen/logrus"
    "net/http"
)
```

```
var log = logrus.New()

func handler(w http.ResponseWriter, r *http.Request) {
    log.WithFields(logrus.Fields{
        "method": r.Method,
        "path":   r.URL.Path,
    }).Info("Received request")
    w.Write([]byte("Hello, Structured Logging!"))
}

func main() {
    log.SetFormatter(&logrus.JSONFormatter{})
    http.HandleFunc("/", handler)
    log.Info("Server started on :8080")
    http.ListenAndServe(":8080", nil)
}
```

Output:

```
{"level":"info","method":"GET","msg":"Received request","path":"/","time":"2025-02-11T12:00:05Z"}
```

The following are the best practices:

- Logs in JSON format for easy parsing.
- Includes fields like method and path.

- **Logging levels in logrus**: The following are the logging levels in `logrus`:

Level	Description
`log.Debug`	Detailed information for debugging.
`log.Info`	General operational information.
`log.Warn`	Indications of potential problems.
`log.Error`	Errors that need attention but are not fatal.
`log.Fatal`	Logs and exits the program.
`log.Panic`	Logs and panics.

***Table 16.5**: Logging levels*

The best practice includes using appropriate log levels for different types of messages.

- **Logging HTTP requests and responses**: Capturing details of incoming HTTP requests and outgoing responses is critical for debugging, auditing, and understanding application usage patterns. Implementing structured request and response logging ensures visibility into your APIs' behavior.
    - **Middleware for request logging**: The following code is an example of middleware for request logging:

```
func loggingMiddleware(next http.Handler) http.Handler {
    return http.HandlerFunc(func(w http.ResponseWriter, r *http.Request) {
        log.WithFields(logrus.Fields{
            "method": r.Method,
            "url":    r.URL.Path,
```

```
            "ip":       r.RemoteAddr,
        }).Info("Incoming request")
        next.ServeHTTP(w, r)
    })
}
```

Refer to the following code to attach middleware:

```
router := mux.NewRouter()
router.Use(loggingMiddleware)
```

The following is the logged data:

- **HTTP method**: GET, POST
- **URL path**: **`/api/users`**
- Client IP address

- **Logging response status codes**: Logs HTTP status codes like **`200 OK`**, **`404 Not Found`**.

  The following code is an example of wrapping response writer to log status codes:

```
type loggingResponseWriter struct {
    http.ResponseWriter
    statusCode int
}

func (lrw *loggingResponseWriter) WriteHeader(code int) {
    lrw.statusCode = code
    lrw.ResponseWriter.WriteHeader(code)
}

func loggingMiddleware(next http.Handler) http.Handler {
    return http.HandlerFunc(func(w http.ResponseWriter, r *http.Request) {
        lrw := &loggingResponseWriter{w, http.StatusOK}
        next.ServeHTTP(lrw, r)
        log.WithFields(logrus.Fields{
            "method": r.Method,
            "path":   r.URL.Path,
            "status": lrw.statusCode,
        }).Info("Response logged")
    })
}
```

- **Monitoring with Prometheus and Grafana**:
  - **Setting up Prometheus metrics**: Refer to the following code to install Prometheus client:

```
go get github.com/prometheus/client_golang/prometheus
go get github.com/prometheus/client_golang/prometheus/promhttp
```

The following code is an example of exposing metrics:

```
package main

import (
```

```
        "net/http"
        "github.com/prometheus/client_golang/prometheus"
        "github.com/prometheus/client_golang/prometheus/promhttp"
    )

    var requestCounter = prometheus.NewCounterVec(
        prometheus.CounterOpts{
            Name: "api_requests_total",
            Help: "Total number of API requests",
        },
        []string{"path"},
    )

    func main() {
        prometheus.MustRegister(requestCounter)

        http.Handle("/metrics", promhttp.Handler())
        http.HandleFunc("/api", func(w http.ResponseWriter, r *http.Request) {
            requestCounter.WithLabelValues("/api").Inc()
            w.Write([]byte("API response"))
        })

        http.ListenAndServe(":8080", nil)
    }
```

Metrics are exposed at the following link:

http://localhost:8080/metrics

- **Visualizing metrics in Grafana**: Use Grafana for real-time visualization of metrics. The steps are as follows:
    1. To visualize and analyze your metrics effectively, start by adding Prometheus as a data source in Grafana. This establishes the connection needed to build rich dashboards and monitor your system's performance.
    2. Create dashboards with panels for the following:
        - API request rates.
        - Error rates.
        - Latency distributions.
- **Distributed tracing with open telemetry**: Traces capture latency and flow of API requests.

  To install OpenTelemetry SDK, refer to the following code:

```
go get go.opentelemetry.io/otel
go get go.opentelemetry.io/otel/exporters/stdout/stdouttrace
```

  The following is an example of tracing API requests:

```
import (
    "context"
    "go.opentelemetry.io/otel"
```

```
    "go.opentelemetry.io/otel/exporters/stdout/stdouttrace"
    "go.opentelemetry.io/otel/trace"
)

func main() {
    exporter, _ := stdouttrace.New()
    tracer := otel.Tracer("api-service")

    http.HandleFunc("/api", func(w http.ResponseWriter, r *http.Request) {
        ctx, span := tracer.Start(context.Background(), "handle-api")
        defer span.End()

        w.Write([]byte("Hello, Tracing!"))
    })

    http.ListenAndServe(":8080", nil)
}
```

- **Best practices for logging and monitoring**: Refer to the following table for the best practices:

Best practice	Description
Use structured logging	JSON format for easy parsing and analysis.
Log request and response details	HTTP method, path, status code, and duration.
Set log levels appropriately	Debug for dev, info for prod, error for failures.
Monitor API metrics	Request rate, error rate, and latency using Prometheus.
Implement distributed tracing	Use OpenTelemetry for tracing across services.
Log errors with context	Include error type, location, and stack trace.

Table 16.6: Best practices in logging and monitoring

- **Summary**:
  - **Logging**: Use logrus for structured logging.
  - **Monitoring**: Capture metrics with Prometheus.
  - **Tracing**: Use OpenTelemetry for distributed tracing.
  - **Best practices**: Ensure log consistency and monitor key metrics.

Implementing API versioning in Go

API versioning is essential for managing changes in RESTful APIs without breaking existing clients. It allows developers to introduce new features, deprecate old ones, and fix bugs systematically. Let us look at it in detail:

- **Key benefits of using API versioning**: Version your API from the start to avoid breaking changes. The key benefits are:
  - **Backward compatibility**: Allows old clients to continue working.
  - **Controlled upgrades**: Enable gradual adoption of new features.
  - **Change management**: Simplifies the process of adding or removing features.

 - **Error reduction**: Prevents breaking changes from affecting live clients.

- **API versioning strategies**: Use URL path versioning for simplicity and clarity. The strategies are mentioned in the following table:

Strategy	Example	Pros	Cons
URL path versioning	`/api/v1/users`	Simple and visible	URL changes for every version
Query parameter versioning	`/api/users?version=1`	Easy to implement	Less visible and less RESTful
Header-based versioning	Accept: `application/vnd.myapi.v1+json`	Clean URLs	Harder for browsers and some clients
Content negotiation	Accept: `application/json;version=1.0`	Flexible and RESTful	Requires custom handling

Table 16.7: *API versioning strategies*

- **URL path versioning**: It is simple and clear for clients and supports parallel version management. The following code is an example of URL path versioning:

```
package main

import (
    "encoding/json"
    "fmt"
    "net/http"
    "github.com/gorilla/mux"
)

type User struct {
    ID   int    'json:"id"'
    Name string 'json:"name"'
}

func getUsersV1(w http.ResponseWriter, r *http.Request) {
    users := []User{{ID: 1, Name: "Venkatesh"}}
    json.NewEncoder(w).Encode(users)
}

func getUsersV2(w http.ResponseWriter, r *http.Request) {
    users := []User{
        {ID: 1, Name: "Venkatesh"},
        {ID: 2, Name: "Shubham"},
    }
    json.NewEncoder(w).Encode(users)
}

func main() {
```

```
    router := mux.NewRouter()
    router.HandleFunc("/api/v1/users", getUsersV1).Methods("GET")
    router.HandleFunc("/api/v2/users", getUsersV2).Methods("GET")

    fmt.Println("Server running at http://localhost:8080")
    http.ListenAndServe(":8080", router)
}
```

Use the following links to test it:

http://localhost:8080/api/v1/users

http://localhost:8080/api/v2/users

- **Query parameter versioning**: It is simple to implement, but less RESTful and less visible in documentation. The following code is an example of query parameter versioning:

```
func getUsers(w http.ResponseWriter, r *http.Request) {
    version := r.URL.Query().Get("version")
    if version == "2" {
        getUsersV2(w, r)
    } else {
        getUsersV1(w, r)
    }
}

router.HandleFunc("/api/users", getUsers).Methods("GET")
```

Use the following links to test it:

http://localhost:8080/api/users?version=1

http://localhost:8080/api/users?version=2

- **Header-based versioning**: Clean URLs without versioning information, but harder to discover for clients. Refer to the following code for using custom headers:

```
func getUsers(w http.ResponseWriter, r *http.Request) {
    version := r.Header.Get("API-Version")
    if version == "2" {
        getUsersV2(w, r)
    } else {
        getUsersV1(w, r)
    }
}

router.HandleFunc("/api/users", getUsers).Methods("GET")
```

Refer to the following code to test with `curl`:

```
curl -H "API-Version: 2" http://localhost:8080/api/users
```

- **Content negotiation**: Flexible and RESTful, but complex for clients to use. Refer to the following code for using `Accept` headers for versioning:

```
func getUsers(w http.ResponseWriter, r *http.Request) {
    accept := r.Header.Get("Accept")
```

```
        switch accept {
        case "application/vnd.myapi.v2+json":
            getUsersV2(w, r)
        default:
            getUsersV1(w, r)
        }
    }

router.HandleFunc("/api/users", getUsers).Methods("GET")
```

To test with **curl**, refer to the following code:

```
curl -H "Accept: application/vnd.myapi.v2+json" http://localhost:8080/api/users
```

- **Handling deprecation and backward compatibility**: Plan a clear upgrade path for clients.
    - **Deprecating endpoints**: When phasing out API endpoints or versions, it is important to communicate these changes clearly to clients to ensure smooth transitions and minimize disruptions.
        - Use the **Deprecation** HTTP header to signal that an endpoint is scheduled for removal, helping clients prepare for upcoming changes. Return **410 Gone** if the version is removed.

      The following code is an example of a **Deprecation** header:

      ```
      w.Header().Set("Deprecation", "true")
      w.Header().Set("Link", "</api/v2/users>; rel=\"latest\"")
      ```

    - **Graceful transition**:
        - Inform clients early about deprecations.
        - Provide a transition period and upgrade guides.
        - Support at least two versions concurrently.

The following are the best practices for API versioning:

Best practice	Description
Start with version 1.0	Ensure versioning from day one.
Prefer URL path versioning	Simple and clear for clients.
Document API versions clearly	Provide examples and changelogs.
Implement graceful deprecation	Warn clients about deprecated endpoints.
Use consistent error responses	Same structure across all versions.
Log version usage	Track API version adoption and usage trends.

***Table 16.8**: API versioning best practices*

Summary:

- API versioning ensures backward compatibility and smooth transitions.
- URL path versioning is the simplest and most widely used approach.
- Header-based and content negotiation offer cleaner URLs but require more setup.
- Deprecation strategies prevent sudden breaks for clients.
- Best practices include starting versioning early, documenting thoroughly, and tracking version usage.

API documentation in Go with Swagger

API documentation is crucial for helping developers understand how to use your API effectively. Swagger, now known as OpenAPI, is a powerful tool for documenting RESTful APIs. It allows you to carry out the following tasks:

- Generate interactive API documentation.
- Provide detailed information about endpoints, request parameters, and responses.
- Simplify testing with an interactive UI.

In Go, we can use **swaggo/swag** to generate Swagger documentation automatically based on code comments.

- **Setting up Swagger:** To set up Swagger in Go, follow these steps:

  1. **Install the swag CLI tool.**

     Run the following command to install the Swagger CLI tool for generating documentation:

     ```
     go install github.com/swaggo/swag/cmd/swag@latest
     ```

  2. **Verify the installation.**

     ```
     swag --version
     ```

  3. **Install Swagger packages.**

     Install the following Go packages:

     ```
     go get -u github.com/swaggo/gin-swagger
     go get -u github.com/swaggo/files
     ```

     These packages help in the following:

     a. Serve Swagger UI (**swaggo/files**).

     b. Generate and host Swagger documentation (**swaggo/gin-swagger**).

  4. **Generate Swagger configuration.**

     Run this command at the root of your Go project:

     ```
     swag init
     ```

     It helps in the following:

     a. Creates a docs folder.

     b. Generates **docs/swagger.json** and **docs/swagger.yaml**.

     c. Builds API documentation based on comments in your Go code.

- **Adding Swagger annotations to Go code**: To automatically generate interactive API documentation, incorporate Swagger annotations directly into your Go code. These special comments serve as metadata for tools like Swagger or OpenAPI, ensuring your API is well-documented and easy to consume. The best practice is to use descriptive comments for better API understanding.

  The following code is an example of adding Swagger annotations:

  ```
  package main

  import (
   _ "code/chapter16/api_documentation/swagger_annotations/docs"
   "github.com/gin-gonic/gin"
   swaggerFiles "github.com/swaggo/files" // Correct import for swagger files
   ginSwagger "github.com/swaggo/gin-swagger"
  ```

```
    "net/http"
)

// @title User API
// @version 1.0
// @description This is a sample server for managing users.
// @host localhost:8080
// @BasePath /api/v1
func main() {
    router := gin.Default()

    // Correct Swagger UI route
    router.GET("/swagger/*any", ginSwagger.WrapHandler(swaggerFiles.Handler))

    // API route
    router.GET("/api/v1/api/v1/users", getUsers)

    router.Run(":8080")
}

// getUsers godoc
// @Summary Get all users
// @Description Get a list of all users
// @Tags Users
// @Accept json
// @Produce json
// @Success 200 {array} User
// @Router /api/v1/users [get]
func getUsers(c *gin.Context) {
    users := []User{
        {ID: 1, Name: "Venkatesh", Email: "Venkatesh@gmail.com"},
        {ID: 2, Name: "Shubham", Email: "Shubham@gmail.com"},
    }
    c.JSON(http.StatusOK, users)
}

// User struct
type User struct {
    ID    int    'json:"id"'
    Name  string 'json:"name"'
    Email string 'json:"email"'
}
```

Key annotations are shown in the following table:

Annotation	Purpose
`@title`, `@version`, `@description`	Metadata for API documentation.
`@BasePath`	Base URL path for API.
`@Summary`	Short description of the endpoint.
`@Description`	Detailed explanation of the endpoint.
`@Tags`	Organize endpoints into categories.
`@Accept` and `@Produce`	Specify request and response formats.
`@Success`	Define HTTP status codes and response types.
`@Router`	Define the HTTP method and endpoint path.

***Table 16.9**: Common Swagger annotations and their purposes*

- **Generate Swagger docs**:

  Run the following command to generate Swagger documentation:

  ```
  swag init
  ```

  The command generates the following:

  - **`docs/swagger.json`**
  - **`docs/swagger.yaml`**
  - HTML files for Swagger UI.

- **Accessing Swagger UI:**

  Start your Go application and access the following link for the Swagger UI endpoint:

  http://localhost:8080/swagger/index.html

  Features of Swagger UI:

  - Interactive API documentation.
  - Try it out feature for testing APIs directly.
  - Displays request and response formats.

  The following is an example of Swagger UI:

  API endpoint: **`/api/v1/users`**

  - **Method**: GET
  - **Description**: Fetch all users.
  - **Response**: JSON array of users.

The following screen will appear. To test it on Swagger UI, click **Try it out** | **Execute** | **View response**:

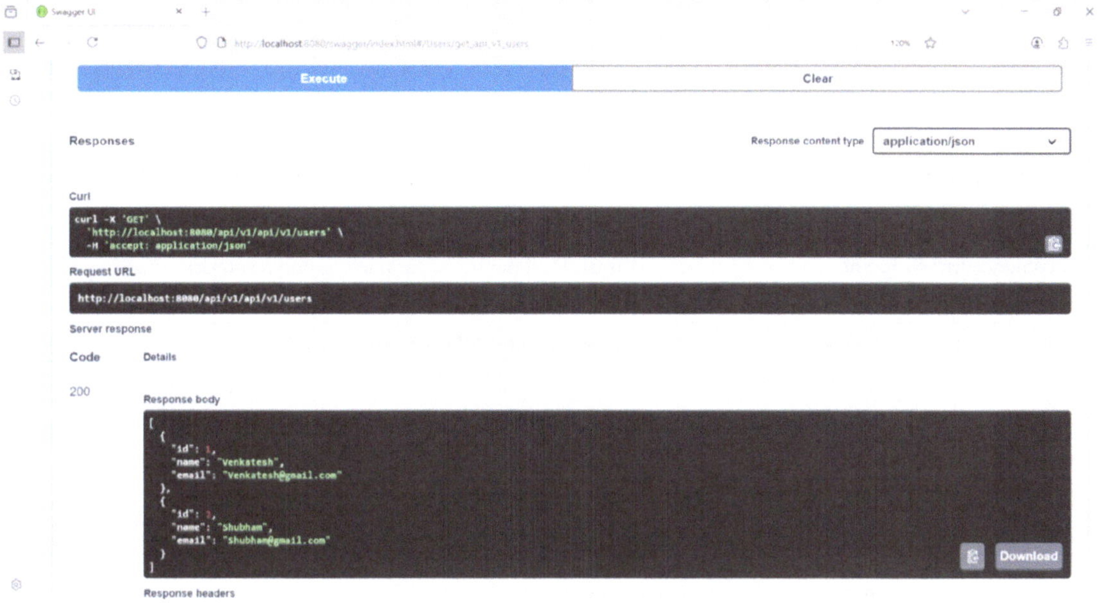

Figure 16.1: Swagger output in browser

- **Customizing Swagger documentation:**
  - **Custom info in Swagger**: Add the following commands above the main function:

```
// @contact.name API Support
// @contact.url http://www.example.com/support
// @contact.email support@example.com
// @license.name MIT
// @license.url http://opensource.org/licenses/MIT
```

    It customizes the following:

    - Contact info
    - License details
    - Support information

  - **Adding authorization in Swagger**:

    The following is an example of JWT authorization:

```
// @securityDefinitions.apikey BearerAuth
// @in header
// @name Authorization
```

    Refer to the following commands for using security definitions:

```
// getUser godoc
// @Security BearerAuth
// @Summary Get a user
// @Tags Users
// @Accept json
```

```
// @Produce json
// @Param id path int true "User ID"
// @Success 200 {object} User
// @Failure 404 {object} ErrorResponse
// @Router /api/v1/users/{id} [get]
```

It adds a `Bearer Token` input in Swagger UI.

- **Best practices for API documentation**: The following table covers the best practices for API documentation:

Best practice	Description
Document every endpoint	Include all methods, parameters, and responses.
Use meaningful summaries and descriptions	Ensure clarity and understanding.
Organize endpoints with tags	Group-related APIs for easier navigation.
Include error responses and examples	Specify possible error status codes and response examples.
Keep documentation in sync with code	Use swag init after every significant change.
Secure sensitive endpoints	Document authentication and authorization requirements.

Table 16.10: API documentation best practices

- **Summary**:
  - Swagger simplifies API documentation with an interactive UI.
  - Use annotations to generate docs directly from code comments.
  - The swag CLI tool generates docs in JSON and YAML formats.
  - Access Swagger UI at `/swagger/index.html`.
  - Follow best practices for clarity, consistency, and security.

Handling rate limiting and throttling in APIs

Rate limiting and throttling are techniques to control the amount of traffic your API can handle. They prevent abuse, safeguard resources, and ensure fair usage, as follows:

- Limiting the number of requests per user or IP.
- Slowing down or rejecting excess requests.
- Protecting the API from DDoS attacks and ensuring fair resource allocation.

The details are as follows:

- **Understanding rate limiting vs. throttling**: Refer to the following table to understand rate limiting and throttling:

Aspect	Rate limiting	Throttling
Definition	Restricts the number of API requests within a time frame.	Slows down the rate of requests to a manageable level.
Goal	Prevent abuse and ensure fair usage.	Prevent server overload by controlling request flow.
Common use cases	Per-user, per-IP, or per-API key limits.	Handling burst traffic or resource-intensive endpoints.
Response status code	429: Too Many Requests	Delayed response or 503 Service Unavailable if overloaded.

Table 16.11: Rate limiting vs. throttling

Best practice: Use rate limiting to prevent abuse and throttling to manage spikes.

- **Implementing rate limiting in Go**: The rate package from Go's extended library (**golang.org/x/time/rate**) provides a token bucket implementation for rate limiting.

  Refer to the following command to install the package:

  ```
  go get golang.org/x/time/rate
  ```

  The following code is an example of a simple rate limiter:

  ```
  package main

  import (
      "fmt"
      "net/http"
      "time"

      "golang.org/x/time/rate"
  )

  var limiter = rate.NewLimiter(2, 5) // 2 requests per second, burst up to 5

  func rateLimitedHandler(w http.ResponseWriter, r *http.Request) {
      if !limiter.Allow() {
          http.Error(w, "429 Too Many Requests", http.StatusTooManyRequests)
          return
      }
      fmt.Fprintln(w, "Request successful")
  }

  func main() {
      http.HandleFunc("/", rateLimitedHandler)
      fmt.Println("Server running at http://localhost:8080")
      http.ListenAndServe(":8080", nil)
  }
  ```

  The following are the key points:

  - **rate.NewLimiter(2, 5)**: Allows 2 requests per second with a burst of up to 5 requests.
  - Returns **429 Too Many Requests** if the limit is exceeded.

  Testing the rate limiter: Test with **curl** using shell manages burst traffic without overwhelming the server. Refer to the following code:

  ```
  for i in {1..10}; do curl -s http://localhost:8080/; echo; done
  ```

  Expected output:

  ```
  Request successful
  Request successful
  429 Too Many Requests
  429 Too Many Requests
  ```

- **Token bucket vs. leaky bucket**: To manage API rate limiting and control traffic flow, two popular algorithms are the token bucket and the leaky bucket. The following tables compare these approaches across various aspects to help you understand when and how to use each:

Aspect	Token bucket	Leaky bucket
Mechanism	Tokens are added at a fixed rate and removed per request.	Requests are processed at a fixed rate; excess is discarded or delayed.
Use case	Allows bursts followed by a fixed rate.	Smooths traffic, preventing bursts.
Implementation	`rate.NewLimiter` in Go.	Requires custom implementation.
Pros	Handles bursts efficiently.	Ensures a consistent traffic rate.

***Table 16.12**: Token bucket vs. Leaky bucket*

  Best practice: Prefer token bucket for most API rate limiting cases.

- **Handling 429 Too Many Requests**:

  The following code is an example of return `Retry` header:

```
w.Header().Set("Retry-After", "10")
http.Error(w, "429 Too Many Requests", http.StatusTooManyRequests)
```

  Effect: Informs clients to retry after 10 seconds.

- **Best practices for rate limiting and throttling**: The following table covers the best practices for rate limiting and throttling:

Best practice	Description
Limit per user or API key	Prevents abuse from specific users or clients.
Set realistic limits	Match rate limits with server capacity.
Use Retry-After headers	Inform clients when to retry after hitting a limit.
Log rate limiting events	Track abuse attempts and adjust limits accordingly.
Prefer token bucket algorithm	Efficiently handles bursts and smooths traffic.
Leverage Redis for distributed systems	Centralized rate limiting across multiple API instances.
Provide clear error messages	Explain the reason for rate limiting to clients.

***Table 16.13**: Rate limiting and throttling best practices*

- **Summary**:
  - Rate limiting controls request volume to prevent abuse.
  - Token bucket is preferred for most cases due to burst handling.
  - Redis-based rate limiting is essential for distributed systems.
  - Throttling ensures consistent traffic by slowing down requests.
  - Follow best practices for security, performance, and user experience.

Building a Docker image and deploying to GKE

Docker and Kubernetes simplify the process of deploying and managing applications at scale. In this section, we will cover the following:

- Build a Docker image for a Go application.

- Push the image to **Google Container Registry** (**GCR**).
- Deploy the container to **Google Kubernetes Engine** (**GKE**).

The details are as follows:

- **Building a Docker image for a Go application**:

  Refer to the following code to create a simple Go web application:

```
package main

import (
    "fmt"
    "net/http"
)

func handler(w http.ResponseWriter, r *http.Request) {
    fmt.Fprintln(w, "Hello from Go on Kubernetes!")
}

func main() {
    http.HandleFunc("/", handler)
    fmt.Println("Server running on port 8080")
    http.ListenAndServe(":8080", nil)
}
```

  Refer to the following code to create a Dockerfile:

```
# Build Stage
FROM golang:1.20 AS builder

WORKDIR /app
COPY . .

# Build the Go app with static linking
RUN go mod init simple_program && go mod tidy
RUN CGO_ENABLED=0 GOOS=linux GOARCH=amd64 go build -o simple_app

# Run Stage - Use a minimal Alpine Linux image
FROM alpine:latest

WORKDIR /app
COPY --from=builder /app/simple_app /app/simple_app

# Expose the port
EXPOSE 8080

# Run the application
CMD ["/app/simple_app"]
```

The following table covers the key concepts in the Dockerfile:

Section	Code	Explanation
Build stage (builder)	`FROM golang:1.20 AS builder`	Uses Golang 1.20 as the base image. The `AS builder` keyword names this stage, so we can reference it later.
Set working directory	`WORKDIR /app`	Sets the working directory inside the container to `/app`.
Copy source code	`COPY`	Copies all project files from the host machine into the container.
Initialize go modules	`RUN go mod init simple_program && go mod tidy`	Initializes Go modules (`go.mod`) and ensures dependencies are correctly installed.
Build the application	`RUN CGO_ENABLED=0 GOOS=linux GOARCH=amd64 go build -o simple_app`	**CGO_ENABLED=0**: Disables CGO to create a fully static binary.
		GOOS=linux GOARCH=amd64: Compiles for Linux on x86_64 architecture.
		go build -o simple_app: Creates a compiled binary named `simple_app`.
Run stage (final image)	`FROM alpine:latest`	Uses Alpine Linux, a minimal base image to keep the final container lightweight.
Set working directory	`WORKDIR /app`	Again sets `/app` as the working directory in the final container.
Copy compiled binary	`COPY --from=builder /app/simple_app /app/simple_app`	Copies the compiled binary `simple_app` from the `builder` stage to the final container.
Expose port	`EXPOSE 8080`	Declares that the application listens on port `8080` (this does not publish the port; that happens at runtime).
Run the application	`CMD ["/app/simple_app"]`	Specifies the default command to run when the container starts, which is our compiled Go binary.

Table 16.14: Key components in Docker file

- **Build and run Docker image locally**:

  To build the Docker image, run the following command:

  ```
  docker build -t go-simple-app:latest .
  ```

  To run the Docker container, run the following command:

  ```
  docker run -p 8080:8080 go-simple-app
  ```

  Use the following link to test:

  http://localhost:8080

  Output: `Hello from Go on Kubernetes!`

- **Pushing Docker image to GCR**:

  Authenticate with Google Cloud Platform: Follow these steps to authenticate with Google Cloud, enable required services, and push your Docker image to Google Container Registry for seamless deployment in Google Cloud environments.

  - Install and authenticate Google Cloud SDK using the following command:

```
gcloud auth login
gcloud config set project YOUR_PROJECT_ID
```

- **Enable GCR API**: Enable GCR API using the following command:

  ```
  gcloud services enable containerregistry.googleapis.com
  ```

- **Tag and push the Docker image**: Tag the image using the following command:

  ```
  docker tag go-simple-app gcr.io/YOUR_PROJECT_ID/go-simple-app:latest
  ```

- **Authenticate Docker with GCR**: To authenticate Docker with GCR, refer to the following command:

  ```
  gcloud auth configure-docker
  ```

- **Push the image to GCR**: To push the image to GCR, refer to the following command:

  ```
  docker push gcr.io/YOUR_PROJECT_ID/go-simple-app:latest
  ```

  Expected output:

  ```
  Pushed gcr.io/YOUR_PROJECT_ID/go-simple-app:latest
  ```

  Use the following link to verify:

  https://console.cloud.google.com/gcr

- **Setting up GKE**:
  - **Enable Kubernetes API**

    ```
    gcloud services enable container.googleapis.com
    ```

  - **Create a GKE cluster**

    ```
    gcloud container clusters create go-cluster --zone us-central1-a --num-nodes 2
    ```

  - **Configure kubectl to use the new cluster**:

    ```
    gcloud container clusters get-credentials go-cluster --zone us-central1-a
    ```

  - **Check cluster status**:

    ```
    kubectl get nodes
    ```

- **Deploying application to GKE**: Once your Docker image is available in Google Container Registry, the next step is to deploy it on GKE. This process involves defining your application's desired state and managing its lifecycle using Kubernetes resources.

  Start by creating a Kubernetes deployment manifest (typically a YAML file). This file describes how your application should run on the cluster, including details like the container image, replicas, and exposed ports.

  Refer to the following code to create a Kubernetes deployment file:

  deployment.yaml

  ```
  apiVersion: apps/v1
  kind: Deployment
  metadata:
    name: go-simple-app
  spec:
    replicas: 2
    selector:
      matchLabels:
        app: go-simple-app
    template:
  ```

```
metadata:
  labels:
    app: go-simple-app
spec:
  containers:
  - name: go-simple-app
    image: gcr.io/YOUR_PROJECT_ID/go-simple-app:latest
    ports:
    - containerPort: 8080
```

Key concepts:

- **Replicas 2**: Ensures high availability with 2 pods.
- **Image**: Uses the GCR-hosted Docker image.

Refer to the following command to apply the deployment:

```
kubectl apply -f deployment.yaml
```

Refer to the following command to check pod status:

```
kubectl get pods
```

- **Expose the deployment as a service**:

  Refer to the following code to create a service file:

  service.yaml

```
apiVersion: v1
kind: Service
metadata:
  name: go-app-service
spec:
  type: LoadBalancer
  selector:
    app: go-simple-app
  ports:
  - protocol: TCP
    port: 80
    targetPort: 8080
```

  Run the following command to apply the service:

```
kubectl apply -f service.yaml
```

  To check service status, run the following command:

```
kubectl get svc
```

- **Access the application**:

  Use the following command to find the external IP:

```
kubectl get svc go-app-service
```

  Output: `Hello from Go on Kubernetes!`

  Use the following link to test it:

  http://EXTERNAL_IP

Note: **Regarding the `gcloud` commands, the testing was conducted in March 2025. Google may update or modify the functionality in future versions.**

Best practices for Docker and Kubernetes deployments: The following table covers the best practices:

Best practice	Description
Use multi-stage builds	Reduce image size by separating build and run stages.
Scan images for vulnerabilities	Use tools like trivy to scan for vulnerabilities.
Use distroless images	Minimize attack surface by avoiding package managers and shells.
Leverage ConfigMaps and Secrets	Manage configuration and sensitive data separately.
Set resource limits for containers	Prevent resource exhaustion and ensure stability.
Implement autoscaling	Use Horizontal Pod Autoscaler for dynamic scaling.

***Table 16.15:** Docker and Kubernetes deployment best practices*

Conclusion

By following the best practices explored in this chapter, you can build RESTful APIs in Go that are not only functional but also robust, secure, and developer-friendly. From choosing the right HTTP methods and status codes to designing clean URLs and consistent JSON responses, each aspect ensures your API is predictable and maintainable. We have also seen how to strengthen APIs with authentication, rate limiting, and caching, while structured logging and monitoring with Prometheus provide deep operational insights. Implementing Swagger documentation further enhances developer experience and adoption. Altogether, these practices lay a strong foundation for scalable and reliable API-driven systems.

In the next chapter, we will build on these concepts by diving into Authentication and Authorization in Microservices, where you will learn how to secure distributed systems using techniques like JWT, OAuth2, mTLS, and RBAC, ensuring your services remain protected in complex, decentralized environments.

Questions

1. Why is it important to use the correct HTTP methods (GET, POST, PUT, PATCH, DELETE) in RESTful API design?
2. How do HTTP status codes contribute to clear communication between client and server in REST APIs?
3. What are the key principles of designing RESTful URLs, and why should verbs be avoided in endpoints?
4. Why is it important to maintain a consistent JSON structure across all API responses?
5. What role do authentication and token-based security (such as JWT) play in protecting REST APIs?
6. How can secure headers (like CORS, HSTS, and content security policy) improve API security?
7. What is the difference between rate limiting and throttling, and why are both needed in API design?
8. How do logging and monitoring (using tools like Logrus, Prometheus, and Grafana) improve API reliability?
9. Why is API versioning critical in microservices, and what are the common strategies for implementing it?
10. How does API documentation with Swagger help developers and clients, and why must documentation be kept in sync with code?

CHAPTER 17
Securing Microservices

Introduction

In microservices architecture, securing individual services is crucial due to the distributed nature of the system. Each service often exposes its own **application programming interfaces** (**APIs**), runs on different hosts, and may communicate over public or semi-public networks. Without proper authentication and authorization, these services are vulnerable to unauthorized access, data leaks, and malicious activity.

Authentication is the process of verifying the identity of a user or system, ensuring that they are who they claim to be. Authorization, on the other hand, involves determining what permissions or access rights this authenticated user or system has, specifying what actions they are allowed to perform within the system. Together, they form the foundation of securing access to microservices.

Structure

We will be covering the following topics in this chapter:

- Importance of microservices
- Token-based authentication
- TLS or SSL for secure communication
- Implementing role-based access control
- Securing communication between services
- Best practices for securing microservices

Objectives

This chapter aims to provide a comprehensive understanding of how to secure microservices architectures, which inherently come with unique security challenges due to their decentralized and distributed nature. We will discuss key concepts such as authentication (verifying identities) and authorization (defining access permissions), and explore methods like API keys, OAuth2, **Security Assertion Markup Language** (**SAML**), mutual TLS, and **JSON Web Tokens** (**JWT**) for implementing secure access. It also delves into **role-based access control** (**RBAC**) and policy-driven authorization using tools like **Open Policy Agent** (**OPA**). Additionally, the chapter focuses on securing service-to-service communication through TLS and **Mutual TLS** (**mTLS**), protecting data in transit. It emphasizes best practices across design, deployment, and runtime, including enforcing least privilege, rotating secrets, and auditing access. By the end, readers will be equipped to architect, implement, and maintain secure microservices environments that protect both data and system integrity.

Importance of microservices

Microservices break applications into many small, independent services that must securely interact over networks. This distributed model increases the risk of attacks, data leaks, and unauthorized access. Each service, often exposed via APIs, becomes a potential entry point for threats. Therefore, security is not optional; it must be deeply embedded into the design. Microservices architecture introduces unique security challenges due to:

- Decentralization of services.
- The need for inter-service communication.
- Multiple entry points for external clients.
- The use of APIs as a communication medium.

Thus, enforcing robust authentication and authorization is mandatory to:

- Ensure each service trusts the caller.
- Prevent privilege escalation.
- Maintain data privacy and system integrity.

Authentication overview

Authentication is about answering the question, *Who are you?*

The following table outlines the common authentication methods in microservices:

Method	Description
API key authentication	A simple token passed in headers, suitable for internal services or low-security scenarios.
OAuth 2.0	A widely used protocol for authorization that supports token-based authentication.
SAML/OpenID Connect	Common in enterprise environments for **single sign-on** (**SSO**) and federated identity.
mTLS	Uses client certificates to validate both parties (used in secure internal communications).

Table 17.1: *Common authentication methods in microservices*

The comparison between centralized and decentralized authentication is as follows:

Model	Pros	Cons
Centralized	Easier to manage and audit.	It can become a single point of failure.
Decentralized	More resilient, closer to service.	Harder to keep consistent policies.

Table 17.2: *Centralized vs. decentralized authentication*

Let us consider the best practice. Use a central identity provider (e.g., Keycloak, Auth0, Okta) to handle authentication and issue tokens that services can verify.

Authorization overview

An authorization answers, *What can you do?*

Once a user or service is authenticated, the system needs to verify:

- The resources they can access.
- The actions (read, write, delete) that they are allowed to perform.

The following table outlines different types of authorization:

Type	Description
Access control lists (**ACLs**)	Lists specific permissions for each user/resource.
Attribute-based access control (**ABAC**)	Grants access based on user, resource, and environmental attributes.
Role-based access control (**RBAC**)	Grants access based on predefined roles.
Policy-based access control (**PBAC**)	Uses external policy engines like **Open Policy Agent** (**OPA**) to manage dynamic rules.

Table 17.3: *Types of authorization*

In a microservices architecture, authorization needs to be applied at multiple layers to ensure robust security. By distributing checks across gateways, services, middleware, and policy engines, you can enforce consistent and fine-grained access control. This layered approach helps mitigate risks even if one layer is bypassed.

Let us see where to enforce authorization:

Layer	Details
API gateway	Central enforcement point for all incoming requests. Useful for simple rule-based access.
Service level	Each service enforces its own access logic, allowing fine-grained control.
Middleware layer	Shared logic implemented via middleware (common in Go, Node, etc.).
Policy engine	An external system like OPA that evaluates policies based on context.

***Table 17.4**: Enforcing authorization scenarios*

Architecture patterns for auth in microservices

In microservices, there is no single place to enforce authentication and authorization. Different patterns are used depending on where and how identity is verified and trusted. Choosing the right pattern is critical for balancing security, performance, and operational complexity. Each approach has trade-offs in trust, scalability, and ease of management.

The following are common patterns employed in microservices authentication and authorization:

- **Gateway authentication and propagation**:
  - External requests are authenticated at the API gateway.
  - The identity context (e.g., user ID, roles) is propagated via headers or tokens to downstream services.
  - Downstream services trust the gateway and enforce authorization.
  - **Pros**: Central point of control.
  - **Cons**: Requires secure communication and trusted gateways.
- **Service-to-service authentication**:
  - Internal services validate the identity of the calling service.
  - Authentication is performed using mTLS or signed tokens (e.g., service accounts).
  - **Use case**: Zero Trust networks where internal traffic cannot be assumed safe.
- **5.3 token-based identity propagation**:
  - A user authenticates once and receives a token.
  - The token is passed to each service that requires user context.
  - Each service verifies and extracts claims from the token to enforce authorization.

Note: This will be explored in-depth in the JWT section.

The following table provides a comparison between authentication and authorization:

Scenario	Authentication	Authorization
Purpose	Identify the user or service.	Define what the identified entity can do.
Question answered	*Who are you?*	*Are you allowed to do this?*
Happens	First	After successful authentication.
Enforced by	Identity provider (e.g., Auth0, Keycloak)	Application, gateway, or policy engine.
Output	Identity token and credentials	Access rights and permissions.

***Table 17.5**: Authentication vs. authorization*

The following are the key security considerations:

- Never trust user input or headers without validation.
- Ensure tokens and identity metadata are cryptographically signed.
- Avoid storing sensitive data (like passwords) in microservices.
- Use short-lived tokens to reduce the risk of misuse.
- Rate limit authentication endpoints to prevent brute force attacks.
- Always log authentication and authorization events for auditing.

The following table outlines the real-world tools and frameworks:

Tool	Use case
Keycloak	Open-source identity and access management.
OAuth2 Proxy	For integrating OAuth2 in services.
OPA	External authorization engine using policies.
Istio + mTLS	Service mesh that supports secure, authenticated service-to-service communication.

***Table 17.6**: Real-world tools and frameworks*

Token-based authentication

Token-based authentication plays a vital role in securing microservices by replacing traditional session-based methods with lightweight, scalable tokens. It allows clients to prove their identity on each request without the server maintaining state. This approach is especially suited for distributed systems, where services need to independently validate user identity and permissions. By leveraging signed tokens like JWTs, microservices can securely propagate identity across the system.

In modern distributed systems like microservices, managing user sessions and securely identifying users without storing session state on the server is critical. Token-based authentication, particularly using JWT, provides a stateless, compact, and secure mechanism to authenticate users and services across multiple components.

A JWT contains claims, user data, and permissions, which are digitally signed, making it tamper-proof and easily verifiable by any service without needing centralized session storage.

Understanding JSON Web Token

A JWT is a base64-encoded token that includes the following:

- **Header**: Token type and signing algorithm.
- **Payload**: Claims (user info, roles, expiration, etc.).
- **Signature**: A cryptographic hash (**Hash-based Message Authentication Code** (**HMAC**) or **Rivest–Shamir–Adleman** (**RSA**)) to ensure integrity.

The following is the JWT structure:

xxxxx.yyyyy.zzzzz

- **xxxxx**: Header that contains metadata about the token (such as algorithm and type).
- **yyyyy**: Payload that carries the user data and claims.
- **zzzzz**: Signature that verifies that the token has not been tampered with.

The following is an example of a JWT decoded:

- **Header**:

```
{
  "alg": "HS256",
  "typ": "JWT"
}
```

- **Payload**:

```
{
  "sub": "1234567890",
  "name": "Venkatesh",
  "admin": true,
  "exp": 1710000000
}
```

- **Signature**: `HMACSHA256(base64UrlEncode(header) + "." + base64UrlEncode(payload), secret)`

Let us consider the need for JWT in microservices.

In a microservices architecture, JWT plays a crucial role by enabling secure, stateless, and efficient communication across distributed services. The following table summarizes the key reasons for using JWT and the benefits they bring:

Reason	Benefit
Stateless authentication	No need to store sessions on the server
Scalable and efficient	Easy to verify the token across services
Portable and compact	It can be stored in cookies, headers, etc.
Secure with a cryptographic signature	Prevents tampering
Cross-service trust	One service can authenticate, and others can authorize

***Table 17.7**: Need for JWT in microservices*

Refer to the following list to understand the ways JWT works in a microservices architecture:

- **Login**: User logs in with username/password.
- **Token issued**: Auth server validates credentials and returns a JWT.
- **Client stores token**: Usually in localStorage (browser) or HTTP-only cookies.
- **Token sent with requests**: Client adds JWT to HTTP headers.
- **Authorization**: Bearer <token>
- **Services verify token**: Each microservice verifies the token and grants/denies access.

Generating and validating JWT in Go

In microservices, services often need to create and verify tokens independently to maintain stateless authentication. Using Go, developers can easily generate JWTs and validate them across services.

The following examples demonstrate how to implement secure token creation and verification in Go applications:

- **Generate JWT in Go (Using github.com/golang-jwt/jwt/v5)**:

```
package main

import (
 "fmt"
 "time"

 "github.com/golang-jwt/jwt/v5"
)

var jwtKey = []byte("my_secret_key")

func GenerateJWT(username string) (string, error) {
 token := jwt.NewWithClaims(jwt.SigningMethodHS256, jwt.MapClaims{
  "username": username,
  "exp":      time.Now().Add(time.Hour * 1).Unix(),
 })
 return token.SignedString(jwtKey)
}

func main() {
 token, err := GenerateJWT("venkatesh")
 if err != nil {
  fmt.Println("Error generating token:", err)
  return
 }
 fmt.Println("Generated JWT:", token)
}
```

- **Output**: Generated JWT:

```
eyJhbGciOiJIUzI1NiIsInR5cCI6IkpXVCJ9.
eyJleHAiOjE3NDM0NDAyMTAsInVzZXJuYW1lIjoidmVua2F0ZXNoIn0.
s0gGqrNhMUA2uCXcK6nCmjO9UMARS5kL6r_cOwH5dqg
```

- **Validate JWT in Go**:

```
package main

import (
 "fmt"
 "github.com/golang-jwt/jwt/v5"
)

var jwtKey = []byte("my_secret_key")

// Validate a JWT and extract the username
func ValidateJWT(tokenString string) (string, error) {
 token, err := jwt.Parse(tokenString, func(token *jwt.Token) (interface{}, error) {
  return jwtKey, nil
```

```
    })
    if err != nil {
     return "", err
    }
    if claims, ok := token.Claims.(jwt.MapClaims); ok && token.Valid {
     return claims["username"].(string), nil
    } else {
     return "", err
    }
}
func main() {
    token := "eyJhbGciOiJIUzI1NiIsInR5cCI6IkpXVCJ9.
eyJleHAiOjE3NDM0NDAxNTMsInVzZXJuYW1lIjoidmVua2F0ZXNoIn0.d8bYb3WjtzlUvD_iPZWcdgCZ-
LCWihomC7I2TXxG-4Q"
    // Step 1: Validate the token
    username, err := ValidateJWT(token)
    if err != nil {
     fmt.Println("Error validating token:", err)
     return
    }
    fmt.Println("Token is valid. Username from token:", username)
}
```

- **Output**:

  `Token is valid. Username from token: Venkatesh`

The following table outlines the differences between standard and custom JWT claims:

Claim type	Example	Purpose
sub	1234567890	Subject identifier (user ID)
name	Venkatesh	User name
iat	1710000000	Issued At
exp	1710003600	Expiration time
role	admin	Custom claim for role-based access

***Table 17.8**: Examples of standard and custom JWT claims*

Let us consider the best practice. Always include **expiration** (**exp**) to limit the token lifetime.

The pros and cons of token storage and transmission are as follows:

Method	Pros	Cons
HTTP headers	Stateless, flexible	Must protect with HTTPS
Cookies (HTTP-only)	Auto-handled by browser, secure	Vulnerable to CSRF without protection
LocalStorage	Easy to use	Vulnerable to XSS

***Table 17.9**: Pros and cons of token storage and transmission*

Use **Hypertext Transfer Protocol Secure** (**HTTPS**) for all API communication when sending JWTs.

Understanding when a token refresh is needed:

- **Use short-lived access tokens and long-lived refresh tokens**:
  - **Access token (e.g., 15 min)**: Used in headers to access APIs.
  - **Refresh token (e.g., 7 days)**: Stored securely and exchanged for new access tokens.

Ways to use JWT in an API gateway:

- **API gateway (like Kong, NGINX, or Istio) can**:
  - Validate JWTs before forwarding requests.
  - Enforce authentication rules.
  - Inject claims into request headers.
  - This offloads auth logic from individual services.

The following table highlights the security best practices for JWT:

Practice	Importance
Use strong signing keys	Prevent brute-force attacks
Always validate exp	Block expired tokens
Use HTTPS for transmission	Prevent token interception
Avoid storing sensitive data in JWT	JWT can be decoded by anyone
Implement token revocation logic	Protect from stolen tokens (e.g., blacklists)
Use short token lifespans	Reduce the impact of compromised tokens

***Table 17.10**: Best security practices for JWT*

The alternatives to JWT are as follows:

Alternative	Use case
Opaque tokens	Where introspection is needed
Session-based	Simpler apps with centralized auth
Mutual TLS	Secure inter-service communication

***Table 17.11**: Alternatives to JWT*

TLS or SSL for secure communication

In a microservices architecture, services often communicate over HTTP or **Google Remote Procedure Calls** (**gRPC**) using networks that may span data centers, cloud regions, or the public internet. To protect sensitive data in transit, it is essential to encrypt all service-to-service communication using **Transport Layer Security** (**TLS**), the modern and secure version of **Secure Sockets Layer** (**SSL**).

TLS ensures the following:

- **Confidentiality**: Data can not be read by unauthorized parties (encryption).
- **Integrity**: Data is not altered in transit (hashing + signatures).
- **Authentication**: The receiver can verify the sender (certificates).

The following table outlines the importance of TLS/SSL for microservices:

Concern	Risk without TLS
Plain-text communication	Exposes data to eavesdropping (e.g., passwords, tokens)
Man-in-the-middle attacks	An attacker could intercept and alter messages
Impersonation or spoofing	One service could pretend to be another
Regulatory compliance failures	Many standards (GDPR, HIPAA, PCI-DSS) require encryption

***Table 17.12**: Importance of TSL and SSL*

TLS addresses all of these by encrypting traffic and verifying identity via certificates.

The key concepts in TLS are as follows:

Term	Explanation
SSL vs. TLS	SSL is outdated; TLS is the modern, secure protocol used today.
HTTPS	HTTP over TLS is used for secure browser/server and API communication.
Certificate	A digital identity used to authenticate a party (issued by a Certificate Authority).
Public/Private key	Used to encrypt and decrypt messages in TLS.
Handshake	The process of negotiating encryption algorithms and verifying certificates.

***Table 17.13**: Key concepts in TLS*

The following table highlights the use cases of TLS in microservices:

Use case	Explanation
API gateway I Microservices	Ensure external traffic is always encrypted.
Service A | Service B (internal)	Secure inter-service communication, especially across networks.
Client | Service (Frontend | Backend)	Encrypt sensitive user data like tokens, passwords, etc.

***Table 17.14**: Use cases of TLS in Microservices*

Configuring TLS in Go using an HTTP server

Let us look at the details:

- **Generating a self-signed certificate (for testing)**:

```
openssl req -x509 -newkey rsa:2048 -nodes -keyout key.pem -out cert.pem -days 365
```

- **Go HTTPS server example**:

```
package main

import (
 "fmt"
 "net/http"
)

func handler(w http.ResponseWriter, r *http.Request) {
 fmt.Fprintln(w, "Secure Go Service with TLS")
}
```

```go
func main() {
 http.HandleFunc("/", handler)
 fmt.Println("Starting HTTPS server on https://localhost:8443")
 err := http.ListenAndServeTLS(":8443", "cert.pem", "key.pem", nil)
 if err != nil {
  fmt.Println("Error starting server:", err)
 }
}
```

This launches an HTTPS server on port 8443 using the provided certificate and key.

The following list outlines the mTLS:

- **mTLS is an enhancement of TLS where**:
  - The client verifies the server.
  - The server also verifies the client.

  Used for service-to-service authentication in Zero Trust architectures.
- **mTLS is ideal for**:
  - Securing internal service mesh traffic (e.g., with Istio or Linkerd).
  - Preventing unauthorized service impersonation.
  - Enabling fine-grained, certificate-based policies.

TLS with reverse proxies or ingress controllers is as follows:

- **In production, TLS is often handled by**:
  - API gateways like Kong or Ambassador.
  - Ingress controllers in Kubernetes (e.g., NGINX, Traefik).
  - Cloud load balancers (GCP HTTPS Load Balancer, AWS ELB).

  Services run on plain HTTP internally, while the gateway or ingress handles TLS termination.

The following table highlights the ways of managing certificates in production:

Approach	Tools/Providers
Self-signed certs	Good for development/testing.
Let us encrypt	Free, automated certs for public domains.
Managed certs	Provided by **Google Cloud Platform** (**GCP**), **Amazon Web Services** (**AWS**), Azure, etc.
Vault/Cert-Manager	Automate issuance and renewal inside Kubernetes.

***Table 17.15**: Certificate management in production*

Rotate certificates regularly to minimize exposure from compromise.

TLS in service meshes (Istio example): With service meshes like Istio, TLS and mTLS can be automatically enforced:

- Injected sidecars manage certificates and secure traffic.
- Policies control which services can talk to each other securely.
- **Example**: Enable mTLS in Istio:

```yaml
apiVersion: security.istio.io/v1beta1
kind: PeerAuthentication
metadata:
```

```
    name: default
  spec:
    mtls:
      mode: STRICT
```

TLS in Go gRPC Services is as follows:

- For gRPC (binary protocol), use `credentials.NewServerTLSFromFile()` to enable TLS:

  ```
  creds, err := credentials.NewServerTLSFromFile("cert.pem", "key.pem")
  grpcServer := grpc.NewServer(grpc.Creds(creds))
  ```

  Works similarly to `http.ListenAndServeTLS` for HTTP servers.

The following table outlines the best practices for TLS in microservices:

Practice	Reason
Always use HTTPS/TLS	Prevents data leaks and MITM attacks.
Use mTLS internally	Enforces mutual trust between services.
Automate certificate renewal	Prevent downtime from expired certs.
Do not use self-signed certs in prod	They are not trusted by clients.
Limit certificate scope	Prevents broad misuse in case of compromise.
Monitor and audit TLS traffic	Detect misconfiguration or expired certs.

***Table 17.16**: Best practices for TLS in microservices*

Implementing role-based access control

RBAC is a popular method for restricting system access to authorized users based on their roles. Instead of assigning permissions directly to users, permissions are grouped into roles, and users are assigned to those roles. This abstraction simplifies permission management and enhances security in scalable systems like microservices.

The following table highlights the role of RBAC in securing microservices:

Challenge	Ways RBAC helps
Complex access rules across services	Centralizes permission logic through role abstraction.
Large user base	The roles scale is better than assigning permissions individually.
Audit and compliance	Easier to trace who has access to what.
Dynamic environments	The roles are flexible and support user mobility and promotion.

***Table 17.17**: RBAC in securing microservices*

The key concepts in RBAC are as follows:

Term	Definition
User	The person or system requesting access.
Role	A collection of permissions (e.g., *admin, editor, viewer*).
Permission	An allowed action on a resource (e.g., `read:user`, `delete:report`).
Resource	The protected entity (e.g., user profile, service endpoint).

***Table 17.18**: Concepts in RBAC*

The following table is an example of role and permission mapping:

Role	Permissions
Admin	Create, read, update, and delete all resources
Editor	Read, update specific resources
Viewer	Read-only access

***Table 17.19**: Role and permissions mapping*

Ways RBAC works in Microservices:

- **High-level flow**:
  - User logs in and receives a token (e.g., JWT).
  - Token contains a role claim (e.g., **`role: editor`**).
  - Each service reads the token, extracts the role, and applies access control logic.
  - If the role has permission to perform the requested action, access is granted.

The following list outlines the ways of implementing RBAC in Go:

- **We will have a service with three endpoints**:
  - **/users (GET)**: It lists all users
  - **/users (POST)**: Create a user
  - **/admin (GET)**: Access admin panel

The following is a sample role-permission map:

```
var rolePermissions = map[string][]string{
    "admin":  {"GET:/users", "POST:/users", "GET:/admin"},
    "editor": {"GET:/users", "POST:/users"},
    "viewer": {"GET:/users"},
}
```

Middleware for role check is as follows:

```
func RBACMiddleware(role string) gin.HandlerFunc {
    return func(c *gin.Context) {
        action := c.Request.Method + ":" + c.FullPath()
        permissions := rolePermissions[role]

        for _, perm := range permissions {
            if perm == action {
                c.Next()
                return
            }
        }

        c.AbortWithStatusJSON(http.StatusForbidden, gin.H{"error": "Access Denied"})
    }
}
```

To apply middleware, follow:

```
r.GET("/users", RBACMiddleware("viewer"), getUsers)
r.POST("/users", RBACMiddleware("editor"), createUser)
r.GET("/admin", RBACMiddleware("admin"), adminPanel)
```

In a real-world app, the role would be extracted from the JWT or session token dynamically.

The following table shows the attribute-based access control in RBAC and ABAC:

Aspect	RBAC	ABAC
Access control by	Role (admin, editor, viewer)	Attributes (user department, time, IP)
Complexity	Simple, easy to manage	More flexible, harder to maintain
Use case	Most common in microservices	Used in dynamic policy-driven systems

***Table 17.20**: RBAC vs. ABAC*

The following table shows ways of enforcing RBAC at different layers:

Layer	Details
API gateway	Enforces roles before requests hit services.
Middleware	Applied in services to restrict access per endpoint.
Business logic	Useful for fine-grained decisions within services.
External policy engine (e.g., OPA)	Enforces access rules based on external policies.

***Table 17.21**: RBAC at different layers*

Token-based RBAC is as follows:

- Most microservices use JWTs to carry user roles:

  ```
  {
    "sub": "user123",
    "role": "editor",
    "exp": 1710000000
  }
  ```

  - Role is read from the JWT (**`claims["role"]`**).
  - The service uses this to determine what the user can access.

  This makes RBAC stateless and easy to enforce in distributed systems.

RBAC in Kubernetes and service meshes is as follows:

- **Kubernetes RBAC**: Controls access to Kubernetes resources (kubectl, API server, etc.).
- **Istio RBAC**: Enforces service-to-service access based on identities and roles.
- **Example (Istio AuthorizationPolicy)**:

  ```
  apiVersion: security.istio.io/v1beta1
  kind: AuthorizationPolicy
  metadata:
    name: admin-access
  spec:
    rules:
  ```

```
        - from:
          - source:
              requestPrincipals: ["admin@your-org.com"]
```

The following table highlights the best practices for implementing RBAC:

Best practice	Importance
Use least privilege	Grant only the access that is required.
Externalize role management	Avoid hardcoding roles inside services.
Audit role assignments	Detect misuse or excessive permissions.
Group permissions logically	Easier to manage large systems.
Combine RBAC with scopes in OAuth2	Allows fine-grained control per endpoint.
Validate roles from secure tokens	Prevent spoofing or injection attacks.

Table 17.22: *Best practices in implementing RBAC*

Securing communication between services

In microservices architecture, services often communicate over the network, either within a cluster, across data centers, or over the internet. Unlike monoliths, this increased surface area makes service-to-service communication a major security concern. Ensuring these communications are secure helps prevent data leaks, spoofing, and man-in-the-middle attacks.

This section explains how to protect internal service traffic, establish trust, and enforce secure access controls between microservices.

The common threats in service communication are:

Threat	Description
Eavesdropping	Unencrypted traffic can be intercepted and read.
MITM	Attackers can alter or inject traffic between services.
Spoofing	One service impersonates another.
Replay Attacks	Malicious actor reuses valid requests.
Privilege Escalation	One service accesses resources beyond its rights.

Table 17.23: *Common threats in service communication*

The goals of securing service communication are as follows:

Security goal	Importance
Encryption in transit	Protect data from being read or altered in flight.
Authentication	Verify the identity of the calling service.
Authorization	Ensure only allowed services can access endpoints.
Auditing and logging	Track communications for compliance and forensics.

Table 17.24: *Goals of securing service communication*

The following table highlights the core techniques to secure service communication:

Technique	Purpose
TLS	Encrypts HTTP or gRPC traffic between services.
mTLS	Authenticates both client and server services.
Service Mesh (e.g., Istio, Linkerd)	Automates mTLS and access control between services.
Token-based auth (JWT/OAuth)	Verifies identities and permissions using tokens.
API gateways and proxies	Enforce access rules, rate limits, and observability.

***Table 17.25**: Core techniques to secure services*

Note: **Use mTLS for trust between services. We have seen mTLS earlier in this chapter.**

Service identity and authorization are as follows:

- **Each service should have a unique identity, such as**:
    - Service account (Kubernetes)
    - JWT claims (subject, issuer)
    - X.509 certificate (TLS/mTLS)
- **Enforce authorization with**:
    - Policy engines like OPA.
    - Identity-aware proxies (e.g., Envoy).
    - Role bindings and namespaces in Kubernetes.

The following list outlines the token-based authentication between services:

- **Services can use short-lived signed tokens (e.g., JWTs or opaque tokens) to**:
    - Prove identity (who they are).
    - Include scopes or permissions.
    - Prevent replay attacks.
- **Tip**: Use service-specific tokens with:
    - **Audience** (**aud**) claim.
    - **Expiry** (**exp**) claim.
    - **Issuer** (**iss**) validation.

The following table highlights the use of an API gateway or service mesh for centralized control:

Component	Role in communication security
API gateway	Handles external traffic, enforces access, and SSL.
Service mesh	Handles internal traffic, mTLS, and traffic policies.
Ingress controller	Securely routes traffic into the cluster.
Sidecars	Attach to services, automatically securing traffic.

***Table 17.26**: API gateway vs. service mesh for control*

Ways to secure DNS and service discovery are as follows:

- Use DNS over TLS or authenticated service discovery.
- Prevent DNS spoofing or misrouting by enforcing certificate checks.
- In Kubernetes, use NetworkPolicies to limit which pods can talk to others.

Ways to audit, monitor, and log service communication are as follows:

- **Logging and monitoring tools help detect suspicious activity**:
    - **Audit logs**: Who accessed what, when.
    - **Service traces**: Distributed tracing with tools like *Jaeger*.
    - **Alerts**: For unauthorized attempts or anomalies.
- **Tools**: Istio telemetry, Prometheus + Grafana, OpenTelemetry, Fluentd

The following table highlights the best practices for securing service communication:

Best practice	Importance
Use mTLS for all internal communication	Ensures authentication and encryption.
Rotate certificates and tokens periodically	Prevents misuse if leaked.
Enforce least privilege between services	Minimize the blast radius of compromise.
Use short-lived and auditable tokens	Enhances traceability and revocation ability.
Automate policy enforcement with a service mesh	Reduces manual configuration and errors.
Log and monitor inter-service requests	Supports audit trails and early detection.

Table 17.27: Best practices for securing services

Best practices for securing microservices

Securing microservices is not just about protecting endpoints with authentication; it is a comprehensive effort involving architecture, design, deployment, and runtime controls. Since microservices are distributed, they introduce more surfaces to attack: APIs, service-to-service communication, databases, and CI/CD pipelines.

The following security best practices help prevent data leaks, unauthorized access, lateral movement within the system, and compliance violations.

The following list outlines the design-time best practices:

- **Apply the principle of least privilege (PoLP)**:
    - Each service should only access the resources it absolutely needs.
    - Restrict roles, credentials, and data access based on minimal requirements.
- **Define clear service boundaries**:
    - Avoid exposing internal logic via public APIs.
    - Clearly define what is internal, partner-facing, and public.
- **Secure APIs by default**:
    - Require authentication and authorization for every endpoint.
    - Implement access control policies even for internal APIs.

- **Avoid monolithic shared secrets**:
  - Do not reuse the same secrets across services.
  - Use scoped and time-limited tokens and rotate them regularly.

The following table outlines authentication and authorization best practices:

Practice	Importance
Use JWT or OAuth2 for auth	Enables a stateless, verifiable identity
Validate the `aud`, `exp`, and `iss` claims	Prevents misuse and replay attacks
Centralized identity management	Ensures consistency across services
Use RBAC and scopes	Enforces fine-grained access control

***Table 17.28**: Authentication and authorization best practices*

Secure communication is as follows:

- Use TLS for all traffic, including internal service-to-service communication.
- Enforce mutual TLS (mTLS) to establish two-way trust.
- Rotate certificates automatically using tools like cert-manager, Vault, or Istio.

The following table outlines container and runtime security:

Area	Recommendation
Docker images	Use minimal base images (e.g., Alpine), and scan for vulnerabilities.
Run as non-root	Avoid running services as root inside containers.
Secrets	Never store credentials in source code or images. Use secret managers.
Namespaces and isolation	Separate services by Kubernetes namespaces or IAM roles.

***Table 17.29**: Container and runtime security*

The following are the ways to secure CI/CD pipelines:

- Scan code and dependencies using tools like Snyk, Trivy, or Dependabot.
- Sign and verify artifacts before deployment (Sigstore, cosign).
- Store secrets securely in CI/CD tools (e.g., GitHub Actions secrets, GitLab CI vaults).
- Automate security testing as part of your CI workflow.

Observability and threat detection are as follows:

- Enable structured logging, auditing, and distributed tracing.
- Monitor for unusual traffic, failed authentication attempts, and service anomalies.
- Use **security information and event management** (**SIEM**) or cloud-native logging (e.g., GCP Logging, AWS CloudTrail) for centralized monitoring.

Zero Trust security principles are as follows:

- Trust no service or user by default, regardless of network location.
- Continuously validate identity, context, and risk before granting access.
- Use identity-aware proxies and service meshes to enforce policies.

The following table outlines ways to protect against common attacks:

Attack	Protection strategy
SQL injection	Use parameterized queries, ORM libraries.
Cross-site scripting (XSS)	Escape input/output, use CSP headers.
Cross-site request forgery (CSRF)	Use CSRF tokens or SameSite cookies.
Rate limiting abuse	Throttle requests with API gateways or service mesh policies.
Replay attacks	Validate token expiration and use nonces.

***Table 17.30**: Ways of protection against common attacks*

The following are the ways to automate and audit:

- Use **infrastructure as code** (IaC) to apply and version security controls.
- Continuously audit user access, tokens, and service permissions.
- Rotate secrets regularly and track who accessed them and when.

The tools to consider are as follows:

Category	Examples
Identity and auth	Keycloak, Auth0, Ory Hydra
Secret management	HashiCorp Vault, AWS Secrets Manager
Service mesh	Istio, Linkerd
API gateway	Kong, Ambassador, Envoy
Security scanners	Trivy, Snyk, Clair
Monitoring and logs	Prometheus, Grafana, Loki, Fluent Bit

***Table 17.31**: Security tools*

Conclusion

This chapter highlighted how critical it is to secure microservices through robust authentication, authorization, and encrypted communication. We explored how authentication verifies identity using mechanisms like OAuth2, SAML, and mTLS, while authorization determines what authenticated entities can access through models such as RBAC and ABAC. Token-based approaches like JWT were discussed for enabling stateless, scalable identity propagation across services. We also examined securing service-to-service communication using TLS and mTLS to protect data in transit and enforce mutual trust. Practical implementations in Go demonstrated generating and validating JWTs, configuring HTTPS servers, and applying middleware for RBAC. Emphasis was placed on best practices, including using strong signing keys, short-lived tokens, rotating secrets, and employing tools like Keycloak, Istio, and Vault. Adopting Zero Trust principles and auditing all access helps prevent privilege escalation, data leaks, and compliance issues. By following these strategies, you can build resilient microservices architectures that withstand modern security threats.

In the next chapter, we will move from securing services to ensuring their quality through unit and integration testing. We will learn how to validate individual functions and interactions between components, using Go's testing libraries and tools to build confidence that your microservices are both secure and functionally reliable.

Questions

1. Why is authentication and authorization particularly important in a microservices architecture compared to a monolith?
2. Explain the difference between authentication and authorization. At what point in a request flow does each typically occur?
3. What are the advantages and disadvantages of centralized versus decentralized authentication models in microservices?
4. Describe the typical structure of a JWT. What are the roles of the header, payload, and signature?
5. How does mTLS enhance security between services compared to standard TLS? Give a use case where mTLS is preferred.
6. What is RBAC, and how does it differ from ABAC? In what situations might you choose ABAC over RBAC?
7. List at least three security best practices for handling JWTs in microservices. Why are they important?
8. How can an API gateway contribute to enforcing authentication and authorization? What are the trade-offs?
9. Explain how token expiration (exp) and short-lived tokens help reduce security risks in distributed systems.
10. Name two tools from the chapter that help manage identity and authorization in microservices, and briefly describe their roles.

Questions

1. Why is authentication and authorization particularly important in a microservices architecture compared to monoliths?
2. Explain the difference between authentication and authorization. At what point in a request flow does each typically occur?
3. What are the advantages and disadvantages of centralized versus decentralized authentication models in microservices?
4. Describe the typical structure of a JWT. What are the roles of the header, payload, and signature?
5. How does mTLS enhance security between services compared to standard TLS? Give a use case where mTLS is preferred.
6. What is RBAC, and how does it differ from ABAC? In what situations might you choose ABAC over RBAC?
7. List at least three security best practices for handling JWTs in microservices. Why are they important?
8. How can an API gateway contribute to enforcing authentication and authorization? What are the trade-offs?
9. Explain how token expiration (exp) and short-lived tokens help reduce security risks in distributed systems.
10. Name two tools from the chapter that help manage identity and authorization in microservices, and briefly describe their roles.

Join our Discord space

Join our Discord workspace for latest updates, offers, tech happenings around the world, new releases, and sessions with the authors:

https://discord.bpbonline.com

CHAPTER 18
Testing Microservices

Introduction

In this chapter, we explore the critical role of testing in microservices architecture, with a particular focus on unit testing, integration testing, mocking dependencies, load testing, performance optimization, and end-to-end validation. Unlike monolithic systems, microservices demand a comprehensive testing strategy because of their distributed, loosely coupled nature and reliance on network interactions. A failure in one service can cascade across others if not identified early through robust testing practices. Different types of testing work together to verify that software systems function correctly and reliably at scale. Unit tests check individual components in isolation, while integration tests examine how those components interact with each other. Contract tests ensure that different services communicate according to agreed-upon interfaces. Performance tests measure how well the system handles expected workloads and identify bottleneck issues. End-to-end tests validate complete user workflows across the entire system. By breaking down test types, tools, best practices, and common pitfalls, this chapter prepares engineers to build confidence in deployments, reduce regressions, and maintain quality at scale. Ultimately, this discussion establishes testing not as an afterthought but as an essential discipline that safeguards business logic, user experience, and long-term system maintainability.

Structure

We covered the following topics in this chapter:

- Unit testing and integration testing in microservices
- Writing tests for RESTful APIs
- Mocking external services and dependencies
- Load testing and performance optimization
- Implementing end-to-end testing
- Best practices for testing microservices

Objectives

By the end of this chapter, we will understand that testing microservices requires a layered and holistic approach. We will learn the distinction between unit testing, integration testing, and end-to-end testing, and how each contributes uniquely to ensuring system quality. We will explore how mocking external services and dependencies allows developers to achieve isolated coverage and faster feedback. The chapter emphasizes best practices for managing test environments, fixtures, and consistent test data to prevent flaws. We will also understand the importance of contract testing in maintaining compatibility between services and preventing breaking changes across teams. Beyond functionality, the role of load testing and performance optimization will be highlighted as essential for ensuring scalability under real-world workloads. Finally, we will gain insights into how automated tests can be integrated into CI/CD pipelines for continuous validation, and we identified common anti-patterns in testing along with strategies to avoid them in order to maintain a reliable and maintainable test suite.

Unit testing and integration testing in microservices

Unit testing and integration testing is a critical part of microservices development. Due to their distributed nature, microservices must be tested at multiple levels to ensure correctness, stability, and reliability. Two fundamental levels of testing are unit testing and integration testing.

Each plays a distinct role in the quality assurance process and serves different goals:

- Unit tests focus on individual components or functions in isolation.
- Integration tests validate interactions between components or services.

Together, they form the foundation of a robust test suite for microservices-based systems.

Unit testing for microservices

Unit testing involves verifying the smallest testable units of an application, typically functions or methods, in isolation. These tests confirm that individual logic components behave as expected.

The following are the goals of unit testing:

- Validate correctness of logic at the function/method level.
- Catch regressions during code refactoring.
- Provide fast feedback during development.
- Serve as executable documentation for business logic.

The following are the characteristics of good unit tests:

Characteristic	Description
Isolated	Does not depend on databases, file systems, or other services.
Deterministic	Produces the same result every time.
Fast	Runs in milliseconds to seconds.
Easy to write and maintain	Clear structure, minimal mocking.

***Table 18.1**: Characteristics of good unit tests*

Unit testing in Go (Example): Go uses the built-in testing package for unit tests.

Example: Unit test for a calculator function is as follows:

```go
// calculator_test.go
import "testing"

func TestAdd(t *testing.T) {
    result := Add(2, 3)
    expected := 5

    if result != expected {
        t.Errorf("Expected %d but got %d", expected, result)
    }
}
```

Run with: `go test`

Output:

```
=== RUN   TestAdd
--- PASS: TestAdd (0.00s)
PASS
```

Unit tests for microservices can be organised as follows:

- Use a separate **`_test.go`** file per module.
- Place tests alongside the code under test.
- Group tests by domain (e.g., user, order, payment).

Integration testing for microservices

Integration testing validates how multiple components work together. This includes service and database. API based communication between ServicesREST client communicating with **`ServicesIntegration`** tests simulate real-world interactions between subsystems.

The goals of integration testing are as follows:

- Verify that contracts between services are adhered to.
- Test interaction with external systems like databases, message brokers, and caches.
- Detect interface mismatches and schema changes.
- Validate configuration and deployment setups.

The key characteristics of integration tests are as follows:

Characteristic	Description
Real environment	Involve real (or simulated) services or databases.
Slower than unit tests	Typically take seconds to minutes to run.
Less frequent than unit tests	Run as part of CI/CD or pre-deployment pipelines.
Often use Docker or test containers	To simulate real environments.

***Table 18.2**: Key characteristics of Integration tests*

Let us look at an integration test example in Go (database layer).

Sample: Testing service with PostgreSQL using Docker is as follows:

```
func TestCreateUser(t *testing.T) {
    db, cleanup := setupTestDatabase()
    defer cleanup()

    repo := NewUserRepository(db)
    err := repo.Create("Venkatesh", "venkatesh@gmail.com")
    assert.NoError(t, err)
}
```

Here, **`setupTestDatabase()`** might spin up a temporary PostgreSQL container or use an in-memory mock database.

Unit testing vs. integration testing is as follows:

Aspect	Unit testing	Integration testing
Scope	Single function/method	Multiple components or services
Speed	Fast	Slower
Dependencies	Mocked or none	Real or simulated (e.g., database, queue)
Failure Feedback	Precise, localized	Broader, can be hard to trace
Environment Setup	Minimal	Often requires containers, databases, etc.

Table 18.3: *Unit testing vs. integration testing*

Integration testing tools for microservices are as follows:

Tool	Purpose
Testcontainers	Spins up disposable Docker containers for testing
GoMock	Mocks interfaces for both unit and integration tests
Docker Compose	Sets up multi-service environments for test suites
WireMock / MockServer	Simulates HTTP services in integration tests
Postman/Newman	API-level integration test runner

Table 18.4: *Integration testing tools*

We can manage test data and environment as follows:

- Use fixtures or seeds to prepopulate test data.
- Clean up databases or queues after test runs.
- Use environment variables to configure test behavior.

Continuous integration and testing:

- Run unit tests on every commit to catch early issues.
- Run integration tests nightly or before merges into main branches.
- Use CI tools like GitHub Actions, GitLab CI, CircleCI to automate tests.

The following are the best practices:

Practice	Why it is effective
Write unit tests before code	Encourages **test-driven development** (TDD)
Mock only what you own	Limit mocking to internal components under your control, avoiding simulations of external public APIs. This prevents unrealistic test scenarios and ensures tests reflect real-world interactions without introducing unnecessary fragility
Keep integration tests deterministic	Avoid flaky tests that fail randomly
Use test tags (**`go test -tags=integration`**)	Apply tags to categorize tests, allowing selective execution during CI runs. This separation enables developers to run only relevant test suites such as unit versus integration, optimizing build times and resource use.
Limit external test dependencies	Keep integration tests fast and self-contained

Table 18.5: *Best practices for testing microservices*

Writing tests for RESTful APIs

RESTful APIs are the core communication layer in most microservice architectures. Ensuring they behave correctly under various inputs and conditions is critical. Testing REST APIs involves verifying that:

- Endpoints return the correct status codes.
- Responses match expected formats and data.
- Input validation and error handling work properly.
- Authorization and business logic constraints are enforced.

This section focuses on testing RESTful HTTP endpoints from within Go services using Go's built-in **`net/http/httptest`** package, as well as external tools.

The following are the types of REST API tests:

Test type	Focus	Example
Unit tests	Handler logic, request parsing, response formatting	Mock request I check response JSON
Integration tests	Full request pipeline: routing I handler I DB	GET /users should return real users
Contract tests	Ensure API contracts match consumer expectations	Validate field types, status codes
Regression tests	Prevent reoccurrence of past bugs	Retest past edge cases

***Table 18.6**: REST API tests*

Unit testing REST handlers in Go

Go provides **`httptest`** and **`http.HandlerFunc`** to create mock requests and inspect responses.

Example: Testing a simple handler:

```
package main

import (
 "net/http"
)

// HelloHandler writes "Hello, world!" to the response
func HelloHandler(w http.ResponseWriter, r *http.Request) {
 w.WriteHeader(http.StatusOK)
 w.Write([]byte("Hello, world!"))
}
```

Unit test:

```
package main

import (
 "io"
 "net/http"
 "net/http/httptest"
 "testing"
```

```
 "github.com/stretchr/testify/assert"
)

func TestHelloHandler(t *testing.T) {
 req := httptest.NewRequest("GET", "/", nil)
 w := httptest.NewRecorder()

 HelloHandler(w, req)

 resp := w.Result()
 body, _ := io.ReadAll(resp.Body)

 assert.Equal(t, http.StatusOK, resp.StatusCode)
 assert.Equal(t, "Hello, world!", string(body))
}
```

Run the following commands:

```
go get github.com/stretchr/testify/assert
go test
```

Output:

```
=== RUN   TestHelloHandler
--- PASS: TestHelloHandler (0.00s)
PASS
```

Testing handlers with path params and JSON

Suppose your endpoint creates a user with a JSON request.

The following is a handler example:

```
package main

import (
    "encoding/json"
    "net/http"
)

type User struct {
    Name  string 'json:"name"'
    Email string 'json:"email"'
}

func CreateUser(w http.ResponseWriter, r *http.Request) {
    var user User
    if err := json.NewDecoder(r.Body).Decode(&user); err != nil {
        http.Error(w, "Invalid input", http.StatusBadRequest)
        return
    }
```

```
    // Simulate saving and respond back
    w.WriteHeader(http.StatusCreated)
    json.NewEncoder(w).Encode(user)
}
```

Test with JSON payload:

```
package main

import (
 "encoding/json"
 "net/http"
 "net/http/httptest"
 "strings"
 "testing"

 "github.com/stretchr/testify/assert"
)

func TestCreateUser(t *testing.T) {
 payload := '{"name": "Venkatesh", "email": "venkatesh@gmail.com"}'
 req := httptest.NewRequest("POST", "/users", strings.NewReader(payload))
 req.Header.Set("Content-Type", "application/json")
 w := httptest.NewRecorder()

 CreateUser(w, req)

 resp := w.Result()
 assert.Equal(t, http.StatusCreated, resp.StatusCode)

 var user User
 err := json.NewDecoder(resp.Body).Decode(&user)
 assert.NoError(t, err)
 assert.Equal(t, "Venkatesh", user.Name)
 assert.Equal(t, "venkateshjramesh@gmail.com", user.Email)
}

func CreateUser(w http.ResponseWriter, r *http.Request) {
    var user User
    if err := json.NewDecoder(r.Body).Decode(&user); err != nil {
        http.Error(w, "Invalid input", http.StatusBadRequest)
        return
    }
    // Simulate saving and respond back
    w.WriteHeader(http.StatusCreated)
    json.NewEncoder(w).Encode(user)
}
```

Let us use router frameworks (e.g., Gin, Chi) in tests as follows:

Main.go:

```
package main

import (
 "net/http"

 "github.com/gin-gonic/gin"
)

type User struct {
 Name  string 'json:"name"'
 Email string 'json:"email"'
}

func CreateUser(c *gin.Context) {
 var user User
 if err := c.ShouldBindJSON(&user); err != nil {
  c.JSON(http.StatusBadRequest, gin.H{"error": "Invalid input"})
  return
 }

 // Simulate save and respond
 c.JSON(http.StatusCreated, user)
}
```

Gin example with integration setup:

```
package main

import (
 "net/http"
 "net/http/httptest"
 "strings"
 "testing"

 "github.com/gin-gonic/gin"
 "github.com/stretchr/testify/assert"
)

func TestCreateUserIntegration(t *testing.T) {
 // Setup Gin router and route
 router := gin.Default()
 router.POST("/users", CreateUser)

 // JSON payload
```

```
    payload := '{"name": "Venkatesh", "email": "venkateshjramesh@gmail.com"}'
    req, _ := http.NewRequest("POST", "/users", strings.NewReader(payload))
    req.Header.Set("Content-Type", "application/json")

    // Record the response
    w := httptest.NewRecorder()
    router.ServeHTTP(w, req)

    // Assertions
    assert.Equal(t, http.StatusCreated, w.Code)
    assert.Contains(t, w.Body.String(), "Venkatesh")
    assert.Contains(t, w.Body.String(), "venkatesh@gmail.com")
}
```

Output:

```
=== RUN   TestCreateUserIntegration
[GIN-debug] [WARNING] Creating an Engine instance with the Logger and Recovery middleware already attached.

[GIN-debug] [WARNING] Running in "debug" mode. Switch to "release" mode in production.
 - using env:   export GIN_MODE=release
 - using code:  gin.SetMode(gin.ReleaseMode)

[GIN-debug] POST   /users                    --> code/chapter18/unit_testing_integration_testing/gin_integration_setup.CreateUser (3 handlers)
[GIN] 2025/05/01 - 19:53:27 | 201 |       616.4µs |                 | POST     "/users"
--- PASS: TestCreateUserIntegration (0.00s)
PASS
```

External tools for API testing are explained as follows:

Tool	Usage
Postman	Manual and automated API testing
Newman	CLI runner for Postman collections
curl/httpie	Quick testing in terminal
RestAssured (Java)	Powerful testing DSL for REST
Dredd	API contract testing

***Table 18.7**: External tools for API testing*

Assertions to perform in API tests are as follows:

- HTTP status code (200, 201, 400, 404, 500)
- JSON body structure and fields
- Response headers (e.g., Content-Type)
- Error messages and codes
- Behavior for invalid inputs
- Authentication-required routes

Organizing API tests in a microservice:

Test file	Purpose
handler_test.go	Unit tests for individual handlers
api_integration_test.go	Tests full API endpoints with DB
router_test.go	Validates routing and middleware
auth_test.go	Tests auth-protected endpoints

***Table 18.8:** Organizing API tests*

Keep tests modular and focused, and use test fixtures or mock DBs where needed. Use test tags for different environments.

Use Go's **-tags** flag to separate fast unit tests from slower API tests:

```
go test -tags=integration ./...
```

Mocking external services and dependencies

Microservices often depend on external components like databases, third-party APIs, message brokers, and internal services. While integration tests validate real interactions, unit tests and fast-running service tests benefit from mocking these dependencies. Mocking allows developers to simulate external behavior without relying on actual external systems, improving test reliability, speed, and isolation.

Need for mocking dependencies is as follows:

Reason	Benefit
Isolate internal logic	Focus on testing service code, not dependencies.
Avoid flakiness	Tests do not fail due to network issues or third-party bugs.
Speed up tests	No real network or I/O delays.
Control test scenarios	Simulate success, failure, timeouts, and edge cases.
Enable testing early	Develop and test services even before external APIs exist.

***Table 18.9:** Need for mocking*

The following can be mocked in microservices:

Component	Mock type
REST API clients	Fake HTTP servers, interfaces
Databases	In-memory mocks, test containers
Message queues (Kafka)	Mock publishers/consumers
gRPC or GraphQL services	Stubbed clients or mock servers
Cloud services (e.g., S3)	Local emulators or fake clients

***Table 18.10:** Mockable components in microservices*

Mocking in Go using interfaces

Go's interface-based design makes mocking simple and powerful. Define dependencies as interfaces and provide mock implementations for testing.

Example: Service with external API dependency:

```
type EmailService interface {
    Send(email string, message string) error
}
```

Actual implementation:

```
type SMTPService struct{}

func (s SMTPService) Send(email, message string) error {
    // connect to SMTP server
    return nil
}
```

Mock implementation for tests:

```
type MockEmailService struct {
    SentEmails []string
}

func (m *MockEmailService) Send(email, message string) error {
    m.SentEmails = append(m.SentEmails, email)
    return nil
}
```

Using GoMock for auto-generated mocks

GoMock is a popular mocking framework that generates mocks from interfaces.

Installation:

```
go install github.com/golang/mock/mockgen@latest
```

Generate mock:

```
mockgen -source=email.go -destination=mocks/email_mock.go -package=mocks
```

Use in tests:

```
mockEmail := mocks.NewMockEmailService(ctrl)
mockEmail.EXPECT().Send("user@example.com", "Welcome!").Return(nil)
```

Mocking HTTP calls

Let us take the following scenario. You want to mock that external API using **`httptest.NewServer`**.

Main.go:

```
package main

import (
 "encoding/json"
 "io"
 "net/http"
)
```

```
// simulate an external call
func NotifyExternalService(url string) (string, error) {
 resp, err := http.Get(url)
 if err != nil {
  return "", err
 }
 defer resp.Body.Close()

 body, err := io.ReadAll(resp.Body)
 if err != nil {
  return "", err
 }

 // parse status from response
 var result map[string]string
 if err := json.Unmarshal(body, &result); err != nil {
  return "", err
 }

 return result["status"], nil
}
```

Using **httptest.NewServer**:

```
package main

import (
 "fmt"
 "net/http"
 "net/http/httptest"
 "testing"

 "github.com/stretchr/testify/assert"
)

func TestNotifyExternalService(t *testing.T) {
 // Step 1: Create a mock downstream server
 ts := httptest.NewServer(http.HandlerFunc(func(w http.ResponseWriter, r *http.Request) {
  w.WriteHeader(http.StatusOK)
  fmt.Fprintln(w, '{"status":"sent"}')
 }))
 defer ts.Close()

 // Step 2: Test the client against the mock server
 status, err := NotifyExternalService(ts.URL)
```

```
    // Step 3: Assert the results
    assert.NoError(t, err)
    assert.Equal(t, "sent", status)
}
```

This is useful for simulating downstream services or third-party APIs.

Output:

```
=== RUN   TestNotifyExternalService
--- PASS: TestNotifyExternalService (0.00s)
PASS
```

Use cases are as follows:

- Mocking third-party APIs (e.g., Twilio, Stripe, SendGrid).
- Testing microservice-to-microservice communication.
- Ensuring stable tests without relying on live endpoints.

Mocking databases

Let us assume you have a service that depends on a **UserRepository** interface to fetch users. For testing, you will create a mock implementation with preloaded data.

In-memory mock (example with custom repo) is as follows:

- **user.go**:

  ```
  package main

  type User struct {
      ID    int
      Name  string
      Email string
  }

  type UserRepository interface {
      FindUser(id int) (*User, error)
  }
  ```

- **mock_user_repo.go**:

  ```
  package main

  type MockUserRepo struct {
      users map[int]*User
  }

  func (m *MockUserRepo) FindUser(id int) (*User, error) {
      if user, exists := m.users[id]; exists {
          return user, nil
      }
      return nil, nil
  }
  ```

- **service.go**:

```go
package main

import "fmt"

type UserService struct {
    repo UserRepository
}

func (s *UserService) GetWelcomeMessage(id int) string {
    user, err := s.repo.FindUser(id)
        if err != nil || user == nil {
            return "User not found"
        }
    return fmt.Sprintf("Welcome, %s!", user.Name)
}
```

- **service_test.go**:

```go
package main

import (
    "testing"

    "github.com/stretchr/testify/assert"
)

func TestGetWelcomeMessage(t *testing.T) {
    mockRepo := &MockUserRepo{
        users: map[int]*User{
            1: {ID: 1, Name: "Venkatesh", Email: "venkatesh@example.com"},
        },
    }

    service := UserService{repo: mockRepo}

    msg := service.GetWelcomeMessage(1)
    assert.Equal(t, "Welcome, Venkatesh!", msg)

    msgNotFound := service.GetWelcomeMessage(2)
    assert.Equal(t, "User not found", msgNotFound)
}
```

Output:

```
=== RUN   TestGetWelcomeMessage
--- PASS: TestGetWelcomeMessage (0.00s)
PASS
```

Benefits of using this pattern:

- Fast, dependency-free unit tests.
- Clear separation of interface and implementation.
- Easily extendable for advanced mocking or error cases.

Mocking message brokers

Instead of running real brokers:

- Use mock consumers and producers.
- Use interfaces for messaging clients (e.g., `Publisher.Send()`, `Consumer.Receive()`).
- Simulate retries, message loss, and dead-letter scenarios.

Tools for mocking in microservices:

Tool	Use case
httptest (Go)	Mock HTTP servers for handlers or clients
GoMock	Interface mocking in Go
Testify/mock	Lightweight mock assertions
MockServer	Simulate real HTTP APIs
WireMock	REST API mocking with scenarios & delays
FakeS3, LocalStack	Cloud service emulation (e.g., AWS S3)

Table 18.11: *Tools for mocking microservices*

Mock should not be conducted in the following scenarios:

Scenario	Solution
You want to test service integration	Use real dependencies or test containers
Your logic depends heavily on DB schemas	Use real DB or test DB
You are validating a deployed contract (OpenAPI, gRPC)	Use contract testing

Table 18.12: *Non-mocking scenarios*

Best practices are as follows:

Practice	Why it matters
Mock only what your service owns	Avoid mocking third-party or external services' internals.
Keep mocks simple	Do not overengineer your mock logic.
Use interfaces for dependencies	Encourages testability and abstraction.
Combine with integration tests	Mocks are fast, but validate with real systems too.
Validate contract compatibility	Ensure mocks behave like real services.

Table 18.13: *Best practices in mocking*

Load testing and performance optimization

As microservices scale, it is not enough for them to be functionally correct; they must also be performant under high traffic and resilient under load. Load testing evaluates how a service behaves under increasing levels of requests, while performance optimization involves tuning the system to meet response time, throughput, and resource usage goals.

Together, these processes ensure your microservices are responsive, scalable, and cost-efficient in real-world conditions.

Need for load testing in microservices:

Reason	Impact
Identify bottlenecks	Find slow endpoints, memory leaks, or DB contention
Verify scalability	Check if services scale under concurrent load
Prevent downtime	Ensure services do not crash under traffic spikes
Size infrastructure correctly	Avoid over-provisioning or under-provisioning

Table 18.14: *Need for load testing*

The following are the key metrics to measure:

Metric	What it tells you
Throughput (RPS)	Requests per second the service can handle
Latency	Time taken to process a request (avg, p95, p99)
Error Rate	Percentage of failed requests
CPU/Memory Usage	Resource consumption under load
Concurrency	Max number of users or connections supported

Table 18.15: *Key metrics in load testing*

The following are the load testing approaches:

Approach	Description
Stress testing	Push the service beyond limits to test failure behavior
Load testing	Simulate expected production load and scale
Spike testing	Introduce sudden load spikes to test elasticity
Soak testing	Run tests for an extended time to check for memory leaks
Capacity testing	Find the max load before service performance degrades

Table 18.16: *Load testing approaches*

Popular load testing tools are as follows:

Tool	Description
k6	Modern CLI-based load testing tool for APIs (JavaScript scripting)
Apache JMeter	Java-based GUI tool for HTTP, database, and messaging load tests
Locust	Python-based load testing framework
Vegeta	Lightweight HTTP load tester written in Go
Gatling	Scala-based performance testing tool with simulation DSL
Artillery	YAML + JavaScript for scenario-based API testing

Table 18.17: *Load testing tools*

Example: Load testing a REST API with k6 is done as follows:

Install k6:

```
brew install k6   # brew is for mac. use Windows/Linux binary equivalent
```

Sample script (test.js):

```
import http from 'k6/http';
import { sleep, check } from 'k6';

export let options = {
  vus: 50,           // virtual users
  duration: '30s',   // test duration
};

export default function () {
  const res = http.get('http://localhost:8080/api/v1/users');
  check(res, {
    'status is 200': (r) => r.status === 200,
    'body is not empty': (r) => r.body.length > 0,
  });
  sleep(1);
}
```

Run the test as follows:

```
k6 run test.js
```

Performance optimization areas are as follows:

Layer	Optimization techniques
Code (Go)	Minimize allocations, use goroutines wisely, avoid locking
API design	Use pagination, limit payload size, minimize N+1 queries
Database access	Use connection pooling, indexing, query optimization
Caching	Use in-memory (e.g., Redis) or client-side caching
Concurrency handling	Use worker pools, channels, and rate limiting
Network	Compress responses (gzip), reduce round-trips

***Table 18.18**: Performance optimization areas*

Profiling and benchmarking in Go

Profiling and benchmarking in Go help developers measure the performance of their code and identify bottlenecks. Benchmarking provides repeatable metrics for function execution speed, while profiling reveals insights into CPU usage, memory allocations, and execution paths. Together, they enable targeted optimization rather than guesswork. By using Go's built-in testing and **pprof** tools, engineers can ensure applications are efficient, scalable, and production ready.

Benchmarking functions are as follows:

```
func BenchmarkAdd(b *testing.B) {
    for i := 0; i < b.N; i++ {
```

```
        Add(1, 2)
    }
}
```

1. **Run with**:
   ```
   go test -bench=.
   ```
2. **Profiling with pprof**:
   ```
   import _ "net/http/pprof"

   go func() {
       log.Println(http.ListenAndServe("localhost:6060", nil))
   }()
   ```
3. Open **http://localhost:6060/debug/pprof/** to explore memory and CPU profiles.

CI/CD integration for load testing can be done as follows:

1. Add load test stages to GitHub Actions, GitLab CI, or Jenkins.
2. Schedule nightly soak tests or pre-release performance checks.
3. Monitor regression trends in latency and throughput.

The best practices for load testing are as follows:

Practice	Benefit
Test in prod-like environments	Ensures accurate results
Set realistic usage patterns	Models actual user behavior
Automate performance thresholds	Prevent regressions
Use dashboards to visualize results	Helps stakeholders and performance tuning
Combine with alerting tools	Detects abnormal slowdowns early
Profile and fix bottlenecks iteratively	Avoid premature optimization

***Table 18.19**: Load testing best practices*

Implementing end-to-end testing

End-to-end (**E2E**) testing verifies the complete functionality of a system by simulating real-world user scenarios that span multiple microservices and components. Unlike unit or integration tests, E2E tests validate the entire workflow from an API request at the gateway, through internal service calls, database interactions, messaging systems, and back to the response.

E2E tests are crucial for confirming that services work together as expected, maintain business flow integrity, and deliver a seamless user experience.

The importance of end-to-end testing is as follows:

Purpose	Benefit
Validate real user flows	Confirms the system behaves correctly from start to end
Catch cross-service issues	Detects contract mismatches, bad configurations, etc.
Ensure business rule enforcement	Verifies features like order processing, user registration
Verify deployment success	Ensures the system is functional after new releases

***Table 18.20**: Importance of end-to-end testing*

In E2E testing we cover the following:

Test scenario	Example
User Registration	API gateway I Auth Service I DB I Email Service
Order Placement	Frontend I Order API I Inventory + Payment Services
Data Flow Between Services	Producer sends event I Message Broker I Consumer
Authorization Enforcement	Ensure protected APIs reject unauthorized access
Error Recovery	Validate retry or fallback logic for failed services

***Table 18.21**: E2E testing scenarios*

Typical architecture for E2E tests is as follows:

```
[Test Script]
     ↓
[API Gateway] -> [Service A] -> [DB]
                      ↓
                [Service B] -> [Queue] -> [Service C]
     ↓
[Assert Response + System State]
```

Tests are run from an external perspective, like a user or external system.

Use real HTTP/gRPC calls and verify responses, side effects, and inter-service messages.

Tools for end-to-end testing are as follows:

Tool	Purpose
Postman + Newman	Manual and automated API workflow testing
Cypress	E2E browser automation for UI + API workflows
RestAssured	Java DSL for end-to-end API tests
k6	Simulates real HTTP flows with scripting
Ginkgo (Go)	BDD-style E2E test framework
Playwright	Automates frontend + backend E2E flows

***Table 18.22**: Tools for end-to-end testing*

Implementing E2E tests in Go

Here is a complete and structured example of implementing an **end-to-end** (**E2E**) test in Go for a simple user creation API. This example uses only the Go standard library and popular testing helpers (require, assert from testify). It simulates a real HTTP request against a running API handler.

Example: Full API flow test is as follows:

main.go:

```go
package main

import (
    "encoding/json"
    "net/http"
```

```
)

type User struct {
    Name  string `json:"name"`
    Email string `json:"email"`
}

var mockDB = make(map[string]User) // Simulated in-memory DB

func CreateUserHandler(w http.ResponseWriter, r *http.Request) {
    var user User
    if err := json.NewDecoder(r.Body).Decode(&user); err != nil {
        http.Error(w, "Invalid input", http.StatusBadRequest)
        return
    }

    mockDB[user.Email] = user
    w.WriteHeader(http.StatusCreated)
    json.NewEncoder(w).Encode(user)
}

func main() {
    http.HandleFunc("/api/v1/users", CreateUserHandler)
    http.ListenAndServe(":8080", nil)
}
```

main_test.go:

```
package main

import (
    "encoding/json"
    "net/http"
    "net/http/httptest"
    "strings"
    "testing"

    "github.com/stretchr/testify/assert"
    "github.com/stretchr/testify/require"
)

func TestUserCreationFlow(t *testing.T) {
    // Start a real HTTP server
    server := httptest.NewServer(http.HandlerFunc(CreateUserHandler))
    defer server.Close()
```

```
    reqBody := `{"name": "Venkatesh", "email": "venkatesh@example.com"}`
    req, _ := http.NewRequest("POST", server.URL, strings.NewReader(reqBody))
    req.Header.Set("Content-Type", "application/json")

    // Send request
    resp, err := http.DefaultClient.Do(req)
    require.NoError(t, err)
    defer resp.Body.Close()

    // Validate response
    assert.Equal(t, http.StatusCreated, resp.StatusCode)

    var user User
    json.NewDecoder(resp.Body).Decode(&user)

    assert.Equal(t, "Venkatesh", user.Name)
    assert.Equal(t, "venkatesh@example.com", user.Email)

    // Validate mock DB state (side effect)
    savedUser, exists := mockDB["venkatesh@example.com"]
    assert.True(t, exists)
    assert.Equal(t, "Venkatesh", savedUser.Name)
}
```

Output:

```
=== RUN   TestUserCreationFlow
--- PASS: TestUserCreationFlow (0.01s)
PASS
```

This tests the following:

- The full HTTP request/response lifecycle.
- JSON parsing and response structure.
- Business logic (e.g., storing user in memory).
- Side effects (mock DB changes).

Use case: If you want, you can do the following:

- Start a full HTTP server with your handler.
- Send a request (like a real client).
- Verify the response and side effects (e.g., DB state).

Running E2E tests in Docker Compose

E2E tests often require a fully deployed system (API gateway, microservices, databases). You can use Docker Compose to spin up all services for testing.

Example Docker Compose setup:

```
services:
  user-service:
    image: myuserapp:latest
    ports: [8080:8080]
  db:
    image: postgres:15
  test-runner:
    build: ./e2e-tests
    depends_on:
      - user-service
      - db
```

Run the E2E test container after the services are up.

Writing maintainable E2E tests:

Practice	Benefit
Use real data flows	Ensures authenticity of test results
Clean up test data after each run	Prevents pollution and flaky tests
Isolate test environments	Avoid conflicts between test runs
Use seed/fake data where needed	Ensures predictability and repeatability
Validate full system behavior	Not just HTTP response also DB, events, logs

***Table 18.23**: Benefits of maintainable E2E testing*

Integrating E2E tests with CI/CD pipelines:

- Run E2E tests after build and deployment to staging.
- Use Docker Compose or Kubernetes job runners.
- Trigger alerts on failures, regressions, or SLA violations.
- Store logs and traces for investigation.

Sample GitHub Actions snippet is a s follows:

```
- name: Run E2E Tests
  run: docker-compose -f docker-compose.test.yml up --abort-on-container-exit
```

Challenges with E2E testing are as follows:

Challenge	Mitigation strategy
Long test execution time	Parallelize tests or run only critical paths
Flaky tests	Use retry mechanisms and proper data cleanup
Environment dependency	Use containerized or mocked environments
Difficult debugging	Add tracing, structured logs, and dashboards

***Table 18.24**: End-to-end testing challenges*

Best practices for testing microservices

In a microservices environment, testing is more than just running a few unit tests. It involves verifying business logic, service contracts, network communication, system interactions, and non-functional aspects like performance and security. Testing must be strategic, automated, and layered to be effective. This section outlines best practices that help teams maintain reliable, fast, and maintainable test suites for modern microservice-based systems.

Isolate tests wherever possible as follows:

- Mock external dependencies in unit tests.
- Use in-memory databases or test containers in integration tests.
- Run tests in isolated environments using containers or namespaces.

Automate tests in CI/CD as follows:

- Run unit and integration tests on every commit.
- Execute end-to-end tests on merges, nightly builds, or pre-deployment.
- Gate deployments with test coverage and success checks.

Continuous testing improves velocity and reduces manual QA overhead.

Maintain test data strategically as follows:

Approach	Benefit
Use fixtures or factories	Create reusable, predictable test data
Seed test DBs	Ensure consistent environment across runs
Clean up after tests	Prevent data pollution and flaky results

Table 18.25: *Test data strategy*

Let us discuss how to focus on contract testing.

Use contract testing (e.g., Pact) to verify that:

- Consumers and providers agree on API contracts.
- Backward compatibility is preserved.
- Service upgrades do not break dependent services.

Especially useful in large microservice environments with multiple teams.

Include non-functional testing:

Test type	Purpose
Performance tests	Detect slow APIs and tune bottlenecks
Security tests	Identify vulnerabilities (e.g., injection, leaks)
Chaos tests	Validate resilience under failure conditions

Table 18.26: *Non-functional testing*

Structure and name tests clearly are as follows:

- Organize test files by domain (**`user_test.go`**, **`order_test.go`**).
- Use clear naming (**`TestCreateUserSuccess`**, **`TestDeleteUserUnauthorized`**).
- Group related tests with subtests (**`t.Run(...)`**).

Make tests observable and traceable as follows:

- Log inputs, outputs, and context in test failures.
- Use structured logs for debugging.
- Add tracing or request IDs in test environments to track flow across services.

Balance test coverage with business value:

- Strive for high coverage in core logic.
- Do not obsess over 100% coverage if it includes trivial or redundant cases.
- Prioritize testing of critical paths, edge cases, and integrations.

Avoid common anti-patterns as follows:

Anti-pattern	What to do instead
Writing overly complex tests	Keep them simple and focused
Mocking everything in all test types	Mock only where isolation is required
Relying only on end-to-end tests	Layer tests with unit and integration levels
Ignoring flaky tests	Fix or remove them immediately

Table 18.27: *Anti-patterns*

Conclusion

We covered a holistic view of testing strategies tailored for microservices. We examined how unit testing secures the correctness of small components, while integration tests validate inter-service and database interactions. We explored the role of mocking to simulate external systems, ensuring tests remain fast, reliable, and isolated. Moving beyond functionality, we highlighted the necessity of load testing and performance optimization to ensure that microservices remain responsive and resilient under varying traffic conditions. End-to-end testing was introduced as the final validation layer, providing confidence that real-world workflows across multiple services function seamlessly. We also emphasized the importance of CI/CD integration, test observability, and contract testing to maintain system health as microservices evolve. Collectively, these practices underscore that testing is not just a quality gate but a continuous enabler of agility, scalability, and trust.

In the next chapter, we will learn that database design in microservices emphasizes autonomy, where each service owns its schema to ensure scalability and independence. We will see polyglot persistence that allows services to adopt SQL or NoSQL databases depending on their unique requirements, supporting flexibility and performance. Schema evolution and migrations are looked upon, with tools like Flyway and Liquibase enabling safe versioning. Advanced patterns such as event sourcing, **Command Query Responsibility Segregation** (**CQRS**), and Sagas that provide resilience, auditability, and eventual consistency in distributed workflows are looked upon.

Questions

1. What is the key difference between unit testing and integration testing, and why are both important in microservices?
2. How does mocking external dependencies help improve the reliability of tests in microservices?
3. Why is load testing important in a microservices environment, and what kind of insights does it provide?
4. Explain how E2E testing ensures system reliability in microservices.
5. What are the risks of relying only on unit tests and skipping integration or system-level tests?
6. Describe how contract testing helps in maintaining compatibility between different microservices.
7. In what ways do testing challenges increase when moving from a monolithic system to microservices?
8. What role does test automation play in maintaining the agility of microservices development?
9. Why is it important to have a clear test strategy covering unit, integration, performance, and E2E tests in microservices?
10. List and explain at least three best practices for testing microservices that help ensure long-term maintainability.

CHAPTER 19
Managing Data in Microservices

Introduction

Designing databases for microservices is fundamentally different from traditional monolithic systems. In a microservices architecture, each service is autonomous, independently deployable, and responsible for its own data. This leads to the principle of database per service, where each microservice owns and manages its own database schema. While this improves service decoupling and scalability, it also introduces challenges around data consistency, schema evolution, and querying across boundaries.

This chapter will explore the principles, patterns, and design strategies for building robust, loosely coupled database architectures tailored to microservices.

Structure

In this chapter, we will cover the following topics:

- Importance of database design in microservices
- Working with SQL and NoSQL databases
- Implementing data migrations and versioning
- Event sourcing and CQRS patterns
- Managing distributed transactions
- Best practices for data management in microservices

Objectives

By the end of this chapter, we will understand the fundamental principles of database design in microservices, including why each service must own its own database and the importance of data autonomy. We will learn how schema design strategies align with bounded contexts, the use of identifiers instead of foreign keys across services, and when to favor denormalization. We will explore approaches for cross-service data access, database technology choices between SQL and NoSQL, and common database design patterns. Additionally, we will gain clarity on key considerations such as schema evolution, consistency management, and avoiding common pitfalls.

Importance of database design in microservices

Designing the database layer is one of the most critical aspects of building microservices because it directly impacts scalability, resilience, and service independence. A poorly designed database can introduce tight coupling and system fragility, while a well-designed one strengthens autonomy and supports polyglot persistence. This section highlights the reasons why database design plays a central role in microservices success.

Refer to the following table:

Reason	Impact
Services own their data	Promotes autonomy and independent scalability
Avoids tight coupling	Prevents shared schema changes from breaking other services
Enables polyglot persistence	Services choose the best-fit database (SQL, NoSQL, etc.)
Enhances resilience	Isolated failures prevent cascading database crashes
Supports domain-driven design	Aligns data storage with business domain boundaries

***Table 19.1**: Importance of database design*

The following are the principles of database design in microservices:

- **Database per service**: Each microservice should have exclusive access to its own database. This encapsulation allows teams to evolve their data models without coordinating with other teams.
- **Decentralized data management**:
  - No shared tables or databases across services.
  - Each service becomes the source of truth for its own data.
  - Services communicate via APIs or events, not direct SQL joins.
- **Loose coupling through data ownership**: Design schemas such that no other service depends on internal data representations or performs joins directly on your tables.

Schema design strategies

The strategies are as follows:

- **Align schema with bounded context**: Use **Domain-Driven Design** (**DDD**) principles to define bounded contexts, then design tables/entities within those boundaries.

  Example:
  - **User Service**: Owns users' table
  - **Order Service**: Owns orders and payments tables
  - **Inventory Service**: Owns products, stock_levels

  Each schema reflects the core business logic and responsibilities of the owning service.
- **Use identifiers and external references**: Avoid foreign key constraints across services. Instead, use reference IDs (e.g., `user_id`, `product_id`) and validate through API calls or event-driven synchronization.

  Why not use foreign keys across services?
  - They couple services tightly.
  - Break autonomy and independent deployability.
  - Assume strong consistency where eventual consistency may be more appropriate.
- **Prefer immutable event history for auditability**: Design databases to capture event history (e.g., `order_placed`, `payment_received`) in addition to the current state. This supports:
  - Auditing
  - Debugging
  - Event sourcing (if used)

- **Use denormalization where necessary**: Microservices often favor denormalized schemas for performance and isolation. Instead of normalized join-heavy schemas:
  - Store duplicated data for local access.
  - Keep it eventually consistent via background sync or messaging.

  Example:

  Order Service includes `user_name` for receipts, even though the user profile is owned by another service.

Handling cross-service data access

In microservices, data rarely exists in isolation, and services often need to access information owned by others. However, directly sharing databases or using joins across services compromises autonomy and scalability. Instead, specialized strategies like API composition and event-driven replication provide controlled, decoupled ways to handle cross-service data access effectively. The details are as follows:

- **Use API composition**: The calling service orchestrates multiple API calls to gather required data from other services.
  - **Pros**: Flexible, keeps services decoupled
  - **Cons**: Latency and complexity at the client level
- **Use data replication via events**: Use a publish-subscribe pattern to replicate key data across services.

  Example:
  - User Service publishes a `UserUpdated` event
  - Order Service consumes it and updates its local copy

  This enables eventual consistency and decouples systems from synchronous calls.

Choosing between SQL and NoSQL

While the actual database technology choice depends on use case, design should prioritize:

- Clear data boundaries
- Scalability needs
- Transaction requirements
- Schema evolution flexibility

We will cover the specifics in the next section.

Service-specific database design patterns

Different services face different data challenges, and no single schema design fits all scenarios. To address diverse requirements, proven database design patterns have emerged that balance scalability, isolation, and maintainability. This section explores service-specific patterns that help microservices manage their data reliably and efficiently.

Refer to the following table:

Pattern	Use case
Aggregate root tables	When you want to isolate key business entities per domain
Append-only tables	For storing event logs or transaction history
Sharded tables	When scaling horizontally across distributed nodes

Pattern	Use case
Partitioned data	For tenant-based isolation (multi-tenancy)
Soft deletes/Archival	To preserve data without deleting records

***Table 19.2**: Service-specific database design patterns*

Key design considerations

While patterns and principles provide guidance, database design for microservices also demands careful attention to practical concerns. From schema evolution to query flexibility and backup strategies, several critical considerations shape the long-term reliability of the system. This section outlines key factors that architects must weigh during design.

Refer to the following table:

Concern	Recommendation
Schema evolution	Use migrations with version control, avoid breaking changes
Data validation	Enforce at the service/API level, not through constraints
Query flexibility	Use projections or materialized views within a service
Consistency	Prefer eventual consistency and idempotent updates
Backups and recovery	Each service must own its backup and recovery policies

***Table 19.3**: Key design considerations*

Common mistakes to avoid in database design

The following are the most common mistakes to avoid in database design:

Mistake	Why it is problematic
Shared database across services	Creates tight coupling and coordination bottlenecks
Direct SQL joins between services	Breaks service boundaries and leads to cascading failures
Enforcing cross-service referential integrity	Violates autonomy, hard to scale
Ignoring schema versioning	Leads to broken deployments and data corruption

***Table 19.4**: Common pitfalls in database design*

Working with SQL and NoSQL databases

Microservices promote polyglot persistence, the idea that each service can choose the database that best fits its needs. This means some services may use relational databases (SQL) for transactional consistency, while others use NoSQL databases for flexibility, scalability, or speed. Selecting between SQL and NoSQL is not about picking a better technology; it is about choosing the right one for the job based on the service's domain requirements.

This section explores when to use SQL vs. NoSQL in microservices, their respective strengths, and how to manage them effectively in a distributed architecture.

Polyglot persistence

Polyglot persistence refers to the practice of using different types of databases (relational, key-value, document, graph, etc.) across different microservices based on their individual use cases.

Example:

- **Order Service**: Uses PostgreSQL for ACID transactions.
- **Catalog Service**: Uses MongoDB for flexible product attributes.
- **Analytics Service**: Uses ClickHouse or Elasticsearch for fast querying and aggregation.

The following are the challenges in polyglot persistence:

Challenge	Mitigation
Learning curve for multiple DBs	Use internal standards and shared libraries
Operational complexity	Automate deployment and monitoring per DB type
Data duplication across systems	Use event-driven sync and eventual consistency
Backup and disaster recovery	Manage DB-specific backup tools separately
Integration in CI/CD pipelines	Add DB migration and readiness checks in tests

***Table 19.5**: Challenges in polyglot persistence*

Relational databases in microservices

The following are the common SQL databases:

- PostgreSQL
- MySQL
- Microsoft SQL Server
- SQLite (for lightweight, embedded use)

Strengths of SQL:

Feature	Advantage
ACID transactions	Ensures consistency for complex workflows
Joins and relations	Model structured, normalized data easily
Mature tooling	Backups, replication, indexing, and migrations
Schema enforcement	Rigid structure helps enforce data integrity

***Table 19.6**: Strengths of RDBMS*

Ideal use cases:

- Payment processing
- Orders and invoices
- Inventory systems
- Auth services with normalized user or session data

NoSQL databases in microservices

NoSQL databases offer high flexibility, horizontal scalability, and speed. There are several types, as shown here:

Type	Example DBs	Best for
Document store	MongoDB, Couchbase	Semi-structured or dynamic JSON-like data
Key-value store	Redis, Amazon DynamoDB	Caching, session storage, fast lookups
Wide-column store	Cassandra, HBase	Write-heavy, time-series, IoT data
Graph DB	Neo4j, ArangoDB	Relationship-heavy data (social networks)

Table 19.7: NoSQL databases

Strengths of NoSQL:

Feature	Advantage
Schema-less design	Easier to evolve data model without migrations
Horizontal scalability	Designed for distributed systems and sharding
High performance	Optimized for specific access patterns
Better fit for large volumes	Handles big data and real-time analytics well

Table 19.8: Advantages of NoSQL databases

Ideal use cases:

- Product catalogs with flexible attributes
- Real-time analytics dashboards
- Logging and monitoring systems
- Shopping cart and session storage

Comparing SQL and NoSQL

The following is a comparison between SQL and NoSQL in a tabular form:

Criteria	SQL (relational)	NoSQL (non-relational)
Data structure	Structured and normalized	Semi-structured or unstructured
Schema	Strict (must define upfront)	Flexible (schema-less or dynamic)
Consistency model	Strong consistency (ACID)	Eventual consistency (BASE)
Scalability	Vertical (scale-up)	Horizontal (scale-out)
Query language	SQL	Varies (MongoQL, CQL, custom APIs)
Transactions	Strong, multi-row	Varies, often limited or requires workaround
use cases	Financial systems, ERP, CRM	Catalogs, caching, analytics, and personalization

Table 19.9: SQL vs. NoSQL

Using SQL and NoSQL together

In microservices, you can combine both:

- Use PostgreSQL in your User Service for relational user data.
- Use Redis in the Session Service for fast, expiring session storage.
- Use MongoDB in the Product Service for flexible, searchable product descriptions.

Ensure clear boundaries and data ownership across services when using mixed database models.

Following are the design guidelines for SQL/NoSQL in microservices:

- Never share the same database between services.
- Define service boundaries based on domain ownership, not data types.
- Abstract data access through repositories or adapters.
- Prefer asynchronous messaging for data replication between services.
- Use schema migration tools (e.g., Flyway, Liquibase, Goose) for SQL changes.

Access patterns and storage decisions

Match the data model to your access pattern:

Access pattern	Suggested database type
Frequent updates and strict integrity	Relational (PostgreSQL, MySQL)
Read-heavy and flexible schema	Document DB (MongoDB, Couchbase)
High-speed key-value lookup	Redis, DynamoDB
Relationship traversal (e.g., friends)	Graph DB (Neo4j)

***Table 19.10**: Access patterns and storage decisions*

Implementing data migrations and versioning

In a microservices architecture, each service is responsible for its own data schema and evolution. Over time, as business requirements change, so must the database schemas, requiring data migrations. Unlike monolithic systems, microservices make schema evolution more complex because each service must manage migrations independently and without breaking existing contracts.

This section covers how to handle schema changes, apply version control, and execute safe and automated migrations in microservices.

Data migration

Data migration refers to the process of:

- Changing the database schema (e.g., adding/removing columns, altering types).
- Migrating data formats (e.g., transforming legacy fields).
- Moving data between systems or versions.

Importance of schema versioning

As microservices evolve, their data models must also change, but uncontrolled schema changes can break deployments and disrupt services. Schema versioning provides a structured way to manage these changes safely, ensuring backward compatibility and auditability. This section explains why versioning is essential for enabling continuous delivery while minimizing risk.

Refer to the following table:

Purpose	Benefit
Enable continuous delivery	Teams can release without waiting for manual changes
Maintain backward compatibility	Avoid breaking existing consumers

Purpose	Benefit
Ensure repeatable, auditable schema changes	Track who changed what and when
Facilitate rollback if needed	Safer deployments and faster recovery

Table 19.11: Schema versioning

Types of schema changes are as follows:

Change type	Example	Risk
Additive	Adding a new column with default	Low (usually safe)
Subtractive	Dropping a column or constraint	High (can break logic)
Transformational	Changing data type or format	Medium

Table 19.12: Types of schema changes

Always prefer backward-compatible, additive changes when possible.

The following are the common migration strategies:

- **Online migrations**:
  - Run migrations without taking the database offline.
  - Useful for zero-downtime deployments.

  Steps:

  1. Add a new column.
  2. Update the application to use the new column.
  3. Backfill data.
  4. Drop old column (optional, and only after full transition).

- **Versioned migration scripts**:
  - Use numbered or timestamped migration files.
  - Stored in version control.

  Example:

```
001_create_users_table.sql
002_add_email_index.sql
003_rename_column_status_to_state.sql
```

- **Blue-green or shadow deployments**:
  - Run both old and new schema versions temporarily.
  - Gradually shift traffic or sync data between them.
  - Useful for critical migrations with high risk.

  The following are the tools for database migrations:

Tool	Language	Features
Flyway	SQL/Java	Easy-to-use, versioned SQL migrations
Liquibase	XML/YAML/SQL	Supports rollback and diff checking
Goose	Go	Lightweight tool for Go projects

Tool	Language	Features
Atlas	Go	Declarative schema-as-code with migrations
Alembic	Python	Popular for SQLAlchemy users

***Table 19.13**: Tools for database design*

Integrate migration tools with CI/CD for automatic deployment.

- **Automating migrations in microservices**: Startup migrations, run migrations automatically when the service starts.

  Example:

```
if err := goose.Up(db, "./migrations"); err != nil {
    log.Fatalf("Migration failed: %v", err)
}
```

  Best for internal services with minimal risk.

- **CI/CD-driven migrations**: Trigger migrations in your deployment pipeline:
  - Before deploying the new version.
  - As part of a rollback process, if needed.

```
- name: Run Migrations
  run: goose up -dir ./migrations
```

- **Managing versioned schemas**: Each schema change should be:
  - Versioned (e.g., 1.0, 1.1, 2.0).
  - Linked to application code version.
  - Tested in staging environments.

  Maintain a clear mapping between:
  - App version | Schema version | Migration script.

- **Handling data transformations**: Sometimes schema changes require data migration (e.g., split full name into first/last). Best practices include:
  - Write migration scripts as pure SQL or data transformation functions.
  - Backfill data asynchronously for large tables.
  - Log the transformation status.

- **Rollback and recovery**: Plan for rollback by:
  - Keeping backup of DB before migration.
  - Making changes reversible (e.g., rename vs drop).
  - Tagging schema state (e.g., schema_version table).

  Use migration tools that support down scripts or version checkpointing.

Following are the best practices:

Practice	Why it is important
Use version control for migrations	Audit trail and rollback support
Prefer additive changes	Minimize impact on dependent services

Practice	Why it is important
Test migrations in staging	Avoid surprises in production
Automate schema migrations	Reduce human error, speed up deployments
Apply migrations with health checks	Ensure DB is in expected state post-deploy

Table 19.14: Best practices for database design

Event sourcing and CQRS patterns

Traditional systems often rely on CRUD-based models, where operations directly update the current state in a database. However, in distributed microservices, this model can limit scalability, auditability, and resilience. To overcome these challenges, advanced architectural patterns like event sourcing and CQRS are used.

These patterns:

- Decouple writes from reads.
- Maintain a log of all changes instead of just the current state.
- Support replayable, audit-friendly, and scalable systems.

Event sourcing

Event sourcing is a pattern where the state of a system is derived by replaying a sequence of events rather than storing the current state directly. Every change to the state is captured as an immutable event and stored in an event log.

Example: Instead of storing:

```
{
  "order_id": 101,
  "status": "Shipped"
}
```

Store a sequence:

```
1. OrderCreated(order_id=101)
2. OrderConfirmed(order_id=101)
3. OrderShipped(order_id=101)
```

The state is reconstructed by applying all relevant events in order.

The following are the benefits of event sourcing:

Benefit	Description
Full audit trail	Track every change in the system's history
Time-travel and debugging	Recreate any state from the past
Replayability	Rebuild projections or fix bugs by reprocessing events
Event-driven integration	Events can be published to other microservices
High write performance	Appending to a log is faster than full-row updates

Table 19.15: Benefits of event sourcing

The following are the challenges of event sourcing:

Challenge	Mitigation strategy
Complex implementation	Use event sourcing libraries/frameworks
Schema evolution	Version events, add metadata
Event storage size	Periodic snapshotting to optimize reads
Learning curve for teams	Start with one bounded context

***Table 19.16**: Challenges of event sourcing*

Command Query Responsibility Segregation

CQRS stands for Command Query Responsibility Segregation. It separates the read and write responsibilities of a system into two distinct models. Refer to the following table:

Command side	Query side
Handles writes (create/update/delete)	Handles reads (queries)
Uses domain models and validation	Uses denormalized or optimized views
Emits events (optional)	Subscribes to events to build projections

***Table 19.17**: Comparison of command side and query side in CQRS*

The following are the benefits of CQRS:

Benefit	Why it is useful
Separation of concerns	Allows independent evolution of read/write logic
Optimized queries	Query models can be denormalized and fast
Scalable architecture	Read and write workloads can be scaled independently
Easier to secure	You can expose read-only APIs and restrict writes

***Table 19.18**: Benefits of CQRS*

CQRS and event sourcing together

These patterns complement each other:

- Use event sourcing to handle the write model.
- Use CQRS to build read models or projections from events.

Example flow:

1. A user places an order | **`PlaceOrderCommand`**.
2. Order Service stores **`OrderPlaced`** event.
3. Projector consumes **`OrderPlaced`** and updates the read model.
4. User queries order status from the read model (e.g., NoSQL or cache).

Implementing event sourcing in microservices

The following are the key components:

Component	Responsibility
Aggregate root	Validates and emits domain events
Event store	Persists events in order
Projector	Builds read models from events
Snapshot	Stores point-in-time state for performance
Event bus	Distributes events across services

Table 19.19: Key components in event sourcing

The following are the technologies used:

Component	Tech options
Event store	Kafka, EventStoreDB, PostgreSQL, NATS
Projection DB	MongoDB, Elasticsearch, Redis, Cassandra
event bus	Kafka, RabbitMQ, Google Pub/Sub

Table 19.20: Technologies used

Practical example: Order microservice

Command side:

```
type Order struct {
  ID     string
  State string
  Events []OrderEvent
}

func (o *Order) Confirm() {
  o.Events = append(o.Events, OrderConfirmed{OrderID: o.ID})
  o.State = "Confirmed"
}
```

Event store: Store **OrderConfirmed** in an append-only event log.

Query side (Projection): Consume events like **OrderCreated**, **OrderConfirmed**, and update a read model:

```
{
  "order_id": 101,
  "status": "Confirmed"
}
```

When to use event sourcing and CQRS:

Use when	Avoid if
You need a full audit trail	You have simple CRUD requirements
System is highly collaborative or temporal	Data is short-lived or does not need change tracking

Use when	Avoid if
Multiple subsystems consume events	Event modeling is too complex for the use case
You want scalable reads and writes	Simplicity and time-to-market are more critical

***Table 19.21**: Event sourcing and CQRS use cases*

The following are the best practices:

Practice	Why it matters
Keep events immutable	Preserves history integrity
Version your events	Helps evolve schemas safely
Use idempotent event handlers	Prevents duplicate side effects
Store events in append-only logs	Ensures ordering and reliability
Generate read models asynchronously	Decouples writes from read workload

***Table 19.22**: Best practices in CQRS*

Managing distributed transactions

In a monolithic system, transactions are typically handled with ACID guarantees through a single relational database. However, in microservices architectures, where each service owns its own data store, distributed transactions become far more complex.

When a business process spans multiple services and databases, coordinating these operations in a consistent, reliable, and failure-resilient way becomes challenging. This section explores patterns, strategies, and best practices for handling distributed transactions in microservices.

Let us understand what a distributed transaction is.

A distributed transaction is a unit of work that involves multiple services and their databases, which must all either commit or roll back the changes together to ensure data consistency.

Example:

- Order Service places an order.
- Payment Service processes the payment.
- Inventory Service reserves stock.

If any one of these operations fails, the entire transaction must be considered unsuccessful.

Let us discuss why distributed transactions are hard in microservices:

Challenge	Description
No global ACID support	Databases are isolated across services
Network unreliability	One service might be unavailable during a transaction
Partial failure scenarios	Some services may succeed while others fail
Long-running processes	Cannot hold database locks indefinitely
Data consistency vs availability	Trade-offs emerge (as per CAP theorem)

***Table 19.23**: Challenges in distributed transactions*

The following are the common patterns to manage distributed transactions:

- **Two-phase commit (2PC)**: A traditional distributed transaction protocol involving:
  - o **Prepare phase**: All participants promise to commit.
  - o **Commit phase**: If all succeed, the coordinator issues a global commit. Refer to the following table:

Pros	Cons
Strong consistency	Blocking, complex, reduces availability
Atomic commits	Does not scale well for modern microservices

***Table 19.24**: Pros and cons of two-phase commit*

It is rarely used in cloud-native microservices due to tight coupling and performance cost.

- **Saga pattern**: The saga pattern is the most widely used approach in microservices. It breaks a transaction into a sequence of local transactions, coordinated via events or commands.

Two types of sagas are as follows:

Type	Mechanism	Failure handling
Choreography	Services listen to events and act	Compensating actions via events
Orchestration	Central coordinator invokes each step	Error handling via orchestration logic

***Table 19.25**: Two types of sagas*

Example: Order processing saga

Flow:

1. Order Service creates order | emits OrderCreated.
2. Payment Service listens | processes payment | emits PaymentSuccessful.
3. Inventory Service listens | reserves items | emits InventoryReserved.

If payment fails:

- o Emit PaymentFailed.
- o Order Service listens and marks the order as cancelled.

- **Compensating transactions**: When a service cannot rollback natively (like in 2PC), we use compensating actions to undo changes made by previous steps.

Example:

- o **Step 1**: Deduct money from wallet.
- o **Step 2**: Reserve inventory.
- o **Compensation**: Refund wallet if inventory reservation fails.

Must design every forward action with a corresponding undo operation.

Implementing the saga pattern:

Component	Responsibility
Saga coordinator	Maintains the workflow (in orchestration pattern)
Local services	Perform actions and optionally emit events
Event bus	Publishes domain events (Kafka, NATS, RabbitMQ)
Compensation logic	Performs rollback in case of failure

***Table 19.26**: Saga implementation*

- **Saga choreography (event-driven)**: Each service listens to events and performs its local transaction autonomously.

  ```
  [Order Service] = emits OrderCreated
  [Payment Service] = emits PaymentSuccessful
  [Inventory Service] = emits InventoryReserved
  ```

  No central controller and services are loosely coupled.

- **Saga orchestration (Command-driven)**: A central orchestrator that tells each service what to do next.

  SagaCoordinator:

  ```
  send =  PaymentService: Deduct()
  on success = InventoryService: Reserve()
  ```

  Better for complex workflows, but introduces coupling to the orchestrator.

Technologies supporting saga and distributed transactions are as follows:

Tool	Description
Axon framework	Saga orchestration in Java + CQRS support
Temporal.io	Durable, fault-tolerant workflows with retry logic
Camunda	Workflow engine supporting BPMN and saga pattern
Kafka/NATS	Event backbones for saga choreography
Dapr	Sidecar-based runtime that supports state, pub/sub, workflows

***Table 19.27**: Technologies supporting saga and distributed transactions*

The best practices for distributed transactions are as follows:

Practice	Why it matters
Prefer eventual consistency	Enables high availability and resilience
Design idempotent and retry-safe services	Prevents unintended side effects on retries
Implement robust compensation logic	Avoids data inconsistency after failures
Use correlation IDs for traceability	Helps track transactions across services
Validate partial failure scenarios	Test how the system behaves under real-world errors

***Table 19.28**: Best practices of distributed transactions*

The following are the trade-offs to consider:

Consistency model	Impact
Strong consistency	Simplifies logic but reduces scalability and availability
Eventual consistency	Improves scalability, but adds complexity to the business logic
CAP theorem	Must choose a trade-off between consistency, availability, and partition tolerance

***Table 19.29**: Trade-offs to consider*

Best practices for data management in microservices

In microservices, data is decentralized, with each service owning its own database and maintaining control over how data is accessed and changed. This independence enhances scalability and agility but introduces challenges in consistency, duplication, migrations, and integrations. Adopting proven best practices ensures microservices remain reliable, maintainable, and efficient as they evolve independently.

This section summarizes the essential guidelines for managing data effectively in a microservices architecture, as follows:

- **Follow the database per service principle**:
  - Each microservice must own its data and must not share a database with others.
  - This ensures loose coupling and independent scalability.
  - Services should never access another service's database directly.
  - Services communicate through APIs or events, not database queries.
- **Embrace polyglot persistence**:
  - Choose the best-fit database (SQL, NoSQL, key-value, document, time-series) per service.
  - Do not enforce a one-size-fits-all database across all services.
  - Base selection on data model, scalability, and access patterns.
  - Use PostgreSQL for transactional data, MongoDB for flexible documents, Redis for caching, etc.
- **Manage schema evolution with versioned migrations**:
  - Track schema changes using tools like Flyway, Liquibase, or Goose.
  - Use incremental, reversible migrations and align them with application releases.
  - Automate migrations as part of your CI/CD pipeline.
  - Prefer additive and backward-compatible schema changes.
- **Apply event-driven communication for cross-service data sync**:
  - Use events (e.g., UserUpdated, OrderCreated) to share data between services.
  - Avoid synchronous API calls for non-critical data syncing.
  - Keep replicated data eventually consistent using message queues like Kafka or RabbitMQ.
  - This pattern supports loose coupling and improves resilience.
- **Use CQRS and projections for scalable reads**:
  - Separate write and read concerns using CQRS.
  - Maintain denormalized read models tailored to specific queries.
  - Build projections asynchronously from event streams.
  - This optimizes read performance and reduces query complexity.
- **Design for eventual consistency**:
  - Accept that in distributed systems, immediate consistency is hard to achieve.
  - Use compensating transactions and retry logic to handle failures.
  - Expose transaction status endpoints (e.g., /order-status) to reflect real-time status.
  - Favor user experience and availability over strict synchrony.
- **Implement data validation at the service boundary**:
  - Validate data on the API level, not just in the database schema.
  - Use strong domain models, input validation, and JSON schema enforcement.

- Prevent bad data from entering the system in the first place.
- Guardrails should exist at every boundary, not just at the DB.

- **Secure data at rest and in transit**:
  - Use TLS for inter-service communication and database connections.
  - Encrypt sensitive data at rest using database-native features or external key managers.
  - Apply row-level security and auditing where necessary.
  - Always comply with relevant data protection regulations (e.g., GDPR, HIPAA).
- **Monitor and audit data access**:
  - Track all reads and writes, especially to sensitive data.
  - Use audit logs and structured logging for observability.
  - Monitor for anomalies, slow queries, and schema drift.
  - Use tools like Prometheus, OpenTelemetry, and DataDog for metrics and alerts.
- **Handle data duplication and reconciliation**:
  - Expect data duplication across services as a trade-off for autonomy.
  - Use unique identifiers, timestamps, and reconciliation jobs to ensure correctness.
  - Ensure idempotency in write operations.
  - It is better to have consistent, duplicated data than brittle, tightly coupled services.
- **Plan for backup and disaster recovery**:
  - Each service should have an independent backup strategy.
  - Use automated backups, versioned snapshots, and disaster recovery plans.
  - Test backup restoration processes regularly.
  - Data ownership also means owning its safety and recoverability.

Let us look at the best practices recap table:

Practice	Why it matters
One database per service	Promotes autonomy and loose coupling
Use appropriate DB technologies	Improves performance and maintainability
Automate schema migrations	Avoid manual errors and ensure traceability
Rely on eventual consistency via events	Enables scalability and fault tolerance
Secure data with TLS, encryption, and policies	Protects sensitive and regulated information
Apply CQRS where needed	Separates reads from writes for better performance
Test data management in CI environments	Prevents drift between environments

***Table 19.30**: Best practices in data management for microservices*

Conclusion

In this chapter, we explored how data management in microservices requires a shift from monolithic thinking to decentralized, domain-driven design. We began with the principle of database per service, highlighting how autonomy and polyglot persistence empower teams to choose the right database for their specific use cases. We learned schema design strategies such as aligning with bounded contexts, using identifiers instead of foreign keys, and applying denormalization where appropriate. Approaches like API composition and event-driven replication were introduced to handle cross-service data access while maintaining decoupling. We also examined design patterns, migration strategies, and the role of schema versioning in ensuring safe evolution. Finally, we emphasized best practices such as embracing eventual consistency, securing data, and planning for recovery. Altogether, the chapter underscored that successful database design in microservices balances autonomy with consistency, scalability with maintainability, and flexibility with long-term reliability.

Questions

1. Why is the principle of database per service critical in microservices, and how does it support autonomy and scalability?
2. What problems arise when services share a common database in a microservices architecture?
3. Explain why foreign keys should be avoided across service boundaries and what alternative approach is recommended.
4. What is polyglot persistence, and why is it particularly suitable for microservices architectures?
5. Compare SQL and NoSQL databases in terms of schema flexibility, scalability, and consistency. Provide typical use cases for each.
6. How do API composition and event-driven replication differ as strategies for cross-service data access?
7. What are the benefits of event sourcing, and how does it differ from traditional CRUD-based data models?
8. Explain the saga pattern in distributed transactions. How does it differ between choreography and orchestration?
9. Why is schema versioning important in microservices, and what best practices should teams follow when evolving schemas?
10. What are the key best practices for ensuring secure, consistent, and reliable data management in microservices?

APPENDIX A
Go Tools and Resources

Introduction

In modern software development, dependency management is critical. For a long time, Go's approach to managing external packages evolved from GOPATH and manual vendoring to the more robust, reliable, and officially supported Go modules system. Today, Go modules are the default for dependency management, making it easier to handle versions, ensure reproducible builds, and support multi-version workspaces.

This appendix will explore how Go modules work, their key commands, and additional tools that complement module-based workflows.

Structure

This chapter covers the following topics:

- Go modules
- Profiling and performance tools
- Debugging tools for Go applications
- Continuous integration and deployment pipelines
- Popular Go libraries and frameworks

Go modules

Go modules is Go's built-in system for managing project dependencies and versions. Introduced officially in Go 1.11 and becoming the default in Go 1.16+, modules replaced the older GOPATH-based dependency management.

Go modules provide a structured and reliable approach to dependency management. They enable the following:

- **Versioning**: Explicit versions of dependencies, ensuring consistent builds.
- **Isolation**: Each project manages its own dependencies, independent of GOPATH.
- **Proxy support**: Faster, secure module fetching through proxy servers.
- **Reproducibility**: Builds always use the same versions defined in go.mod.

Key Go modules files

Go modules rely on two primary files viz, `go.mod` and `go.sum`, that together define, track, and verify all dependencies within a project. These files ensure that your application remains consistent across environments, reproducible during builds, and secure against dependency tampering. They act as the foundation of Go's dependency management system, promoting transparency and stability. Understanding these files is essential for effective project version control and long-term maintainability.

go.mod

The manifest file declares:

- The module's name.
- Required dependencies and their versions.
- Go language version.

Example:

```
module github.com/yourusername/myapp

go 1.20

require (
    github.com/gin-gonic/gin v1.9.0
    github.com/go-redis/redis/v8 v8.11.5
)
```

go.sum

Stores cryptographic hashes of the exact module content used. It helps ensure the integrity and tamper-proofing of dependencies:

```
github.com/gin-gonic/gin v1.9.0 h1:N4h...
github.com/gin-gonic/gin v1.9.0/go.mod h1:Lt...
```

Core Go commands for modules

The Go commands for modules are shown in the following table:

Command	What it does
`go mod init`	Initializes a new module in the current directory.
`go get example.com/pkg`	Adds/updates a dependency to your module.
`go mod tidy`	Adds missing and removes unused modules.
`go list -m all`	Lists all modules needed for building.
`go mod vendor`	Copies dependencies to a vendor/ directory.
`go mod verify`	Checks that dependencies match expected checksums.

***Table Appendix A.1**: Go commands for modules*

Typical workflow example

```
go mod init github.com/yourusername/myapp
go get github.com/gin-gonic/gin@v1.9.0
go mod tidy
```

Dependency proxy and security

Go ensures a secure and reliable dependency management system through its built-in proxy and checksum verification features. These mechanisms help developers fetch modules faster, verify their authenticity, and maintain consistent builds across environments. By using trusted proxies and checksum validation, Go prevents tampered or malicious dependencies from entering your project. Together, these features form the foundation of Go's commitment to integrity, speed, and reproducibility in dependency handling, as follows:

- **Go Proxy**: The Go Proxy acts as an intermediary that caches and serves Go modules, reducing the need to fetch them directly from source repositories. It improves reliability and performance by storing verified copies of modules and ensuring they remain available even if the original source is removed.

By default, go uses **https://proxy.golang.org**, which:

- Speeds up downloads.
- Improves availability.
- Keeps immutable copies for reproducibility.

To see or change proxies, use:

```
go env GOPROXY
# Change to a private mirror or multiple proxies
go env -w GOPROXY=https://proxy.golang.org,direct
```

- **Dependency integrity**: `go.sum` verifies downloaded modules match their expected cryptographic hashes, preventing tampering.
- **Vendoring dependencies**: For strict environments or air-gapped deployments, you can vendor all your dependencies.

  ```
  go mod vendor
  ```

  This copies all external packages into a local vendor/ folder. Add `-mod=vendor` during builds to force usage:

  ```
  go build -mod=vendor
  ```

- **Tools for managing modules**: While `go mod` covers most needs, advanced tools can enhance workflows.

  Refer to the following table:

Tool	Description
`golangci-lint`	Ensures your module adheres to style & correctness.
`go-licenses`	Audit the licenses of your dependencies.
`gopkgs`	Quickly lists available packages.
`gomodifytags`	Modifies struct tags across your module.
`go mod graph`	Visualizes dependency graphs.
`vgo`	Historical, early experiment that led to modules.

Table Appendix A.2: Common Go modules, tools, and utilities

- **Managing versions**: Use go get to update dependencies:

  ```
  go get github.com/gin-gonic/gin@v1.9.0
  ```

  - Or upgrade all minor/patch versions:

    ```
    go get -u ./...
    ```

  - Use replace directives in `go.mod` to test local modules:

    ```
    replace github.com/other/service => ../local/service
    ```

- **Multi-module repositories**: For larger projects, each module can have its own `go.mod`. This is common in monorepos.

  ```
  /project
    --/service1/go.mod
   -- /service2/go.mod
  ```

  - Use `go work` (introduced in Go 1.18) to manage multi-module builds:

    ```
    go work init ./service1 ./service2
    ```

  - This creates a `go.work` file to coordinate multiple modules together.

Best practices for using Go modules are as follows:

Best practices for using Go modules	Its importance
Keep modules small and domain-focused	Easier to test, maintain, and version.
Commit **go.mod** and **go.sum**	Ensures reproducibility for the team and CI/CD.
Run **go mod tidy** frequently	Keeps module definitions clean and minimal.
Pin to specific versions	Avoids surprises from upstream breaking changes.
Review **go.sum** diffs in PRs	Prevents malicious dependency injection.
Use replace only for local/testing	Do not ship production code with replace.

Table Appendix A.3: *Best practices for using Go modules*

Profiling and performance tools

Writing correct programs is just the first step; ensuring they run efficiently under production load is equally critical. Go provides powerful profiling and performance analysis tools out of the box, along with a vibrant ecosystem of third-party tools. These tools help you identify CPU bottlenecks, memory leaks, excessive goroutines, blocking I/O, and more.

This section introduces the most important profiling and performance tools that will help you build high-performance Go applications.

Built-in profiling with pprof of GO

pprof is Go's built-in tool for capturing and analyzing runtime profiles, as shown in the following table:

Profile type	Use case
CPU profile	Find CPU-intensive functions.
Heap profile	Detect memory usage and leaks.
Goroutine profile	See all active goroutines and stacks.
Block profile	Identify blocking on the mutex or I/O.

Table Appendix A.4: *Built-in profiling in Go*

Let us look at the details:

- **Enabling pprof in your code**: Go's **pprof** package helps developers profile their applications to identify performance bottlenecks such as CPU, memory, and goroutine usage. Before you can collect profiling data, you must enable **pprof** within your Go application to expose runtime metrics through an HTTP endpoint.
- **Add this import to automatically expose debugging endpoints**: Importing the **net/http/pprof** package registers several useful debugging routes (like **/debug/pprof/**) in your application. These endpoints can then be accessed via a web browser or command-line tools to view or download profiling data.

```
import _ "net/http/pprof"
```

  - Start an HTTP server (often on a separate port):

```
go func() {
    log.Println(http.ListenAndServe("localhost:6060", nil))
}()
```

- **Then visit**:
  - **http://localhost:6060/debug/pprof/**
  - Download profiles or use live views.

- **Using the pprof CLI tool**: To analyze a CPU profile:

```
go test -bench=. -cpuprofile=cpu.prof
go tool pprof cpu.prof
```

  - Run interactive commands like **top**, **list**, **web**, **callgrind**.

Visualizing profiles

Profiling data becomes most insightful when visualized, allowing developers to intuitively understand performance hotspots and call relationships. Go provides multiple tools to transform raw profile data into visual formats such as flamegraphs and call graphs for deeper analysis. These visualizations make it easier to identify inefficient code paths, memory leaks, or functions that consume excessive CPU or memory resources, as follows:

- **Graphviz**: Graphviz helps visualize program execution by rendering function call relationships as detailed graphs. It provides a clear picture of which functions dominate CPU or memory usage, aiding developers in performance tuning.
  - Use the Go tool **pprof** to generate call graphs:

    ```
    go tool pprof -http=":8081" cpu.prof
    ```

    Or output a PNG:

    ```
    go tool pprof -png ./myapp cpu.prof > cpu.png
    ```

- **Speedscope**: Speedscope offers an interactive and browser-based visualization of profiling data through flamegraphs. It makes performance analysis intuitive by displaying how much time functions spend executing and how they call each other.
  - Convert profiles to JSON for interactive flamegraphs:

    ```
    go tool pprof -json cpu.prof > cpu.json
    ```

    When uploading to **https://www.speedscope.app**.

- **Memory leak and allocation analysis**: Use heap profiles to find memory-heavy objects:

```
go test -bench=. -memprofile=mem.prof
go tool pprof mem.prof
```

Look for functions allocating large amounts of memory.

- **Goroutine profiling**: Diagnose leaks or excessive concurrency:

```
curl http://localhost:6060/debug/pprof/goroutine?debug=2
```

Or run from CLI:

```
go tool pprof http://localhost:6060/debug/pprof/goroutine
```

- **Benchmarking with testing**: Go's testing package has built-in micro-benchmarks:

```
func BenchmarkAdd(b *testing.B) {
    for i := 0; i < b.N; i++ {
        Add(1, 2)
    }
}
```

Run with:

```
go test -bench=.
```

- **Third-party profiling**: Third-party profiling and performance tools are shown in the following table:

Third-party tool	Use case
go-torch	Generates flame graphs from pprof.
pprof-plus	Advanced profiles with more diffing tools.
go-tracer	Distributed tracing for microservices.
Parca	Continuous profiling for cloud workloads.
Jaeger/Tempo	For tracing across services (OpenTelemetry).

Table Appendix A.5*: Third-party profiling and performance tools*

- **Continuous profiling**: Use continuous profilers to capture data over long periods in production:

Tool	Description
Parca	Open source always-on Go profiler.
Pyroscope	Pulls `pprof` data for live flamegraphs.
Google Cloud Profiler	Production profiler for GCP workloads.

Table Appendix A.6*: Continuous profilers*

- **Best practices**: The best practices for profiling are given in the following table:

Practice	Its importance
Profile with realistic workloads	Avoid misleading optimizations.
Combine CPU, heap, and goroutines	Get a full picture of performance.
Run multiple short profiles	Helps find transient spikes.
Look for long-tail issues (p95, p99)	Not just average performance.
Keep profiling lightweight in prod	Use sampling, avoid constant high overhead.

Table Appendix A.7*: Best practices for profiling*

Debugging tools for Go applications

Debugging is an essential part of any development workflow. While Go is famous for its simplicity and strong compile-time checks, bugs, logic errors, concurrency issues, or misconfigurations are inevitable. Fortunately, Go offers a range of powerful debugging tools, both built-in and external, that make finding and fixing these issues much more effective. This section explores popular tools and techniques to debug Go applications, covering interactive debuggers, advanced logging, and tracing tools.

Print debugging and structured logs

Let us look at the details:

- **Simple print debugging**: The simplest way to debug in Go is still by printing values:

```
fmt.Println("Value of x:", x)
```

Use **`fmt.Printf`** for formatted output and type visibility:

```
fmt.Printf("Processing item: %+v\n", item)
```

- Structured logging uses libraries like:

Library name	Features supported
`logrus`	JSON logs, fields, hooks
`zap`	Extremely fast, structured logging
`zerolog`	Zero-allocation JSON logging

Table Appendix A.8: Logging libraries

Structured logs help when debugging distributed systems or when logs are aggregated in tools like ELK or Grafana Loki.

- Interactive debugging with Delve:
  - **Delve explanation**: Delve is the standard debugger for Go, offering breakpoints, step-through, and variable inspection.
  - **Installing delve**:

```
go install github.com/go-delve/delve/cmd/dlv@latest
```

  - Running a program under delve:

```
dlv debug
```

- This compiles and runs the program in debug mode. Use commands like:
  - `break main.main` to set a breakpoint
  - `continue` to run to the next breakpoint
  - `next` to step over
  - `step` to step into functions
  - `print x` to inspect variable x
- **Remote debugging**: Delve supports debugging inside containers or on remote servers:

```
dlv debug --headless --listen=:2345 --api-version=2
```

- **IDE integration**: Modern IDEs integrate Delve under the hood.

IDE	Features supported
GoLand (JetBrains)	Advanced breakpoints, goroutine dumps, and memory view
VS Code (Go plugin)	Debug panels, inline variables, and breakpoints
LiteIDE	Native Go support with a simple debugger

Table Appendix A.9: IDE integration

Set breakpoints by clicking in the gutter, inspect variables inline, and use watch expressions:

- **Tracing and live analysis**: Go's execution tracer

  Run:

```
go test -trace=trace.out
go tool trace trace.out
```

  - Open the web interface to analyze:
    - Goroutine scheduling
    - Network latency

- Syscall blocking
- Goroutine Dumps

You can capture a live snapshot of all currently running goroutines to inspect their state and detect deadlocks or performance bottlenecks. Run the following command in your terminal:

```
curl http://localhost:6060/debug/pprof/goroutine?debug=2
```

This command fetches detailed information about each goroutine, including stack traces, function calls, and waiting states that are similar to what you would see in panic stack traces, but available on demand.

- **Concurrency debugging**: Go's concurrency can create subtle bugs like race conditions. **Use**:
  - The race detector
  - Compile with `-race` to catch data races:

```
go run -race main.go
go test -race ./...
```

- **Profiling for debugging**: Sometimes performance profiling is part of debugging.

  Use:

```
go tool pprof http://localhost:6060/debug/pprof/profile?seconds=10
```

  Then run `list` or `top` to see slow functions that may be blocking or misbehaving.

- **Logging state for reproducibility**:
  - Dump structured logs with timestamps and request IDs.
  - Save request/response payloads to files for replay during debugging.

  Helps reproduce production issues locally.

- Popular third-party debugging tools are given in the following table:

Tool	Use case
sentry-go	Captures panics and reports stack traces.
Jaeger/OpenTelemetry	Traces requests across services.
mockery	Generates mocks for easier test debugging.
errcheck	Ensures you handle errors everywhere.

***Table Appendix A.10**: Third party debugging tools*

- **Best practices for debugging Go**:

Tip	Effectiveness reason
Use `-race` early and often	Catch data races before they hit prod.
Prefer `zap` or `logrus` for logs	Easier to filter structured output.
Write minimal reproducible examples	Isolate bugs faster.
Combine logging with tracing	See both system-wide and local context.
Always handle errors	Unchecked errors are a major bug source.

***Table Appendix A.11**: Best practices for debugging in Go*

Continuous integration and deployment pipelines

Modern Go applications, especially microservices, must be delivered quickly, safely, and consistently. This is achieved through robust **continuous integration** (**CI**) and **continuous deployment** (**CD**) pipelines. The features are as follows:

- CI ensures that code is automatically built, tested, and validated on every commit.
- CD automates the deployment of these tested builds into environments like staging or production.

This section explores best practices, popular CI/CD tools, and examples tailored for Go projects.

Importance of CI/CD for critical Go projects

Refer to the following table:

Reason	Benefit
Catch bugs early	Automated builds and tests on every pull request.
Consistent builds	Ensures binaries are built the same way every time.
Fast feedback loops	Developers see failures in minutes, not days.
Safe, automated releases	Reduces human error and manual deployment mistakes.

***Table Appendix A.12**: Reasons to use CI/CD*

Common CI/CD workflow for Go projects

Typical pipeline steps:

1. **Checkout code**: Clone the repository.
2. **Run unit tests**: Validate logic correctness.
3. **Run linters**: Check code style and potential bugs.
4. **Build binary**: Compile the Go application.
5. Run race detector/tests with `-race`, catch concurrency bugs.
6. Run integration/API tests.
7. Build Docker image (if applicable).
8. Push to registry (Docker Hub, ECR, GCR).
9. Deploy to Kubernetes/VM.
10. Run smoke tests on the deployed service.

Popular CI/CD tools for Go are given in the following table:

Tool	Use cases
GitHub Actions	Native CI/CD for GitHub with easy YAML workflows.
GitLab CI	Powerful integrated pipelines in GitLab.
Jenkins	Flexible, extensive plugin ecosystem.
CircleCI	Quick setup, Docker-first, great caching.
Drone CI	Go-native, YAML, container-based pipelines.
ArgoCD	Kubernetes-native GitOps deployment (CD focus).

***Table Appendix A.13**:Popular CI/CD tools*

Example: Go CI with GitHub actions:

Following is the YAML file that defines a GitHub Actions workflow for automating **continuous integration** (**CI**) in a Go project. It ensures that every time code is pushed or a pull request is created, GitHub automatically builds, tests, and validates the Go application. This setup helps maintain code quality, catch issues early, and ensure consistent builds across environments.

github/workflows/ci.yml

```
name: Go CI

on:
  push:
    branches: [main]
  pull_request:

jobs:
  build:
    runs-on: ubuntu-latest

    steps:
    - uses: actions/checkout@v3
    - name: Set up Go
      uses: actions/setup-go@v4
      with:
        go-version: 1.21
    - name: Run Linter
      run: go vet ./...
    - name: Run Tests
      run: go test -race ./...
    - name: Build
      run: go build -o app
```

- **Adding Docker builds and push:**

  ```
  - name: Build Docker image
    run: docker build -t myrepo/myapp:${{ github.sha }} .

  - name: Push to Docker Hub
    run: docker push myrepo/myapp:${{ github.sha }}
  ```

  Tagging with the commit **Secure Hash algorithm** (**SHA**) ensures you can trace exactly what code went to prod.

- **CD**: Kubernetes deployment example: Integrate with tools like kubectl, Helm, or ArgoCD:

  ```
  - name: Deploy to Kubernetes
    run: |
      kubectl set image deployment/myapp myapp=myrepo/myapp:${{ github.sha }}
      kubectl rollout status deployment/myapp
  ```

- Running Go tools in pipelines is shown in the following table:

Tool used	Purpose in CI/CD
`golangci-lint`	Run comprehensive linters.
`go test -race`	Detect concurrency issues.
`go test -coverprofile`	Ensure code coverage thresholds are met.
`go mod tidy` + `go mod verify`	Maintain clean, secure deps.

***Table Appendix A.14**: Go tools used in CI/CD*

- **Deploying artifacts and caching**: Cache Go module downloads for faster pipelines:

```
- uses: actions/cache@v3
  with:
    path: ~/go/pkg/mod
    key: ${{ runner.os }}-go-${{ hashFiles('**/go.sum') }}
```

- **Store binaries or test reports**:

```
- name: Upload build artifacts
  uses: actions/upload-artifact@v3
  with:
    name: myapp
    path: ./app
```

- **Best practices for Go CI/CD**:

Practice	Its importance
Fail fast	Place lint and test early in the pipeline.
Run tests with `-race` and `-cover`	Ensure concurrency safety and quality.
Automate schema migrations in the pipeline	Keeps DB and app in sync.
Tag builds with version or commit hash	Guarantees traceability.
Separate the deploy pipeline from CI builds	Avoid accidental production pushes.
Use staged environments (dev | staging | prod)	Safer progressive rollout.

***Table Appendix A.15**: Best practices in CI/CD for Go*

Popular Go libraries and frameworks

One of the reasons Go has become such a dominant language for modern backend and cloud-native systems is its rich ecosystem of mature libraries and frameworks. Whether you are building REST APIs, microservices, CLI tools, or working on data processing pipelines, Go has high-performance, production-grade libraries that save time and help enforce best practices.

This section highlights widely used Go libraries and frameworks, categorized by typical use cases.

Web frameworks

The web frameworks are as follows:

- **Gin**:
  - We use Gin because it is extremely fast HTTP router with a martini-like API, perfect for REST APIs.

- **The features of Gin are as follows**: Middleware support, JSON validation, grouping routes, and recovery from panics.

```
r := gin.Default()
r.GET("/ping", func(c *gin.Context) {
    c.JSON(200, gin.H{"message": "pong"})
})
r.Run()
```

- **Echo**:
  - Focuses on high performance with extensive middleware support.
  - Has built-in HTTP/2, WebSocket, and template rendering.
- **Fiber**:
  - Inspired by Express.js, designed for minimal overhead.
  - Use cases like Lightning-fast JSON APIs, microservices, etc., can be solved.
- **RPC and gRPC**:
  - **gRPC-Go**:
    - Efficient binary protocol built on HTTP/2. Great for inter-service communication.
  - **go-micro**:
    - Has a microservice toolkit that includes service discovery, load balancing, pub/sub.
- **Database libraries**:
  - **GORM**: The most popular ORM for Go. Handles CRUD, migrations, transactions:

```
db.Create(&User{Name: "Alice"})
```

Note: Always watch performance; sometimes plain database/sql + sqlx is faster.

  - **Sqlx**:
    - Extensions to database/sql that simplify working with structs and queries.
  - **go-pg**:
    - Rich PostgreSQL client with ORM features.
- **MongoDB (official driver)**:

```
go.mongodb.org/mongo-driver/mongo
```

- **Caching and messaging**:
  - **Redis:**
    - Use **github.com/go-redis/redis/v8**
    - Supports clusters, pub/sub, and Lua scripting.
  - **Kafka:**
    - Use **github.com/segmentio/kafka-go** for a native Go client.
    - Great for building event-driven microservices.
- **Testing and assertions**:
  - **Testify**:

        - Simplifies writing assertions (`assert.Equal`, `require.NoError`).
        - Has a powerful mocking library.
    - **Ginkgo + Gomega**:
        - BDD-style test framework with expressive matchers.
    - **GoMock**:
        - Generates mocks from interfaces. Used heavily in unit testing.
- **Logging and observability**:
    - **Zap**:
        - Extremely fast structured JSON logger.
        - Ideal for production.
    - **Zerolog**:
        - Zero-allocation JSON logger, even faster for high-volume logging.
- **OpenTelemetry**:
    - Unified standard for traces, metrics, logs.
- **Configuration and validation**:
    - **Viper:**
        - Reads from JSON, YAML, ENV, and flags.
        - Great for twelve-factor microservices.
    - **go-playground/validator:**
        - Popular package for struct field validation:

```
validate := validator.New()
err := validate.Struct(User{Name: "", Email: "invalid"})
```

- **CLI applications**:
    - **Cobra**:
        - Used by Kubernetes and Docker CLIs.
        - Automatically generates help and completion scripts.
    - **urfave/cli**:
        - Minimal, expressive CLI building.
- **Security**:
    - **JWT**:
        - **github.com/golang-jwt/jwt/v5** is widely used for token-based auth.
    - **Bcrypt**:
        - **golang.org/x/crypto/bcrypt** for hashing passwords securely.
- **Miscellaneous utilities**:

Library used	Purpose
`github.com/google/uuid`	UUID generation.
`github.com/mitchellh/mapstructure`	Decode maps to structs.
`golang.org/x/sync/errgroup`	Manage goroutines + error handling.

***Table Appendix A.16**: Miscellaneous utilities*

Join our Discord space

Join our Discord workspace for latest updates, offers, tech happenings around the world, new releases, and sessions with the authors:

https://discord.bpbonline.com

Appendix B
Glossary

- **Application programming interface (API)**: A collection of functions, types, and rules that allow software components to interact. In Go, APIs are exposed through packages, interfaces, or REST/gRPC services.
- **API gateway**: A centralized entry point that routes client requests to services. Also handles authentication, rate limiting, and logging.
- **Append function**: A built in function to add elements to slices. It grows the slice if required and returns the updated slice.
- **Array**: A fixed size collection of elements of the same type. The length of an array is part of its type and cannot change.
- **Benchmark**: Tests that measure performance using the testing package. Run with `go test -bench`.
- **Blocking**: Occurs when a goroutine waits for a channel or resource. Channels block when full (send) or empty (receive).
- **Buffered channel**: A channel with a predefined capacity. It allows sending without an immediate receiver until full.
- **Cap (Capacity)**: The maximum size of a slice before it reallocates. Returned using the built in `cap()` function.
- **Channel**: A typed conduit for communication between goroutines. Send and receive operations on channels synchronize concurrent code.
- **Close channel**: A built in function `close(ch)` closes a channel. Sends after closing cause a panic.
- **Compiler**: A tool that converts Go source code into executable machine code. Go includes an official compiler as part of its toolchain.
- **Concurrency**: Executing multiple tasks that overlap in time. Go's concurrency model is based on goroutines and channels.
- **Constants**: Declared with `const`, these are immutable values. They are evaluated at compile time and remain fixed.
- **Context**: Carries cancellation signals, deadlines, and metadata. Essential for cooperative goroutine cancellation.
- **CQRS**: Separates read and write models in microservices. Improves scalability and clarity.
- **Deadlock**: A state where goroutines are stuck waiting on each other. Deadlocks often occur when channels are misused.
- **Deadlock detection**: Identifying and preventing circular waiting between goroutines. Tools and careful channel design help avoid deadlocks.
- **Defer**: Schedules a function to run after the current function finishes. Often used for resource cleanup, like closing files.
- **Dependency management**: The process of managing external libraries for your project. In Go, this is achieved with modules.

- **Dereferencing**: Accessing the value stored at the memory address of a pointer. Performed with the `*` operator.
- **Embedding**: The practice of including one struct type inside another. This allows promoting fields and methods to the embedding struct.
- **Empty interface (interface{})**: An interface type that has no methods. It can hold values of any type.
- **Error**: The built-in type for representing runtime problems. Errors are returned as values rather than thrown as exceptions.
- **Event sourcing**: Stores all changes as a series of immutable events. Allows replaying events to rebuild state.
- **Exported identifier**: Names that start with a capital letter and are accessible from other packages. For example, `fmt.Println` is exported from the `fmt` package.
- **Function**: A block of reusable code declared using the `func` keyword. Functions can return multiple values.
- **Go toolchain**: The suite of tools like compiler, linker, `go` command, profiler, and `gofmt`. It is used for building, testing, formatting, and profiling Go applications.
- **Goroutine**: A lightweight, independently scheduled function. Created using the `go` keyword.
- **Google Remote Procedure Calls (gRPC)**: A high performance communication protocol over HTTP/2. Generates Go code from `.proto` files.
- **Handler**: A function that responds to an HTTP request. Implements the `http.Handler` interface.
- **Heap**: A memory region used for dynamic allocation. Go's garbage collector manages objects stored on the heap.
- **HTTP package**: Standard library package `net/http` for building servers and clients. Provides utilities for routing, requests, and responses.
- **Idempotent**: An operation that can be applied multiple times safely. Common in distributed systems for reliability.
- **Immutable**: A value that cannot be modified after it is created. Constants in Go are immutable by definition.
- **Implicit implementation**: A type satisfies an interface if it implements all required methods. This happens automatically, without explicit declarations.
- **Import path**: The path you use to import packages, like `fmt` or `math/rand`. It can be standard library paths, local, or remote repositories.
- **Interface**: A type that defines a set of method signatures. Any type implementing those methods implicitly satisfies the interface.
- **JSON**: A lightweight data exchange format. Handled using the encoding/json package.
- **JSON Web Token (JWT)**: A compact token used for securely transmitting information. Often used for authentication.
- **Keywords**: Reserved words like `func`, `for`, `if`, `struct` that have special meaning. They cannot be used as variable or function names.
- **Map**: A built in associative data type storing key value pairs. Maps are reference types and grow dynamically.
- **Method**: A function with a special receiver argument. Methods allow behavior to be attached to a type.
- **Mock**: A fake implementation used in testing. Helps isolate code under test.
- **Modules**: A unit of versioned Go code defined by a `go.mod` file. Modules replace the older GOPATH system.
- **Mutual exclusion (Mutex)**: A synchronization primitive to protect shared data. Available in the sync package.

- **Nil**: The zero value for pointers, slices, maps, interfaces, and channels. Represents the absence of a value.
- **Package**: A collection of related Go files grouped together. Packages enable modularity and code reuse.
- **Panic**: A runtime state that abruptly stops execution. Panic should be used only in severe conditions.
- **Pointers**: Variables that store the memory address of another variable. Declared using the * operator.
- **Race condition**: A bug caused by unsynchronized access to shared data. Can be detected with `go run -race`.
- **Receiver**: The parameter before a method name that binds it to a type. It can be a value receiver or a pointer receiver.
- **Recover**: Used with defer to regain control after a panic. It helps prevent abrupt program termination.
- **Select statement**: A statement for handling multiple channel operations. It blocks until one of the operations is ready.
- **Service discovery**: Mechanism to locate services dynamically. Essential in microservice ecosystems.
- **Slice**: A flexible, dynamically sized abstraction over arrays. Slices store a pointer to an underlying array, along with length and capacity.
- **Stack**: Memory used for local variables and function calls. Stacks are automatically managed by Go runtime.
- **Standard library**: A set of core packages bundled with Go. It covers I/O, networking, crypto, HTTP, math, and more.
- **Struct**: A composite type used to group related fields. Structs are often used to model entities or data structures.
- **Swagger/OpenAPI**: Specifications and tools for documenting and testing APIs. Helps generate client **software development kits** (**SDKs**) and visualize endpoints.
- **Synchronization**: The act of coordinating multiple goroutines. Ensures correct order and safe data access.
- **Test coverage**: A metric showing which parts of code are executed by tests. Run with `go test -cover`.
- **Ticker**: Generates events at regular intervals using a channel. Part of the time package.
- **Timeout**: A mechanism that cancels an operation if it takes too long. Often implemented with `select` and `time.After`.
- **Transport Layer Security (TLS)**: Cryptographic protocol for secure communication. Ensures encryption and integrity of data in transit.
- **Type assertion**: Extracts the underlying value stored in an interface.
- **Type switch**: A special switch that branches based on an interface's dynamic type. Useful when handling different concrete types at runtime.
- **Value receiver**: A method receiver that operates on a copy of the value. Changes to the receiver do not affect the original type.
- **Variable**: A named storage for holding a value. Declared using `var`, `:=`, or inside a function.
- **Vendor directory**: A local folder storing all external dependencies. Useful for offline builds or locked dependencies.
- **Worker pool**: A pattern where a fixed number of goroutines process tasks from a queue. Useful for controlled concurrency.

Join our Discord space

Join our Discord workspace for latest updates, offers, tech happenings around the world, new releases, and sessions with the authors:

https://discord.bpbonline.com

Appendix C
Answers to Exercises

Chapter 1

1. Go, also called Golang, is an open-source programming language developed at *Google* in 2009 by *Robert Griesemer*, *Rob Pike*, and *Ken Thompson*. It was designed to overcome the shortcomings of languages such as C++ and Java when building large-scale, cloud-based, and concurrent systems. Go's creators sought a language that combined the performance and type safety of C with the simplicity and rapid development cycle of scripting languages, enabling developers to build efficient, reliable, and maintainable software.
2. Go's suitability for cloud and microservice architectures stems from its fast compilation, built-in concurrency (via goroutines and channels), and simple deployment model. The language produces statically linked binaries that run without external dependencies, which is ideal for containers and Kubernetes. Its automatic garbage collection, strong standard library (including **`net/http`** and **`encoding/json`**), and lightweight memory model further make Go a first-class choice for scalable, distributed systems.
3. Here are the steps to install Go on your machine:
   a. To install Go, visit **https://go.dev/dl** and download the correct installer for your operating system.
   b. After installation, configure two environment variables: **`GOROOT`** (the Go installation directory) and **`GOPATH`** (the workspace directory).
   c. Add Go's bin folder to the system **`PATH`** so commands like **`go run`** and **`go build`** are recognized. Finally, verify the setup by running go version and go env in the terminal.
4. The **`main()`** function is the entry point of any Go application. It resides within the main package and is executed automatically when the program starts. Without it, the Go compiler cannot generate an executable. The **`main()`** function orchestrates initialization, function calls, and overall program logic, serving as the central control hub for application execution.
5. Go modules, introduced in Go 1.11, provide a standardized way to manage project dependencies outside **`GOPATH`**. A **`go.mod`** file defines the module's path and dependency versions, ensuring reproducible builds. Modules simplify dependency resolution, version control, and portability, eliminating many manual tasks required by earlier **`GOPATH`**-based workflows.
6. Dependency management in Go is handled using module commands such as **`go get`**, **`go mod tidy`**, and **`go mod vendor`**. The **`go get`** command adds or updates packages; **`go mod tidy`** removes unused ones and ensures **`go.mod`** and **`go.sum`** are accurate; and **`go mod vendor`** creates a local copy for offline builds. This system promotes clean, versioned, and repeatable dependency handling.
7. The **`go build`** command compiles source files into an executable binary. For example, running **`go build main.go`** produces main on Linux or main.exe on Windows. The command automatically resolves imports, checks syntax, and includes dependencies to generate a fully self-contained binary ready for deployment.
8. **`GOPATH`** points to the root of the Go workspace, traditionally containing **`src`**, **`pkg`**, and **`bin`** folders. Before modules, it defined where Go looked for source code and where compiled binaries were stored. Though optional in modern Go, it remains useful for legacy projects and certain tools that rely on the **`GOPATH`** structure.

9. **go mod tidy** analyzes the source code to ensure dependency lists are accurate. It adds any missing modules required for compilation and removes unused ones. This keeps **go.mod** and **go.sum** clean, avoids redundant dependencies, and ensures consistent, reliable builds across environments.

Chapter 2

1. A **for** loop in Go typically includes three components: the initialization statement, the condition expression, and the post statement. The initialization sets up the loop variable, the condition determines when to continue or terminate the loop, and the post statement updates the variable after each iteration. Together, these provide a compact and readable mechanism to perform repetitive tasks or iterate through sequences in Go.
2. When used without conditions, the **for** loop becomes an infinite loop that runs continuously until explicitly stopped. This construct is often used in long-running services, background daemons, or continuous monitoring routines. Developers can use break or return statements to safely terminate it when required.
3. The **range** keyword simplifies iteration over data structures such as arrays, slices, maps, and strings. For arrays and slices, it returns both the index and the element value. For maps, it provides the key and the corresponding value. This construct eliminates manual index management and improves readability and safety.
4. The **break** statement immediately stops the loop's execution, skipping any remaining iterations. For instance, a **break** can end a loop when a desired value is found in an array. This helps improve efficiency and prevents unnecessary iterations once the target condition is met.
5. The **continue** statement is useful when certain iterations should be skipped without stopping the loop entirely. For example, when processing a list of numbers, you might use **continue** to skip negative values while still iterating over the rest. It enhances control over conditional flow within iterative logic.
6. In Go, omitting the initialization and post statements in a **for** loop allows it to behave like a **while** loop. The loop continues as long as the condition is true. This pattern is concise and avoids unnecessary syntax while maintaining clarity and simplicity.
7. The **range** keyword improves readability, safety, and efficiency when working with collections. It automatically handles indexing and boundaries, reducing the chance of out-of-range errors. Additionally, it clearly conveys the intent of iterating over items, which enhances code maintainability.
8. The loop would look like this:

   ```
   for i := 1; i <= 10; i++ {
     if i == 5 {
      continue
     }
     fmt.Println(i)
   }
   ```

   This prints 1 through 10, excluding 5, demonstrating the use of continue for conditional skipping.
9. Infinite loops should be avoided when termination conditions can be predicted or when system resources are limited. They can be safely terminated using break statements, context cancellations, or signal interrupts. Proper termination ensures that programs do not hang or consume excessive CPU.
10. The **goto** statement transfers control unconditionally to a labeled statement. While it can simplify some error-handling flows, it disrupts structured programming and makes code harder to follow. Go supports it for completeness, but encourages structured control mechanisms like **for**, **break**, and **continue** instead.

Chapter 3

1. A Go function follows the syntax **`func functionName(parameter type) returnType`**. Parameters and return types are explicitly declared, ensuring type safety. For example:

   ```
   func add(a int, b int) int {
    return a + b
   }
   ```

   This function takes two integers and returns their sum, demonstrating Go's clarity and simplicity.

2. In Go, functions are first-class citizens, meaning they can be stored in variables, passed as arguments, or returned from other functions. This enables functional programming patterns. For example, a function can be assigned to a variable and later invoked just like any other object.

3. Variadic functions accept a variable number of arguments using an ellipsis (...). They differ from regular functions because they can take zero or many arguments. A slice can be passed using the spread operator (slice...). This makes them ideal for flexible functions like **`fmt.Println`**.

4. Go passes parameters by value by default, meaning a copy is made. To modify the original variable, a pointer must be passed instead. The called function then dereferences the pointer to access and modify the actual value, allowing safe and controlled data manipulation.

5. Anonymous functions have no name and can be declared inline. Closures extend this by capturing variables from their surrounding scope. For example, a counter function that increments a captured variable each time it is called illustrates how closures maintain state effectively across calls.

6. Go promotes explicit error handling rather than exceptions. Errors are treated as values returned alongside normal results, encouraging developers to check and handle them immediately. This approach leads to clearer, more predictable, and maintainable error management compared to implicit exception propagation.

7. Custom errors are implemented by defining a struct that satisfies the error interface's **`Error()`** method. For instance, a **`ValidationError`** struct can hold context about invalid inputs, and its **`Error()`** method can format a descriptive message, enhancing debugging and error tracing.

8. **`fmt.Errorf`** with **`%w`** wraps an existing error, preserving its context while adding new information. This allows errors to be layered and later unwrapped using **`errors.Unwrap`**, facilitating better traceability and structured debugging across application layers.

9. **`errors.Is`** checks whether an error matches a specific target, even when wrapped, while errors. As an extract of an error of a specific type. It is ideal for equality checks and for type assertions. Together, they make advanced error handling more precise and expressive.

10. **`errors.Join`** allows combining multiple errors into a single composite error. This is useful in concurrent operations where several errors may occur simultaneously. It improves reporting by collecting related issues under one structured error object.

Chapter 4

1. A struct in Go is a composite data type that groups related fields. It can be initialized using named fields for clarity or positional fields for brevity. For example, **`Person{Name: "Venkatesh", Age: 40}`** uses named fields, while **`Person{"Venkatesh", 40}`** uses positional initialization.

2. Exported fields start with an uppercase letter and are visible outside their package. Unexported fields start with lowercase letters and remain private. This naming-based access control enforces encapsulation, ensuring internal fields remain protected from external modification.

3. Anonymous structs are defined inline without a type name. They are useful for short-lived or localized data structures, such as temporary JSON responses or quick grouping of variables within a function. They reduce boilerplate where reuse is unnecessary.

4. A function is independent, while a method is associated with a specific type via a receiver. For example:

```
func (p Person) Greet() {
  fmt.Println("Hello,", p.Name)
}
```

Here, **Greet** is a method bound to the **Person** struct, providing type-specific behavior.

5. Value receivers operate on a copy, preserving immutability, while pointer receivers modify the original object. Pointer receivers are recommended for large structs or when mutation is needed, offering efficiency and consistent method behavior.

6. Method chaining allows multiple methods to be called sequentially on the same object. Returning a pointer receiver enables this by maintaining state continuity. This pattern improves code fluency, especially in builder-like APIs or configuration objects.

7. Embedding includes another struct directly, inheriting its fields and methods implicitly. Composition involves referencing another struct as a field. Embedding simplifies reuse but can cause naming conflicts if embedded types share field names.

8. Yes, embedded methods can be accessed directly as if they belong to the parent struct. If the embedding struct defines a method with the same name, it overrides the embedded version, enabling controlled customization of behavior.

9. Structs can be compared directly if all their fields are comparable. Fields like slices, maps, and functions are not comparable, causing compilation errors. This restriction ensures type safety and prevents undefined comparison semantics.

10. A shallow copy duplicates only top-level fields, whereas a deep copy replicates all referenced data. When structs contain slices or pointers, shallow copies may lead to shared data mutations. Deep copies prevent such unintended interference by fully cloning nested structures.

Chapter 5

1. Arrays in Go have a fixed length defined at compile time, while slices are dynamically sized views over arrays. Arrays are best used when the size is known and fixed, ensuring memory predictability. Slices, on the other hand, offer flexibility and are commonly used for variable-length collections in practical Go programs.

2. When **append()** adds elements beyond the slice's current capacity, Go allocates a new underlying array with larger capacity, copies existing elements to it, and returns a new slice referencing the new array. This resizing mechanism is automatic and efficient, but may involve memory reallocation.

3. Maps are initialized using the **make()** function or map literals. For example, **make(map[string]int)** creates an empty map ready for use. Attempting to add elements to a nil map causes a runtime panic because it lacks the necessary internal data structures.

4. The **json:"field_name"** tag specifies how a struct field maps to a JSON key during encoding and decoding. It enables consistent field naming between Go code and JSON payloads, supporting lowercasing, renaming, or omitting fields as needed for clean API communication.

5. Multidimensional arrays have a fixed grid-like structure with all dimensions pre-allocated. Slices of slices are more flexible, allowing each inner slice to vary in length. Arrays provide predictable memory layout and faster access, while slices offer flexibility and simpler memory management.

6. A sample program:

```
students := map[string]int{"Venkatesh": 95, "Shubham": 85, "Parth": 92}
for name, score := range students {
```

```
    if score > 90 {
     fmt.Println(name, score)
    }
   }
```

This iterates over the **map** and conditionally prints students with scores above 90.

7. The slice can be created using slicing syntax:

```
arr := [5]int{1, 2, 3, 4, 5}
 sub := arr[1:4]
 fmt.Println(sub)
```

This prints **[2 3 4]**, effectively excluding the first and last elements.

8. A filtering function can loop through the slice and collect even numbers into a new slice. Using modulus (**%**) ensures only numbers divisible by two are selected, demonstrating practical use of slice manipulation.
9. This can be done by creating a slice of slices, initializing each row, and modifying the middle index. It demonstrates Go's ability to handle nested slices dynamically, enabling easy matrix representation.
10. Sub-slices share the same underlying array as the original slice. Therefore, modifying elements in a subslice reflects in the original. This behavior highlights the need for caution when sharing slices to avoid unintended data modification.

Chapter 6

1. A pointer is a variable that holds the memory address of another variable. Unlike regular variables that store actual values, pointers store references to those values. They enable direct memory access and efficient data manipulation without unnecessary copying.
2. The **&** operator retrieves a variable's memory address, while ***** dereferences a pointer to access the value stored at that address. For instance, **p := &x** creates a pointer to **x**, and ***p** accesses or modifies **x** through that pointer.
3. Pointer receivers modify the actual struct instance rather than a copy, ensuring changes persist. They also improve performance by avoiding value copying, especially for large structs, and maintain consistent method sets across receivers.
4. Advantages include memory efficiency and direct manipulation of large data structures. However, improper use can lead to nil pointer dereferences and complex debugging. Careful design ensures safe and effective pointer handling.
5. Go prevents pointer arithmetic and automatically manages memory via garbage collection. These mechanisms eliminate common issues such as dangling pointers or memory leaks, balancing low-level control with safety.
6. The function dereferences both pointers and exchanges their values. By manipulating values directly in memory, it demonstrates Go's pointer semantics for efficient in-place data modification.
7. A pointer receiver method, such as **func (p *Person) Birthday()**, can increment **p.. Age++**, updating the actual struct instance. This illustrates the use of pointer receivers for mutable object methods.
8. Dereferencing a **nil** pointer causes a panic because it refers to no valid memory. Defensive programming involves **nil** checks (if **p != nil**) before dereferencing or using **new()** or **make()** to properly initialize values.
9. Using a struct with a slice field and pointer methods, the stack can be implemented to mutate internal data efficiently. Pointer receivers ensure operations directly modify the stack instance.

10. `new()` allocates memory and returns a pointer to a zero value of the type, while `make()` initializes and returns slices, maps, or channels. They serve distinct purposes: new for basic types, make for built-in reference types.

Chapter 7

1. Go uses structural typing, where a type automatically satisfies an interface if it implements its methods. Unlike explicit declarations in languages like Java, this approach reduces boilerplate and promotes flexibility in design.
2. The empty interface represents any type, allowing highly generic functions. While flexible, overuse can reduce type safety and clarity. It is often replaced by any in newer Go versions for readability.
3. Interface embedding allows one interface to include another, composing larger interfaces from smaller ones. This modular design promotes reusability and cleaner abstraction across components.
4. Struct embedding deals with data reuse, while interface embedding combines behavior contracts. Struct embedding shares fields and methods, whereas interface embedding merges method sets, enhancing abstraction rather than state.
5. Keep interfaces small (narrow interfaces), name them after behavior (e.g., `Reader`, `Writer`), and define them near consumers. This results in clearer and more adaptable codebases.
6. Any type implementing an interface's methods can be used polymorphically. This enables writing functions that operate on different concrete types through a unified interface, increasing code flexibility.
7. Narrow interfaces improve clarity and maintainability by limiting method sets. They are easier to implement and mock, fostering modular design aligned with Go's simplicity philosophy.
8. By defining interfaces for dependencies, developers can substitute mock implementations during testing. This isolates components and enhances test reliability and coverage.
9. Type assertions extract concrete values from interface types, while type switches handle multiple possible types dynamically. Together, they provide controlled access to underlying implementations.
10. Common issues include over-abstracting, premature interface definition, and misuse of empty interfaces. Adhering to minimal design and defining interfaces at usage boundaries prevent such pitfalls.

Chapter 8

1. Go distinguishes between executable packages (main) and library packages. The main package produces executables, while library packages provide reusable functions or types for other programs.
2. The `init()` function executes automatically before the main function. It is commonly used to initialize package-level variables, register resources, or configure dependencies safely.
3. Exported identifiers begin with uppercase letters and are accessible outside the package. Unexported identifiers start with lowercase letters and remain private, reinforcing encapsulation through naming convention.
4. A module is a collection of packages versioned together. It simplifies dependency management and ensures reproducible builds. Modules decouple projects from `GOPATH`, providing clarity and version control.
5. The `go.mod` file defines module dependencies and versions, while `go.sum` ensures integrity through cryptographic checksums. Together, they maintain dependency consistency and security.
6. Avoid cyclic imports, mismatched package names, and deep directory hierarchies. Following Go's simple package layout prevents confusion and dependency issues.
7. Initialize a module with go mod init, commit it to a public repository, and tag releases using semantic versioning. Other projects can then import it via its repository path.
8. Descriptive package names improve readability, while shallow hierarchies simplify navigation. Deep nesting increases complexity and reduces maintainability, violating Go's design simplicity.

9. Commands like **go get**, **go mod tidy**, and **go mod vendor** manage dependencies efficiently. They handle fetching, cleaning, and localizing modules, ensuring smooth project builds.
10. Group related functionality, expose minimal public APIs, and document packages thoroughly. Consistent naming, proper testing, and adherence to Go's idioms promote scalable and maintainable architecture.

Chapter 9

1. Concurrency involves managing multiple tasks that make progress independently, while parallelism executes them simultaneously. Understanding this distinction helps design responsive systems that scale effectively across CPUs.
2. Goroutines are lightweight, requiring only a few kilobytes of stack space, and are multiplexed onto OS threads by Go's scheduler. This allows thousands of goroutines to run efficiently compared to limited, heavy threads.
3. **sync.WaitGroup** synchronizes multiple goroutines by tracking task completion. It must be passed by pointer so all goroutines modify the same counter instance, ensuring accurate coordination and preventing data races.
4. Channels provide a safe communication mechanism between goroutines. By passing data rather than sharing memory, they eliminate race conditions and enforce structured synchronization.
5. In web scraping or data processing pipelines, fan-out distributes tasks across worker goroutines, while fan-in aggregates results. This pattern maximizes CPU utilization and throughput.
6. Use proper synchronization (**WaitGroup**, **Context**), limit concurrency levels, and handle errors gracefully. Always ensure goroutines terminate properly to prevent leaks.
7. The pipeline pattern connects goroutines through channels where the output of one stage becomes the input for the next. It is ideal for data streaming, ETL systems, and event processing pipelines.
8. Select enables non-blocking operations across channels, enhancing responsiveness. However, it introduces complexity when dealing with dynamic channel sets or fairness in scheduling.
9. Context propagates cancellation and deadlines across goroutines, enabling coordinated shutdowns and resource cleanup. It prevents orphaned tasks and improves system reliability.
10. Worker pools are effective for distributing identical tasks among fixed workers, while publish-subscribe decouples senders and receivers for event-driven systems. Both patterns enhance scalability in distinct contexts.

Chapter 10

1. Buffered channels allow asynchronous communication with limited capacity, while unbuffered channels block until both sender and receiver are ready. Buffered channels suit bursty workloads; unbuffered ensure tight synchronization.
2. Channels coordinate send and receive operations atomically, preventing simultaneous access conflicts. They inherently serialize data transfer, maintaining data integrity without explicit locks.
3. On unbuffered channels, senders and receivers block until paired. In buffered channels, send blocks when full and receive blocks when empty. This behavior provides flow control and safety.
4. Directional channels restrict usage to send-only or receive-only contexts, enforcing intended communication flow. They make APIs safer by preventing misuse and clarifying function contracts.
5. Deadlocks occur when all goroutines wait indefinitely for sends or receives. Avoid them by closing channels correctly, ensuring matching operations, or using select statements with timeouts.

6. The range keyword iterates over values until a channel is closed. Closing a channel signals completion, preventing further sends and allowing receivers to exit cleanly.
7. Select enables concurrent channel listening, timeouts, and default non-blocking cases. It increases responsiveness and control in complex communication scenarios.
8. Always close channels from the sender side, avoid double closure, and prevent sends on closed channels. Proper lifecycle management ensures program safety.
9. Channels encapsulate data transfer, replacing shared memory with message passing. This avoids the need for explicit locks and reduces the risk of race conditions.
10. `WaitGroup` tracks goroutine completion while channels coordinate data flow. Used together, they form robust synchronization primitives for orchestrating concurrent workflows.

Chapter 11

1. The `select` statement lets a goroutine wait on multiple channel operations simultaneously, proceeding with whichever is ready first. Unlike a `switch`, which matches values, select synchronizes concurrent channel events, providing elegant coordination among goroutines.
2. A `default` case executes immediately if no other channel is ready, making the select non-blocking. It is useful for polling, timeout checks, or preventing goroutines from blocking when work is not available.
3. Using `select`, a goroutine can monitor multiple input channels and print the first response received. This pattern is often used for race conditions, mirrored requests, or redundancy in distributed systems.
4. `time.Returns` a channel that delivers the current time after a specified duration. Combining it with select allows implementing timeouts, ensuring goroutines do not block indefinitely when waiting for events.
5. Goroutines and channels enable coordinated termination through signal propagation. For example, a server can broadcast a stop signal to worker goroutines via channels, ensuring all processes finish cleanly before exit.
6. `time.After` creating a one-off timer returning a channel, whereas `time.NewTimer` gives a reusable timer object that can be reset or stopped. Use `NewTimer` when fine-grained control is needed across multiple timeout cycles.
7. A ticker repeatedly sends events at fixed intervals, ideal for periodic tasks like heartbeat signals or metric reporting. Timers, by contrast, trigger only once.
8. Improper default-case use can cause busy loops that hog CPU. To avoid this, introduce small sleeps, back-off strategies, or block on channels when possible to maintain efficiency.
9. WaitGroup tracks active goroutines and blocks until all complete, ensuring orderly shutdown. It prevents premature program exits and resource leaks by enforcing lifecycle synchronization.
10. First, propagate cancellation via context; second, close channels properly; third, ensure deferred cleanup (e.g., closing files or sockets). Together, these yield a reliable and recoverable system termination.

Chapter 12

1. A worker pool limits concurrent task execution by distributing jobs among fixed worker goroutines. This approach controls resource usage, prevents oversubscription, and improves throughput under heavy load.
2. WaitGroup coordinates completion by counting active workers. It ensures the main routine waits for all tasks to finish before proceeding, providing predictable synchronization in concurrent systems.
3. Results are typically sent through a shared results channel. Once all workers finish, the channel is closed and results aggregated, ensuring concurrent data collection without shared-memory conflicts.

4. Fixed pools use constant worker counts for stable workloads; dynamic pools adjust worker numbers based on load. Dynamic pools are suited for variable demand or bursty tasks needing elasticity.
5. A pipeline chains stages of goroutines connected via channels. Each stage processes data and passes results onward. This modularity promotes reusability and enables streaming of large datasets efficiently.
6. Errors can be sent on a dedicated error channel or aggregated via **`errors.Join`**. The main goroutine can monitor these channels without halting normal operations, allowing non-blocking error recovery.
7. A race condition arises when multiple goroutines access shared data unsafely. Running tests with **`go test -race`** detects such issues at runtime by instrumenting memory access patterns.
8. Mutex enforces exclusive access, while RWMutex allows concurrent reads with single-writer exclusion. Use RWMutex when reads dominate writes for higher concurrency.
9. Rate limiting caps the number of requests over time, whereas throttling delays or queues excess requests. Implement them using tickers, channels, or time-based algorithms like token buckets.
10. Condition variables (**`sync.Cond`**) excel when goroutines must wait for complex state changes - e.g., a bounded queue notifying producers only when space becomes available.

Chapter 13

1. Simultaneous goroutines can produce multiple errors concurrently, making collection and reporting difficult. Coordinating these safely without data races is a key concurrency design challenge.
2. Context provides cancellation signals, deadlines, and scoped values, enabling coordinated termination. It prevents orphaned goroutines and facilitates structured cancellation hierarchies.
3. Deadlocks occur when goroutines cyclically wait on each other's resources, such as unfulfilled channel sends or mutex locks. Proper ordering, timeouts, and select statements help avoid them.
4. Running with the **`-race`** flag triggers Go's race detector, which observes concurrent memory accesses at runtime and reports conflicts, enabling early bug identification during testing.
5. Recover catches panics within deferred functions, allowing graceful recovery instead of abrupt termination. It is useful in concurrent systems to isolate failures and maintain uptime.
6. Centralization aggregates errors from multiple goroutines into unified logs or channels. This simplifies analysis, reduces duplication, and provides a holistic system-level error view.
7. A goroutine leak happens when goroutines continue running after their work or parent context ends. Such leaks consume memory and CPU indefinitely; proper cancellation prevents them.
8. **`sync.RWMutex`** allows many readers simultaneously but only one writer at a time. It optimizes performance for read-heavy workloads while preserving data integrity.
9. Atomic operations are faster for simple counters or flags since they avoid lock overhead. They are best used for lightweight, independent updates without complex critical sections.
10. Stack traces reveal execution paths leading to panics, making debugging easier in concurrent environments. Logging them ensures failures can be diagnosed even after program recovery.

Chapter 14

1. A microservice is a small, independently deployable service that performs a specific business function. It communicates with other services through lightweight APIs, typically over HTTP. Each microservice can be developed, tested, and deployed separately, allowing greater agility and scalability in software systems.
2. Key benefits of microservices over monolithic architecture are:
    - First, microservices enable independent development and deployment, reducing dependencies across teams.

- Second, they enhance scalability services that can be scaled individually based on load, optimizing resource use and performance.

3. Microservices often communicate via RESTful APIs using HTTP/JSON or via asynchronous messaging systems such as RabbitMQ or Kafka. REST ensures simplicity, while message brokers provide resilience and decoupling.
4. An API gateway typically manages client requests, routing them to appropriate backend services. It handles cross-cutting concerns such as authentication, rate limiting, and load balancing.
5. Go's speed, lightweight concurrency model, and static compilation make it ideal for microservices. It creates self-contained binaries, ensuring fast startup, low memory overhead, and easy container deployment.
6. Service discovery automatically tracks and locates active service instances. It allows services to find each other dynamically without hard-coded endpoints, improving resilience and scalability.
7. *Netflix* employs microservices to deliver content globally. Each service handles specialized functions such as user profiles, recommendations, or streaming, allowing independent scaling and fault isolation.
8. It means each microservice should focus on one core business capability. This ensures clarity, reduces coupling, and simplifies both maintenance and testing.
9. Kubernetes is the most widely used orchestration tool. It automates deployment, scaling, and management of containerized applications across distributed clusters.
10. Microservices should be avoided for small, simple applications or teams lacking operational maturity. Their distributed nature adds complexity in communication, deployment, and monitoring that may outweigh the benefits for small projects.

Chapter 15

1. The `net/http` package provides a lightweight yet powerful framework with built-in concurrency, routing, and request handling. It adheres closely to HTTP standards and allows developers to build scalable APIs with minimal dependencies.
2. Graceful shutdowns let servers finish ongoing requests before termination. This prevents data loss, incomplete transactions, and abrupt connection resets, ensuring better reliability and user experience.
3. Middleware wraps request handling logic to perform actions like authentication, logging, and rate limiting. It encourages modular, reusable code and clean separation of concerns across the request lifecycle.
4. Proper timeout configuration prevents resource exhaustion from slow or malicious clients. It helps maintain responsiveness and safeguards against denial-of-service vulnerabilities.
5. `http.FileServer` serves files directly from a directory. When combined with `http.StripPrefix` efficiently handles assets like images, CSS, and JavaScript within the same server context.
6. GET retrieves data, POST creates new resources, PUT updates existing ones, and DELETE removes them. Following these semantics ensures adherence to REST principles and predictable API design.
7. Structured JSON responses allow clients to programmatically interpret errors. Including fields like code, message, and details improves consistency and aids debugging and automation.
8. Frameworks like Gorilla Mux offer advanced features such as named routes, URL parameters, and middleware chaining, simplifying large API design while maintaining performance.
9. Go's `encoding/json` package provides seamless data conversion between Go structs and JSON. Struct tags map field names to JSON keys, ensuring consistent data exchange with clients.
10. Follow clean architecture, modularize handlers, implement logging and configuration management, and always validate inputs. Using environment variables and containerization further ensures scalability and maintainability.

Chapter 16

1. Proper use of HTTP verbs ensures predictable behavior, making APIs intuitive and interoperable. It enforces REST conventions and simplifies client-side integration.
2. Status codes such as 200 (OK), 404 (Not Found), and 500 (Server Error) clearly express the result of API calls. This standardization enables consistent error handling and debugging.
3. RESTful URLs should represent resources, not actions. Using nouns like `/users` instead of verbs like `/getUsers` improves clarity, aligning endpoints with resource-based design philosophy.
4. Consistency in response format simplifies client integration and reduces parsing errors. It allows predictable handling of success and failure responses across endpoints.
5. Token-based authentication ensures that only authorized users access protected resources. JWTs embed claims and signatures, enabling stateless, secure identity validation.
6. Secure headers protect against common web vulnerabilities. CORS manages cross-origin access, HSTS enforces HTTPS, and CSP prevents injection attacks by restricting resource loading.
7. Rate limiting restricts request counts over time, while throttling slows or queues excessive requests. Both safeguard performance and fairness among API consumers.
8. Logging captures detailed runtime behavior, while Prometheus and Grafana visualize metrics and alerts. Together, they enable proactive performance monitoring and troubleshooting.
9. Versioning ensures backward compatibility when APIs evolve. Common strategies include path-based (`/v1/users`), header-based, or query-parameter approaches.
10. Swagger generates interactive API documentation from code annotations, enhancing discoverability and testing. Keeping documentation synchronized prevents confusion and accelerates onboarding.

Chapter 17

1. In microservices, many distributed components communicate across networks, increasing security exposure. Robust authentication and authorization ensure that each service interaction remains trusted and compliant.
2. Authentication verifies identity (who you are), while authorization checks permissions (what you can do). Authentication occurs first during login or token validation; authorization follows for access control.
3. Centralized models simplify management and auditing but introduce single points of failure. Decentralized approaches enhance resilience and flexibility but may complicate token synchronization and consistency.
4. A JWT contains three parts: a header (specifying algorithm), a payload (holding user claims), and a signature (ensuring integrity). Together, they form a compact, secure credential for stateless authentication.
5. mTLS verifies both client and server certificates, ensuring bidirectional trust. It is ideal for inter-service communication within secure networks such as financial or healthcare systems.
6. RBAC grants permissions by role, while ABAC uses contextual attributes like time or location. ABAC suits dynamic, policy-driven environments.
7. Use short expiration times, validate signatures, and store tokens securely (never in URLs). These practices mitigate replay attacks and unauthorized token use.
8. An API gateway centralizes policy enforcement, reducing redundancy and ensuring consistency. However, it adds operational complexity and potential bottlenecks if not scaled properly.
9. Short-lived tokens limit exposure by reducing the time window for misuse if compromised. They force periodic re-authentication, ensuring active session validation.
10. Keycloak provides centralized identity and access management, while OAuth2 Proxy handles authentication delegation. Both integrate easily with Go-based microservices for secure access control.

Chapter 18

1. Unit tests validate individual functions, while integration tests ensure that services interact correctly. Together, they verify both internal logic and system-wide reliability.
2. Mocks replace real dependencies with controlled simulations, enabling deterministic, repeatable testing without network or database dependencies.
3. Load testing evaluates system performance under stress, revealing bottlenecks, scalability limits, and potential failure points before production deployment.
4. E2E testing validates the entire workflow across multiple services, ensuring that all integrations, data flows, and business rules function as expected from the user's perspective.
5. Exclusive focus on unit tests can miss interaction errors and network issues, leading to fragile production systems. Comprehensive test coverage is essential.
6. Contract testing ensures that a provider's API conforms to consumer expectations, catching breaking changes early and maintaining compatibility in evolving systems.
7. Challenges include distributed dependencies, data consistency, environment setup, and asynchronous communication. Effective automation and monitoring mitigate these complexities.
8. Automation accelerates feedback cycles, enabling continuous integration and delivery. It ensures regression prevention and consistency across frequent deployments.
9. A structured test strategy ensures comprehensive validation at every layer, balancing speed and confidence. It minimizes production risks and supports reliable scaling.
10. Isolate environments, use data stubs or mocks, and automate repetitive scenarios. Additionally, maintain clear documentation and versioned test contracts for sustainable quality.

Chapter 19

1. Each service owning its database enforces autonomy, allowing independent schema evolution and deployment. It prevents cross-service coupling and enhances scalability.
2. Shared databases introduce tight coupling, coordination overhead, and risk of schema conflicts. They hinder independent scaling and slow down deployment cycles.
3. Foreign keys across services break isolation and require cross-database joins. Instead, reference identifiers and asynchronous data replication are used to maintain logical relationships.
4. Polyglot persistence means using different database technologies per service based on needs. It allows optimized performance in relational databases for transactions and NoSQL for flexibility.
5. SQL enforces strict schemas and ACID transactions, ideal for financial systems. NoSQL offers flexible structures and horizontal scalability, better for analytics or caching layers.
6. API composition aggregates data by calling multiple services at runtime, while event-driven replication pushes updates asynchronously. The former suits real-time queries; the latter supports decoupled synchronization.
7. Event sourcing stores immutable state changes as a sequence of events. It provides auditability, replayability, and improved consistency compared to mutable CRUD operations.
8. The saga pattern breaks long transactions into steps coordinated via events. In choreography, services react to events independently; in orchestration, a central controller directs flow.
9. Schema versioning maintains backward compatibility across evolving systems. Practices include semantic versioning, additive changes, and deprecating old fields gradually.
10. Adopt data ownership boundaries, implement encryption, use proper replication strategies, and automate backups. Monitoring data flows ensures integrity and fault tolerance.

Index

A

Anonymous Functions 44
Anonymous Functions, demonstrating 44-48
Arrays 82
Arrays, features 82
Arrays, integrating 82-84
API Documentation 346
API Documentation, illustrating 346-350
API First Communication 301
API Requests 338
API Requests, illustrating 338-341
API Versioning 342
API Versioning, illustrating 342-345
Asynchronous Communication 301
Autonomy 300

B

Bidirectional Channel, converting 199
Bidirectional Channel, practices 201
Built-In Profiling 424
Built-In Profiling, configuring 424, 425
Built-In Profiling, integrating 425, 426

C

Channel Direction 197
Channel Direction, benefits 199
Channel Direction, configuring 197, 198
Channels 185, 186
Channels, anatomy 186
Channels, mechanisms
- Blocking Nature 193
- Error Handling 195
- Non-Blocking 194
- Receiving Data 192
- Sending Data 191

Channels, mistake 187
Channels, practices 187
Channels, reasons 186
Channels, types
- Buffered 188
- Unbuffered 187

CI/CD 429
CI/CD, reasons 429
CI/CD, steps 429
Compare/Copy Structs 76
Compare/Copy Structs, illustrating 76-79
Complex Numbers 17
Complex Numbers, ensuring 17-19
Concurrency 161, 162
Concurrency, advantages 163
Concurrency, architecture 162
Concurrency, challenges 163
Concurrency, configuring 162
Concurrency Model, comparing 164
Concurrency Model, scenarios 164, 165
Concurrency, patterns
- Fan-Out/Fan-In 176
- Pipeline 177
- Propagate Cancellation 181
- Publish-Subscribe 179
- Rate Limiting 183
- Select 180
- Worker Pool 178

Concurrency-Safe Applications 256
Concurrency-Safe Applications, concepts 260
Concurrency-Safe Applications, outlines 256
Concurrency-Safe Applications, principles 256
Concurrency-Safe Applications, techniques
- Atomic Operations 258
- Channels 257
- Context Package 259
- Synchronization 257

Condition Variables 252
Condition Variables, applications 255, 256
Condition Variables, ensuring 253, 254
Constants, configuring 11-13
Control Structures 21
Control Structures, integrating 21-25
CQRS 413
Custom Errors 52
Custom Errors, illustrating 52-56

D

Data Types 13
Data Types, ensuring 13-17

Database Design 403
Database Design, concerns 406
Database Design, mistake 406
Database Design, patterns 405
Database Design, principles 404
Database Design, terms
  Cross-Service Data Access 405
  Schema Design 404
  SQL/NoSQL 405
Data Management 417
Data Management, integrating 418, 419
Data Migration 409
Data Migration, process 409
Deadlock 273
Deadlock, applications 278
Deadlock, configuring 273, 274
Deadlock, integrating 274-277
Deadlock, issues 274
Debugging 426
Decentralized Data Management 300
Deadlock 250
Declare/Call Functions 36
Declare/Call Functions, configuring 36, 37
Distributed Architecture 406
Distributed Architecture, terms
  NoSQL Databases 407
  Polyglot Persistence 406
  Relational Databases 407
Distributed Transactions 415
Distributed Transactions, illustrating 415-417
Docker Compose 399
Docker Compose, configuring 400
Docker/Kubernetes 352
Docker/Kubernetes, illustrating 352-356

E

Embedding/Composition 71
Embedding/Composition, demonstrating 71-75
Empty Interface 138
Empty Interface, integrating 139, 140
Error Handling 48
Error Handling, illustrating 48-51
Error Handling, practices 57
External Libraries 153
External Libraries, importing 153-155
External Libraries, integrating 156-160
External Libraries, reasons 153
E2E Testing, configuring 396, 397
E2E Testing, implementing 397, 399
E-Commerce Microservices 304
End-to-End (E2E) Testing 396
Error Handling 267
Error Handling, archiecture 268
Error Handling, challenges 268
Error Handling, practices 268-272
Event Sourcing 412
Event Sourcing, integrating 414, 415

F

Fan-Out/Fan-In Pattern 176
Fault Tolerance/Resilience 301

G

Go 1
Go, configuring 4, 5
Go, evolution 4
Go, features 1, 2
Go Microservices 294
Go Microservices, reasons
  CI/CI Integration 298
  Cloud Native 297
  Concurrency 295
  Ecosystem Community 298
  gRPC 298
  High Performance 296
  HTTP/Networking 296
  Simplicity/Readability 294
  Small Binary Size 297
Go Microservices, usages 299
Go Modules 421
Go Modules, commands 422
Go Modules, files 421
Go Methods 63
Go Methods, demonstrating 63-67
Go Modules 6, 150
Go Modules, steps 151, 152
Go Program 5
Go Program, breakdown 6
Go Program, steps 5
Go, reasons
  Community/Ecosystem 4
  Concurrent Programming 4
  Performance 4
Goroutines 165
Goroutines, applications
  File Processing 171
  Web Server 170
Goroutines, ensuring 167, 168
Goroutines/Functions, differences 170
Goroutines, syntax 166
Goroutines/Threads, differences 172
Goroutines/Threads Sheduler, differences 174
Go, use cases 2, 3
Graceful Shutdowns 224
Graceful Shutdowns, configuring 224, 225

Graceful Shutdowns, mechanism
Goroutines 226
Long-Running Tasks 228
OS Signals 227
Web Servers 229
Graceful Shutdowns, practices 230, 231

H

HTTP Requests/Responses 310
HTTP Requests/Responses, illustrating 310-316

I

Integration Testing 381
Integration Testing, ensuring 381, 382
Interface 119
Interface, advantages 124
Interface Embedding 128
Interface Embedding, illustrating 128-131
Interface, ensuring 121-123
Interface, features 123
Interface, implementing 124-127
Interface, practices 141, 142
Interface Satisfaction 132
Interface Satisfaction, characteristics 132
Interface Satisfaction, configuring 132-134
Interface Satisfaction, methods
Combining 135
Single/Multiple 134
Iterating Over Maps/Slices 94
Iterating Over Maps/Slices, preventing 94-98

J

JavaScript Object Notation (JSON) 98
JSON, demonstrating 98-102
JSON Encode/Decode 321
JSON Encode/Decode, integrating 321-326
JSON Web Token (JWT) 362
JWT, configuring 362, 363
JWT, integrating 363-366

L

Locks 251
Loops 26
Loops, demonstrating 26-32
Load Testing 393
Load Testing, ensuring 393-395
Loose Coupling 300

M

Main Function 6
Maps 87
Maps, illustrating 87-91
Microservices 289, 359
Microservices, advantages 291
Microservices, architecture 289
Microservices, challenges 292
Microservices, characteristics 290
Microservices, components 291
Microservices Deployment, strategies
CI/CD Pipelines 293
Containerization 292
Serverless Computing 293
Service Mesh 293
Microservices Design 299
Microservices Design, principles
API First Communication 301
Asynchronous Communication 301
Autonomy 300
Decentralized Data Management 300
Fault Tolerance/Resilience 301
Loose Coupling 300
Observability 302
Single Responsibility Principle (SRP) 299
Microservices, industries 292
Microservices, patterns 361
Microservices, services
Authentication 360
Authorization 360
Microservices Testing 400
Microservices Testing, integrating 401, 402
Microservices, use cases 293
Mocking 388
Mocking, components
Auto-Generated Mocks 389
HTTP Calls 389
Interface-Based Design 388
Message Brokers 393
User Databases 391
Monolithic/Microservices, comparing 290
Multidimensional Arrays/Slices 91
Multidimensional Arrays/Slices, illustrating 91-94
Multi-Stage Pipeline 242
Mutex 246
Mutex, ensuring 247-249
Mutex, scenarios 250

N

Non-Blocking Operations 214

O

Observability 303
Operators 19
Operators, evaluating 19-21

P

Package 145
Package, architecture 145
Package, initializing 147-149
Package, steps 146
Package, types
Executable 146
Library 146
Panic Recovery 278

Panic Recovery, architecture 278
Panic Recovery, configuring 278, 279
Panic Recovery, integrating 280-282
Panic Recovery, practices 282
Pipeline Pattern 177
Pipelines 240
Pipelines, advantages 242
Pipelines, applications 245
Pipelines, architecture 240
Pipelines, components 240
Pipelines, initializing 241
Pipelines, stages 240
Profiling/Benchmarking 395, 396
Pointer Receiver Methods 112
Pointer Receiver Methods, advantages 115, 116
Pointer Receiver Methods, architecture 113
Pointer Receiver Methods, practices 118
Pointer Receiver Methods, ptifalls 117
Pointer Receiver Methods, syntax 113
Pointers 67, 105
Pointers, ensuring 105-108
Pointers, evaluating 108-112
Pointers, illustrating 67-71
Producer-Consumer Problem 252
Propagate Cancellation Pattern 181
Publish-Subscribe Pattern 179

R

Race Conditions 245
Race Conditions, configuring 245
Rate Limiting 350
Rate Limiting, illustrating 350-352
RBAC, illustrating 369-372
RESTful API 334
RESTful API, demonstrating 334-337
RESTful API, tests
  Handlers 384
  Unit 383
Role-Based Access Control (RBAC) 369
Routing 317
Routing, illustrating 317-321
Rate Limiting 260
Rate Limiting, architecture 260
Rate Limiting, concepts 260
Rate Limiting, implementing 261, 262
Rate Limiting Pattern 183
Return Types/Function Parameters 37
Return Types/Function Parameters, illustrating 37-40

S

Schema Versioning 409
Schema Versioning, illustrating 410, 411
Secure Service Communication 372
Secure Service Communication, integrating 372-374
Securing Microservices 374
Securing Microservices, illustrating 374-376
Single Responsibility Principle (SRP) 299
SQL/NoSQL, comparing 408
Select Pattern 180
Select Statement 207
Select Statement, advantages 212
Select Statement, architecture 207
Select Statement, capabilities
  Channel Multiplexing 211
  Continuous Monitoring 210
  Multiple Receives 208
  Send/Receive Operations 209
  Timeout Handling 212
Select Statement, characteristics 208
Select Statement, practices 212
Select Statement, syntax 208
Slices 84
Slices, ensuring 84-87
Structs 59
Structs, illustrating 59-63
Synchronization 201
Synchronization, channels
  Buffered 202
  Non-Blocking 203
  Unbuffered 201
Synchronization, practices 205
Synchronization 283
Synchronization, applications 287
Synchronization, architecture 283
Synchronization, integrating 283-286

T

Threads 172
Throttling 264
Throttling, implementing 264
Ticker 220
Ticker, ensuring 220, 221
Ticker/Timer, differences 222
Ticker/Timer, illustrating 222, 223
Ticker/Timer, practices 224
Timeouts 213
Timeouts, implementing 213
Timeouts/Non-Blocking Operations, advantages 216
Timeouts/Non-Blocking Operations, integrating 215

Timeouts/Non-Blocking Operations, pitfalls 217
Timeouts/Non-Blocking Operations, practices 218
Timeouts/Non-Blocking Operations, scenarios 216, 217
Timer 218
Timer, configuring 218-220
TLS/SSL 366
TLS/SSL, configuring 366, 367
TLS/SSL, ensuring 367-369
Token-Based Authentication 362
Type Assertions/Switches 135
Type Assertions/Switches, illustrating 135-138

U

Unbuffered/Buffered Channels, differences 189
Unit Testing 380
Unit Testing, configuring 380, 381

V

Variables 10
Variables, configuring 10, 11
Variadic Functions 40
Variadic Functions, integrating 40-43

W

Web APIs 327
Web APIs, demonstrating 327-331
Web Frameworks 431
Web Frameworks, illustrating 431-433
Web Server, illustrating 305-310
Worker Pool Pattern 178
Worker Pools 233
Worker Pools, architecture 234
Worker Pools, components 234
Worker Pools, features
  Dynamic Worker Count 237
  Results Collecting 236
Worker Pools, reasons 234
Worker Pools, use cases 240
Workspace 5